MENTAL DISORDERS IN THE COMMUNITY

PROCEEDINGS OF THE AMERICAN PSYCHOPATHOLOGICAL ASSOCIATION

Vol. I (33rd Meeting): *Trends of mental disease*. Joseph Zubin (Introduction), 1945.*

Vol. II (34th Meeting): *Current therapies of personality disorders*. Bernard Glueck (Ed.), 1946.

Vol. III (36th Meeting): *Epilepsy*. Paul H. Hoch and Robert P. Knight (Eds.), 1947.

Vol. IV (37th Meeting): *Failures in psychiatric treatment*. Paul H. Hoch (Ed.), 1948.

Vol. V (38th Meeting): *Psychosexual development in health and disease*. Paul H. Hoch and Joseph Zubin (Eds.), 1949.

Vol. VI (39th Meeting): *Anxiety*. Paul H. Hoch and Joseph Zubin (Eds.), 1950.

Vol. VII (40th Meeting): *Relation of psychological tests to psychiatry*. Paul H. Hoch and Joseph Zubin (Eds.), 1951.

Vol. VIII (41st Meeting): *Current problems in psychiatric diagnosis*. Paul H. Hoch and Joseph Zubin (Eds.), 1953.

Vol. IX (42nd Meeting): *Depression*. Paul H. Hoch and Joseph Zubin (Eds.), 1954.

Vol. X (43rd Meeting): *Psychiatry and the law*. Paul H. Hoch and Joseph Zubin (Eds.), 1955.

Vol. XI (44th Meeting): *Psychopathology of childhood*. Paul H. Hoch and Joseph Zubin (Eds.), 1955.

Vol. XII (45th Meeting): *Experimental psychopathology*. Paul H. Hoch and Joseph Zubin (Eds.), 1957.

Vol. XIII (46th Meeting): *Psychopathology of communication*. Paul H. Hoch and Joseph Zubin (Eds.), 1958.

Vol. XIV (47th Meeting): *Problems of addiction and habituation*. Paul H. Hoch and Joseph Zubin (Eds.), 1958.

Vol. XV (48th Meeting): *Current approaches to psychoanalysis*. Paul H. Hoch and Joseph Zubin (Eds.), 1960.

Vol. XVI (49th Meeting): *Comparative epidemiology of the mental disorders*. Paul H. Hoch and Joseph Zubin (Eds.), 1961.

Vol. XVII (50th Meeting): *Psychopathology of aging*. Paul H. Hoch and Joseph Zubin (Eds.), 1961.

Vol. XVIII (51st Meeting): *The future of psychiatry*. Paul H. Hoch and Joseph Zubin (Eds.), 1962.

*This volume was published by King's Crown Press (Columbia University). Volumes II through XXVI were published by Grune & Stratton. Volumes XXVII through XXXI were published by The Johns Hopkins University Press. Volumes XXXII through XXXIX were published by Raven Press. Volumes XL through XLI were published by The Guilford Press.

Mental Disorders in the Community:
Progress and Challenge

Edited by James E. Barrett and Robert M. Rose

PROCEEDINGS OF THE 75TH ANNUAL
MEETING OF THE AMERICAN
PSYCHOPATHOLOGICAL ASSOCIATION,
NEW YORK CITY, FEBRUARY 28–MARCH 2, 1985

THE GUILFORD PRESS
NEW YORK   LONDON

Library of Congress Cataloging-in-Publication Data

American Psychopathological Association. Meeting
    (75th : 1985 : New York, N.Y.)
    Mental disorders in the community.

    Includes bibliographies and index.
    1. Psychiatric epidemiology—Congresses.
2. Community mental health services—Congresses.
I. Barrett, James E. (James Elmer), 1934–   .
II. Rose, Robert M. (Robert Marc), 1936–   .
III. Title. [DNLM: 1. Community Mental Health
Services—congresses. 2. Mental Disorder—occurrence—
congresses. W3 Am632 75th 1985m / WM 100 A5122 1985m]
RC455.2.E64A44 1986   362.2′042   86-14311
ISBN 0-89862-376-6

Preface

During the 1980s the field of psychiatric epidemiology has come into increasing prominence. Epidemiologic data has been used to guide policy makers in planning programs to reduce or eliminate particular mental disorders. There has been a growing interest in prevention research, with epidemiologic findings used to identify potential risk factors in the development of particular disorders. The field has been stimulated by the appearance of a new technology: standardized assessment instruments for case identification, coupled with a psychiatric nosology of which the categories have greater reliability than ever before. The development of diagnostic systems such as the Research Diagnostic Criteria or DSM-III, together with case identification instruments of established reliability relating to each system, the Schedule for Affective Disorders and Schizophrenia (SADS) and the Diagnostic Interview Schedule (DIS), have expanded the opportunities for carrying out large scale community surveys. Beginning in 1981, one such survey, the Epidemiologic Catchment Area (ECA) project, was fielded under the auspices of the National Institute of Mental Health. This ambitious undertaking was eventually to involve community surveys of over 3,000 probands each in five separate United States communities.

The chapters in this volume are concerned with contributions from psychiatric epidemiology, and in particular from community survey findings. The first section is devoted to the ECA project. Gerald Klerman presents the background of the ECA project, the planning for it, and its goals, and findings are then presented from the research teams at three of the ECA sites. The chapter by Lee Robins and her associates introduces the ECA project methodology and reports findings related to substance abuse and to antisocial personality. Dan Blazer and his colleagues, utilizing data from the North Carolina ECA site, provide new and provocative insights into rural–urban differences in mental disorders and their relationship to aging. In the next chapter Philip Leaf, Myrna Weissman, and members of the ECA research team in Connecticut, present new data examining risk factors for the development of depressive illness.

The next section presents findings from earlier community surveys. One of the most famous is the Lundby Project, a community survey initiated in 1947 by Eric Essen-Möller and his colleagues, which examined all inhabitants from a defined geographic area in Sweden. Dr. Essen-Möller himself gives the background to this project, including its focus on the relationship of personality to mental disorders, utilizing the conceptual system developed by Henrick Sjöbring. The initial data from this field study became the baseline data for a longitudinal study, with re-examination of the original probands on two occasions, 10 years and 25 years respectively, after the initial assessment. Selected results from this longitudinal data are presented in the chapter by Olle Hagnell, with a focus on depression, alcoholism, and disorders of aging. Results from an equally famous North American study, the Stirling County Study carried out by Alexander Leighton and his associates, are presented next. Dr. Leighton gives the background for that epidemiologic field study, emphasizing the questions approached and why in the original survey. Data from the Stirling County Study were also used as baseline assessment for longitudinal examination of particular disorders, leading to the next chapter in which Jane Murphy examines the changing prevalence of depressive and anxiety disorders.

The focus shifts in the next section to the use of epidemiologic methods in understanding and planning services for those with a schizophrenic disorder. The chapter by John Wing reviews his experience, using epidemiologic techniques, in developing and evaluating programs of benefit to schizophrenics, particularly chronic schizophrenics. In the next chapter, Bruce Dohrenwend and his associates, using data from a follow-back study, examine risk factors for the development of schizophrenia compared to depressive disorders. Their findings serve as a guide to the direction for future research on the development of these disorders, with implications for possible prevention programs.

The fourth section is concerned with methodologic issues central to psychiatric epidemiology in general and to field surveys in particular. The chapter by James Barrett presents longitudinal outcome data for selected outpatient neurotic disorders, and uses the results to caution researchers that, when validation of individual diagnostic categories is a goal, assessment methodologies should be different, for certain disorders at least, than those used in community surveys. Another issue related to case identification, the source of the data used to make a diagnostic categorization, is explored in the chapter by Salvatore Mannuzza and Rachel Gittelman. In the following chapter, Jack Burke examines evidence related to the validity of the Diagnostic Interview Schedule, the principal case identification instrument used in the ECA project to identify the specific disorders examined in that project. In the final chapter of this section, Patrick Shrout and his colleagues make a compelling case for the need for a two-stage assessment in community surveys.

The fifth section focuses on the use of epidemiologic data as an aid in program planning and its implications for public policy. Using recent data from the ECA project, Sam Shapiro and his colleagues estimated the need for services in one urban community. This provocative chapter raises questions both about who is not receiving services who should be, as well as who is receiving services in the specialty sector who might be better served elsewhere. Darrel Regier picks up this theme in the next chapter, but with a particular focus on the need for new data as an aid in program planning and the need for caution in interpreting recent findings. Herbert Pardes, utilizing his background within NIMH, examines the use of epidemiologic data to influence the legislative process. His advice on what is necessary to prevent needed programs from disappearing in times of fiscal austerity, and on getting the legislative process to provide new programs when indicated, is timely. The section concludes with a panel discussion, with representation from the legislative branch of Congress, from within programs of NIMH, and from sources outside of government. The focus is on the relationship between research findings and the legislative process in a climate of budget reductions.

This review of the content of the individual chapters serves to emphasize the broad goals of this volume. Stated succinctly, these goals are to explore current findings from psychiatric epidemiologic research, including prevalence and incidence of mental disorders, risk factors for particular disorders, changes over time in the outcome and frequency of disorders, and the health services utilization associated with particular disorders. This volume brings together the methodologies and findings from two separate generations of epidemiologic studies, those done in the 1940s and 1950s, and the current large-scale survey, the ECA project, done in the 1980s. The old and the new thus serve to provide perspective and renewed insight in the continuing quest by psychiatric epidemiologists to understand mental disorders in the broadest sense, those that may never come to the attention of formal psychiatric services. Since that quest is never complete, but is an ongoing process, this volume is a snapshot, albeit a rather broad one, of where we have been, where we are now, and directions for the future.

J.E.B.
R.M.R.

Contents

SECTION III. FINDINGS FROM OTHER EPIDEMIOLOGIC STUDIES: TREATMENT AND RISK FACTORS FOR SCHIZOPHRENIA

SECTION IV. METHODOLOGIC ISSUES FOR EPIDEMIOLOGIC STUDIES: THE PROBLEM OF CASE IDENTIFICATION

SECTION V. IMPLICATIONS OF EPIDEMIOLOGIC FINDINGS FOR POLICY AND PROGRAM PLANNING

MENTAL DISORDERS IN THE COMMUNITY

FINDINGS FROM THE UNITED STATES EPIDEMIOLOGIC CATCHMENT AREA (ECA) PROGRAM

1

Scientific and Public Policy Perspectives on the NIMH Epidemiologic Catchment Area (ECA) Program

GERALD L. KLERMAN
Harvard Medical School and Massachusetts General Hospital

The NIMH Epidemiologic Catchment Area Program, which has come to be known as the ECA, has already established itself in many respects as a landmark epidemiologic project with important scientific and public policy implications. In this chapter, I will offer some perspectives on the scientific and policy aspects which gave impetus to the initiation of the ECA.

SCIENTIFIC IMPORTANCE

The scientific significance of the ECA is that it represents an important transition from the epidemiology of *mental health* to an epidemiology of *mental disorders* (Weissman & Klerman, 1978).

Following World War II, a large number of important epidemiologic studies were instituted in North America. These years were a "golden era" of social epidemiology represented by studies such as the study of treated prevalence in New Haven conducted by Hollingshead and Redlich (1958), the Stirling County Project developed by Leighton (1963), and the Midtown Manhattan Study initiated by Rennie and completed by Srole, Langer, Michael, Opler, & Rennie (1962).

These studies, particularly the community surveys, demonstrated the feasibility of large-scale sampling and documented the importance of social factors as risk factors for mental illness. Social class, urban anomie, and social change from rural to industrial economies were highlighted as risk factors for poor mental health.

However, these studies did not provide estimates of incidence or prevalence of specific disorders, in part, because of theoretical controversy over the nature of mental illness and mental health. Instead of categorical diagnoses, many of these studies utilized dimensional measures of mental disability. Mental health was conceptualized on a continuum from normality through psychoses, in contrast to the view of mental illness as a series of separate disorders in the classic medical model.

Perhaps even more important than the theoretical issues were the problems of unreliability in psychiatric diagnosis. The problem of unreliability and diagnosis was highlighted in the findings from the United States–United Kingdom cross-national study initiated by Morton Kramer (1969) and Joseph Zubin (1969). Reported rates of hospitalization for schizophrenia were higher in the United States, while rates of depression were higher in the United Kingdom. A cross-national study was undertaken to determine the validity of these findings and to explore possible factors contributing to the reported differences and rates. It soon became evident that the major factor in U.S.–U.K. differences was the different diagnostic criteria used by hospital psychiatrists in the two countries. The experience of this study established the value of training and structured interviews in improving reliability. The Present State Examination (PSE) developed by Wing (1967), was used in this study and later in the World Health Organization (WHO) International Pilot Study of Schizophrenia (IPSS) (WHO, 1978). Moreover, a group of young psychiatric investigators on both sides of the Atlantic participated in this study. Researchers such as Gurland, Spitzer, Barrett, Sartorius, Kendell, and Cooper, who later were to become important leaders of psychiatry, had their early clinical and epidemiology research experience in this project.

It is well known that considerable progress on the problems of reliability and validity was made through the late 1960s and early 1970s, particularly because of the efforts of the group at Washington University in St. Louis led by Robins, Guze, and Goodwin, and their collaboration with Spitzer, Endicott, and Fleiss at the New York State Psychiatric Institute.

Meanwhile, the NIMH leadership in Washington was devoting considerable effort during the same period to the federal program of community mental health centers geared to meeting the mental health needs of defined population groups in catchment areas, comprising between 75–250,000 individuals. It was important to have means to assess the mental health service needs of communities and to evaluate the impact of the community mental health centers, not only on service utilization but also on incidence and prevalence as it affects public health.

In these efforts Mort Kramer again plays an important role. As the major figure in the NIMH activities in biometrics and epidemiology through the 1950s and 1960s and into the 1970s, Kramer and Ben Locke had proposed a set of programs to develop measures of community needs and to provide modes of assessment of community mental health programs. One proposal was for creation of a number of field stations. Ben Locke developed the Center for Epidemiologic Studies–Depression (CES-D) for screening and assessment of depression, which was then tested at the field station in Kansas City. Another of the proposals developed by Kramer and his associates was for field studies of prevalence and incidence in a defined population. This proposal came to be called the Epidemiologic Catchment Area project. The term "catchment area" is of significance since this sampling design linked the efforts in epidemiology to the federal program in community mental health centers, which were also designed to provide services for individuals in defined population areas.

Kramer left NIMH to join the faculty at Hopkins and was succeeded by Darryl Regier, who has carried the ECA project vigorously through its implementation.

The first use of structured interview and diagnostic algorithms for community epidemiologic surveys took place in the New Haven area in a project led by Jerry Myers, a sociologist, who had worked with Hollingshead and Redlich in the earlier survey of New Haven. Recognizing the importance of developing epidemiologic and evaluation methods, he applied a community survey methodology for assessing the needs of the Hill–West Haven neighborhood, the catchment area to be served by the Connecticut Mental Health Center. The first waves of community survey were undertaken by Myers in 1967 and 1969.

In 1975, Myrna Weissman (a graduate student in epidemiology) joined Myers. They decided to utilize the Schedule for Affective Disorders/Research Diagnostic Criteria (SADS/RDC), newly developed by the NIMH Collaborative Program on the Psychobiology of Depression, for the third wave of the New Haven community survey. The SADS/RDC was originally intended for assessment of patients who were relatives, and there were serious questions as to the feasibility and validity of using such techniques in community surveys.

Lee Robins and her associates at Washington University in St. Louis, who had been developing the Renard Interview which was linked to the Feigner Diagnostic Criteria (1981), contributed the next scientific advance. When it was decided in the late 1970s to initiate the ECA project, it was necessary to develop a structured interview capable of being used in community surveys. Out of that effort came the NIMH Diagnostic Interview Schedule (DIS), developed by Robins, Helzer, Croughan, and Ratcliff (1981), which was specifically geared for administration by nonclinical personnel and, when coupled with computer algorithms, was capable of generating DSM-III, Feigner criteria, and RDC diagnoses. By 1979, field interviewing had begun.

PUBLIC POLICY PERSPECTIVES

Perceptions as to the frequency of mental disorders frequently have played an important role in policy decisions. For example, the first community survey in the United States, by Jarvis in Massachusetts, was prompted by the needs of the legislature in Massachusetts for accurate information concerning the two important diagnostic groups on the classification of that time—lunacy and idiocy—so as to be better able to plan the number and location of two types of public institutions: asylums for the lunatics and schools for the retarded (Jarvis, 1971). The first public institution in Massachusetts, in Worcester, opened in 1832 and rapidly became overcrowded, forcing the legislature to construct other facilities. The public policy decisions accepted the diagnostic distinction between lunacy and idiocy, conditions which today are labeled "psychotic mental illness" and "mental retardation."

During the late 1970s, the Carter administration was actively involved in a number of public policy decisions relevant to mental health. This time the focus was at the federal level: the President's Commission on Mental Health (1978), the future of the community mental health centers' program, and the proposal to develop national health insurance.

President Carter appointed a President's Commission on Mental Health, with his wife Rosalyn as honorary chairperson, soon after his election. David Mechanic and Bruce Dohrenwend were commissioned to collect and evaluate existing information as to the magnitude of the problem. Out of this effort came the volume authored by Dohrenwend which reviewed the available evidence from community surveys and other sources (B. P. Dohrenwend & B. S. Dohrenwend, 1978). At the same time, Darryl Regier (1978) summarized available data from NIMH surveys. Based on these reviews the commission recommended more intensive epidemiological studies.

The NIMH, with support from the Executive Branch and Congress, made plans to implement these recommendations. The DIS was commissioned and its testing was under way. A request for proposal was issued for community sites to participate in the ECA and five awards were made—first to Baltimore, New Haven, and St. Louis, and later to Los Angeles and North Carolina. It had been planned that a sixth center would be located in San Francisco to intensively sample Asian-Americans, but funding did not allow the sixth center.

Meanwhile, the Carter administration was busily involved in developing legislation for national health insurance, promised to NIH as part of the election campaign. Through 1977 and 1978 there were intensive efforts at the Congressional and Executive Branch levels to plan various programs and estimates. At that time there were active discussions about what type of mental health benefits to include in the proposed NHI. During these planning sessions, the question frequently arose as to the magnitude of mental health problems and the estimates of the incidence and prevalence of disorders, as well as the degree of disability involved and the duration of effective treatment, whether inpatient or outpatient. The perception was widespread among planners, particularly economists and political scientists, that there were no limits to mental health problems, and that provision of mental health services for the population would be a "bottomless pit." In this context, accurate information, even preliminary, such as from the New Haven survey and that summarized by the Prsident's Commission, allowed formulations of rough estimates of prevalence of major disorders, particularly schizophrenia, alcoholism, depression, phobias, and dementia. In all levels of government the need was apparent that more accurate information was needed. In this context it was possible to provide the necessary funds for the development of the DIS and for the initiation of the community surveys in five communities.

CONCLUSIONS

The ECA represents the largest community survey sample yet studied and has demonstrated the feasibility of structured interviews and computer diagnosis in generating rates of prevalence. We look forward to hearing the detailed results and to the continued discussion of their implications for science and public policy.

Although the political and legislative climate has changed considerably since the ECA program was initiated, the scientific importance of the data being generated will ultimately have impact on public policy.

REFERENCES

Dohrenwend, B. P., & Dohrenwend, B. S. (1978). *Psychiatric disorders and susceptibility to stress: Reactions to stress of varying magnitudes and varying origins.* Paper presented at the World Psychiatric Association, Section Committee on Epidemiology and Community Psychiatry, Triennial Meeting, St. Louis, MO.

Endicott, J., & Spitzer, R. L. (1978). A diagnostic interview: The schedule for affective disorders and schizophrenia. *Archives of General Psychiatry, 35,* 837–844.

Helzer, J. F., Robins, L. N., Croughan, J. L., & Welner, A. (1981). Renard Diagnostic Interview: Its reliability and procedural validity with physicians and lay interviewers. *Archives of General Psychiatry, 38,* 393–398.

Hollingshead, A., & Redlich, F. (1958). *Social class and mental illness.* New York: Wiley.

Jarvis, E. (1971). *Insanity and idiocy in Massachusetts. Report of the Commission on Lunacy, 1855.* Cambridge, MA: Harvard University Press.

Kramer, M. (1969). Cross-national study of diagnosis of the mental disorders: Origins of the problem. *American Journal of Psychiatry, 125*(Suppl.), 1–11.

Leighton, D., Harding, J., Macklin, D. B., Hughes, C. C., & Leighton, A. H. (1963). Psychiatric findings of the Stirling County study. *American Journal of Psychiatry, 119,* 1021–1026.

Redlich, F. C., Klerman, G. L., McDonald, R., & O'Connor, J. F. (1966). The Connecticut Mental Health Center: A joint venture of state and university in community psychiatry. *Connecticut Medicine, 30,* 656–662.

Regier, D. A., Goldberg, I. D., & Taube, C. A. (1978). The de facto U.S. mental health service system. *Archives of General Psychiatry, 35,* 685–693.

Report to the President's Commission on Mental Health, Vol. I. (1978). Washington, DC: U.S. Government Printing Office.

Robins, L. N., Helzer, J. E., Croughan, J., & Ratcliff, K. S. (1981). National Institute of Mental Health Diagnostic Interview Schedule. *Archives of General Psychiatry, 38*, 381–392.

Spitzer, R. L., Endicott, J., & Robins, E. (1978). Research Diagnostic Criteria: Rationale and reliability. *Archives of General Psychiatry, 35*, 773–782.

Srole, L., Langer, T. A., Michael, S. T., Opler, M. K., & Rennie, T. A. C. (1962). *Mental health in the metropolis.* New York: McGraw-Hill.

Weissman, M. M., & Klerman, G. L. (1978). Epidemiology of mental disorders. *Archives of General Psychiatry, 35*, 705–712.

Weissman, M. M., Myers, J. M., & Harding, P. (1978). Psychiatric disorder in a U.S. urban community. *American Journal of Psychiatry, 135*, 459–462.

Wing, J., Birley, L. T., Cooper, J. et al. Reliability of a procedure for measuring and classifying "Present Psychiatric State." *British Journal of Psychiatry, 113*, 499–515.

World Health Organization. (1973). *International pilot study of schizophrenia.* Geneva: Author.

Zubin, J. (1969). Cross-national study of diagnosis of the mental disorders: Methodology and planning. *American Journal of Psychiatry, 125*(Suppl.), 12–20.

2

Substance Abuse in the General Population

LEE N. ROBINS, J. E. HELZER, AND THOMAS PRZYBECK
Washington University School of Medicine

It is well known that substance abusers have an abundance of social problems such as marital breakups, job loss, fights, and arrests. They are also believed to have high levels of associated psychiatric disorders, such as depression. What is not yet clear is the extent to which substance-abuse disorders account for these problems and disorders. Many of the childhood predictors of substance abuse also predict social problems. Introduction to alcohol and drugs usually occurs in the middle and late teens. Often those who go on to have problems with these substances have had behavior problems at school and home even before first using these psychoactive substances, behavior problems associated with later social difficulties of all kinds. It is therefore possible that the adult social difficulties characteristic of substance abusers would have appeared whether or not these children with behavior problems began excessive use of drugs or alcohol. While it is commonly believed that abusing drugs and alcohol account for these problems, that view is not universally held. For example, there have been heated arguments among the proponents and adversaries of methadone treatment as to the possibility that substituting methadone for heroin would markedly reduce crimes committed by addicts. Critics of methadone programs have argued that heroin addicts who commit property crimes were criminals long before they used heroin, and if they are relieved of the necessity for stealing to support a heroin habit, they will just shift from buying heroin to buying fancy clothes with the profits from their thefts (Lukoff, 1977). Our own research provided some modest support for the idea that many of the consequences of abuse might actually be consequences of preexisting predispositions in our study of Vietnam veterans. The only alcoholic veterans who reported committing violent crimes in the three years after their return from Vietnam were those with a preservice history of fighting (Robins, 1979). Further, the number of adverse adult outcomes associated with heroin abuse was no larger than the number associated with the abuse of "milder" drugs, such as amphetamines, once we

9

held constant the level of preabuse deviant behavior and the number of other drugs used simultaneously (Robins, unpublished report to NIDA). Finally, preservice behavior was a better predictor of veterans' use of drugs after return than was even dependency on heroin in Vietnam (Robins, Helzer, Hesselbrock, and Wish, 1980).

While childhood behavior problems often precede substance abuse, there are also substance abusers who do not have an early history of deviance. It could be the case that they instead had depressive or anxiety symptoms that led them to overuse psychoactive substances in an attempt originally to treat these symptoms. An excess of later psychological problems might then not be attributable to the substance abuse, but rather to the continuation of the problems that originally accounted for the abuse.

However, it is certainly also possible that substance abuse has serious consequences of its own that are not expressed entirely in symptoms of the disorder itself. Support for the idea that drug abuse might have serious consequences of its own independent of its association with deviant behavior came from our study of young black men. Although lacking the low IQ and early school problems that are the precursors of delinquency, men who began drug abuse in early adolescence had a frequency of high school dropout equal to that of delinquents, and their rates of adult antisocial behavior were as high as the rates for delinquents (Robins, 1980).

The extent to which it is the prior predisposition to deviance or psychological difficulties that accounts for the social problems and psychological symptoms associated with substance abuse or the independent effect of the substance abuse itself appears answerable if we can contrast abusers with and without preabuse histories of deviance and psychiatric disability with non-abusers with similar histories. It is also of interest to know whether substance abuse which arises in the context of childhood deviance is a different disorder from that which does not in terms of its symptoms and course.

This chapter uses data from the St. Louis ECA site to begin to address these issues. The ECA data are appropriate for several reasons. First, they come from a representative sample of the general population, so that the substance abusers include both those with and without treatment experience or contact with social agencies. In clinical and justice system samples, one would not expect to find cases without some of the more noxious associated social and emotional problems because it is often these problems rather than the substance abuse itself that leads to treatment or contacts with agencies. On the other hand, samples that exclude treated cases may be concentrating on milder cases and so underestimate the effect of substance abuse. The ECA project incorporated samples from both household and institutional populations, including mental hospitals, jails and prisons, chronic hospitals, Veterans' Administration facilities, and nursing and boarding homes, thus providing access to the full population of those with and without substance abuse.

Furthermore, a census of these institutions with respect to their inmates from the sampled areas makes it possible to weight them appropriately so that final results are truly representative of the total population resident in these areas.

To measure psychiatric disorders in the population, the ECA sample was given the Diagnostic Interview Schedule (DIS). This interview covered many DSM-III diagnoses. Among these were alcohol abuse and dependence and the abuse of six classes of illicit drugs: sedatives and tranquilizers, opiates, cocaine, other stimulants, hallucinogens, and cannabis. Of particular importance to answering the questions posed by this chapter was the fact that antisocial personality was also assessed. To do so, the age of onset was determined for each of the childhood behavior problems that serve as the childhood criteria for antisocial personality. These included age of onset of first drug use and first drunkenness, as well as behaviors typically considered to represent delinquent behavior. Since three-quarters of those who developed alcohol abuse or dependence had their first symptom at age 17 or later, delinquent behaviors occurring before age 15 were almost certain to have predated the first symptoms of substance abuse. The St. Louis site also included other childhood information of special relevance to the questions posed in this chapter: parental history of substance abuse, broken homes in childhood, parents' occupation when the respondent was 16, and initiation of heavy smoking before 15.

The review of adult symptoms of antisocial personality provided information about the frequency of the social problems most often associated with substance abuse, problems such as arrests, job loss, marital breakup, fighting, vagrancy and homelessness, and illegal occupations. Therefore, there is considerable information about adverse outcomes that might be attributable to substance abuse or to preexisting childhood behavior problems.

The other psychiatric disorders covered by the DIS included disorders that might be outcomes or antecedents of substance abuse. The DIS interviews in St. Louis included broader diagnostic coverage than in other sites. As indicators of possible psychiatric disorder in addition to symptoms, St. Louis respondents were asked about others' perceptions of them as depressed, anxious, bizarre, or psychopathic. Therefore, it is possible to study the relation of substance abuse to psychiatric disorder when there was and was not a prior history of childhood deviance.

The design of the ECA project called for three interviews with the respondents at 6-month intervals. In each interview, respondents were asked about the use of treatment in the previous six months, and in St. Louis, we also asked in each about the experience of certain adverse life events in the previous six months. As a result of these three interviews, we are able to look over an 18-month interval at treatment and recent life events that are not only clearly subsequent to the onset of substance abuse and therefore not confounded with its possible causes. Review of an 18-month period gives us a frequency of these relatively rare events high enough to make it possible to study them as consequences of substance abuse.

These data would not enable us to answer questions about the relation of early antisocial behavior and substance abuse to later outcome if there was a high rate of error in the detection of a lifetime history of substance abuse or poor recall of childhood behavior. These areas are often thought to be difficult ones in which to get reliable self-reports; however, this has not been our experience in prior research (Robins, 1966, 1973) when we had police, school, and military records with which to compare self-reports. While we lack these objective records in the current study, we have carried out two studies comparing DIS reinterviews by psychiatrists with the interview as given by lay interviewers in the ECA. The first (Robins, Helzer, Ratcliff, & Seyfried, 1982) was done with 216 persons, a mix of clinical samples and persons registered with the Washington University Medical Care Group; the second was with 13% of the household portion of the ECA sample reinterviewed a few weeks to a few months after their first ECA interview (Helzer *et al.*, 1985). In both, levels of diagnostic agreements for the substance-abuse disorders were very satisfactory (Table 2.1). In fact, agreement between psychiatrists and lay interviewers was higher for substance abuse diagnoses than for any of the other 13 diagnoses tested.

METHODS

Results will be reported for the St. Louis ECA site, which includes 3207 persons who responded to questions about substance abuse in at least one interview. This sample consists of 2961 household members and 246 residents of institutions. While the total sample was 3499, 259 of the 495 institutional residents were too demented, mentally retarded, or physically ill to be able to complete the interview, as were 43 of the 3004 residing in independent households. These respondents represent residents of three mental health catchment areas: an inner city area, an inner suburb, and three counties made up of rural areas and small towns. In some of our analyses, we will be looking only at persons who were interviewed in all waves of the study and able to answer questions about substance abuse—a total of 2474 such individuals.

Diagnoses were made by computer using algorithms based on DSM-III criteria. Lifetime diagnoses are presented, indicating that respondents met criteria based on symptoms occurring at any time in their lives. The diagnosis of illicit drug abuse and dependence indicates that the respondent has met criteria for one or more of the 15 drug-abuse and dependence diagnoses in DSM-III. Preemptions of one diagnosis by another as listed in DSM-III are not used as exclusion criteria.

Table 2.1. Reliability of the Substance-Abuse Diagnoses

	Alcohol Abuse/ Dependence	Drug Abuse/ Dependence
*Clinical Reinterview**		
Numbers: Total	216	216
Positive—Lay interview	68	34
—Psychiatrist	77	26
Kappa	.86	.73
Sensitivity	86%	88%
Specificity	84%	94%
General Population Reinterview (weighted)**		
Numbers: Total	359	357
Positive—Lay interview	65	41
—Psychiatrist	61	38
Kappa	.68	.70
Sensitivity	70%	64%
Specificity	96%	99%

*From Robins *et al.* (1981).
**From Helzer *et al.* (1985).

To assess the presence of childhood behavior problems that might indicate a predisposition to deviance antedating substance abuse, we will use nine of the 12 behaviors used as childhood symptoms of antisocial personality: stealing, lying, fighting, truancy, misbehavior in school, running away from home, vandalism, school expulsion for bad behavior, and official delinquency. We selected these because they are usually thought of as "delinquent-like," although not all children with them come into contact with police or juvenile authorities. We considered persons who had experienced two or more of these behaviors before age 15 to have had a history of childhood delinquency. We excluded early drunkenness and drug use because they are confounded with substance abuse; school underachievement because it is not clearly delinquent; and early sexual activity because it was asked only in St. Louis, and so could not be replicated in the future in other sites. It should be noted that the "delinquents" referred to below do not necessarily have official police or juvenile court records.

We also counted the number of adult symptoms of antisocial personality experienced by substance abusers. These included job problems, neglect of children, arrest or illegal earnings, problems with sexual partners whether or not formally married, violence, debt and credit problems, vagrancy, frequent lying, and multiple moving-traffic offenses. We considered persons with two or more of these nine difficulties to have significant adult antisocial behavior. Persons with antisocial behavior need not meet criteria for a diagnosis of antisocial personality, which requires at least four of these adult behaviors plus three or more childhood indicators of deviance.

RESULTS

Substance-abuse disorders were found to be extremely common (Table 2.2). Overall more than one-third of the St. Louis population met criteria for tobacco abuse, one-sixth for alcohol abuse or dependency, and one in twenty met criteria for drug abuse or dependency. Since tobacco-use disorder was not investigated in all ECA sites, we do not know whether this finding was uniform across sites, but alcohol abuse was equally common in Baltimore and only slightly less common in New Haven and North Carolina, while rates of drug abuse were about the same everywhere. In St. Louis, substance abuse of one kind or another was more common than any other type of disorder explored.

Institutional residents did not differ from household residents in the frequency of tobacco abuse, but they had more than double the rates of alcohol disorders and more than four times the rates of drug abuse as those living at home. Their very high rates are due to the fact that many of the hospitalized elderly and mentally retarded, who would have had low lifetime

Table 2.2. Lifetime Frequency of Substance Abuse and Antisocial Personality in St. Louis (Weighted)

	Of Those Well Enough for Interview			
	Household (2961) %	Institutions (246) %	Total (3207) %	I:H Ratio
Substance-abuse disorders				
Tobacco	36.6	35.6	36.6	1.0
Alcohol	15.7	37.6	15.9	2.4
Drug	5.5	22.3	5.6	4.1
Cannabis	3.7	17.2	3.8	4.6
Stimulants	2.0	12.6	2.1	6.3
Sedatives	1.1	10.5	1.2	9.5
Opiates	0.7	11.2	0.8	16.0
Hallucinogens	0.2	2.4	0.2	12.0
Cocaine	0.1	3.9	0.1	39.0
Antisocial personality (ASP)	5.0	27.3	5.2	5.5

Table 2.3. Lifetime Alcohol and Drug Abuse and/or Dependence in the General Population (*2474 St. Louis area residents interviewed twice**)

	f	%
Alcohol only	302	12%
Drug only	66	3
Both	80	3
Either	448	18

*Omits persons so demented that they could not answer drug and alcohol questions.

rates, were too incoherent to be interviewed. Thus the interviewable institutional sample is particularly loaded with prisoners, who are both young and deviant enough to have high substance-abuse rates. Their contribution can also be seen in the high level of antisocial personality in the institutional population, among whom over one-fourth of the sample met criteria, more than five times the rate in the household sample.

In both household and institutional samples, problems with marijuana were the most common form of drug abuse, with abuse of stimulants next. Abuse of other drug classes dropped off sharply in the household sample and more slowly in the institutionalized sample, so that the largest ratio between institutional and household users was found for the drug least often producing problems for the household group cocaine.

Despite the heavy level of substance abuse in the institutional population, weighting them into the total sample increases the overall rates by only 0.1 or 0.2% because there are so few people in institutions, compared with the number living in households.

Alcohol and drug disorders tend to occur in the same people, although the overlap is by no means complete (Table 2.3). Half of all drug abusers also met criteria for an alcohol disorder, while one-fifth of alcohol abusers also had a drug-abuse disorder. As we shall see, this lack of symmetry is primarily because only the younger members of the sample were at risk for drug abuse.

Alcohol and drug abuse are more highly intercorrelated than most psychiatric disorders (Table 2.4), although the presence of any disorder tends to increase the likelihood that any other will be present (Boyd *et al.*, 1984). When we compare associations among diagnoses grouped under the major headings in DSM-III for which more than one diagnosis was made in the DIS, that is, affective disorders, anxiety disorder, and substance-abuse disorders, alcohol and drug disorders have the highest association. (There are still higher associations across diagnostic groupings, panic disorder and depressive episode being still more closely associated. This association is found, of course,

Table 2.4. High Correlations (.20+) among Lifetime Diagnoses without Exclusions (St. Louis ECA Data)

Within major DSM-III diagnostic headings		
Anxiety	Phobia vs. panic	.20
Affective	Manic vs. depressive episode	.24
Substance abuse	Alcohol vs. drug	.27
Across Diagnostic Headings		
Anxiety-affective	Obsessive compulsive vs. manic	.21
	Obsessive compulsive vs. depressive	.23
	Phobia vs. depressive	.27
	Panic vs. depressive	.29
Anxiety-substance	None	
Affective-substance	None	
Anxiety-antisocial personality	None	
Affective-antisocial personality	None	
Substance-antisocial personality	Drug vs. antisocial	.37
	Alcohol vs. antisocial	.38

only because diagnostic exclusions, which would rule out the diagnosis of panic disorder in the presence of depression, are not being used.)

It is of special interest to our investigation that both drug and alcohol disorders are more closely associated with antisocial personality, on Axis II, than they are either with each other or with *any* Axis I diagnosis. The substance-abuse disorders are the only Axis I disorders with which antisocial personality is highly associated. This finding underscores the importance of determining whether the social problems associated with substance abuse are truly the effect of the substance abuse. They might be the symptoms of antisocial personality, which by definition begins in childhood with at least three types of childhood behavior problems before age 15, and therefore typically predates the onset of substance abuse.

As expected from these correlations, we found that having two or more of the nine childhood behaviors that we had selected as representing delinquent-like activity before age 15 was strongly related to developing substance abuse (Table 2.5). Their presence increased the relative risk of having an alcohol disorder by almost four times, a drug disorder by five times, and both disorders by more than seven times. Nonetheless, most children with behavior problems did not develop substance abuse.

Likewise, most persons who developed an alcohol or drug abuse disorder did not have a previous childhood history of delinquency as we have defined it (Table 2.6). Only when both disorders were present was prior delinquency more common than not, but even in that group, about one-third had no history of delinquency.

Table 2.5. Childhood Delinquent Behavior* as a Predictor of Substance Abuse

	Delinquent (480) %	Nondelinquent (1994) %	Relative Risk
Alcohol	37.5	10.2	3.7
Drug abuse	16.9	3.3	5.1
Both	10.6	1.5	7.1

*"Delinquent behavior" = Two or more of truant, expelled, arrested, runaway, lying, stealing, vandalism, discipline problems at school, starts fights before age 15.

The adult outcomes for substance abusers were equally variable. While substance abusers were much more likely than nonabusers to have the adult social problems that are used to diagnose antisocial personality, unless they had both disorders, a substantial minority had only one or two of these social problems. If both disorders were present, almost all (90%) had a significant number of antisocial symptoms.

Thus there was no identity between either the childhood or adult symptoms of antisocial personality and substance abuse, unless both disorders were present simultaneously. About half the substance abusers had early delinquent behavior, and half to two-thirds had significant adult social problems. There remains the question of whether these adult social problems are a result of the substance abuse or are simply consequences of the childhood behaviors that simultaneously predict both social problems and substance abuse.

To explore that question we compared substance abusers who had had no significant childhood delinquency (i.e., they had at most one of the nine behaviors we had counted) with delinquents to see whether they had much

Table 2.6. Proportions of Substance Abusers without Antisocial Behavior in Childhood and as Adults

	Alcohol Only (302) %	Drug Only (86) %	Both (80) %	Neither (2026) %
Not more than one delinquent behavior before 15	57	55	36	85
Not more than two adult antisocial personality (ASP) symptoms	37	48	10	82
No adult ASP symptoms	6	2	0	30

Table 2.7. How Substance Abuse Makes Up for Delinquency in Determining Adult Life-Style

| | Nondelinquents | | Delinquents (480) % | Nondelinquent Nonabusers (1756) % |
	Alcohol (134) %	Drug (65) %		
Legal				
Nontraffic arrest				
ever	29	29	34	6
in last 18 mos.	10	9	17	3
4+ traffic offenses	48	34	41	13
Ever incarcerated	5	3	8	1
Family				
Marital problems				
ever	57	57	57	31
Broke up with mate in last 18 mos.	17	31	26	11
Lived common-law	34	31	36	14
Job				
Job problems				
ever	66	80	73	43
Job loss, last 18 mos.	32	49	41	20
Violent	50	55	55	20
Vagrant	17	23	20	4
Robbery Victim	28	34	34	19

lower rates of common social problems (Table 2.7). We found very little difference between the outcomes of nondelinquent substance abusers and delinquents. Even in the absence of a history of childhood delinquency, half the substance abusers reported fighting as adults or wife- or child-beating; almost all had had job troubles, and most had had serious marital problems. Only with respect to problems with the law—arrest and incarceration—did delinquents exceed both alcohol and drug abusers by even 3%. Both substance abusers and delinquents had many more adult social problems than those with neither substance-abuse nor delinquent behaviors. We included being a *victim* of robbery, break-in, or mugging as an outcome of interest because it was a recent life event predicted by substance abuse, along with arrests, job loss, and marital breakup. It is part of our street lore that drunks are easy robbery victims. The same appears to be true from these data with respect to drug abusers and delinquents. Perhaps for all three it is their residence in high-crime areas and their spending more time on the streets than their neighbors that matters rather than their appearing intoxicated.

One objection to interpreting these findings as showing that substance abuse itself can create adverse outcomes is that we do not have temporal information for all of these outcomes. It is possible that the substance abuse was a response to marital breakup or job loss, for example. However, three of these outcomes were included in our list of life events inquired about as having occurred within 6 months of interview—arrests, marital breakup, and job loss. Since substance abuse typically began in the early twenties, events within 18 months of the time of final interview were almost all subsequent to the onset of the disorder. And we found *recent* marital and job problems in nondelinquent substance abusers as similar to the rates for delinquents as were lifetime measures.

We conclude then that substance abuse and delinquency are alternate routes to the same adverse outcomes. Having found that substance abuse can lead to the same kinds of outcomes as delinquency raises a possibility that had not occurred to us in our original formulation of the problems: substance abuse might be an important route through which childhood deviance leads to adult social problems. Our own earlier studies (Robins, 1979) found that only about half the children with serious conduct problems developed antisocial personality. Was adolescent substance abuse essential to the continuity between childhood and adult problems?

To investigate that possibility, we divided the delinquents into those with and without substance abuse (Table 2.8). We found that abuse of either alcohol or illicit drugs substantially increased the risk that delinquents would show each of these adult social problems. However, even in the absence of substance-abuse disorders, delinquents had strikingly more adverse outcomes than nondelinquents. Thus, substance abuse seemed to contribute to the continuity of behavior problems into adult life, but was not necessary to that continuity. Of particular interest was the fact that delinquents, with or without substance abuse, had increased rates of very recent adverse life events, showing the long-lasting predictive power of childhood antisocial behavior.

We found that delinquency and substance abuse appear to be independent and additive factors in predicting social problems. When both were present, very high rates of social problems occurred. For example, four out of five drug abusers with a history of delinquency had marital problems, and almost three-quarters of the delinquents who were also substance abusers had a history of fighting or violence. Nearly half the drug abusers with a history of delinquency had been victims of robbery, mugging, or break-in in the last 18 months. The only exception to the additive rule was job problems. The rate of job problems was so high in drug abusers that even if they were not previously delinquent, the history of delinquency made little further contribution.

We had thought that if delinquent and nondelinquent substance abusers had different outcomes, their substance-abuse symptoms might also differ.

Table 2.8. Substance Abuse and Adult Social Problems in Delinquents (D) and Nondelinquents (ND)

	Alcohol		Drugs		Neither	
	D (180) %	ND (134) %	D (81) %	ND (65) %	D (269) %	ND (1756) %
Legal						
Non-traffic arrest						
ever	52*†	29†	65*†	29†	20*	6
in last 18 mos.	24†	15†	32*†	9	12	3
4+ traffic offenses	60*†	48†	62*†	34†	27*	13
Ever incarcerated	13	5	11	3	5	1
Family						
Marital problems						
ever	73*†	57†	79*†	57†	46*	31
Broke up with mate, last 18 mos.	27*	17	40†	31†	23*	11
Lived common-law	44*†	34†	59*†	31†	30*	14
Job						
Job problems						
ever	79*†	66†	83†	80†	68*	43
Job loss, last 18 mos.	46*	32†	51†	49†	38*	20
Violent	74*†	50†	72*†	55†	41*	20
Vagrant	29*†	17†	43*†	23†	13	4
Victim last 18 mos. of robbery, break-in, mugging	35	28	48*†	34†	33*	19

   *Delinquents > ND by 10%.
   †Abusers > Nonabusers by 10%.

Those who came to substance abuse through delinquency might report as substance-related, the fighting and job problems which were in fact simply a continuation of the aggression and resistance to authority that had typified their presubstance abuse behavior. If so, the substance-abuse symptoms of those with no prior deviance should center on heavy intake, inability to control their intake, and withdrawal symptoms, rather than social complications. However, once we found that substance abusers who developed their disorders in the absence of childhood delinquent behavior shared a variety of social problems with those previously delinquent, it was not clear that their substance abuse would have different symptom patterns.

Nonetheless, we compared the frequency and ranks of the symptoms used to diagnose substance-abuse disorders (Tables 2.9 and 2.10). First, we found that delinquent alcohol abusers tended to have more symptoms than nondelinquents (Table 2.9). Of the 16 common alcohol symptoms examined, rates were higher in the delinquents for 12; however, differences were not great. In only three instances did delinquents exceed nondelinquents by more than 10%. These three symptoms included one we had initially expected— delinquents reported more fighting when drunk. However, the other two had not been expected. Delinquents drank larger amounts and showed more physiological withdrawal symptoms. Almost all of them (87%) had drunk a fifth in one day more than once, while less than half of the nondelinquents had done so, and a third of the delinquents had had the classic alcoholic's withdrawal symptom, the "shakes," while about a quarter of the nondelinquents had done so. In general, the same symptoms tended to be rare or common in both groups. There were no alcohol symptoms that distinguished the nondelinquent abuser. Among the four symptoms in which they exceeded the delinquents, the greatest excess was 4%, for an indicator of dependence, drink before breakfast, but only about a quarter of either group reported this symptom. The rank-order correlation between the two groups with respect to the frequency of symptoms was .87.

The picture with respect to the symptoms of drug disorders was similar (Table 2.10). Delinquents exceeded nondelinquents in six out of seven symptom groups, and they exceeded nondelinquents by 10% or more in two— heavy use (daily for two weeks or more) and developing tolerance (needed

Table 2.9. Common Symptoms of Delinquent and Nondelinquent Alcohol Abusers (20% or more in either)

	Delinquents (180) %	Nondelinquents (202) %
*Fifth in one day	87	44
Family objected	66	59
*Fighting	64	38
Two weeks of 7 drinks/day	61	56
Blackouts	61	52
Thinks excessive	58	59
Friends, others think excessive	43	37
Arrest	34	33
*Shakes	34	23
Driving problem	33	30
Binges	31	29
Liver Problem	30	21
Rules about when	26	27
Drink before breakfast	23	27
Job, school problem	21	18
Couldn't stop	19	21

*Delinquents > nondelinquents by 10%.

Table 2.10. Symptoms of Drug Abuse among Delinquents and Nondelinquents

	Delinquents (81) %	Nondelinquents (65) %
*Daily use for 2 weeks	84	72
Emotional, psychiatric problems	70	77
*Developed tolerance	69	55
Social, police problems	48	43
Felt dependent	48	42
Withdrawal symptoms	31	28
Couldn't stop	26	18

*Delinquents exceeded nondelinquents by 10% or more.

larger amounts to get high). Emotional and psychiatric problems related to drug use was the only symptom that was higher in nondelinquents, but emotional problems occurred in the great majority of both groups. The rank-order correlation for frequencies of the seven symptom groups was .96.

Our comparison of the delinquent with nondelinquent abusers for both drugs and alcohol, then, indicates only that the delinquents tend to have more symptoms overall, and they particularly exceed nondelinquents in their heavier intake and resultant physical dependence. They also get more aggressive when drinking. Their higher incidence of social problems, therefore, seems attributable more to their greater overall severity than to any special abuse type.

These results would seem to indicate that the symptoms used by DSM-III to describe substance abuse are appropriate. The definition is not one that results in labeling deviant behaviors that would have occurred in any case in predisposed individuals as symptoms of substance abuse simply because the individual happens to be a heavy user of psychoactive substances. The very same symptoms that occur in nondelinquent abusers also occur in delinquent abusers, and vice versa. The difference between the two groups is more one of severity than kind.

Even though the social problems and symptoms associated with substance abuse did not differ for delinquents and nondelinquents, the emotional and psychiatric concomitants of substance abuse might differ for the two groups as well as their readiness to seek care for their problems. We looked at the psychiatric concomitants of their substance abuse from two points of view—in terms of whether they had ever in their lifetimes met criteria for the more common affective and anxiety disorders, and in terms of their assessment of whether they have been perceived by others as psychiatrically disturbed. We anticipated that the nondelinquents might have more associated depression or anxiety disorders because these could have accounted for their abusing substances in the absence of a predisposition to deviance.

We found very little difference between the two groups in this regard (Table 2.11). Both delinquent and nondelinquent abusers of illicit drugs tended to have more of each of the common psychiatric disorders explored than either alcohol abusers or nonabusers, but they differed little from each other. Delinquent and nondelinquent alcohol abusers were also similar. Among nonabusers, delinquents had somewhat higher levels of each disorder, further evidence that childhood behavior problems are no protection against depression or anxiety, as we noted many years ago (Robins, 1966).

When we ask how substance abusers think others perceive them, we find that delinquent and nondelinquent substance abusers do not differ in the frequency with which they say others perceive them to be nervous or depressed, though drug abuse seems to trigger such perceptions a bit more than alcohol abuse. However, delinquent abusers are more often perceived as bizarre and cold, presumably as a result of the impulsiveness and lack of empathy for others so frequently described as elements of antisocial personality. When not substance abusers, delinquents appear more often than nondelinquents to be regarded as nervous and depressed as well, although only a small minority report such perceptions.

Table 2.11. Association of Delinquent (D) and Nondelinquent (ND) Substance Abuse with Other Psychiatric Disorders

	Alcohol		Drugs		Neither	
	D (180) %	ND (134) %	D (81) %	ND (65) %	D (269) %	ND (1756) %
Psychiatric diagnoses in lifetime:						
Phobic	17	16	23	22	15	11
Generalized anxiety	14	20	22	20	12	7
Depressive episode	8	9	20	26	10	5
Obsessive-compulsive	7	2	11	4	6	1
Seen by others as:						
Nervous	26	24	36	37	19	11
Crazy, odd	27*	9	37*	23	14*	4
Cold, hard	27	19	43*	31	13	5
Depressed	10	8	16	18	7	3
Received health care for mental problem	45	42	62	57	27	20

*D > ND by 10%.

Delinquent and nondelinquent substance abusers did not differ in the frequency with which they had received care for some emotional or psychiatric problem, including their substance abuse. About half the alcohol abusers had at some time received some care, as had somewhat more of the drug abusers. Alcohol abusers were about twice as likely to have had care than those without substance abuse, whether or not they were delinquent, and drug abusers were about three times as likely to seek care.

In summary, there was little difference between delinquent and nondelinquent substance abusers in their rates of affective and anxiety disorders, in how they appeared to others, and in their willingness to seek care for their problems. Substance abusers had more of these psychiatric problems than did nonabusers, particularly if they abused illicit drugs, but whether or not the abuse had delinquent roots seemed immaterial. These findings do not support a theory that substance abuse has two nonoverlapping causes—a predisposition to deviance *or* efforts to self-medicate psychiatric symptoms. Since the nondelinquents lack a distinct tendency toward these disorders, the increased rate of disorders associated with substance abuse seem best understood as the effects of the substance abuse rather than its cause.

If we cannot explain substance abuse by nondelinquents as a response to some other psychiatric disorder, we wondered if there were other precursors that could account for it in the absence of an apparent predisposition to deviant behavior. The available candidates were sex, race, date of birth (which indicated the historical era in which the individual reached the age of risk for developing substance abuse), the age at which he or she first smoked tobacco regularly, first got drunk, and first used illicit drugs, school success measured by whether he or she reported doing poorly in school or repeating grades and by failure to graduate from high school, a broken home, parents' psychiatric problems, and parents' occupations during his or her childhood. Table 2.12 shows those variables which were related to substance abuse among delinquents, nondelinquents, or both, when the criterion for having an effect was that they increased the relative risk of abuse at least 1.66 times.

It is worth noting first the variables that do not appear. Broken homes, breadwinner's occupation, and high school graduation did not predict substance abuse in either delinquents or nondelinquents. Nor did race explain substance abuse in nondelinquents, although being white increased the risk of alcohol abuse in delinquents. Several variables were powerful predictors of abuse for both delinquents and nondelinquents. For alcohol abuse, these predictors were being male and getting drunk before 15 rather than later; for drug abuse these variables were using drugs before age 15 rather than later and being born after 1936. (It should be noted that we are contrasting early with later drunkenness and drug use, excluding those who never got drunk or never used drugs, and so were never at risk for developing problems, so that age at exposure is not confounded with whether there was any exposure at

Table 2.12. Childhood Predictors of Substance Abuse in Nondelinquents

| | | Delinquents | | | Non-Delinquents | | |
			Alcohol Abusers	Drug Abusers		Alcohol Abusers	Drug Abusers
		N	%	%	N	%	%
Total		478	37	17	1990	10	3
Alcoholic parent(s)							
Yes		92	41	22	155	23	10
No		376	36	15	1811	9	3
	R.R.		*	*		2.6	3.3
Drugs							
Before 15		49	57	47	17	6	41
Later		233	39	25	441	22	13
	R.R.		*	1.9		*	3.2
Poor grades							
Yes		75	48	12	119	19	7
No		403	35	18	1865	10	3
	R.R.		*	*		1.9	2.3
Smoking							
Before 15		147	49	19	136	26	8
Later		207	49	20	932	13	5
	R.R.		*	*		2.0	*
Drunk							
Before 15		130	59	15	128	27	8
Later		302	34	8	1198	14	5
	R.R.		1.7	1.9		1.9	*
Male		280	51	19	674	21	4
Female		198	19	13	1317	4	3
	R.R.		2.7	*		5.3	*
Born since 1936		376	38	21	1090	11	5
Before 1936		102	36	0	901	9	0.5
	R.R.		*	∞		*	10.0
White		273	49	18	1213	11	3
Black		197	21	13	744	9	3
	R.R.		2.3	*		*	*

*Relative Risks < 1.67.

all.) All four of these items may be related to exposure to substances. Males are typically much more exposed to heavy drinking than are females, and persons over 25 at the time of the beginning of the drug epidemic in the 1960s have had relatively little opportunity to use drugs because their use was so strictly age-graded. These results show that the effect of early use of a substance on the likelihood of developing a problem with it is independent of the fact that delinquents tend to start drinking and using drugs earlier than other children do.

We looked for predictors that were unique to nondelinquents. Two variables met the relative risk criterion of 1.67 for predicting both alcohol and drug abuse only in nondelinquents: having an alcoholic parent and making poor grades in school. There are similar trends in delinquents with respect to parents' drinking problems, although the relative risk is much lower. Poor grades in school also increased the risk of alcohol abuse for delinquents by 13%, but failed to make the 1.67 relative risk criterion because delinquents had such a high risk for drinking problems whether or not they failed at school. School failure, however, had no relationship to drug abuse in delinquents. Becoming a regular smoker before age 15 also increased the risk of alcohol abuse among nondelinquents, and there was a trend toward more drug abuse as well among nondelinquent smokers. Smoking was not a risk factor at all for delinquents. Alcohol problems in parents, school failure, and early smoking were thus the three risk factors for substance abuse that affected nondelinquents more than delinquents, while birth cohort, sex, and age at introduction to abusable substances affected both.

DISCUSSION

We have explored substance abuse in the general population in terms of its precursors and correlates. We found it to be extremely common, often predicted by delinquent childhood behavior, and closely related to the adult diagnosis of antisocial personality. Its correlates with adult problem behaviors are consistent with its association with both delinquency in childhood and antisocial personality. Substance abusers have high rates of job problems, aggression, marital disruption, and arrest. Nonetheless, there is a substantial minority of substance abusers who have no prior delinquent history. We inquired as to whether this minority had different patterns of alcohol symptoms and different outcomes. Few substantial differences were found, although nondelinquents had somewhat fewer symptoms and somewhat less severe social problems. But even in the absence of a delinquent history, their levels of social problems were well above those of persons who were not substance abusers. We also inquired about their level of affective and anxiety disorders, thinking that they might exceed delinquent abusers in these areas. Instead we found that they closely resembled delinquent abusers. Drug abusers, whether delinquent or nondelinquent, had a somewhat elevated rate of these disorders as compared with nonabusers, but alcohol abusers had no striking excess. Our findings thus did not support a theory of two subtypes of substance abuse, one associated with deviant behaviors visible from childhood and another growing out of attempts to medicate symptoms of depression or anxiety.

Having found no distinctive symptom patterns, associated disorders, or outcomes for nondelinquent substance abusers, we sought distinctive predictors in their childhood histories. Three such predictors were found: alcoholism in parents, poor school success, and early regular smoking. These results suggest several hypotheses. First, in the absence of a general propensity to deviant behavior, a genetic factor specific to dependence liability may be required. On the other hand, the effect of the parents' alcoholism may be chiefly that it leads to growing up in a home in which there is increased access to liquor and the presence of models of excessive drinking. Such access may be more important to the nondelinquent than the delinquent, who usually associates with deviant peers who can provide access to alcohol and are models of excessive drinking. A third possibility is that school failure creates the same low self-esteem in the nondelinquent that behavior problems create in the delinquent, encouraging substance abuse to lift spirits and make the youthful user feel more adult and thus more worthy. Why smoking should be a predictor only for nondelinquents is more difficult to understand. It may serve as a mark of being "grown-up" only for children who are otherwise conforming. Among delinquents, smoking may be perceived as so common—and so tame—as to have lost any symbolic meaning.

It is notable that each of the predictors of abuse in nondelinquents might serve to lower the age at which trying these substances begins. This study as well as previous studies have unanimously indicated that beginning use of psychoactive substances before the mid-teens (except under prescription) is a particularly dangerous behavior. The current study shows that it is equally dangerous for delinquents and nondelinquents. This observation has important implications for preventive efforts. It suggests that urging youngsters to postpone their exposure to abusable substances may be important. The fact that many will eventually go on to use them should not be seen as program failure. Postponement alone may be sufficient to protect many from excessive and problem use.

Finally, we need to underscore the fact that substance abuse, particularly in early adolescence, has adverse effects on life chances that are additive with whatever underlying predisposition may have led to the use of these substances in the first place. Therefore, preventive efforts are valuable both with normal conforming children, who will not necessarily recover from substance abuse unscathed just because they began without known pathology, and with deviant children, whose deviance is more likely to be preserved into adult life if they become involved with drugs and alcohol.

This study of drug and alcohol abuse in the general population has endeavored to show some of the diverse purposes which psychiatric epidemiology can serve. Most earlier surveys asking about experience with drugs and alcohol have been limited to assessing lifetime exposure and recent quantity and frequency of use, and perhaps a few indicators of problems resulting from use. The present study shows that general population surveys can also produce reliable estimates of the prevalence of alcohol and drug disorders, in the past as well as currently. Its results underscore the pervasiveness of substance-abuse disorders in our society compared with other types of psychiatric disorder. Epidemiological studies can also suggest hypotheses about causes and consequences of disorder, and when samples are sufficiently large, can allow the study of deviant cases—in this instance, substance abuse that arises independently of a history of childhood delinquent behavior. However, they are efficient sources of such hypotheses only if historical as well as current information is covered. In addition, epidemiological studies can evaluate current nosological systems and find them adequate, as we did in this study, or discover that lumping or splitting diagnoses would more accurately delineate boundaries consistent with naturally appearing symptom patterns. Finally, epidemiological studies can be a source of suggestions for policy with respect to preventive activities, as in this chapter we note the implications for making postponement of exposure a major thrust of preventive activities.

ACKNOWLEDGMENTS

This research was supported by the Epidemiological Catchment Area Program (ECA). The ECA is a series of five epidemiologic research studies performed by independent research teams in collaboration with staff of the Division of Biometry and Epidemiology (DBE) of the National Institute of Mental Health (NIMH). The NIMH principal collaborators are Darrel A. Regier, Ben Z. Locke, and Jack D. Burke, Jr.; the NIMH Project Officer is Carl A. Taube. The principal investigators and coinvestigators from the five sites are: Yale University, UO1 MH 34224—Jerome K. Myers, Myrna M. Weissman, and Gary L. Tischler; Johns Hopkins University, UO1 MH 33870—Morton Kramer and Sam Shapiro; Washington University, St. Louis, UO1 33883—Lee N. Robins and John E. Helzer; Duke University, UO1 MH 35386—Dan Blazer and Linda George; University of California, Los Angeles, UO1 MH 35865—Marvin Karno, Richard L. Hough, Javier I. Escobar, M. Audrey Burnam, and Dianne M. Timbers. This work acknowledges support of this program as well as AA 03539, MH 31302, and Research Scientist Award MH 00334.

REFERENCES

Boyd, J. H., Burke, J. D., Gruenberg, E., Holzer, C. E., III, Rae, D. S., George, L. K., Karno, M., Stoltzman, R., McEvoy, L., & Nestadt, G. (1984). Exclusion criteria of DSM-III: A study of co-occurrence of hierarchy-free syndromes. *Archives of General Psychiatry, 41*, 983–989.

Helzer, J. E., Robins, L. N., McEvoy, L. T., Spitznagel, E. L., Stoltzman, R. K., Farmer, A., & Brockington, I. F. (1985). A comparison of clinical and DIS diagnoses: Physician reexamination of lay interviewed cases in the general population. *Archives of General Psychiatry, 42*, 657–666.

Lukoff, I. F. (1977). Consequences of use: Heroin and other narcotics. In J. D. Rittenhouse (Ed.), *The epidemiology of heroin and other narcotics.* NIDA Research Monograph Series 16, DHEW Publication No. 1 (ADM) 78–559.

Robins, L. N. (1973, April). *A follow-up of Vietnam drug users.* Special Action Office Monograph, Series A, No. 1, Executive Office of the President, Washington, DC.

Robins, L. (1966). *Deviant children grown up: A sociological and psychiatric study of sociopathic personality.* Baltimore: Williams & Wilkins. (Reprinted by Robt. E. Krieger, Huntington, N.Y., 1974.)

Robins, L. N. (1979). Sturdy childhood predictors of adult outcomes: Replications from longitudinal studies. In J. E. Barrett, R. M. Rose, & G. L. Klerman (Eds.), *Stress and mental disorder.* New York: Raven Press, 1979.

Robins, L. N. (1980). The natural history of drug abuse. In L.-M. Gunne (Ed.), *Evaluation of treatment of drug abusers. Acta Psychiatrica Scandinavica, 62*(Suppl. 284), 7–20.

Robins, L., & Murphy, G. E. (1967). Drug use in a normal population of young Negro men. *American Journal of Public Health, 57*, 1580–1596.

Robins, L. N., Hesselbrock, M., Wish, E. D., & Helzer, J. E. (1979). Alcohol and crime in veterans. In L. Otten (Ed.), *Colloquium on the correlates of crime and the determinants of criminal behavior.* McLean, VA: Mitre.

Robins, L. N., Helzer, J. E., Hesselbrock, M., & Wish, E. (1980). Vietnam veterans three years after Vietnam: How our study changed our view of heroin. In L. Brill & C. Winick (Eds.), *Yearbook of substance use and abuse.* New York: Human Sciences Press.

Robins, L. N., Helzer, J. E., Croughan, J., & Ratcliff, K. S. (1981). The NIMH Diagnostic Interview Schedule: Its history, characteristics, and validity. *Archives of General Psychiatry, 38*, 381–389. (Reprinted in J. K. Wing, P. Bebbington, & L. N. Robins (Eds.), *What is a Case?: The problem of definition in psychiatric community surveys.* London: Grant McIntyre, 1981.)

Robins, L. N., Helzer, J. E., Ratcliff, K. S., & Seyfried, W. (1982). Validity of the Diagnostic Interview Schedule, Version II: DSM-III diagnoses. *Psychological Medicine, 12*, 855–870.

DISCUSSION

Robert Hirschfeld: You spoke about three routes to substance abuse: the antisocial, the genetic, and the low self-esteem. I wonder whether your results would change if you were to control for social class differences among the three routes?

Robins: We found remarkably little effect of social class in our sample. Parents' occupation when the respondent was age 16 did not predict substance abuse; it also did not predict delinquency. There was a trend toward more delinquency in lower-status families, but it was a very weak relationship.

Vasant Tanna: In your data showing that nondelinquent drug users had no more psychiatric problems (such as nervousness and depression) than delinquent drug users, were the rate of drug use and the type of drug comparable between the two groups? Certain drugs have particular side effects, and this might introduce a spurious element to the findings. For example, if delinquent drug users were on amphetamines, they would have more tachycardia, palpitations, and so on, than the nondelinquent drug users.

Robins: You are interested in whether the depressive symptoms might result from the substance abuse. That may well be the case. We think that the causal relationships probably go in both directions—that is, substance abuse may cause depression and depression may cause substance abuse. In addition, delinquent behavior also seems to cause substance abuse but not depression. If we look at the substance-abuse-as-a-cause-of-depression direction, we do not expect to find any relationship between delinquent behavior and depression, because substance abuse that arose from delinquent behavior would be neither more nor less likely to cause depression than would other substance abuse. However, when we look at the other causal direction—depression as a possible cause of substance abuse—we do expect to find that delinquency is more strongly associated with substance abuse when there was no preexisting depression. That is because in the absence of depression, some other predictor was probably present, and delinquency is a likely candidate. We will be able to test these hypotheses when we use age of onset of depression and substance abuse to see which appeared first.

Joseph Zubin: This striking finding, that the more you postpone the first taking of the substance-abuse agent, the better are your chances in the future, raises the question of whether a selective factor is working there. Is it possible that those people who tend to be well adjusted in life will tend to take longer to succumb to the temptation of drug abuse?

Robins: You have brought up the important point that epidemiologic research is not an experiment. We can only identify correlations which suggest causal hypotheses; an experiment is required to test these hypotheses. We do not really know whether early age of onset is a cause of later problems or only an indicator of some other causal factor. It looks as though age of onset could be causal because of the fact that when delinquents, whom we know are predisposed to having adult problems, postpone their drug use, they do better.

Still, I can think of many reasons why that causal inference could be wrong. Some kids, for one reason or another, stop being delinquent, and perhaps the fact that they do not start using drugs and alcohol is a sign that they have already reformed. At this point, all we can say is that postponement of use is worth testing in an experimental fashion. We cannot prove a causal relationship from our data.

Bruce Dohrenwend: You mentioned that the class, the socioeconomic relationships were weak. Was that true also for racial differences and for gender?

Robins: We found that overall there was no relationship between race and either alcohol or drug abuse. However, when we split our sample on the basis of delinquency, we found that among delinquents, whites were at higher risk for alcohol abuse than blacks. No difference was found for drug abuse. Regarding the relationship with gender, I do not think a difference existed between male and female, but we have not looked exhaustively at that. We have done one logistic regression, throwing in all of these precursors, and we did not find any striking interactions, but we have much more to do in that area.

Blumenthal: Alcoholism, chemical dependence, aggressivity, and anti-social behaviors have been linked with suicide and suicidal behaviors. Does the ECA study provide any evidence about this?

Robins: That is a very interesting question that can be explored with ECA data. We have asked people whether they have ever had suicidal thoughts, ever wished they were dead, or ever made a suicide attempt. So we can certainly look for association between those suicidal behaviors, substance abuse, and aggressivity. We have not done it yet; we have not looked at individual depressive symptoms, only at whether criteria for a depressive episode were met.

James Halikas: While we have no evidence that there should be differential treatment for the two groups, might they have differential treatment responses?

Robins: We have no idea. We do know whether people have been treated, and, because we have a first and second interview, when we put all 20,000 respondents together from the five sites, there may be enough substance abusers who had treatment shortly before the first interview so that we can compare their outcomes one year later. We may find that one group seems to profit from treatment more than the other. However, our information about the particular type of treatment they received is so sketchy that we still would have no prescription for the best treatment to offer various types of abusers.

3

Urban–Rural Differences in Depressive Disorders: Does Age Make a Difference?

DAN BLAZER, BRADFORD A. CROWELL, Jr., LINDA K. GEORGE, AND RICHARD LANDERMAN
Duke University

INTRODUCTION

Urban–rural differences in the prevalence of psychiatric disorders, especially depressive disorders, have intrigued epidemiologists and sociologists for many years and also have been popular topics among professional and lay audiences (Dohrenwend & Dohrenwend, 1974). Most studies to date, however, have assessed generalized psychological well-being or examined levels of depressive symptoms, rather than probing specific psychiatric disorders. In addition, previous comparisons were usually across studies, thus confounding urban–rural differences with regional, cultural, and/or methodological differences. Investigators with the Piedmont Health Survey (the Duke Epidemiologic Catchment Area Project), a part of the multisite epidemiologic catchment area (ECA) collaborative programs sponsored by the National Institute of Mental Health, surveyed five rural and urban counties in the Piedmont region of North Carolina.

Although there is general consensus that affective disorders are biologically determined to a significant extent, the social origins of depressive disorders in particular continue to receive much attention in the literature. For example, stressful life events have been connected frequently with the etiology of both physical and psychiatric disorders, especially depression (Brown & Harris, 1978; Paykel, 1974; Schwab & Schwab, 1978). Of all ecological and social environments, cities are generally considered to be among the more stressful in that they bear the brunt of technological and social dislocations in modern society. Urban environments are viewed as crime-ridden, riot-torn, and without strong loyalties and consistent values (Dohrenwend & Dohrenwend, 1974). In contrast, rural settings have been viewed as supportive, integrated, and stable (Leighton, Harding, Mackline, Macmillan, & Leighton). Though opinions vary about the degree to which these perceptions of urban versus rural areas are realistic (Hassinger, 1976), especially given the relative rigidity of values and the lack of health services in rural areas, the urban environment still is thought to be an environment particularly conducive to the onset of depressive disorders. Contributory factors include the lack of and/or weak social ties secondary to the transitory nature of urban life, increased frequency of marital separation and divorce (thought to be a risk factor for men), and increased work pressures experienced by upwardly mobile young professionals.

The risk factors generally associated with major depression, such as being separated or divorced, also are more likely to be found among young adults. For this reason, a consideration of urban–rural differences in depressive disorders should control for age. This is especially important in that age is also a risk factor for depression (i.e., depression is most prevalent among adults age 18–44) (Myers, Weissman, & Tischler, 1984). In a previous study based on the Duke ECA data, we reported that major depressive episodes were more common among urban residents and that this increased prevalence persisted even when the sample was stratified for sex, race, marital status, and education (Blazer *et al.*, in press). This chapter reports findings concerning the effects of age and urban–rural residence upon the prevalence of depressive disorders.

The findings reported in this chapter are from the Piedmont Health Survey, a survey of nearly 4000 community-based subjects in the Piedmont region of North Carolina. The study was designed to compare contiguous counties, one urban and four rural. Unlike previous studies, these data permit urban–rural comparisons in the same geographic region. The urban county is dominated by a single city (Durham, North Carolina). The four rural counties (Vance, Granville, Warren, and Franklin) consist of small towns, farms, and undeveloped acreage.

A major focus of this study is comparison of current major depressive episodes with the more chronic dysthymic disorder (depressive neurosis). By definition, an individual had to complain of significant depressive symptoms for at least 2 years (though not for every day) in order to obtain a diagnosis of dysthymic disorder, in contrast to the criteria for diagnosing major depression (depressive affect plus criteria symptoms for 2 weeks). The investigators hypothesized that major depression, in contrast to dysthymic disorder, would be influenced by residence. It is recognized that, among the depressive disorders, bipolar disorders and major depressive disorders are influenced by genetic factors (Weissman, Kidd, & Prusoff, 1982; Winokur, Clayton, & Reich, 1969). Nevertheless, the criteria for a major depressive episode are broadly defined in DSM-III to include both melancholic and nonmelancholic depressive episodes. In addition, studies to date do not demonstrate that genetic and/or biological factors explain all or even the majority of the variance in the distribution of these disorders. Moreover, the work of Brown and Harris (1978) (though limited to females) suggests that social factors are important determinants of even the more severe of the depressive disorders. Dysthymic disorder, however, is more constitutional, related to personality traits, and therefore less subject to environmental influence.

We also hypothesized that the impact of urban–rural residence on the prevalence of depressive disorders would be greater for younger than for older respondents. Some of the psychosocial risk factors that have been associated with the depressive disorders appear to diminish with increasing age. For example, the presence of young children in the household, a risk factor identified by Brown and Harris (1978), would obviously be less prevalent among older persons. In addition, older persons actually suffer fewer stressful life events than individuals at earlier stages of the life cycle (Mellinger, Balter, Manheimer, Cisin, & Perry, 1978) and appear to "rehearse" exit events prior to the actual occurrence of these events, thus buffering their impact (Neugarten, 1970). With regard to urban–rural residence, the particular stresses of urban living that might lead to increased prevalence of major depression, such as the pressures experienced by upwardly mobile professionals, would be less salient among the elderly. In addition, older persons in rural areas may suffer unique stressors, such as lack of transportation and social isolation, that would also mitigate urban–rural differences in that age group.

METHODS

This chapter reports results from the National Institute of Mental Health Epidemiologic Catchment Area Program. Five sites geographically distributed throughout the continental United States—Greater New Haven, East Baltimore, Greater St. Louis, the Piedmont region of North Carolina, and East Los Angeles–Venice—were each sampled to yield approximately 3000 interviews, one from each household, in the respective communities. Of the five ECA sites, the North Carolina sample contained the highest number of rural residents and was designed to facilitate urban–rural comparisons. In the Piedmont Health Survey, a sample was drawn to yield an additional 900 interviews from elderly (age 60+) community residents. Although the survey included both community and institutional residents, this chapter reports results from community respondents only.

The five counties surveyed in North Carolina provide an excellent opportunity for urban–rural comparisons. Durham County is a major metropolitan center in the midst of the Research Triangle, an area that contains more than 500,000 persons and three major universities as well as a large industrial park (Research Triangle Park) which is the site of the research facilities for a number of industrial firms. Twenty-four percent of the population have at least a college education, and mean per capita family income exceeds $20,000. Nevertheless, the city of Durham has not escaped many of the problems of larger metropolitan areas. For example, the decline in employment among the tobacco and textile industries has paralleled the increase in employment in higher technology industries, thus leaving a number of unskilled and semiskilled laborers without jobs. Overall unemployment rates are lower in Durham County than in other urban centers, however.

The four rural counties, in contrast, are most representative of the rural South in transition. There are no major industries in the four counties, though approximately one-third of the residents are employed in some form of manufacturing. The proportion of persons employed in professional and related occupations, however, is only one-half as high as in Durham County. Migration from the rural areas to the urban counties has left a residual population in rural areas that is disproportionately black and poorly educated. Of particular significance is the fact that the city of Durham does not extend into the rural counties, leaving them relatively isolated.

The Piedmont Health Survey team randomly sampled all housing units from segments throughout the five-county area in the north-central Piedmont region of North Carolina. The segments were selected to represent accurately the demographic characteristics of the population within the five counties with regard to race, urban–rural residence, and socioeconomic status. As noted above, elderly residents were oversampled in all of the segments. Once a household was selected and rostered for all residents 18 and over, the Kish (1965) method was used to select one potential participant from each household. This method ensures that, regardless of the size and the composition of the household, a random selection of the respondents is effected. For the elderly oversample, the same method was applied to select one potential participant 60 years of age and older. In the general community survey, 3911 households were screened and an additional 3371 households were screened for the elderly oversample, yielding 3015 respondents in the community sample and 906 respondents in the elderly oversample.

There were 3798 interviews usable for this study. Certain interviews were not used owing to the lack of availability of information from a "proxy" respondent ($n = 80$), a partial interview ($n = 37$), and a determination by the research team that interview information was not reliable ($n = 6$). The overall response rate was 79%. Reasons for nonresponse included inability to obtain a listing of household members for random selection of respondents (10%) and the refusal of a designated respondent to participate in the survey (11%).

These analyses are based on unweighted data and on data weighted to reflect adult population estimates of prevalence for the disorders studied. This weighting procedure took into account household probability selection, nonresponse, and the 1980 census demographic profiles of adults in the five-county catchment area. For significance tests, the data were downweighted to the original number of subjects, but the weighted adjustments remained. The elderly oversample was therefore taken into account in the weighting of the sample.

Urban–rural residence was determined by county of residence. Durham County, which contains the city of Durham, is part of a standard metropolitan statistical area (SMSA) and has a population of 152,785 according to 1980 U.S. census figures. Four counties to the northeast of Durham in the North Carolina Piedmont—Granville, Vance, Warren, and Franklin—are not part of a standard metropolitan statistical area and have a combined population of 117,078. These four counties are contiguous and form a catchment area for one mental health center whereas Durham County is served by a separate mental health center. The demographic profile of the respondents by urban–rural residence is presented in Table 3.1. As is readily apparent, the unweighted demographic characteristics are skewed, reflecting the oversample of the elderly, but the sampled respondents do not differ otherwise from the general population of these five counties.

Each participant in the survey completed an approximately 2-hour interview which included the Diagnostic Interview Survey (DIS), a highly structured interview schedule designed for use by lay interviewers in epidemiologic studies and capable of generating computer-based diagnoses for certain DSM-III disorders (Robins *et al.*, 1981). Robins *et al.* compare the 6-month prevalence of major depressive episodes and the lifetime prevalence of dysthymic disorder among urban–rural residents and in relation to other demographic characteristics. The DIS does not generate a current (6-month) diagnosis of dysthymia and assumes that all cases of dysthymia are lifetime cases. Nevertheless, the vast majority of individuals suffering from a dysthymic disorder in fact have current symptomatology.

Data analysis is based upon crosstabular analysis of weighted data to determine significance of findings across the demographic characteristics of interest.

RESULTS

Table 3.1 presents the demographic profile of subjects participating in the Piedmont Health Survey. The totals for some distributions do not equal 3798 because of missing data. For example, race could not be determined for four subjects. Prevalence data for major depression and dysthymia are presented in Table 3.2. Note the significantly increased prevalence of major depressive episodes among urban as compared to rural residents. Current major depressive episodes are nearly three times more frequent among urban as among rural residents. In contrast, the lifetime prevalence of dysthymia is virtually the same in both the urban and the rural counties. Those individuals who

Table 3.1. Demographic Profile of Community Subjects Participating in the Piedmont Health Survey ($n = 3,798$)

	Rural			Urban			Total		
	No.	%	(Wtd%)	No.	%	(Wtd%)	No.	%	(Wtd%)
Total	1936	51	(44)	1862	49	(56)	3798	100	(100)
Age									
18–24	156	8	(17)	217	12	(19)	373	10	(18)
25–44	560	29	(37)	656	35	(43)	1216	32	(40)
45–64	553	29	(29)	496	27	(26)	1049	28	(27)
65+	667	34	(17)	493	26	(13)	1160	31	(14)
Sex									
Male	718	37	(44)	771	41	(47)	1489	39	(46)
Female	1218	63	(56)	1091	59	(53)	2309	61	(54)
Race									
White	1143	59	(53)	1256	68	(69)	2399	63	(62)
Nonwhite	791	41	(47)	604	32	(31)	1395	37	(38)
Marital status									
Married with spouse	1001	52	(59)	899	48	(56)	1900	50	(57)
Separated/divorced	243	13	(11)	262	14	(12)	505	13	(12)
Widowed	466	24	(11)	350	19	(8)	816	21	(9)
Nonmarried	226	12	(19)	351	19	(24)	577	15	(22)
Education									
Less than high school	1095	57	(49)	696	38	(29)	1791	47	(38)
High school graduate	837	43	(51)	1160	62	(71)	1997	53	(62)
Move within past year									
No	1745	90	(89)	1500	81	(77)	3245	86	(82)
Yes	188	10	(11)	362	19	(23)	550	14	(18)

Note: Wtd% = weighted percentage. Weighted percentages reflect the probability of respondent selection within the household, the nonresponse rate, and the demographic characteristics of the community.

have concurrent diagnoses of dysthymia and current major depressive episodes are included in both the major depressive episode category and the dysthymia category.

As can be seen in Table 3.3, there is some tendency (though not significant) for dysthymia to be more common among urban residents age 18–24 and among rural residents age 25–44. Nonetheless, the general trend across age groups is a relatively even distribution of dysthymia by residence. In contrast, major depression is significantly more prevalent among urban than rural residents in the two younger age groups. The same trend is apparent among respondents age 45–64, but is not apparent among respondents age 65 and older. These data suggest that urban–rural differences are specific to major depressive episodes and to younger age groups. This interaction be-

Table 3.2. Six-Month Prevalence of DIS/DSM-III Major Depression and Dysthymia Stratified by Residence

	Urban		Rural		Total	
	%	(Wtd.%)[a]	%	(Wtd.%)[a]	%	(Wtd.%)
Major depressive episode (*n* = 65)	2.4	(2.70)*	1.1	(0.93)	1.70	(1.90)
Dysthymia (*n* = 96)	2.8	(2.40)	2.3	(2.00)	2.50	(2.20)

*$p < .01$.

[a]Weighted percentages adjust the actual response percentages to take into account household probability selection, response rate, demographic characteristics, and the elderly oversample of the 196,790 persons in the five-county survey area who were 18+ years of age. (Total five-county population, based on 1980 census data, was 269,863.)

tween age and urban–rural residence also explains, in part, the overall decreased prevalence of major depression in the North Carolina ECA data as compared to results from the first three ECA sites (Myers *et al.*, 1984). In fact, when the urban rates in North Carolina are stratified by age and sex, they are similar to those found in New Haven, East Baltimore, and St. Louis.

In an earlier study, the investigators recognized the potential for a number of factors to confound simple urban–rural comparisons (Blazer *et al.*, in press). These factors include age, marital status, sex, race, education,

Table 3.3. Prevalence of DIS/DSM-III Dysthymia and Major Depression (in %) by Age and Residence

	Dysthymia		
Age	Rural	Urban	Total
18–24	1.3 (0.9)[a]	1.9 (1.9)	1.7 (1.5)
25–44	2.7 (2.3)	2.0 (1.6)	2.4 (1.9)
45–64	2.4 (2.0)	3.2 (2.4)	2.8 (2.2)
65+	1.5 (1.3)	1.8 (1.7)	1.6 (1.5)
	Major Depression		
Age	Rural	Urban	Total
18–24	0 (0)	3.2 (3.6)**	1.9 (2.1)
25–44	1.2 (1.1)	3.5 (3.0)*	2.2 (2.0)
45–64	1.8 (1.6)	2.2 (2.3)	2.0 (1.9)
65+	0.6 (0.5)	0.6 (0.9)	0.6 (0.6)

*$p < .05$.
**$p < .01$.
[a]Weighted percentages are in parentheses.

and whether the individual had moved during the year prior to survey. Each of these confounders was differentially distributed between the rural and urban counties, and none was evenly distributed across both major depression and dysthymia. Although stratification would be one method of testing the significance of each of these independent factors, progressive stratification decreased cell size to the point that tests of significance could not be performed effectively. Certain tendencies did arise, however. For example, racial differences were almost totally eliminated when race was stratified by education.

Given this problem with crosstabular techniques, logistic regression was used to predict dysthymia and major depressive disorder, on the basis of the following independent variables: age, sex, race, education, marital status, and whether the respondent had moved during the past year. Major depressive disorders were positively associated with urban residence at a $p < .05$ level, and the estimate of the odds ratio suggested that major depression was almost twice as prevalent among urban residents. Yet, as suggested in Table 3, the effects of age on major depression are nonlinear and therefore somewhat difficult to interpret.

The investigators then returned to the strategy of stratification, splitting the sample into two age groups: 18–44 and 45+. As can be seen in Table 3.4, the higher prevalence in the urban area is almost exclusively found in the

Table 3.4. Six-Month Prevalence of DIS/DSM-III Major Depression (in %) by Sex, Race, and Residence

	Age 18–44						
	Male			Female			
	White	Other	Total	White	Other	Total	Total
Urban	1.7 (1.5)[a]	0.9 (0.7)	1.5 (1.3)*	4.5 (4.1)**	5.8 (6.5)	5.0 (5.0)**	3.4 (3.2)*
Rural	0 (0)	0 (0)	0 (0)	0 (0)	3.6 (2.8)	1.7 (1.4)	1.0 (0.7)
	Age 45+						
	Male			Female			
	White	Other	Total	White	Other	Total	Total
Urban	1.5 (1.8)	0 (0)	1.1 (1.3)	1.4 (2.4)	2.0 (2.3)	1.6 (2.4)	1.4 (1.9)
Rural	1.2 (1.4)	0.6 (0.4)	1.0 (1.2)	1.4 (1.3)	1.0 (1.3)	1.2 (1.3)	1.1 (1.2)

*$p < .05$.
**$p < .01$.
[a]Weighted percentages are in parentheses.

younger age group. This is true for both sexes, but is most dramatic in the white female. Specifically, there were no white females in the 18–44 age group who suffered from major depression in the rural setting, compared to 15 in the urban setting. As females are at higher risk for major depression, this finding was of particular interest. This trend persists in the 45+ age group, but not nearly to the degree seen in the younger age groups. No findings among the respondents age 45 and older reached significance, partially due to their lower prevalence of depression. It is interesting to note that the urban prevalence of major depression in North Carolina, stratified by age and sex, is similar to that found in the New Haven, Baltimore, and St. Louis ECA projects. The lower rural prevalence in North Carolina, particularly among the young, explains in part the overall decreased prevalence of major depression at the North Carolina site (Myers *et al.*, 1984).

CONCLUSION

These findings emphasize the importance of differentiating major depression from dysthymia when studying the relationship between depressive disorders and urban–rural residence, for the pattern varies according to the disorder. Neff (1983) has critically reviewed the evidence for a relationship between urbanicity and depression. He suggests that selective migration may be one factor that contributes to increased levels of depression, and several studies have indicated higher levels of psychiatric disorders among urban migrants than among natives (e.g., Hagnell, 1965). In this sample, the increased risk for current major depression in urban areas persists when moving in the last year was controlled in logistic regression analysis. Yet given the finding of increased major depression in younger persons in the urban setting, these individuals may have had a predisposition to the disorder, moved to an urban setting, and then at a later point in time developed the overt symptomatology.

Another factor that must be taken into account is the fact that "symptom levels" and the actual diagnosis of major depression may be correlated but not identical. For example, a number of studies suggest that the prevalence of depressive symptomatology is higher in the elderly whereas the prevalence of major depressive episodes is lowest in late life when compared to other stages of the life cycle (Blazer, 1983). Therefore, the etiology and meaning of depressive symptomatology may be different across the life cycle. For example, depressive symptomatology elicited through symptom scales (and even the dysthymia algorithm of the DIS) may be more closely related to those etiological factors that precipitate major depression in the younger age group and more related to general life satisfaction in the older age group. Regardless, depressive symptom scales and DIS/DSM-III dysthymia (though being more common in females) do not follow the distribution of major depressive episodes across age and urban–rural residence.

In summary, despite the inherent genetic and biological factors that are undoubtedly precipitants of major depressive episodes, psychosocial factors continue to be associated with their distribution. In these analyses, urban–rural differences in major depressive disorder persist even when race and sex are controlled. These differences are more pronounced among younger females, suggesting that future analyses should focus on those features of urban–rural residence that are especially salient for young adults.

ACKNOWLEDGMENTS

The Epidemiologic Catchment Area Program is a series of five epidemiologic research studies performed by independent research teams in collaboration with staff of the Division of Biometry and Epidemiology (DBE) of the National Institute of Mental Health (NIMH). The NIMH principal collaborators are Darrell A. Regier, Ben Z. Locke, and Jack Burke; the NIMH project officer is Carl A. Taube. The principal investigators and the coinvestigators from the five sites are: Yale University, UO1 MH 34224—Jerome K. Myers, Myrna M. Weissman, and Gary L. Tischler; Johns Hopkins University, UO1 MH 33870—Morton Kramer, Ernest Gruenberg, and Sam Shapiro; Washington University, St. Louis, UO1 MH 33883—Lee N. Robins and John Helzer; Duke University, UO1 MH 35386—Dan Blazer and Linda George; University of California, Los Angeles, UO1 MH 35865—Richard Hough, Marvin Karno, Javier Escobar, Audrey Burnam, and Dianne Timbers.

REFERENCES

Blazer, D. G. (1983). The epidemiology of psychiatric disorder in the elderly population. In L. Grinspoon (Ed.), *Psychiatric update: The American Psychiatric Association Annual Review* (Vol. 2; pp. 87–95). Washington, D.C.: American Psychiatric Press.

Blazer, D. G., George, L. K., Landerman, R., Pennybacker, M., Melville, M. L., Woodbury, M., Manton, K. G., Jordan, K., & Locke, B. (in press). Psychiatric disorders: A rural/urban comparison. *Archives of General Psychiatry.*

Brown, G. W., & Harris, T. (1978). *Social origins of depression: A study of psychiatric disorder in women.* London: Tavistock Publications.

Dohrenwend, B. P., & Dohrenwend, B. S. (1974). Psychiatric disorders in urban settings. In G. Kaplan (Ed.), *Child and adolescent psychiatry: Sociocultural and community psychiatry* (Vol. II of the *American handbook of psychiatry*; pp. 424–449). New York: Basic Books.

Hagnell, O. (1966). *A prospective study of the incidence of mental disorder.* Lund: Scandinavian University Books.

Hassinger, E. W. (1976). Pathways of rural people to health services. In E. W. Hassinger & L. R. Whiting (Eds.), *Rural health services: Organization, delivery and use.* Ames, IA: Iowa State University Press.

Kish, L. (1965). *Survey sampling.* New York: Wiley.

Leighton, D. C., Harding, J. S., Mackline, D. B., Macmillan, A. M., & Leighton, A. H. (1963). *The character of danger.* New York: Basic Books.

Mellinger, C. D., Balter, M. B., Manheimer, D. I., Cisin, I. H., & Perry, H. J. (1978). Psychic distress, life crisis, and the use of psychotherapeutic medications: National household survey data. *Archives of General Psychiatry, 35*, 1045–1052.

Myers, J. K., Weissman, M. M., & Tischler, G. L. (1984). Six month prevalence of psychiatric disorders in three communities. *Archives of General Psychiatry, 41*(10), 959–970.

Neff, J. A. (1983). Urbanicity and depression reconsidered: The evidence regarding depressive symptomatology. *Journal of Nervous and Mental Diseases, 171*(9), 546–552.

Neugarten, B. L. Adaptive and life cycle. *Journal of Geriatric Psychology, 4*(1), 71.

Paykel, E. S. (1974). Life stress in psychiatric disorder. In B. S. Dohrenwend & B. P. Dohrenwend (Eds.), *Stressful life events: Their nature and effects* (pp. 135–149). New York: Wiley.

Robins, L. N., Helzer, J. E., Croughan, J., & Rathcliff, K. S. (1981). National Institute of Mental Health Diagnostic Interview Schedule: Its history, characteristics and validity. *Archives of General Psychiatry, 38*, 381–389.

Schwab, J. J., & Schwab, M. E. (1978). *Sociocultural routes of mental illness: An epidemiologic survey.* New York: Plenum Medical Book Company.

Weissman, M. M., Kidd, K. K., & Prusoff, B. A. (1982). Variability in rates of affective disorders in relatives of depressed and normal probands. *Archives of General Psychiatry, 39*, 1397–1403.

Winokur, G., Clayton, P. J., & Reich, T. (1969). *Manic depressive illness.* St. Louis: C. V. Mosby.

DISCUSSION

Bruce Dohrenwend: In our 1974 paper that Dr. Blazer mentioned, we did find higher rates in urban areas of what was then lumped together as "neurosis." I think this finding was present in five out of the six studies that had an urban–rural contrast. If, as is likely, most cases of what is now called major depression were in that broad neurotic category, then your difference would be consistent with results from first- and second-generation studies.

Blazer: We have just done some preliminary analysis looking at a much looser approach to diagnosing generalized anxiety disorder, something that we included in our Wave II analyses and which was included at other ECA sites as well. We found that the rates of generalized anxiety disorder did not differ appreciably across urban–rural boundaries. We were surprised to see that, because we felt that overall they would. They did not show the degree of difference that major depression showed. However, when we broke that group down by race, we found that the differences did not hold up for whites; in fact, whites seemed to be protected against generalized anxiety disorders in rural areas as opposed to urban areas.

In fact, although I cannot speak conclusively about this yet, in our findings a trend is beginning to emerge, that in our area a rural residence is more protective for whites than it is for blacks. We have not controlled for socioeconomic status, which is very important, but at least the crude rate suggests that urban–rural differences are more likely to be found among whites than among blacks, both in generalized anxiety disorder, major depression, and also in alcoholism.

Murray Raskind: How did you deal with the possible problem of the reluctance of older persons to endorse depressive symptoms, and perhaps other psychopathologic symptoms in general?

Blazer: We think that this is actually not the case in community surveys. We went into an analysis that I did not report today, looking at the self-report of psychological symptoms of depression as opposed to somatic symptoms of depression. We thought that those individuals who were diagnosed with major depressive episode would have more somatic symptoms and fewer psychological symptoms. This we did not find. They did have more somatic symptoms, but they also had more psychological symptoms.

In general, if you looked at those individuals with no DIS diagnosis whatsoever, the rate of reporting most of the psychological symptoms for depression is virtually the same for the middle-aged and the elderly. If you look at the individuals who are diagnosed as having a major depressive episode, they actually report more of these psychological symptoms than what you find typically. So I think this concern that older persons do not report psychological symptoms may be unique to the hospital and possibly unique to those individuals who are suffering from a severe endogenous depression as opposed to individuals who fall into the broader category of a major depressive disorder.

We also looked at those individuals who self-endorsed the item "Have you been depressed for the past two weeks?" and again, no age difference appears when you look at diagnosis across that particular endorsement.

Myrna Weissman: I wanted to say something about that too. In the 1975 survey using the SADS, although we had a very small sample of people over 65, we also found the same types of lower rates in the elderly. More important, in our family studies where we have information from multiple informants, rather than just from the subject, we still find the same low rates. So it may just be that it is a cohort effect.

Blazer: I guess the bottom line is we think that low rates of depression are real in the elderly.

Gerald Klerman: In the classical sociological literature about urban–rural differences that goes back to Farris and Dunham, there is always mention of social drift. Are you involved in a situation where people with depression, or proneness to depression, are more likely to migrate into the city, and in your analysis can you control for the role of migration? If it is a migration effect, then you have an antecedent–consequence problem. Is it that certain personality types or depression-prone individuals are more likely to migrate, or is there something about the stress of migration and the changes in social bonding that cause those who move to be more prone to disorders?

Blazer: I can comment very specifically on how we attempted to control for it, and Dr. Dohrenwend can tell us whether I was right or not. We were looking at 6-month prevalence of depression. We looked in terms of drift at those individuals who had moved within the past year and included moving as a control variable in our logistic regression. When moving was included, the urban–rural differences persisted.

Now, that only addresses the last depressive episode. What we cannot control for is the predisposition to depression, and we have not yet examined our data in terms of selecting individuals who have had a recurrence of depression and where that 1-year factor would not be taken into account. However, we do have some ability to control for it in our analyses, and we have made an attempt to do so.

Dohrenwend: In the earlier review, we had no way of ruling out selection alternatives. However, I do not know of any literature reporting that depressives are more likely to migrate, that they move around a lot. I haven't seen anything like that. You would be much more likely to expect it of schizophrenics, where there happens to be no consistent urban–rural difference in the past studies. So you certainly cannot rule it out, since you have no premigration baseline, and no study has ever come up with one.

Leo Srole: Farris and Dunham were not the first to refer to the drift to the cities from the outlying sections. In the follow-up of the Midtown Manhattan Study, we found considerable drift from the city *out* into the suburbs, the countryside, and the exurbs. In a preliminary test to see whether there was any selective difference between those who stayed put and those who left, we found none; that is, those who left the city were approximately the same as those who had stayed in terms of their mental health.

Joseph Zubin: With reference to the low rate of depression in the elderly, is it possible that there is a survival phenomenon at work, namely, differential mortality? By the time they reach the older age, might those people who had a tendency to depression have died off, leaving only those with a lower risk for depression?

Blazer: I think Dr. Zubin raises an excellent question. We have given considerable thought to this lower rate of depression in the elderly, not only for methodologic reasons, but also for policy reasons. Those of us who work with mental illness in later life and depend upon funding are concerned when we see statements in Congress suggesting "the myth of mental illness in the elderly." We believe a number of factors may be operative. It is possible that we may see some selective mortality. What may be more likely, however, is what Dr. Weissman just mentioned, that in this particular cohort of older persons we see lower rates of major depressive episodes. I believe that younger cohorts, especially people in midlife, are now showing fairly high levels of major depression, and the rates are not going to drop as those individuals get into late life. So the idea that depression is not a problem among the elderly appears to be a temporary illusion.

Also, we find that the individuals who currently report major depression in later life are less likely to report a previous episode than people at early stages of the life cycle. It is fairly rare to find an individual reporting a past history of major depression who does not also report a present history of major depression. So we tend to believe that the findings are real. In older persons we must also consider problems with memory, problems with conceptualizing the construct of major depression, and, as Dr. Raskind mentioned, the problem of differential symptom endorsement. But I believe the cohort effect is a major contributor.

Ernest Gruenberg: I would like to comment on the migration issue. Migration has been discussed as though it were only important in terms of what one might call numerator factors: people with the disorder or about to develop the disorder are likely to move in a particular direction. But the concept is one of differential migration. It was first developed in epidemiology by Ørnulv Ødegaard in his study of mental disorders among migrants from Norway to the United States. His concept was a greater migration for the cases than for the noncases. There are situations, as Wade Hampton Frost pointed out, in which a whole population has a tendency to migrate and the presence of disabling disorders inhibits the tendency to migrate. I don't know what the situation has been at Duke. Perhaps the whites living in the rural area were professionals who tended to move out from the city to more attractive places. Chronic illness could inhibit such migration. That is the other side of the coin of differential migration that we ought to keep in mind.

Blazer: This is an important issue, and we feel that it is why our particular sample may be unique. It is a characteristic of our area that individuals do not tend to move into these four counties if they continue to work in the urban area, and therefore the migration of individuals into the "suburbs" actually means into the suburbs of Durham County, which we continue to classify as urban.

Durham County provides a rather wide border around the central city of Durham per se. You would have to be there to appreciate the distance between the inner city of Durham and the county line. So we don't think that migration out is playing a significant role. Upper-class and middle-class whites certainly do live in the rural counties, but they tend to be individuals who have lived there for generations, not those who have moved out from the urban areas.

Jules Angst: We have studied a very young cohort only, age 20–23, and we did not find any urban–rural differences. But it is also true that the difference between urban and rural life-style is probably not as marked as in your setting.

Does the decrease of prevalence of depression with age that was found in the Yale study, and in your ECA sample also, hold for all depressive syndromes? Does it hold for primary depression, secondary depression, and so on?

Blazer: If you use a typical symptom checklist, such as the Zung scale or the CES-D, you do not see this decline with age nearly as markedly. That is one of the paradoxes of understanding depression in the elderly: you may actually see an increase in the levels of those symptoms that we generally associate with depression, but a decrease in the rate of major depression.

I have some ideas about this finding. Many older persons may score high on depression scales when, in fact, they are suffering from decreased life satisfaction, which I think is a separate construct. Also, depression for a number of older persons may not fit easily into the procrustean bed of DSM-III; in fact, they may be suffering from an "atypical" depression, which may not be atypical at all for the elderly. It actually may be the most common variant of depression.

4

Psychosocial Risks and Correlates of Major Depression in One United States Urban Community

PHILIP J. LEAF, MYRNA M. WEISSMAN, JEROME K. MYERS,
CHARLES E. HOLZER III, AND GARY L. TISCHLER
Yale University

INTRODUCTION

One of the most important aspects of epidemiologic research is its community-based orientation. Focusing on the full range of psychopathology, epidemiologic research has potential for uncovering important etiologic findings reflecting both the causes and consequences of psychiatric disorders (Weissman & Klerman, 1978). To the extent that these investigations eliminate the selection biases inherent in studies dealing only with treated cases (Cohen & Cohen, 1984), epidemiologic research provides important insights into factors related to receiving treatment for a psychiatric disorder and prognosis. In addition, epidemiologic studies represent an additional strategy for the validation of clinical concepts.

This chapter represents our initial attempt to identify psychosocial risks and correlates of current major depression based on DSM-III in a sample of residents from one U.S. urban community (New Haven, Connecticut). The data derive from the first wave of interviews from the Yale Epidemiologic Catchment Area (ECA) study, one of five ECA projects being conducted in five U.S. sites. The purpose of this chapter is twofold. First, we describe some of the unique aspects of the ECA projects deriving from their focus on specific, well-defined populations. Second, we present results from the first attempt to apply DSM-III criteria for major depression in a community survey and discuss the extent to which demographic and social factors are correlated with increased risk of major depression.

Epidemiologic Precursors to the ECA Project

The Epidemiologic Catchment Area (ECA) project reflects both a long history of descriptive epidemiology and an important break with earlier conceptual models and methodologies. Community studies of mental illness are not a recent tool for either scientists or policymakers. Large-scale surveys of the prevalence of psychiatric disorders have been conducted since the late 1820s when Halliday conducted an extensive survey of individuals receiving treatment for mental illness in Scotland and supplemented this information with an extensive inventory of key informants (Halliday, 1828, cited in Schwab & Schwab, 1978).

Efforts in this area were not limited to Europe. As early as 1840, the U.S. government attempted to enumerate all "insane and idiotic" through its Decennial Census. In 1855, Edward Jarvis conducted an extensive survey of the prevalence of idiocy and insanity in Massachusetts by supplementing data from institutional records with reports from physicians, clergy, and community leaders. In the 1880 census, the usual house-to-house canvass was expanded to include correspondence with approximately 80,000 physicians in order to obtain an enumeration of mania, melancholia, paresis, dementia, dipsomania, and epilepsy. Other early studies include Rosanoff's study of Nassau County and the studies of the Eastern Health District of Baltimore in the early 1930s (Lemkau, Tietze, & Cooper, 1942). Jablonsky (in press) has recently reviewed over one hundred epidemiologic studies, many utilizing quite sophisticated longitudinal designs.

Innovations of the ECA Project

But if so many other epidemiologic studies have been conducted, why should particular attention be paid to the ECA project? The answer to this question is fourfold. First, the ECA project represents the first attempt to apply DSM-III diagnostic criteria in a community setting. Many of the earlier studies do not allow for the differentiation of specific psychiatric disorders or apply criteria no longer in general use. Second, the ECA project will eventually consist of over 30,000 interviews, from over 18,000 different individuals. These large samples allow for the testing of hypotheses concerning specific disorders not possible with more limited epidemiologic surveys. Third, the ECA project allows for replication across communities with comparable assessment procedures being used in five distinct communities. The ability to contrast rates and risk factors will greatly increase the generalizability of the data.

Fourth, the ECA project allows for design-based analyses incorporating effects of the study design making statistical tests of significance. Statistical tests of significance utilized in previous epidemiologic studies of psychiatric disorders relied on the "assumption" of simple random sampling even though few studies actually utilized simple random sampling. Because of the focus on defined populations, the ECA Project takes advantage of statistical techniques previously utilized by only the largest and most sophisticated national health surveys (Cohen & Kalsbeek, 1981). These design-based analyses incorporate estimates of variance based on observed data and allow for tests of significance more closely tied to the actual procedures generating the sample (Hansen, Madow, & Tepping, 1983; Sarndal, 1984). Cohen and Kalsbeek (1981) have demonstrated that the consequence of assuming simple random samples generated from complete surveys is nonconservative statistical inferences.

Risks and Correlates of Major Depression

In this chapter we focus on the relationship between social factors and the prevalence of major depression in the New Haven ECA. Previous studies using samples of treated cases have identifying factors that are related to the onset of major depression such as chronic stress and family history (Weissman, Kidd, & Prusoff, 1982), genetic factors (Kidd, 1982), early childhood relationships (Orvaschel, Weissman, & Kidd, 1980) and personality (Hirschfeld & Klerman, 1979). The data we are presenting do not include indicators of these factors or deal with the incidence of new cases. The extent to which factors identified in previous studies as being related to major depression are related in the New Haven area and the extent to which these relationships simply reflect the effects of sex and age on the prevalence of major depression will be determined in this chapter. This exercise is important because much of what we know about risk factors and correlates for major depression is based on clinical data (Hirschfeld & Cross, 1982; Keller, Lavori, Endicott, Coryell, & Klerman, 1983). In addition, little research incorporates the current DSM-III criteria. We will not attempt to review the huge volume of research that has investigated correlates of major depression because several comprehensive assessments of this literature already exist. Instead, we will review those findings most relevant to the current study.

In their comprehensive review of psychosocial risk factors for major depression, Hirschfeld and Cross (1982) found a consistent relationship between sex and age. The highest rates of major depression were in women and persons under age 40. No studies reporting association between major depression with race were found.

Marital status has also been identified frequently as an important correlate of major depression. For example, divorce has been found to be a frequent consequence of major depression (Briscoe & Smith, 1973). Marital friction is the most common event reported by depressed patients prior to the onset of depression (Paykel, Myers, Dienelt, Klerman, Lindenthal, & Pepper, 1969). Marital problems have also been found to be overrepresented in depressed patients coming to treatment (Coyne, 1976; Weissman & Paykel, 1974) and a lack of a confiding heterosexual relationship was found to be a major vulnerability factor by Brown and Harris (1978).

METHODS

Sample

The data in this chapter are from the first wave of community interviews at the New Haven ECA. The methodology used has been discussed in detail elsewhere so we will only briefly review the procedures (Eaton & Kessler, 1985). Interviews were obtained from 5034 residents of a 13-town region of south-central Connecticut. In 1980, the area had a total population of 420,000 persons living in 150,000 housing units. Of these 300,110 were persons age 18 and older living outside of institutions. The area includes three general hospitals, a large community mental health center, a major medical school, a Veterans' Administration hospital, and a small private psychiatric hospital. Since the study includes data from an oversample of 1977 individuals age 65 and older, poststratification procedures have been used to obtain estimates that represent relationships for the community studied. The overall completion rate was 77%.

Diagnostic Interview Schedule (DIS)

The interview used in this study included version 2 of the NIMH Diagnostic Interview Schedule (DIS) (Robins, Helzer, Croughan, & Ratcliff, 1981) and questions concerning general health, functional disability, sociodemographic characteristics, barriers to care, role performance, and utilization of general medical, mental health, and human service facilities. All interviewing was conducted in the field by trained lay interviewers. The entire interview took approximately one hour to complete. In instances where the respondent was too ill to be interviewed or where the respondent spoke a language other than Spanish or English, an informant interview was utilized.

    Briefly, the DIS is a highly structured interview designed for use by lay interviewers in epidemiologic studies and capable of generating a set of computer diagnoses according to DSM-III. The DIS elicits the elements of a diagnosis, including severity, frequency, distribution over time of symptoms, and whether or not they can be explained by physical illness, drug or alcohol use, or another psychiatric diagnosis. The instrument contains structured questions and probes and is precoded so that after editing, answers can be entered directly into the computer. Diagnosis can be generated to cover a range of time periods: within the last 2 weeks, 1 month, 6 months, 1 year, or lifetime. We discuss only 6-month prevalence rates.

Criteria for Major Depression

In earlier ECA reports (Myers, Weissman, Tischler, Holzer, & Leaf, 1984; Robins, Helzer, Weissman, Orvaschel, & Gruenberg, 1984), we presented rates of depressive episodes rather than major depressive disorder. In this chapter, we focus only on those individuals who met criteria for major depression during the 6-month period prior to being interviewed. Individuals who experienced an episode of major depression during the 6-month period but who also reported an earlier episode of mania are excluded from these analyses. Individuals reporting a depressive episode lasting 12 months or longer that occurred after a significant loss are also included. Although bereavement is an exclusion criteria in DSM-III, in these data bereavement lasting for more than one year and of sufficient severity to otherwise meet criteria for a depressive disorder is considered indicative of major depression.

Weighting Data

There are two reasons for weighting data prior to conducting analyses. In the New Haven sample, individuals were selected inversely proportional to the size of their households. In addition, individuals age 65 or older were over-sampled because of special interest in obtaining a large enough sampling of elderly to be able to study psychopathology in this group. In order to correct for these differences in selection probability, data were weighted inversely to the actual probability of selection into the sample.

Because we were interested in generalizing to a specific, well-defined population, the New Haven ECA, poststratification procedures were also incorporated in order to improve the fit between the estimates generated from our sample and the known characteristics of the catchment area (Holt & Smith, 1979). This correction takes into account nonresponse and inadequacies in the sampling frame (Holzer *et al.*, 1985). The weighted sample produces population estimates that correspond precisely to those obtained by the U.S. census.

Statistical Analysis

Since conventional statistical procedures assume simple random sampling and are not appropriate for the analysis of complex weighted samples (Cohen, 1983), all tests of statistical significances reported in this chapter incorporate estimates of the design effects using the SURREGR statistical programs (Hansen, Horwitz, & Madow, 1953; Kessler *et al.*, 1985; Shah & LaVange, 1981). These procedures utilize weighted least-squares rather than ordinary least-squares estimates and are therefore equivalent for large samples to the maximum-likelihood estimators. In almost all cases, this procedure produces a more conservative test of statistical significance than would be produced by estimates of variance assuming simple random sampling.

In order to examine the relationship between social factors and major depression we first determined whether the 6-month prevalence rates of major depression varied by the levels of the social factor. The relationships were then reexamined adjusting for age (18–44/45–64/65+) and sex. In the tables presented in this chapter, the actual sample size is presented along with percentages and rates based on the weighting procedures described earlier.

RESULTS

Demographic Characteristics of Sample

As Table 4.1 indicates, over half the residents in this community were female, under age 45, and currently married. Almost three-quarters of the residents had completed high school. Over 86% of the sample was white. The median age of our sample was 41. Over half the respondents had a household income of $20,000 or more.

Table 4.1. Sociodemographic Characteristics of New Haven Epidemiologic Catchment Area

	Unweighted N	Weighted Percent
Sex		
Male	2,062	46.4
Female	2,972	53.6
Age (years)		
18–44	1,655	54.2
45–64	803	29.8
65+	2,576	16.0
Race		
White	4,440	86.6
Black	420	10.1
Other	139	3.3
Marital Status		
Married	2,492	59.9
Widowed	1,231	8.1
Sep/Div	517	9.5
Single	792	22.5
Education (years)		
0–8	1,167	11.8
9–11	751	13.3
12	1,339	30.9
13–15	831	21.0
16+	931	23.1
Annual Household Income		
0–$9,999	1,618	19.6
$10,000–19,999	1,237	28.1
$20,000–34,500	994	34.2
$35,000+	482	18.2

Table 4.2. Six-Month Prevalence Rates for Major Depression in the Yale ECA by Age and Sex

		Rates per 100		
		Males ($N = 2,062$)	Females ($N = 2,972$)	Full Sample ($N = 5,034$)
18–44	($N = 1655$)	2.0	5.8	3.9
45–64	($N = 803$)	1.2	2.2	1.7
65+	($N = 2576$)	0.5	1.6	1.2
Overall		1.5	3.9	2.8

Correlates of Major Depression

Demographic. The primary goal of this analysis is to investigate the relationships between a variety of social factors and the prevalence of major depression in residents of a well-defined geographic area.

Sex and Age. Table 4.2 shows the 6-month prevalence rates of major depression by sex and age. Both sex ($\chi^2 = 18.85$, 1 df, $p < .001$) and age ($\chi^2 = 19.86$, 1 df, $p < .001$) exhibit direct effects on the rates of major depression. Rates are higher in females (female-to-male ratio 2.5:1), and younger persons age 18–44, particularly age 25–44. There is, however, also a significant sex:age interaction ($\chi^2 = 9.06$, 1 df, $p < .025$) with young females having particularly high rates of depression. Within sex, the rates decrease with increasing age.

Race. There is no statistically significant relationship ($\chi^2 = 0.22$, 1 df, NS) between major depression and race (nonwhite is mainly black Americans) with the rate of major depression 2.8/100 among whites and 3.0/100 among nonwhites (Table 4.3).

Table 4.3. Six-Month Prevalence Rates for Major Depression for Yale ECA: Race

	Rates per 100	
	White ($N = 4,440$)	Nonwhite ($N = 559$)
Males		
18–44	1.9	2.5
45–64	1.2	0
65+	0.6	0
Females		
18–44	5.9	5.3
45–64	2.4	0
65+	1.5	3.2
Overall	2.8	3.0

Education. The relationship between education and major depression appears to be somewhat curvilinear when the sex and age of the respondent is not considered. As Table 4.4 indicates, however, the relationship between education and major depression is quite complex with the data indicating a significant three-way interaction between education, sex, and age ($\chi^2 = 15.8$, 8 df, $p < .05$). Males (age 18–44) with less than 9 years of education report very high rates of major depression (7.4/100). The highest rates of depression appear to be concentrated in the younger females with moderate levels of education. For females in the highest education group we do not find the inverse relationship between age and depression found in other groups.

Economic Status

Personal and Household Income. The assessment of the relationship between income and major depression further illustrates the importance of taking age and sex into account when examining these data. Personal income (Table 4.5) shows a significant relationship with major depression in the absence of controls for age and sex ($\chi^2 = 9.1$, 3 df, $p < .05$). Individuals with less personal income have higher rates of depression than individuals with higher personal incomes with those earning less than $5000 per year twice as likely to have depression as those earning $20,000 per year or more (3.9% vs. 1.7%). The data in Table 4.5, however, show no relationship between personal income and major depression once the age and sex are taken into account ($\chi^2 = 4.6$, 3 df, NS). There is clearly no relationship between personal income and major depression in the elderly and only trends that are difficult to interpret such as the inconsistency of income relationship among middle-aged women.

Table 4.4. Six-Month Prevalence Rates for Major Depression for Yale ECA: Education

	Rates per 100 Years of Education				
	0–8 (N = 1,167)	9–11 (N = 751)	12 (N = 1,339)	13–15 (N = 831)	16+ (N = 931)
Males					
18–44	7.4	1.3	1.5	1.6	2.4
45–64	1.8	0.9	1.9	1.1	0
65+	0.6	1.2	0.6	0	0
Females					
18–44	0	10.7	6.1	5.9	3.4
45–64	0	1.2	2.4	2.5	3.6
65+	1.7	1.1	1.4	0.7	3.4
Overall	1.5	3.5	3.1	3.2	2.4

Table 4.5. Six-Month Prevalence Rates for Major Depression for Yale ECA: By Personal Income

Income	Rates per 100 Annual Personal Income			
	0–4,999 (N = 1,763)	5,000–9,999 (N = 1,156)	10,000–19,999 (N = 1,061)	20,000+ (N = 549)
Males				
18–44	3.5	1.8	1.1	2.3
45–64	2.6	2.2	1.3	0.8
65+	1.0	1.0	0	0
Females				
18–44	6.1	5.9	4.4	2.6
45–64	2.1	3.0	0.4	4.7
65+	2.0	1.5	2.4	1.9
Overall	3.9	3.4	1.8	1.7

A different situation appears to exist for household income. Although the relationship between household income and major depression is not as consistent as with personal income, Table 4.6 indicates that the most affluent households have the lowest rates of major depression. However, the overall relationships are not statistically significant suggesting that household and personal income may be substantively different indicators.

Employment Status

When the relationship between employment status and major depression was investigated (Table 4.7), we found that employment status was significantly

Table 4.6 Six-Month Prevalence Rates for Major Depression for Yale ECA: By Household Income

Income	Rates per 100 Annual Household Income			
	0–9,999 (N = 1,618)	10,000–19,999 (N = 1,237)	20,000–34,999 (N = 994)	35,000+ (N = 482)
Males				
18–44	5.6	2.1	2.3	0.3
45–64	3.9	1.0	1.4	0
65+	1.2	0.2	0	0
Females				
18–44	8.2	5.1	5.4	6.1
45–64	0.6	1.9	4.2	0
65+	2.3	0.2	6.4	1.4
Overall	3.9	2.5	3.4	1.9

Table 4.7. Six-Month Prevalence Rates for Major Depression for Yale ECA: Employment

	Rates per 100		
	Working Full Time (N = 1,638)	Not Working Now (N = 3,061)	Never Worked (N = 306)
Males			
18–44	1.8	3.2	0
45–64	0.6	3.2	0
65+	0	0.6	0
Females			
18–44	4.6	5.3	12.0
45–64	1.6	2.0	10.1
65+	3.6	1.4	2.8
Overall	2.2	2.9	8.0

related to major depression ($\chi^2 = 7.7$, 2 df, $p < .025$). However, when the data were adjusted for the age and sex of the respondents, we found a more complex relationship between employment and depression with both a direct effect of employment status ($\chi^2 = 15.2$, 2 df, $p < .001$) and a sex:employment interaction ($\chi^2 = 11.2$, 2 df, $p < .005$). Few men in the sample had never worked, and none of these reported having a recent case of major depression. Females age 18–64 who had never worked exhibited very high rates of major depression. At all ages, males who were not currently employed exhibited more depression than those who were working full-time. For females, this effect was less consistent with females age 65 or older who were working having higher rates of major depression than other females in that age group.

Number and Ages of Children

There is a significant relationship between number of children and major depression. However, as shown in Table 4.8, the relationship is not linear. Persons with one child have the highest rates. This finding is particularly strong among younger parents (age 18–44) and for females, although the only interactions that are statistically significant are the age:sex interaction ($p < .025$).

Marital Status

Marital status is significantly related to major depression, only when we compare the widowed/separated with all others ($\chi^2 = 5.34$, 1 df, $p < .025$), but these data suggest that this relationship is much more complex than

Table 4.8. Six-Month Prevalence Rates for Major Depression for Yale ECA: Number of Children

	Rates per 100		
	0 (N = 1,305)	1 (N = 800)	2+ (N = 2,029)
Males			
18–44	2.2	4.8	0.7
45–64	1.4	1.4	1.1
65+	0.9	0	0.6
Females			
18–44	3.6	10.1	6.3
45–64	0	3.7	2.8
65+	1.2	2.7	1.5
Overall	2.5	5.4	2.4

usually acknowledged. When we adjust for age and sex, this relationship is no longer statistically significant. Rates are significantly higher in the separated and divorced (5.7/100) and are lowest in the currently married (2.3/100) and widowed (2.1/100). The rates are highest in females and in persons under age 45. The highest rates (10.8%) are in separated women age 18–44.

On the other hand, Table 4.9 indicates that even among the lower-risk groups, there exist individuals with relatively high rates of major depression. We find that when both marital status and satisfaction are taken into account, there are significant differences in rates of disorder ($\chi^2 = 14.2$, 4 df,

Table 4.9 Six-Month Prevalence Rates for Major Depression for Yale ECA: Marital Status and Satisfiction Rates per 100

	Sep/Div (N = 517)	Single (N = 792)	Widowed (N = 1,231)	Married— gets Along w/Spouse (N = 2,364)	Married— Does Not get Along w/Spouse (N = 47)
Males					
18–44	5.9	2.6	0	0.5	10.9
45–64	2.1	0	4.9	0.6	34.3
65+	0	0	0.5	0.6	0
Females					
18–44	9.4	14.4	17.9	4.0	68.7
45–64	1.6	0	2	2	19.6
65+	3.2	1.2	1.6	1.5	0
Overall	5.7	3.1	2.1	1.7	30.5

$p < .01$). For example, the rates are significantly higher in persons who are married but who report that they do not get along with their spouses (30.5/ 100). There is nearly an 18-fold increase in risk of major depression for a person who complains of marital discord as contrasted with persons who report fair to excellent marital harmony. Widowed females age 18–44 report high rates of major depression (17.9/100). The rates of major depression are slightly higher in separated men (11.2/100) as compared to separated women (9/100), one of the few instances of a reversal in the sex ratios. These findings suggest that care must be taken when generalizing from overall rates of disorder to rates for specific subpopulations. In addition, statistical analysis of marital status is limited by the relatively small number of widowed, separated, and single individuals in certain age ranges.

SUMMARY

We have investigated the demographic correlates of major depression in one specific community. Certain subpopulations were found to exhibit increased risk of major depression: the young, individuals with unhappy or disrupted marriages, and individuals with a single child and/or who are not currently working. Other demographic factors, such as personal income, were significantly related to major depression only in the absence of controls for the effects of age and sex.

An important finding is that susceptibility to major depression may be greater at specific stages of the life cycle than at others. These findings suggest that studies not controlling for the effects of age and sex may attribute risk to factors not having independent effects on rates of depression. Likewise, these findings suggest that studies of different communities or subpopulations may appear to produce contradictory findings simply as the result of the samples containing different age and sex distributions. In future investigations, we need to focus more clearly on identifying vulnerability and stress factors that operate only at specific points in the life cycle or for specific subgroups.

Comparison with Other Studies

A major finding of this study is the similarity of data from the Yale ECA and data from other epidemiologic and clinical studies of major depression. For example, when the data from the Yale ECA are compared with data from an earlier New Haven study (Weissman & Myers, 1980), we find that in both studies the rates of major depression were higher in females than in males and in separated/divorced persons. In the 1975 survey, social class, which is a composite of education and income, did not show a significant relationship with rates of major depression. The current relationship between these variables appears to be quite complex. However, the communities sampled in the two studies are not exactly comparable with the variation in socioeconomic status being much less in the earlier study than in the current study.

A major difference in findings between the two studies is the association of major depression with age. The present study found higher rates of major depression in persons age 26–44 than did the earlier 1975 survey. The rates in persons age 46–65 and 66+ are similar. The rapid decline in prevalence rates of major depression in the elderly found in the ECA was not found in the 1975 New Haven survey. However, there were only 111 persons age 66+ in the 1975 survey. In addition, the 1975 survey consisted of individuals originally interviewed in 1967 and 1969. Having lived in the community for at least 8 years, the survivors in this study had more stable housing patterns and social networks. This may explain the somewhat lower rates of disorder in the 1975 study.

The association between marital problems and depression is one of the most consistent findings in the clinical literature. Depressed patients as compared with normal controls report marital discord as the most common event in the 6 months before the onset of depression (Weissman & Paykel, 1974). Marital dispute is one of the most common problems noted in depressed patients seeking treatment (Rounsaville, Weissman, Prusoff, & Herceg-Baron, 1979a). Depressed women patients, as compared with matched normal neighbors, report more problems in marital relationships during the acute phase of the depression. These problems persist 1–4 years after the acute illness when they are symptomatically recovered (Weissman & Paykel, 1974).

The absence of an intimate confiding heterosexual relationship has been related to an increase of the risk of depression in the face of life events (Brown & Harris, 1978). The presence of depressive symptoms has been shown to be associated with degree of marital stress (Ilfeld, 1977). Divorced rates are higher among depressed patients when compared with the national average (Merikangas, Ranelli, & Kupfer, 1979). Women with unresolved marital disputes have a poor outcome on treatment as compared with those without partners or those reporting satisfactory marriages (Rounsaville, Weissman, Prusoff, & Herceg-Baron, 1979b). Our analysis suggests the importance of not treating married individuals as representing a single homogeneous social status and of recognizing that certain married individuals are actually at high risk for depression.

In the only longitudinal epidemiologic study partially related to the issue of separating cause from consequence, Henderson (1977) confirmed the clinical association between weak social bonds and neurosis (mostly depression). He showed that lack of social bonds is a risk factor for the onset of neurosis. However, the crucial aspect of social bonds was not their availability but how adequately they are perceived by the individual, suggesting that the personality and perception of the individual may be a more important determinant. While there are methodologic issues in this study which preclude its direct comparability (e.g., diagnostic criteria, measure of marital discord), the results point out the importance of not making assumptions about causation from cross-sectional data. The relationship between marital discord and depression may likely be a reflection of as well as a risk for depression.

CONCLUSION

This is the first time that risk factors and correlates for major depression based directly on DSM-III criteria have been examined in a probability sample of a community. The use of similar methods, but independent studies, in separate geographic areas will allow for replication of analyses in the other ECA sites. The findings do not yet point to areas of preventive intervention except possibly secondary prevention, perhaps during marital breakup. The data do suggest that earlier descriptions of simple linear relationships between social and demographic factors and major depression may have reflected the limited statistical analysis possible with small samples or samples not drawn from a defined population. The failure to find a strong inverse effect of either education or income suggests that social class may serve only as a limited risk factor, with personal and household income measuring different types of risk.

Our current analyses represent only the starting point of our study. For example, we are now attempting to explain why young women in New Haven have such high rates of major depression. In addition, we can monitor these individuals in order to determine whether these high rates of depression persist.

These findings should also be considered in light of the increasing evidence for family history as an important risk factor for major depression as well as increasing evidence for the heterogeneity of major depression. The most fruitful approach for future research might be to incorporate these identified correlates of depression into a family-study framework and to test their impact with varying subtypes of depression. An important question is whether the risk factors for major depression operate in the absence of family history of major depression and whether they operate for all subtypes of major depression (Weissman *et al.*, 1984). What is clear from these studies is the benefit of constituting entire communities as research labs and the future need to integrate epidemiologic, clinical, biologic, and family methodologies.

ACKNOWLEDGMENTS

This research was supported by the Epidemiologic Catchment Area Program (ECA). The ECA is a series of five epidemiologic research studies performed by independent research teams in collaboration with staff of the Division of Biometry and Epidemiology (DBE) of the National Institute of Mental Health (NIMH). The NIMH Principal Collaborators are Darrel A. Regier, Ben Z. Locke, and William W. Eaton; the NIMH Project Officer is Carl A. Taube. The principal investigatators and coinvestigators from the five sites are: Yale University, UO1 MH 34224—Jerome K. Myers, Myrna M. Weissman, and Gary L. Tischler; Johns Hopkins University, UO1 MH 33870—Sheppard Kellam, Ernest Gruenberg, and Sam Shapiro; Washington University, St. Louis, UO1 MH 33883—Lee N. Robins and John Helzer; Duke University, UO1 MH 35386—Dan Blazer and Linda George; University of California, Los Angeles, UO1 MH 35865—Marvin Karno, Javier Escobar, and Audrey Burnam.

REFERENCES

Briscoe, C. W., & Smith, J. B. (1973). Depression and marital turmoil. *Archives of General Psychiatry, 28,* 811–817.

Brown, G. W., & Harris, T. (1978). *Social origins of depression: A study of psychiatric disorders in women.* London: Tavistock.

Cohen, P., & Cohen, J. (1984). The clinician's illusion. *Archives of General Psychiatry, 41,* 1178–1182.

Cohen, S. B. (1983). Present limitations in the availability of statistical software for the analysis of complex survey data. *Review of Public Data Use, 11,* 338–344.

Cohen, S. B., & Kalsbeek, W. D. (1981). *National medical care expenditures survey: Estimation and sampling variances in the household survey.* National Center for Health Services Research, Instruments and Procedures Series, No. 2, (DHHS Publication No. 81-3281. Washington, DC: U.S. Government Printing Office.

Coyne, J. C. (1976). Depression and the response of others. *Journal of Abnormal Psychology, 85,* 186–193.

Eaton, W. W., & Kessler, L. G. (Eds.). (1985). *Epidemiologic field methods in psychiatry: The NIMH Epidemiologic Catchment Area program.* New York: Academic Press.

Hansen, M. H., Horwitz, W. N., & Madow, W. G. (1953). *Sample survey methods II.* New York: Wiley.

Hansen, M. H., Madow, W. G., & Tepping, B. J. (1983). An evaluation of model-dependent and probability sampling inferences in sample surveys. *Journal of the American Statistical Association, 78,* 776–793.

Henderson, S. (1977). The social network, support and neurosis: The function of attachment in adult life. *British Journal of Psychiatry, 131,* 185–191.

Hirschfeld, R., & Klerman, G. L. (1979). Personality attributes and affective disorders. *American Journal of Psychiatry, 136,* 67–70.

Hirschfeld, R., & Cross, C. K. (1982). Epidemiology of affective disorders. *Archives of General Psychiatry, 39,* 35–46.

Holt, D., & Smith, T. M. F. (1979). Poststratification. *Journal of the Royal Statistical Society, 33,* 191–198.

Holzer, C. E., Spitznagel, E., Jordan, K., Timbers, P. M., Kessler, L. G., & Anthony, J. C. (1985). Sampling the household population. In W. W. Eaton & L. G. Kessler (Eds.), *Epidemiologic methods in psychiatry: The NIMH Epidemiologic Catchment Area program.* New York: Academic Press.

Ilfeld, F. W. (1977). Current social stressors and symptoms of depression. *American Journal of Psychiatry, 134,* 161–166.
Jablonsky, A. (in press). Epidemiologic surveys of mental health of geographically defined populations in Europe. In M. M. Weissman, J. K. Myers, & C. Ross (Eds.), *Community surveys, Vol. 4. Monographs in psychosocial epidemiology.* New Brunswick: Rutgers University Press.
Keller, M. D., Lavori, P. W., Endicott, J., Coryell, W., & Klerman, G. L. (1983). Double depression: Two year follow-up. *Archives of General Psychiatry, 140,* 689–694.
Kessler, L., Folsom, R., Royall, R., Forsythe, A., McEvoy, L., Holzer, C. E., Rae, D. S., & Woodbury, M. (1985). Parameter and variance estimation. In W. W. Eaton & L. G. Kessler (Eds.), *Epidemiologic methods in psychiatry: The NIMH Epidemiologic Catchment Area program.* New York: Academic Press.
Lemkau, P., Tietze, C., & Cooper, H. (1942). Complaint of nervousness and the psychoneuroses. *American Journal of Orthopsychiatry, 12,* 214–223.
Merikangas, K. R., Ranelli, C., & Kupfer, D. (1979). Marital interaction in hospitalized depressed patients. *Journal of Nervous and Mental Disorders, 167,* 689–695.
Myers, J. K., Weissman, M. M., Tischler, G. L., Holzer, C. E., & Leaf, P. J. (1984). Six-month prevalence of psychiatric disorders in three communities: 1980–1982. *Archives of General Psychiatry, 41,* 959–967.
Orvaschel, H., Weissman, M. M., & Kidd, K. K. (1980). Children and depression: The children of depressed parents; the childhood of depressed patients; depression in children. *Journal of Affective Disorders, 2,* 1–16.
Paykel, E. S., Myers, J. K., Dienelt, M. N., Klerman, G. L., Lindenthal, J. J., & Pepper, M. P. (1969). Life events and depression: A controlled study. *Archives of General Psychiatry, 21,* 753–760.
Robins, L. N., Helzer, J. E., Croughan, J., & Ratcliff, K. S. (1981). National Institute of Mental Health Diagnostic Scale: Its history, characteristics and validity. *Archives of General Psychiatry, 38,* 381–389.
Robins, L. N., Helzer, J. E., Weissman, M. M., Orvaschel, H., & Gruenberg, E. (1984). Lifetime prevalence of specific psychiatric disorders in three sites. *Archives of General Psychiatry, 41,* 949–958.
Rosanoff, A. J. (1917). Survey of mental disorders in Nassau County, New York, July–October 1916. New York: National Committee on Mental Health.
Rounsaville, B. J., Weissman, M. M., Prusoff, B. A., & Herceg-Baron, R. L. (1979a). Process of psychotherapy among depressed women with marital disputes. *American Journal of Orthopsychiatry, 49,* 505–510.
Rounsaville, B. J., Weissman, M. M., Prusoff, B. A., & Herceg-Baron, R. L. (1979b). Marital disputes and treatment outcome in depressed women. *Comprehensive Psychiatry, 20,* 483–490.
Sarndal, C. E. (1984). Design-consistent versus model-dependent estimation for small domains. *Journal of the American Statistical Association, 79,* 624–631.
Schwab, J. J. & Schwab, M. E. (1978). *Socio-cultural roots of mental illness.* New York: Plenum.
Shah, B. V., & LaVange, L. M. (1981). Software for inference on linear models from survey data. Cary, N.C.: Research Triangle Institute.
Weissman, M. M., & Paykel, E. S. (1974). *The depressed woman: A study of social relationships.* Chicago: University of Chicago Press.
Weissman, M. M., & Klerman, G. L. (1978). Epidemiology of mental disorders: Emerging trends in the United States. *Archives of General Psychiatry, 35,* 705–712.
Weissman, M. M., & Myers, J. K. (1980). Psychiatric disorders in a U.S. community: The

application of Research Diagnostic Criteria to a resurveyed community sample. *Acta Psychiatrica Scandinavica, 62*, 99–111.

Weissman, M. M., Kidd, K. K., & Prusoff, B. A. (1982). Variability in rates of affective disorders in relatives of depressed and normal probands. *Archives of General Psychiatry, 39*, 1397–1403.

Weissman, M. M., & Boyd, J. H. (1983). The epidemiology of affective disorders: Rates and risk factors. In L. Grinspoon (Ed.), *Psychiatry update: The American Psychiatric Association Annual Review* (Vol. II). Washington, DC: American Psychiatric Press.

Weissman, M. M., Wickramaratne, P., Merikangas, K. R., Leckman, J. F., Prusoff, B. A., Caruso, K. A., Kidd, K. K., & Gammon, G. D. (1984). Onset of major depression in early adulthood: Increased familial loading and specificity. *Archives of General Psychiatry, 41*, 1136–1143.

DISCUSSION

James Barrett: In the association you found between depression and the variables "trouble getting along with spouse" and "lack of an intimate confidant," how much of what you are picking up is difficulty with relationships in general? Can you tap into that as a risk factor for depressive illness?

Weissman: We will need the longitudinal data to separate cause from consequence. If we have a large enough sample who were well during the first wave and who then developed a depression for the first time, over the course we can see whether problems in the marriage or the depression came first. We do have some other information on satisfaction in relationships with friends and work associates. The data show that if you are depressed, you are not getting along with those people, but relationships with spouse are the most dramatic. These findings are similar to what we have noted on our case-control studies of depressed compared to normal women.

Ben Pasamanick: Concerning the ECA project, I have some comments and questions.

In these studies we are dealing largely with disorders for which we have no good criteria so far as validity is concerned. Occasionally we come across a disorder with such criteria, and, when I was listening to Lee Robins, I thought of the possibility of testing the validity of the criteria to establish drug or alcohol abuse. The strategy would be to use point prevalence rates in drug and alcohol dependence by merely doing urine or blood tests at the same time that you have your interview, which would give you an indication of whether or not your interview was really valid.

Our Baltimore study was a point prevalence study. The three recent ECA papers in the *Archives* did not report point prevalence, and I have wondered why. If you intended to make comparisons with earlier studies, it would be nice to have something on which to compare. I, of course, would like to have seen point prevalence.

I still have the old data, and I rediagnosed the cases to make them conform to modern diagnostic nomenclature. Frankly, there is no great difference between what existed 30 years ago and what exists now for those diagnoses that are listed in the recent articles in *Archives*. The reason our study did not give specific diagnoses at that time was that we, as part of the Chronic Disease Commission Study, were primarily interested in need for care rather than diagnostic associations. Nevertheless, we do have them, and I hope in time to report them.

Now, a question: I wonder if you have tested reliability between psychiatrists and the DIS in Baltimore, and if so, what that reliability was?

Weissman: Let me make several comments. First, it is reassuring to know that when you went back and analyzed the data from your very important studies which had a different purpose, some of the findings were the same as those in the ECA.

Jane Murphy has recently been doing similar reanalysis on the Nova Scotia studies, applying DSM-III criteria to that data, and she has been finding some similarities in rates of depression and anxiety with the rates in the ECA data.

Concerning the reliability or the agreement (our concordance studies) between psychiatrists and lay interviewers, that is a very important issue. In the ECA we established a workgroup that has met throughout the last few years to discuss how to analyze the data on the various concurrent diagnosis studies done at the different ECA sites. We have looked at DIS completed by psychiatrist compared with lay interviewer. We have looked at the SADS completed by a psychiatrist compared with DIS completed by a lay interviewer. Other studies have also been done. Later, Dr. Jay Burke will be presenting a review of the studies that were done as part of the ECA, as well as the studies that other people have done using the DIS.

In regard to the comment about point prevalence, why did we present 6-month rates rather than point prevalence in the first papers, or even today? As you mentioned, in your important studies your focus was need for care. One important issue in the ECA studies was the relationship between diagnosis and utilization. The decision was made by the ECA Scientific Advisory Group, which consists of the NIMH and all the ECA Principal and Co-Principal Investigators, that it would be best to analyze utilization data in terms of 6 months. Therefore, we analyzed prevalence data for the first go-round in terms of 6 months. Since the data were set up that way and since you do get larger samples with 6 months, we chose to present 6-month prevalence. There will be subsequent presentations which will present point prevalence rates.

As for criteria for validity, that could be a whole session, and I will not begin to try to assess it, but I would like to make a few statements. One can look at the validity of the diagnoses in many ways. If you looked at blood levels for alcohol or urine levels for drug abuse, that would tell you something about the reliability of reporting of current (although not past) episodes. But what do you do for depression or schizophrenia, where blood or urine levels are not going to tell you anything? The dexamethasone suppression test might be better, but it would not tell you all that much. What are your criteria? With the improved reliability of psychiatric diagnoses, there has been considerable research activity using different approaches to validity, looking at differential treatment response, family aggregation, and follow-up studies.

My view is that epidemiologic studies can be another approach to validity. For example, if we find that major depression has a different set of risk factors and a different clinical course and pattern than, say, bipolar depression, and if this finding is repeated across all the sites, this would be consistent with some of our other evidence that bipolar depression and major depression are distinct disorders. It would be another example of the potential validity of this diagnostic distinction.

John Helzer: I want to respond also to what Dr. Pasamanick said. At the St. Louis ECA site we hope to do one of the things that Dr. Weissman has mentioned—longitudinal follow-up of lay- and physician-diagnosed cases over time—to try to get better estimates of the predictive validity of the two sets of diagnoses.

I also have an anecdote in response to the issue of urine tests as a validator. Lee Robins and I were faced with this same problem in a study of Vietnam veterans, in which we wanted to establish the credibility of their verbal reports of drug use. One of the ways that we devised for this was taking urine samples from them at the time of interview. We did not ask for the specimens until the end of the interview, so we already had their verbal report about their drug use before we asked for the urine.

When we approached the people who would do the urine analyses with this idea, their response was: "Well, the error of the analytic method can be hard to interpret. Why don't you just ask them whether or not they are using drugs?" And indeed we did test the analytic method by sending them spiked urines, and the error of that method was at least as great as the error of our method of asking directly.

Alfred Dean: I was curious as to why you have concluded that this decline in prevalence is, in fact, a cohort effect. Obviously a key issue is: to what extent is it a life-stage or life-course event, as well as possibly a cohort effect?

Weissman: The conclusion about the presence of cohort effect is still tentative. I think it would take a whole session to discuss all the possibilities. We have looked at different modeling, though. Using some of the techniques from vital statistics, we have looked at age, period, and cohort models in all four of the sites. This work was done by a statistician colleague of ours at

Yale, Dr. Wickaramaktne, who is experienced with vital statistics modeling. We find that the model which best fits the data at all ECA sites is a cohort effect. Now that does not mean that the data that went into the model are trouble-free. These are early results, and we are still hesitant to draw a definite conclusion.

General Discussion

Robert Spitzer: I would first like to congratulate all of the people associated with the ECA. The material presented here and that in the October 1985 issue of the *Archives of General Psychiatry* illustrate the wealth of data now available for study.

I have a question about one aspect of the DIS evaluations. Consider a disorder, such as schizophrenia or obsessive-compulsive disorder, that tends to be chronic in its course. Once you have the diagnosis, you are likely to have it for the rest of your life. For such diagnoses, the ratio of lifetime prevalence to 6-month prevalence should be close to one. On the other hand, disorders such as major depression or bipolar disorder tend to have episodic courses; for such disorders, the ratio of lifetime prevalence to 6-month prevalence should be quite large, since most individuals who have the diagnosis at one point in their lives would not be expected to have it during the previous 6 months. What is puzzling about the DIS data is that this ratio is usually 2:1 or 3:1 for all DIS/DSM-III diagnoses, and does not seem to vary much according to whether the disorder tends to be chronic or episodic. Does this not raise questions about the validity of the prevalence estimates?

Lee Robins: What Dr. Spitzer is asking requires putting together data from two sources. He is not asking whether the results in my paper on the 6-month ratio were right or wrong, but why they don't have the expected ratio. First, it is not the case that all the ratios are identical. There is a greater cessation of alcohol and drug abuse than there is, say, of depression, though you might expect just the opposite. One of the suggested hypotheses is that current state influences recall of depressive symptoms. Perhaps what current state influences is not whether the occurrence of the symptom is recalled, but rather whether it is recalled as having been severe enough to be worth mentioning in an interview.

I can readily imagine that if you accurately recalled it took you an average of 45 minutes to get to sleep for several weeks, you might define this as "trouble falling asleep" if you were feeling depressed at the time of interview, but not if you were feeling good. If the willingness to report such experiences as symptoms varies with current mood state, that would certainly help to explain why current depressive episodes are high relative to lifetime rates. This happens less with alcohol and drug abuse because there are often indisputable external markers. It is not as difficult to determine whether you have ever been arrested for drunk driving as whether you have had trouble falling asleep. Either you have or have not been charged with drunk driving; whether or not you tell the interviewer about it is just a matter of your willingness to admit it. In contrast, when reporting purely subjective symptoms that lie on a continuum with everyday experience, there is always a censuring operation on the part of the respondent, in which he or she must decide if it is a reportable experience; thus, the respondent's current state may influence that censoring function.

One of the ECA project's most valuable by-products has been the many fascinating methodologic problems, such as this one, which it has raised.

Dan Blazer: I have been curious across the life cycle about the issue raised by Dr. Spitzer. People who are younger tend to recall more episodes of past depression than people who are older, which brings up the question of whether selective recall may be different across the life cycle. But I would hasten to add that one thing that certainly is occurring in this data set is the cohort effect. We were looking at people across the entire life cycle, and those trends that are presently receiving a lot of attention are trends that we may be seeing in younger and middle-aged individuals; since we are also including older persons, the degree of the ratios may not be as great as expected. The other issue that must be considered is that major depression as defined in DSM-III casts a rather wide net. Some of what it includes may very likely not be similar to the types of depressions seen in the elderly. Evidence from clinical settings suggests that depression in late life often has more endogenous features or is more severe.

Virginia Ryle: What are the implications of high rates of depression on offspring, particularly since it is occurring so predominantly among women of childbearing age?

Weissman: As you probably know, we have been studying the children of depressed and the children of normal parents. We and others doing similar studies (Gershon at NIMH; Keller and Beardslee at Harvard) are finding very high rates of depression in the children. Maybe DSM-III is not suitable for children, but we have been looking at depression according to the children's reports and the mothers' reports about the children. The impact is serious. We would expect that there will be more children who will have problems.

Gerald Klerman: There are, as Dr. Weissman mentions, at least four research groups that are looking at the offspring of families where one or more parent has been diagnosed depressed. The findings are all consistent that, if there is one parent ill, the rate in the children is higher than in the control group. If there are two parents ill, by age 18 the rates run as high as 40–50% of children having significant depression. It is very hard to disentangle whether you are dealing with a genetic or an environmental transmission, and you also have a problem of assortative mating, but it does appear that having a depressed parent has a powerful effect on the offspring. The apparent decrease in older groups must take into account the factors of recall, selective mortality, and selective migration. To control for these factors in the NIMH Collaborative Study we truncated the sample below the age of 50, and we still got a very powerful cohort effect. And when we just looked at siblings, we still got the effect. So it appears that there may be two phenomena. One is an apparent decrease in depression in the current older age group, compared with expectations, and an apparent increase in young adults, particularly those born since the Korean conflict.

Darrel Regier: A careful reading of the paper that Dr. Robins and a number of us presented in the *Archives* will show that we considered several alternative ways of measuring lifetime prevalence. Before we assume that the higher rates of disorder among the young represent a cohort effect, which roughly means that there is a higher rate of specific disorders in the younger age group than was present at that age in the older age group, we have to be very careful about methodologic difficulties. Using this particular measure of lifetime prevalence, which is very dependent on recall and is the only measure that the ECA had available, limits our ability to address this issue fully. Other prospective ways exist to determine whether or not there is an increasing rate of mental disorder in the younger age groups.

The fact that there are lower rates for the disorders in the older population has to be looked at first in terms of whether or not the older population has a problem with recall of symptoms that occurred 20 or 30 years earlier. There are other problems, as Dr. Klerman pointed out, of selective mortality, migration, institutionalization, and the like that tend to decrease the pool of individuals who would have had the disorder in the earlier time frame. So we have been very cautious in trying to interpret these ECA data until it is clear what is the methodologic impact of this particular approach to assessing lifetime prevalence of a disorder.

I have one other point, referring back to Dr. Pasamanick's comment on the need for physiologic measures to correlate with diagnostic data obtained from this kind of study. We are planning to have the affective disorders portions of the DIS included in the NCHS National Health Examination Survey. This will permit correlation between DIS diagnoses and physical diagnosis results (including laboratory studies of biological fluids and specimens) and will provide, on a national basis, the type of information requested. It was simply impossible to add a physical examination to this very complex epidemiological and services research study, but some such data will eventually come out of studies using the DIS instrument.

Judith Rapoport: Dr. Robins, I am concerned about underreporting of drug use in the data you presented because of an experience I had a few years ago, as part of a consultation I did for the two doctors who screen all prospective employees for the CIA. Everybody applying for a job with the CIA has to fill out a very extensive personal questionnaire, which includes a section on drug use. As they are about to fill out the questionnaire, they are told that they will repeat it in two days under a lie-detector test.

The results were surprising with respect to the high drug-use rates reported even on the first questionnaire. There now were fewer "eligible" applicants than needed to fill the large numbers of jobs. In addition to recreational use, many applicants had had "bad trips." It was hard to advise these physicians what to do with data collected in this unusual manner, but the experience suggested that there might be a need to do something "extraordinary" to check on the validity of the usual interview approach.

Robins: I think it matters a great deal in what context the respondent is being asked these questions. There is a famous old study using the Cornell Medical Index that found quite high rates of complaints in a general population, but when job applicants filled out the questionnaire, they were all totally healthy—as you and I would be if we were filling out a job application. In a survey, where nothing is riding on the answers, one expects quite a high level of honesty. We got hard evidence for this honesty in the study of Vietnam veterans that Dr. Helzer mentioned. Without the respondents' knowledge of the fact, we had access to their army medical records. We also collected urines at the end of the interview without any prior warning, because we were afraid that they would be hiding drug abuse from us. It turned out that, of all the people who had a positive record of heroin use in the army record, 97% reported heroin use in the interview. And the results of our urine screenings after the interview showed the same low rate of current use that we found in the interviews. An anonymous interview by a stranger provides a special relationship in which people tend to be more honest than they are in their daily lives, because they expect no consequences and don't even expect to see the interviewer ever again. It is simply more trouble to lie than to tell the truth, and, if nothing is riding on it, there is little motivation to take the extra trouble.

Robert Rose: Is there a possibility of circularity in the findings reported between antisocial personality and the diagnosis of substance abuse? Since the early use of drugs and alcohol is part of the criteria for the diagnosis of antisocial personality, some of the relationships which you found between antisocial personality and the diagnosis of substance abuse might be explained by this definitional relationship.

Robins: The rules for diagnosing antisocial personality are that you have to have at least three problem behaviors before the age of 15, one of which could be substance abuse. In the adult criteria, that is after the age of 18, you have to have at least one symptom in four different areas of antisocial behavior. Substance abuse is *not* included as one of those adult areas.

On a superficial level, then, the adult symptoms of substance abuse and antisocial personality don't overlap at all. But on a deeper level they certainly could. For example, one criterion for alcohol problems is fighting when drunk, and one criterion for antisocial personality is fighting. A person who admits fighting is not asked whether the fighting occurred only when he or she was drunk. Therefore, the same behavior could qualify that person for symptoms of both disorders. While this danger of overlap exists, it is not overwhelming, as shown by the fact that people qualify for substance abuse without qualifying for antisocial personality, and there are even a considerable proportion of people with antisocial personality who do not have substance abuse. Because there was a certain circularity if we used the DSM-III definition of childhood conduct problems in predicting later outcomes, we created a new variable, "childhood delinquent behavior," which *excludes* early substance abuse. What we showed is that delinquent behavior, so defined, greatly increases the risk of substance abuse and of many other adverse adult outcomes.

Glorisa Canino: In our preliminary findings for DIS lifetime prevalence, we have found the exact opposite: an increase in the prevalence of lifetime disorders with age and no decline at all in any age group. Since the difference between our findings and the five ECA catchment areas is so dramatic, I would like to ask this panel to discuss what might be some of the possible explanations.

Robins: Did your study include those over 65, the group in which the ECA finds such a low rate?

Canino: No, we do not have the 65-and-older group. However, you did find differences in the younger age groups that we did not find.

Robins: The differences were not nearly as dramatic between the 25–44 and the 45–64 age groups as they were between either of these and the 65+ age group. It is this oldest group that really had the extremely low rates in our studies. So we would have to look carefully at findings in the earlier age brackets to be sure that your results and ours are different.

Weissman: The change in rates comes at the cohort born around 1930; that is the one that starts having the low rates.

Hans Huessy: I have a further comment about the findings reported by Dr. Weissman concerning the children of depressives. In the DSM-III classification, many adults with attention deficit disorder, residual type, can qualify for a DSM-III major depression diagnosis, and yet I think they are a very different group. They have a very high rate of marital problems, and ADD is heavily genetic, so you would expect problems in their children. In the discussions about ADD, it should be remembered that one of the consequences of being an attention deficit child is a very poor self-image. Whenever there is a failure or stress they overreact, and with their poor self-image they feel desperate, hopeless, and qualify for a DSM-III depression diagnosis. We have to learn how to separate this group—grown-up ADDs with depression—from what we used to call endogenous depression. They are quite different, both by family history and clinical response to treatment.

Klerman: Any comment on this issue of adult ADD presenting as major depression, and the differential diagnosis of the two conditions?

Rapoport: There is still a question about such an association. The few careful prospective studies that have been done on hyperactive children suggest that, while they may continue symptoms of hyperactivity or impulsivity, depression (at least up through the early 20s) is not prominent.

Klerman: Does childhood ADD emerge as a risk factor in any of the ECA studies on adult depression?

Weissman: It has not yet been examined.

Alfred Dean: A comment about the lower lifetime prevalence rate for depression in the elderly. There is evidence that, if you use the CES-D scale to assess current depressive symptoms, the elderly show less (current) depression. In other words, I think there is a consistent trend that the elderly report fewer depressive symptoms, and this may be what is affecting your DIS diagnosis rates.

Blazer: I think that the CES-D is different from some of the other depressive symptom scales in that it includes a time scale; the severity of the symptom is based on the number of days during the past week that a person has experienced that symptom. The data from studies using that particular scale is as you reported it—a fall-off occurs with age, but I had not noticed it as being so dramatic as you did. It is not as dramatic as the fall-off that we see with our DSM-III diagnoses.

In contrast, if you look at a recent study in Florida where a variant of the Zung scale was used (a scale which inquires about symptoms at one point in time), the rates for depression progressively increase with age. What we have hypothesized is that older people probably have a number of transient episodes of fairly significant symptoms, but if you ask them, "Have you persistently had those symptoms over a period of time, say one or two weeks?" they are less likely than younger people to endorse such a symptom item.

Joseph Zubin: I would like to propose an explanation for this drop in old age, beyond the other factors that we have proposed—cohort effect, mortality, and so on. Barry Gurland recently published a book, *The Mind and Mood of Aging*, in which he took up this question of the drop in depression with age. He found a V-shaped distribution. Depression went down, with a trough around age 60, and then went up again after that, up to ages 80 and 90. The tentative explanation for the dip at age 60 was that this is around the age of retirement, when the need for a job and working hard declines, so that the triggers for depression tend to get less potent. After passing that particular stage and getting adjusted to it, the older person begins to experience such things as feelings of isolation, bereavement, and the greater frequency of relatives' deaths. It is at this point that depression rises again.

REFERENCES

Gurland, B. J. (1983). *The mind and mood of aging: Mental health problems of the community elderly in New York and London.* New York: Hawood Press.
Robins, L. N., Helzer, J. E., Weissman, M. M., Orvaschel, H., Gruenberg, E., Burke, J. D., Jr., & Regier, D. A. (1984). Lifetime prevalence of specific psychiatric disorders in three sites. *Archives of General Psychiatry, 41,* 949–958.

FINDINGS FROM EARLIER COMMUNITY SURVEYS: THE LUNDBY AND STIRLING COUNTY STUDIES

5

Paul Hoch Award Address

Individual Traits and Morbidity in a Circumscribed Population: The Cross-Sectional Beginnings of a Longitudinal Study

ERIK ESSEN-MÖLLER
University of Lund

BIOGRAPHY BY JOSEPH ZUBIN

Erik Essen-Möller was born in Lund, Sweden on February 4, 1901 and spent most of his life in this university town. He matriculated there in 1919, received his B.A. in genetics and statistics in 1926, and his M.D. in 1931.

It is difficult to trace the stages of development of Professor Essen-Möller's career, because unlike artists he did not have blue or black or white periods. Three powerful interests dominated his research and permeated his entire career simultaneously—statistics, genetics, and psychiatry. He inherited from his father, Professor Elis Essen-Möller, a gynecologist, (whether genetically or environmentally is difficult to tell) an interest in studying the similarity existing in the two types of twins (mono- and dizygotic) and even devised a statistical table to help his father in determining duration of pregnancy.

At the University of Lund he came under the influence of the famous statistician, Charlier, and the eminent professor of genetics, Nilsson-Ehle, whose evening lectures attracted him and apparently converted him. His psychiatric/genetic career began in earnest after meeting Rüdin in Munich, where he also began life-long interaction with Kallman, Schultz, Luxenburger, and Slater. His clinical psychiatry he learned at the feet of Sjöbring.

Among his many accomplishments, three are especially noteworthy: first, his contributions to classification and diagnosis and psychiatric studies for which he was feted with a Festschrift at the time of his so-called retirement in 1967; second, his contributions to psychiatric epidemiology for which he is being feted today; and third, in addition to his worldwide fame as a psychia-

trist, he has also merited acclaim from scientists, physicians, and lawyers concerned with the problem of contested paternity trials. He is truly the father of the scientific development of this field. I will attempt to give you a layman's understanding of it.

Before the 1930s anthropologists used to evaluate similarities in appearance between kinfolk, especially between a child and its alleged father, subjectively and emotionally. The problem was how to convert the perceived evidence for similarity into a numerical index, especially in cases of contested paternity. Essen-Möller was the first to provide this index in the form of the equation $W = X/(X + Y)$, *where* W *is the index,* X *is the probability of paternity, and* Y *is the probability of nonpaternity which on an a priori basis he assumed to be .50. The proportion of observed similarities and dissimilarities had to deviate from .50 to be acceptable as proof or disproof of paternity. His intuitive grasp of the problem and its solution led him to adopt a probability measure instead of an absolute measure, which was more commonly in use in those days, and led him to anticipate (unknowingly) the use of Bayes' theorem, before it was rediscovered, and to the use of a technique not too different from that which underlies kappa in our measures of reliability—a truly creative ingenious leap of intuition before the slowly moving science of statistics caught up with him.*

I will not review his contributions to diagnosis and psychiatric genetics except to point out that he was the father of multiaxial diagnosis.

His incisive reasoning was demonstrated in 1958 when an advocate of the theory of "schizophrenogenic mothers" had pointed out that the incidence of schizophrenia among mothers of probands was twice that among fathers. Essen-Möller was able to explain this phenomenon: At the time of marriage, mothers are generally younger than fathers, and, on the average, women become schizophrenic at a later age than men; accordingly, in statistical terms the risk of mothers becoming schizophrenic must be greater.

A word must be said regarding his lifelong devotion to his teacher, Sjöbring, an original theoretician and observer who exerted an extraordinary influence on his students and collaborators. Sjöbring can be likened somewhat to Adolf Meyer. The writings of both were rather obscure and incomprehensible to most, but despite this barrier they made themselves felt through their students. Essen-Möller interpreted Sjöbring, collected and edited his writings, and made them intelligible to the next generation.

Essen-Möller served on the World Health Organization panel of experts from 1959–1967 and again from 1981 to the present. He is a corresponding member of the Danish Society of Psychiatry, and honorary member of both the Royal Medico-Psychological Association and the Gesellschaft für forensische Blutgruppenkunde. His bibliography extends to more than 80 articles and 11 books.

In honoring Essen-Möller we are recognizing his tremendous contributions to psychopathology. In a sense, he honors us by accepting the award, adding luster to those who preceded him on the list of Hoch Award recipients.

In looking for a suitable phrase to end his laudatio, *one which would give you a feeling for his humaneness, I found the following. When Tzu Chang asked Confucius the meaning of the word "virtue" the sage said: "Five things constitute virtue. They are courtesy, magnanimity, sincerity, earnestness, and kindness. With courtesy, you avoid insult. With magnanimity you win all. With sincerity men will come to trust you. With earnestness and kindness you can achieve success." Erik Essen-Möller truly embodies these virtues.*

INTRODUCTION

Our population study, later called the Lundby Project, was started in 1947 by four psychiatrists of similar schooling (Essen-Möller, Larsson, C. E. Uddenberg, & White, 1956). We set out to estimate the frequency of the milder mental disorders, not merely the psychoses. Above all, however, we hoped to be able to shed some light on the role of personality as a possible etiologic or pathoplastic factor. This may appear to be a somewhat vague and unprecise objective, yet we were in a position to share a certain basic outlook that had been instilled in us by our teacher in psychiatry, the late Professor Sjöbring, a highly interesting, speculative, and theoretically minded person, too little known internationally.

SJÖBRING'S OBSERVATIONS AND THEORIES

Sjöbring was born in 1879, graduated at the age of 26, and then specialized in psychiatry at the University of Uppsala. His lifelong interest was in the problem of personality, that is, in our normal mental functioning, for which he devised a theory—not a theory of psychological contents or events but rather a kind of psychophysiological model at a formal and elemental level, where our cognitive, volitional, and emotional functions were comprised under the aspect of a unitary, continuing development. Within this general framework he tried to find a number of typical ways along which individual personalities may develop and differ. [For an extensive survey in English see Sjöbring (1973). Shorter accounts are given by Nyman (1956) and Essen-Möller (1980).]

Sjöbring imagined that within the infinite mixture of different personalities, there would exist a number of hidden lines of variation, each following the Gaussian distribution, which is so frequent in biology. In such a distribution the majority, as situated closely around the mean, will not be possible to distinguish. What we might hope to identify are some of the minorities that have developed beyond the average in a particular respect, and those who are lagging behind. The lingerers were thought to be somewhat less adaptable in certain respects and therefore liable to some particular type of mild mental illness when exposed to stress. In order to disentangle some of the unknown lines of variation, an investigation into the personalities of patients who displayed a typical functional disorder appeared to be indicated.

Three such investigations had in fact already been published. Janet (1909), of Paris, had described a certain type of personality that was frequent among his obsessional neurotics. They are retiring and diffident, ambivalent, and cautious, with a difficulty in concluding a work and in relaxing, getting stuck in details. They prefer customary work, if possible one task at a time, and they try to avoid distractions and situations which tend to make them anxious and tense. Janet interpreted this personality as resulting from a low supply of mental energy (psychasthenia). Sjöbring called it "subvalidity," and he ventured to reconstruct or extrapolate the "supervalids" which he postulated to exist at the other end of the Gaussian distribution. These people would be forceful and confident, calm and relaxed, have a broad outlook, and make decisions decisively. Such people were easily found in the population.

In a similar way Sjöbring worked out another set of observations made by Janet regarding patients with a hysteric or primitive reaction. A major group of them were described as of childish impressibility and mobility, with rapid learning as well as rapid forgetting, reacting subjectively to the momentary situation, often endowed with particular charm and considerable verbality. In pursuit of Janet's concept of "dissociability," Sjöbring spoke of "subsolidity," and again he extrapolated the supervariants to be more consolidated, slowly reacting and circumspect, consistent and conservative, objective, mature, and perhaps a bit unromantic.

A third type of personality, described by the Kraepelinian school, was the one often seen in patients with deep depression. These were recognized as participating with nature and with fellow creatures in a genuinely warm and emotional manner. Their interest is directed essentially toward realities, and their motility is somewhat heavy. Sjöbring assigned this constitution to a low capability of habituation, called "substability," and from this he extrapolated the superstables to be skilled and elegant in motility, directed toward abstraction and ideas, with cool detachment, and with an interest in people that is more analyzing than participating.

Brief descriptions alone cannot, however, provide a sufficient guide to Sjöbring's system, as was stressed by Barrett (1975) when adapting a self-rating test of the variants to be used in American epidemiology. A fuller understanding requires some acquaintance with Sjöbring's general theory, with the caveat that words should not be overrated. It may be appropriate to describe as "energetic" a supervalid person who pursues untiringly his or her far-reaching aims. However, the same word, energetic, might also apply to a subvalid who cannot stop working for mere lack of confidence or because of perfectionism and tension. Similarly, if a subvalid person is said to be cautious, it does not follow that the supervalid would be careless. The point is that the extrapolation should be based not on words but rather on the hypothesized underlying variable, in this case the supply of energy. This is why the supervalid is not supposed to be careless but rather confident.

Once agreed upon this principle, many clinicians found the Sjöbring variants a handy tool for a comprehensive description of personality from three different aspects—supply of energy, cohesion (maturity), and habituation—each of them graded around a neutral average. It is interesting to find that very much the same traits have been used in quite a number of other inventories, like those of Burt, Cattell, Eysenck, Halstead, Heymans, Kretschmer, and Sheldon (all quoted in Nyman, 1956). Even for the experimental dogs of Pavlov (1951), quite similar variants of "personality" were suggested!

LATER DEVELOPMENTS OF SJÖBRING'S CONCEPTS

The principal elaboration of the typology described took place while Sjöbring was still working in mental hospitals. At 50 years of age he became a professor of psychiatry at the University of Lund and director of the psychiatric department of the general teaching hospital. In general patients here were only mildly disordered, providing an ideal population for Sjöbring to apply his ideas of normal subvariants of personality. There was little support for the expected histories of conflicts and stresses, but a history of physical ailments appeared frequent, particularly in the guise of banal infections.

To Sjöbring, this experience meant a reorientation. In his search for normal subvariants (and lines of variation) he had intentionally restricted himself to patients with a functional mental disorder, discarding the well-known organic and even the schizoid conditions. This discrimination now appeared to be perhaps not sharp enough. Could a banal infection occasionally bring about a lasting change in the personality? It would be a subtle change, to be sure, but one that possibly predisposes a personality to what we normally call a functional mental disorder.

Sjöbring approached this problem from two different angles. One of them has already been touched upon: the ordinary clinical judgment of whether or not the patient's history and personality provided a reasonable explanation. The second approach consisted in looking out for minimal traits that might be tentatively interpreted as diluted organic symptoms. Here Sjöbring's extraordinary ability in clinical observation came to use. The task was, for instance, to separate organic rigidity and stubbornness from normal supersolid conservatism, or to separate organic affective lability from subsolid dissociability.

With increasing diagnostic confidence Sjöbring considered his organic findings in their own right; that is, he accepted them even when they could not always be referred to any particular causative event or when neurological and experimental findings were missing. This generated some opposition in the 1930s when Sjöbring's expansion of lesional diagnoses took place. It was chiefly Sjöbring's clinical assistants who realized that his observations were plausible and at least essentially correct. The desired substantial support for the lesional aspect came later and was largely delivered from child psychiatry, for example by Knobloch and Pasamanick (1959) and G. Uddenberg (1956). From adult psychiatry the findings made by Slater (1943, 1950) in the war neuroses ought to be mentioned. Today the concept of minimal brain dysfunction is widely and independently considered.

In a way Sjöbring's description of minor lesional deviations in adults seems to represent an even greater achievement than that of his normal variants. It is true that these were more or less instrumental when he traced the lesional, but on the other hand the lesional variants were genuinely observational, while the normals were partly constructed. Be this as it may, I do not know that inventories for adults would in general attempt to separate lesional personality from normal. To Kretschmer (1925), for instance, schizothymic normality was on the same scale as schizoid abnormality and even schizophrenic psychosis. Similarly Kurt Schneider (1923) conceived the psychopathic personalities as extremes of normal variation. With the character neuroses it is essentially the same (Essen-Möller, 1943).

I think it will now be understood how an interest arose in Sjöbring's department to search an unselected population for alleged normal and lesional traits in the sense described. So far our population study might have been called an experiment in diagnostics.

THE LUNDBY STUDY

A primary requirement for our study was that every member of the study population had to be investigated face to face by someone familiar with the Sjöbring ratings. A test, or outside information alone, would as a rule not be sufficient for our purpose. A second requirement for the census that we were planning was that it had to be performed in that part of Sweden where we had become fluent in the local dialect and familiar with the local ways of nonverbal communication. One may wonder how far the importance of such factors are considered by doctors who frequently change regions for their practice.

At the particular key date the population registers of the selected area contained 2550 inhabitants including about 600 children. We obtained the consent of the leading officials and foremen, and we saw to it that they were the first to be interviewed. Fliers were sent to all households, explaining that we were four doctors from the neighboring hospital who were interested in holding personal interviews for all regarding their health, both past and present. No physical examination would be made, and there would be no expenses. All information would be treated confidentially.

We then took lodgings in the area and set up the interviews, with roughly one quarter of the population assigned to each doctor. Interviews were held in homes or workplaces. Each of us completed on an average about 12 interviews a day during two summer months, children included, and we succeeded in meeting in person almost 99% of the population.

We brought individual cards for annotations, physical as well as mental, on which were many items to be considered in arbitrary sequence. Interviews were conducted in terms of a conversation rather than as an interrogation, thus enabling every interviewed person to talk as freely as possible. This was achieved by bringing up, as in the Stirling County study (Leighton, 1950), a number of topics of interest to the subject—health, work, family, leisure time, and aspects of his or her own personality. This gave us an opportunity to observe behavior while collecting the desired factual information. The conversation was carried on at least until we had formed a reasonably satisfactory impression, comparable perhaps to that of a first consultation.

In subsequent years much work was devoted to comparing the direct information with doctors' and hospitals' records. A systematic control with the aid of certain registers was also performed and some additional information from well-informed sources gathered. Finally the entire material had to be classified and worked up, at that time with the aid of punched cards.

RESULTS AND CONCLUSIONS

Three figures exemplify some of our findings. In Figure 5.1 the normal variants were found to be distributed bilaterally, in conformance with Sjöbring's ideas. All inhabitants, and in fact all human beings, are supposed to have a place within each of the three lines of variation—or four, if intellectual variation (Capacity) is included.

Figure 5.2 presents the frequency of various descriptive diagnoses, while Figure 5.3 shows the degree of confidence with which we assumed a lesional etiology. Clearly these items pertain to a fraction of the population only, and they have no positive counterpart. They must not be understood as alterna-

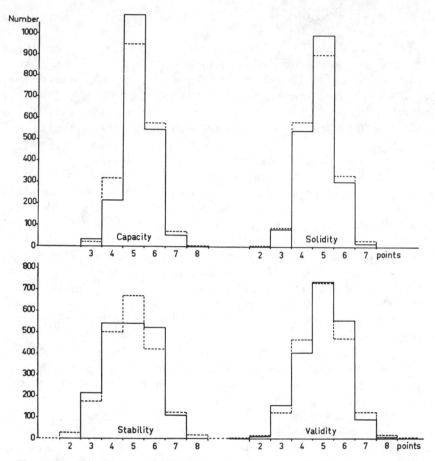

Figure 5.1. Distribution of Sjöbring variants by age and subjective gradation.

tives to the respective normal sub-, medium-, or supervariants but rather as
being superimposed upon them. Thus normal and lesional variants, when
present, interact in molding the clinical picture and reactions, an example of
multifactorial classification.

The interrelations between our various findings were extensively investigated. Of particular interest was a statistically significant association of
certain asthenic–lesional deviations, on the one hand, and the item called
"proneness to infections" on the other hand. This was entirely in agreement
with expectation according to Sjöbring's teachings.

However, the very fact that certain expected associations were actually
demonstrable suggests the possibility of subjective bias in our observations.
To be sure, we were conscious of such risks, and we had tried to remain
neutral in judgment. As for the bias that may nevertheless have been present,

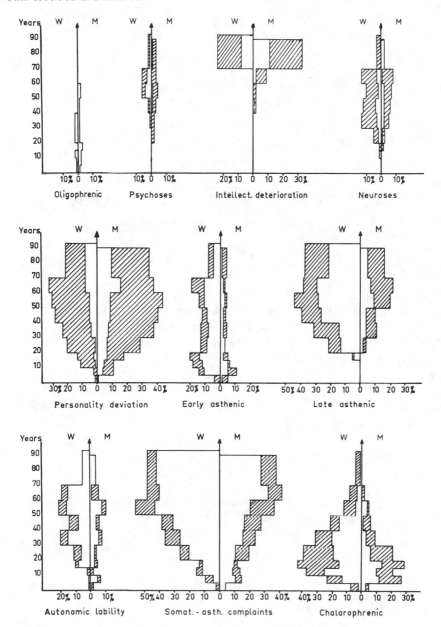

Figure 5.2. Mental diagnoses in percents within groups by sex and age.
Note. White areas = severe, major, or present. Lined areas = mild, minor, or previous.

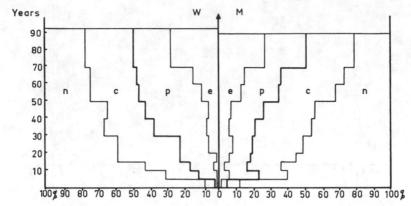

Figure 5.3. Evident, probable, and and conceivable lesions in percents within sex and age groups.

Note. n = no pathology.

we hoped that it would be reduced if we could repeat the survey of the same population longitudinally after some years' lapse. It ought to be possible to compare the degrees of future health and impairment with the present cross-sectional groupings.

In fact, a longitudinal review, such as we had hoped for, was realized on two separate occasions, after 10 and 25 years, respectively. At the first occasion the field work was carried out by Dr. Hagnell (1966), and at the second by him and Dr. Öjesjö in collaboration. Dr. Hagnell's following chapter will provide some of these results.

REFERENCES

Barrett, J. E. (1975). Sjöbring's personality dimensions: Norms for some American populations. *Acta Psychiatrica Scandinavica, 52,* 107–115.

Essen-Möller, E. (1943). Uber den Begriff des Funktionellen und Organischen in der Psychiatrie. *Acta Psychiatr. Neurol, 18,* 1–44.

Essen-Möller, E. (1980). The psychology and psychiatry of Henrik Sjöbring (1879–1956). *Psychological Medicine, 10,* 201–210.

Essen-Möller, E., Larsson, H., Uddenberg, C. E., & White, G. (1956). Individual traits and morbidity in a Swedish rural population. *Acta Psychiatrica et Neurologica Scandinavica* (Supplement 100).

Hagnell, O. (1966). *A prospective study of the incidence of mental disorder.* Stockholm: Scandinavian University Books, Svenska Bokförlaget/Norstedts-Bonniers.

Janet, P. (1909). *Les neuroses.* Paris: Flammarion.

Knobloch, H., & Pasamanick, B. (1959). The syndrome of minimal damage. *Journal of the American Medical Association, 170,* 1384–1387.

Kretschmer, E. (1925). *Physique and character* (2nd ed.). New York: Harcourt, Brace & World.

Nyman, E. (1956). Variations in personality. *Acta Psychiatrica et Neurologica Scandinavica* (Supplement 107).

Leighton, A. H. (1950). Epidemiology of mental disorder. New York: Milbank Memorial Fund.

Pavlov, I. A. (1951). General types of animal and human higher nervous activity. Latest reports on the physiology and pathology of higher nervous activity. *3*, 5–41.

Schneider, K. (1950). *Psychopathic personalities* (9th ed.). Vienna: S. Deuticke. (Original work published 1923)

Sjöbring, H. (1973). Personality structure and development, a model and its application. *Acta Psychiatrica Scandinavica* (Supplement 244)

Slater, E. (1943). The neurotic constitution. *The Journal of Neurology and Psychiatry, 6*, 1–16.

Slater, E. (1950). Kriegserfahrungen und Psychopathiebegriff. *Monatschrift für Psychiatrie und Neurologie, 119*, 207–226.

Uddenberg, G. (1956). Diagnostic studies in prematures. *Acta Psychiatrica Scandinavica* (Supplement 104).

DISCUSSION

Ernest Gruenberg: The first time I visited Professor Essen-Möller in Lund, Olle Hagnell had just begun his field interviewing. Hagnell excused himself because he had to do some of these interviews. He said, politely, that I should stay behind, because the Swedish interviewing would bore me. I said, politely, that I would be fascinated to watch the interviews, but that he and his subjects would be constrained by my presence. We each repeated our position the conventional three times, and then I joined him.

I happened to have one of the first portable tape recorders, which I had bought on impulse. He asked what kind of camera I was carrying, and when I explained what it was, he suggested that I put the tape recorder in front of us when he interviewed his subjects in Swedish. Of course, I did not understand what was said, but I watched the emotional give and take.

That evening I met Professor Essen-Möller and two of his colleagues with whom he had done the survey of 1947. They wanted to hear the tapes, and Hagnell had no objection. What impressed me was that at first they didn't discuss anything but were absolutely silent through the whole thing. Each pulled out a scrap of paper and a pencil to make notes. After it was all over, they had a discussion of how the subject should be classified on these normal personality variants. They would not discuss the interview's contents until they had decided how to account for the slight discrepancies that existed among the four of them present in the room. When I saw them do that over and over again, I realized that I was witnessing a local custom: they insisted on reliability of their appraisal of these variants. I am still mystified by some of the variants but am impressed by their reliability.

I would also like to point out that Dr. Essen-Möller kept referring to the "lesions," to the abnormal, to the minimum brain dysfunctions—the not-obvious examples of brain syndromes that have been a continuing preoccupation for decades in psychiatry and psychology. We all know that people with brain damage have certain mental symptoms. They have attention deficits, are irritable or impulsive, and are sometimes slack. In other people we see these same mental symptoms, but we cannot be sure that a brain injury is present because we don't have nonmental evidence for it. We wonder whether these symptoms are due to the same kind of brain damage with only mental manifestations. We once called such cases "minimum brain damage"; now we have "minimum brain dysfunction." We keep trying to find a name for what I call the "organoid syndrome."

That is an attempt to summarize what I heard Professor Essen-Möller say, having read most of his work before.

Joseph Zubin: It is, of course, very difficult in a limited time period to really describe the system of personality which Sjöbring developed and which Essen-Möller elaborated on, and which has done so much, at least in Lund, for explaining the differences that exist between individuals, even within the same diagnosis. I became infatuated with the system and tried to learn it. It is still highly subjective and intuitive, but in the hands of the group at Lund they were able to get agreement about the ratings from the 7-step scale for each of those diagnostic items that he was talking about. I would like to appeal to those of you who are young enough to still be seeking to make a name for yourselves in this field: here is a chance to develop an interview based upon the Sjöbring method which might perhaps bring personality out of the lamentable stage in which it now exists, despite the multiplicity of inventories. We still lack a sufficiently basic approach to evaluation of personality, especially when it comes to the question of personality disorders. I do hope that some younger colleague will become inspired with the idea and perhaps visit Lund or confer with Jim Barrett, who has already begun to lay the foundation for converting the intuitive, subjective system into a systematic interview.

6

The 25-Year Follow-up of the Lundby Study: Incidence and Risk of Alcoholism, Depression, and Disorders of the Senium

OLLE HAGNELL
University of Lund

INTRODUCTION

The follow-up studies within the Lundby Project have become very extensive. In the following only some hints from various substudies will be presented.

After Essen-Möller's 1947 study of the persons in the community of Lundby, we made two follow-up studies (Table 6.1). Ten years after the first study, in 1957, Hagnell examined all the persons from the 1947 study irrespective of domicile (Hagnell, 1966). At that time almost 700 probands had moved from Lundby and 253 had died. Hagnell interviewed the nearest relatives or other persons who had been well acquainted with the deceased person during the last years of his/her life. In addition all persons who were newcomers into the community (1013), that is, who were in the population registers of Lundby in 1957 but not in 1947, were examined.

In 1972 Hagnell and Öjesjö reexamined the same persons (Hagnell, Lanke, Rorsman, Öjesjö, 1986). At this assessment we limited the study to those persons who had lived in Lundby either in 1947 or in 1957. Thus, newcomers to Lundby in 1972 were *not* included. The field examinations were all made by psychiatrists trained at the same psychiatric institute at the University of Lund.

The Lundby Study thus comprises two prevalence studies of all inhabitants in Lundby (a geographically defined area in southern Sweden); in 1947 this was a population of 2550 persons (Essen-Möller, Larsson, Uddenberg, & White, 1956), and in 1957 of 2612 persons (Hagnell et al., 1986). This gives us two prospective longitudinal studies, one over 10 and 25 years, from July 1, 1947 to June 30, 1957 and June 30, 1972, of 2550 persons, and another over 15 years, from July 1, 1957 to June 30, 1972, of 3310 persons.

Table 6.1. The Lundby Study

In 1947	2,550 persons
In 1957	2,550 + 1,013 persons
In 1972	2,550 + 1,013 persons

1947 COHORT

In the following I will deal primarily with the 1947 cohort (Table 6.2), that is, the 2550 persons from the 1947 survey. A single example from the 1957 cohort will be given.

As in the previous two surveys, in 1972 the dropout was only a few percent. Even for those persons we often could get enough information for a satisfactory evaluation of the proband's mental health. Over half of the probands not personally examined were elderly people who died before our planned visit. The survey in 1972 took a long time to perform, since the probands were so scattered over the country and even abroad. About half of those alive still lived in Lundby; 613 had died and for these, as in 1957, information was collected from the nearest relatives and other persons who had known the deceased well, especially during his/her later years.

The residence in 1972 of the 1947 Lundby cohort is shown in Table 6.3. Only 20% lived in rural areas and more than 15% lived in big cities (cities with more than 100,000 inhabitants). The first Lundby Study in 1947 dealt mainly with a rural population, but the two later studies, especially the one in 1972, dealt mainly with an urban population. The demographic development has followed the pattern seen in areas around big, expansive cities in the Western world.

Table 6.2. Survey of Residence and Obtained Information in 1972 of the 1947 Lundby Cohort ($N = 2,550$)

Residence	Total persons	Personally examined, 1972		With enough information, 1972	
		n	%	n	%
Men ($N = 1,312$)					
Remainders in 1972	481	475	(98.8)	481	(100.0)
Moved	471	454	(96.4)	466	(98.9)
Deceased	360	—	—	357	(99.2)
Women ($N = 1,238$)					
Remainders in 1972	461	455	(98.7)	461	(100.0)
Moved	464	454	(97.8)	463	(99.8)
Deceased	313	—	—	310	(99.0)

Table 6.3. Residence in 1972 of the 1947 Lundby Cohort

	Rural area	Small towns	Big city area	Other densely built-up area
Men	202	124	166	460
Women	193	122	142	468
Total	395	246	308	928

The three surveys were done in a similar way, although, with more experience, we were able to improve our methods. The field examinations were performed with a direct examination. The psychiatrist met the probands face to face, mostly in their homes, and conducted a semistructured interview. A description of the probands and their social milieu was made as well. Table 6.4 shows the various sources we have used to perform an evaluation of each proband. These evaluations were always made by psychiatrists.

1957 10-YEAR FOLLOW-UP STUDY

During the 40 years that the Lundby Study has been going on, many aspects of it have evolved. Essen-Möller has described how they tried in 1947 to classify each inhabitant according to the Sjöbring hypotheses of normal and

Table 6.4. Sources of Data about Probands

1. Field Examination:
   Interview
   Description
2. Information from Other Sources:
   Parish and central population registration
   The Swedish Central Bureau of Statistics
   Social Insurance Office
   Inland Revenue Office
   Criminal register
   County temperance boards
   Hospital case notes, psychiatric
   Hospital case notes, nonpsychiatric
   Key informants
   Official death certificates
   Autopsy reports
   Regional archives
   Postal investigation in 1962

abnormal personality traits. One of his main points was the identification of those with a "lesion" (see Chapter 5; Essen-Möller & Hagnell, 1975).

It should be emphasized that this was a socially healthy population, and when "contracting a mental illness" is mentioned below, it is for the first time in previously healthy persons. In my ten-year follow-up of 1957 I registered all subjects in the population who had contracted a mental illness. Figure 6.1(a) is a graph showing the rate, for lesional and for nonlesional women, of experiencing at least one episode of mental illness during the ten years after 1947. Women who were scored lesional in 1947 were more likely to contract a mental illness. Calculated otherwise, this excess is about 60% for lesional

Figure 6.1(a). Rate of first episode of mental illness, by age, in women (10-year period, 1947–1957).

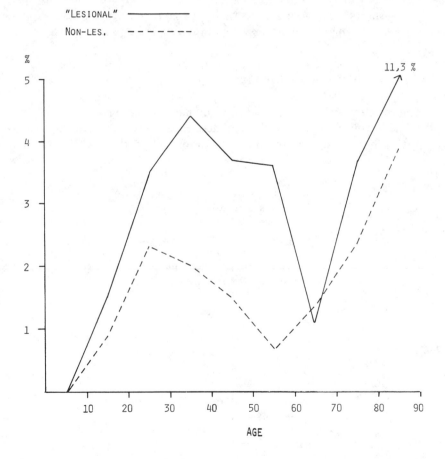

women, which is statistically highly significant. There is also an excess, about 20%, of contracting a mental illness for men classified as lesional in 1947 (Hagnell, 1966).

Figure 6.1(b) shows data for the following 15 years, 1957–1972. Here the excess for lesional women has disappeared, but to expect a significant outcome 10–25 years after the initial examination is unlikely in an epidemiological study such as ours.

As for normal Sjöbring variants (see Sjöbring, 1973), only solidity seems to show a relationship to contracting a mental illness. Subsolids fall ill more often than mediosolids, and mediosolids more often than supersolids.

Some somatic disorders seem to be of importance in determining who

Figure 6.1(b). Rate of first episode of mental illness, by age, in women (15-year period, 1957–1972).

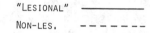

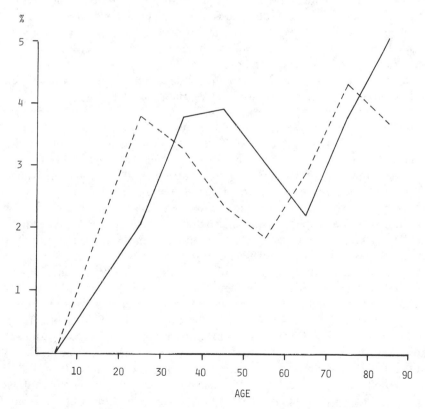

contracts a mental disease. As shown in Table 6.5, proneness to infections, endocrine disturbances, and encephalomeningitis in women, and circulative diseases and peptic ulcer in men show such a relationship (Hagnell, 1966).

INCIDENCE OF MENTAL ILLNESS DURING 25 YEARS, 1947-1972

Figure 6.2 illustrates the way observation years have been calculated in this study. By following the horizontal line we get different cohorts passing through the same ages. One person supplies information years to different age groups. Observation years are cut off when a proband dies or is taken ill with the actual disease studied. When recovered he/she again starts to supply observation years and is again participating in the calculations of risk.

Table 6.6 shows data for all first-time episodes of mental illness over the 25-year period 1947-1972. It comprises all degrees of impairment and all of our diagnoses of mental illness. In the Lundby Study "mental illness" denotes disorders that are acute, clear-cut, and pronounced as regards mental symptoms and onset. Personality deviations, such as character neurosis, are not classified among neuroses, not even in instances where their abnormality might be looked upon as the result of a long-term neurotic development. These cases as well as alcoholism, psychosomatic diseases, and psychopathy, among other diagnostic entities, are handled separately. This system has been used throughout all three field studies (see Hagnell, 1966, 1981).

Of the original 2550 persons, 905 (402 men and 503 women) had a mild, medium, or severe episode of mental illness from the time of the first examination in 1947 up to July 1, 1972. Looking only at episodes of a severe impairment we find 200 first episodes (100 men and 100 women) (Table 6.7).

The cumulative probability of contracting a mental illness for a newborn baby until he/she reaches 90 years of age, if that age is attained (= lifetime probability), is for men 85.6% and for women 92.6%. This is of course a conditional figure. The exact incidence is given under "cases," and the incidence rate per year is given in the fifth column from the left. However, it is easier and possibly more convenient, and in some ways more correct, to compare the cumulative probability of illness for the entire lifespan.

This is what we have done in Figures 6.3-6.5, which attempt to summarize the incidences and probabilities of contracting a particular mental illness during the 25-year period 1947-1972. The illnesses are divided into main groups: neuroses (Fig. 6.3) with six subgroups; psychoses (Fig. 6.4) with two; and organic brain syndromes (Fig. 6.5) with three subgroups. (For an explanation of what is an illness in the various subgroups, see Hagnell, 1966, 1981.)

In the Figures the incidences and the cumulative probability of contracting the disease before the age of 90 are given. The small marks on the bars

Table 6.5. Physical Ailments.

Item	Person years observed 1947-57	Observed number with mental disease O	Crude average annual incidence /100	Age specifically expected number with mental disease E	O/E	p
Men						
Proneness to infections	1818.0	20	1.1	16.5	1.2	
Orthopedics	1351.5	16	1.2	11.2	1.4	
Chronic polyarthritis	30.0	0	0.0	0.3	—	.10
Rheumatic fever	280.0	2	0.7	2.6	0.8	
Encephalitis and meningitis[1]	182.0	2	1.1	1.7	1.2	
Endocrine disturbances[1]	48.5	0	0.0	0.4	—	
Circulative diseases[1]	303.5	8	2.6	2.8	2.9	.001
Peptic ulcer	197.5	3	1.5	1.3	2.3	
Peptic ulcer 40–59 years[1]	187.5	3	1.6	1.2	2.5	.05
Women						
Proneness to infections	1885.5	64	3.4	43.0	1.5	.00001
Orthopedics	250.0	9	2.4	17.6	1.1	
Chronic polyarthritis	200.0	3	1.5	4.1	0.7	
Rheumatic fever	240.0	6	2.5	5.2	1.1	
Encephalitis and meningitis[1]	203.5	8	3.9	4.5	1.8	.05
Endocrine disturbances[1]	350.0	13	3.7	7.9	1.7	.025
Circulative diseases	500.0	14	2.8	10.3	1.4	
Peptic ulcer	120.0	3	2.5	2.5	1.2	
Peptic ulcer 40–59 years[1]	80.0	2	1.8	1.4	1.4	

[1]Chi-square test used, age group 15–59 years.

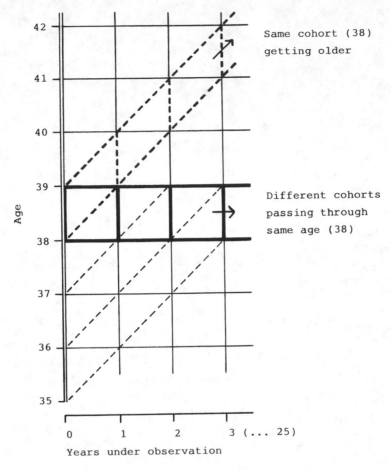

Figure 6.2. Two ways of using follow-up cohorts entering at double lines.

indicate limits of degrees of impairment. The whole bar equals all degrees of impairment of the illness in question.

Psychoses are few (Fig. 6.4). However, those of the senium and other psycho-organic psychoses are not included.

For organic syndromes and multi-infarct dementia (Fig. 6.5) a slight excess for men has been found. The same is the case for age neuroses. Some of the age neuroses might be of organic origin. These are the only diagnostic groups where we find more men than women.

CHANGES OVER TIME: THE FIRST 10 YEARS COMPARED WITH THE LAST 15 YEARS

The long observation time, 25 years, the same population followed during that time, and the same criteria for diagnosing give us an opportunity to find out if the incidences of diseases have changed over time.

Table 6.6. The Incidence and Risk of Contracting a Mental Illness for the First Time.

MEN

Age interval	Observation years under risk	Cases	Rate per year	Probability of disease during age interval	Cumulative probability of disease
00–09	1059.7	5	.0047	.046	.046 (.020)
10–19	2790.2	20	.0072	.069	.112 (.024)
20–29	4145.8	76	.0183	.167	.261 (.025)
30–39	3887.9	60	.0154	.143	.366 (.025)
40–49	3706.9	51	.0138	.129	.448 (.024)
50–59	3411.9	48	.0141	.132	.520 (.023)
60–69	2469.6	55	.0223	.200	.616 (.022)
70–79	1530.2	44	.0288	.250	.712 (.021)
80–89	549.5	38	.0692	.499	.856 (.019)
90–99	46.1	5	.1084	—	—
100–109	.0	0	—	—	—
0+	23597.7	402	.0170	—	—

WOMEN

Age interval	Observation years under risk	Cases	Rate per year	Probability of disease during age interval	Cumulative probability of disease
00–09	1025.4	3	.0029	.029	.029 (.016)
10–19	2843.5	40	.0141	.132	.156 (.024)
20–29	3317.3	104	.0314	.269	.384 (.026)
30–39	2667.3	92	.0345	.292	.564 (.024)
40–49	2549.3	75	.0294	.255	.675 (.021)
50–59	2420.4	59	.0244	.217	.745 (.018)
60–69	2057.8	45	.0219	.197	.795 (.016)
70–79	1329.4	49	.0369	.309	.858 (.013)
80–89	505.9	33	.0652	.479	.926 (.011)
90–99	67.1	3	.0447	—	—
100–109	2.6	0	.0000	—	—
0+	18785.9	503	.0268	—	—

Note. Data from a total population during the 25-year period 1947–1972. Degree of impairment: Severe + Medium + Mild.

Table 6.7. The Incidence and Risk of Contracting a Mental Illness for the First Time.

MEN

Age interval	Observation years under risk	Cases	Rate per year	Probability of disease during age interval	Cumulative probability of disease
00–09	1072.3	0	.0000	.000	.000 (.000)
10–19	2940.9	1	.0003	.003	.003 (.003)
20–29	4560.9	14	.0031	.031	.033 (.009)
30–39	4449.9	9	.0020	.020	.053 (.011)
40–49	4286.5	7	.0016	.016	.068 (.012)
50–59	3793.6	10	.0026	.026	.092 (.014)
60–69	2776.4	14	.0050	.049	.136 (.018)
70–79	1687.2	20	.0119	.112	.233 (.026)
80–89	634.4	23	.0363	.304	.466 (.044)
90–99	64.6	2	.0310	—	—
100–109	.0	0	—	—	—
0+	26266.6	100	.0038	—	—

WOMEN

Age interval	Observation years under risk	Cases	Rate per year	Probability of disease during age interval	Cumulative probability of disease
00–09	1030.4	0	.0000	.000	.000 (.000)
10–19	2988.6	3	.0010	.010	.010 (.006)
20–29	4085.5	10	.0024	.024	.033 (.009)
30–39	3643.3	6	.0016	.016	.049 (.011)
40–49	3355.3	15	.0045	.044	.091 (.015)
50–59	3181.9	10	.0031	.031	.118 (.017)
60–69	2607.1	12	.0046	.045	.158 (.020)
70–79	1618.5	24	.0148	.138	.274 (.028)
80–89	590.9	19	.0322	.275	.474 (.044)
90–99	73.3	1	.0137	—	—
100–109	2.6	0	.0000	—	—
0+	23177.3	100	.0043	—	—

Note. Data from a total population during the 25-year period 1947–1972. Degree of impairment: Severe.

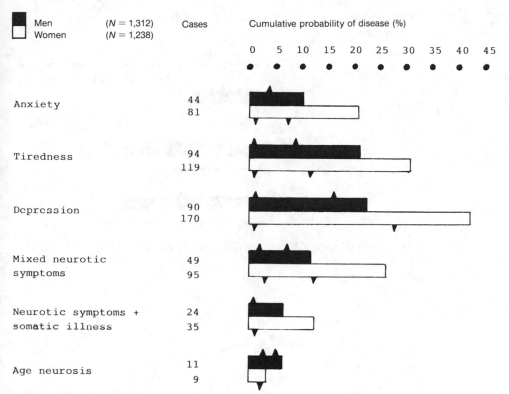

Figure 6.3. Incidence of neuroses in the Lundby Study, 1947–1972 (*N* = 2,550).

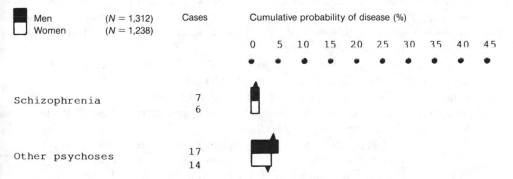

Figure 6.4. Incidence of psychoses in the Lundby Study, 1947–1972 (*N* = 2,550).

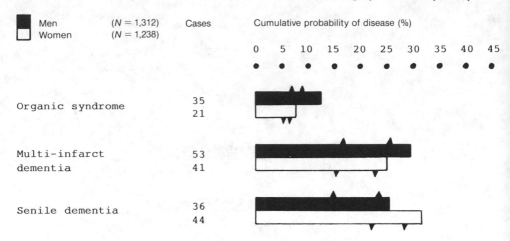

Figure 6.5. Incidence of organic brain syndromes in the Lundby Study, 1947–1972 ($N = 2,550$).

Depressions

At the end of the 1960s some psychiatrists (e.g., Gerald Klerman and John Schwab in the United States) claimed that an increase of depression was under way. Today, as far as the Lundby population is concerned, we can concur. This is illustrated by the bar graphs in Figure 6.6. During the first 10-year period versus the later 15-year period there has been an increase in depression for both sexes. However, for severely impaired depressives, there is no increase, but rather a slight decrease. An explanation for this phenomenon is that people with depressions come under treatment earlier now, so the illness has less opportunity to develop into a severe impairment (Hagnell, Lanke, Rorsman, & Öjesjö, 1982).

But is the increase similar in all subgroups? To date in our analysis of the depressions we have found age group differences. For males [Fig. 6.7(a)], young and middle-aged males have the greatest increase. For example, the probability of contracting a depression during the age interval of 30–39 years has increased tenfold for males, from 0.6 to 6.0% [see Fig. 6.7(a)]. For women the figures for depression in the first 10-year period were already high, but for women in late middle age the probability of contracting a depression is four to five times greater during the last 15-year period [Fig. 6.7(b)].

Mental Disorders of the Senium

Another group of diseases of great interest in our time is mental illness of the senium. The cumulative probability of contracting senile dementia before the age of 90 has decreased (Fig. 6.8). Thus the incidence in 1957–1972 compared with 1947–1957 is lower for both men and women (Hagnell, Lanke, Rorsman, Öhman, and Öjesjö, 1983).

The trend for multi-infarct dementia is similar. The probability of contracting multi-infarct dementia before the age of 90 has decreased, from the 10-year period to the 15-year period, with the exception of the most severely impaired women (Fig. 6.9). One explanation for the decrease might be the better treatment of patients with hypertension.

Figure 6.6. Cumulative probability of contracting depression before the age of 90.

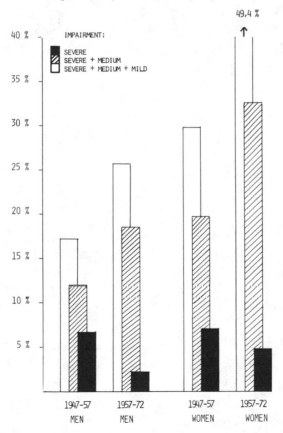

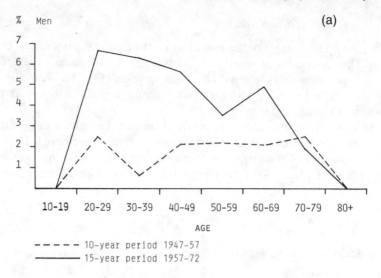

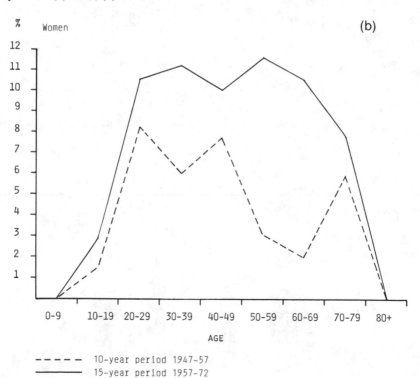

Figure 6.7. Probability of contracting depression, by ages, during the two time periods: (a) Men, (b) Women.

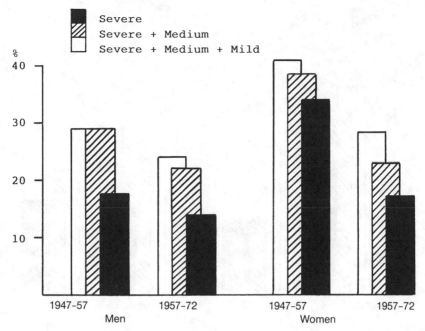

Figure 6.8. Cumulative probability of contracting senile dementia before the age of 90.

Alcoholism

The following definition of alcoholism has been used in the Lundby Study:

1. An increased tolerance for alcohol and thereby a significantly increased consumption.
2. Changed behavioral pattern:
   a. Trigger mechanism (i.e., a pathological desire for alcohol after ingestion of small quantities—a "trigger dose").
   b. Recovery requirement (the need of a drink the morning after abuse).
   c. Blackout (loss of memory).

We classified alcoholism into three groups: chronic alcoholism, alcohol addiction, and alcohol abuse. Chronic alcoholism is at least two of the three symptoms above plus sequence symptoms (as cirrhosis of the liver, polyneuritis, deterioration). Alcohol addiction is at least two of the three symptoms above. Alcohol abuse is an increased tolerance for alcohol and thereby a significantly increased consumption of the same (DSM-III 305.0).

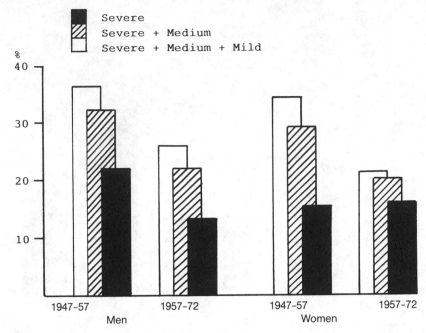

Figure 6.9. Cumulative probability of contracting multi-infarct dementia before the age of 90.

Chronic alcoholism and alcohol addiction are together called alcohol dependence (DSM-III 303.0). Alcoholism in this study is defined as alcohol dependence and alcohol abuse.

Alcoholism, especially hidden alcoholism, is difficult to detect, and therefore the true incidence of alcoholism is very hard to establish. To get a population as free from alcoholics as possible, we sorted them out from the 1947 cross-sectional study, from the 10-year period 1947–1957, as well as in the 1957 prevalence study (Hagnell & Tunving, 1972). Since alcoholism among women was rare, we calculated the incidence of alcoholism for men only. In the 1947 prevalence study, of the 1312 men, 90 were or had been alcoholics. Among the 862 nonalcoholic males of the 1947 cohort studied in 1957, 41 became alcoholics (Table 6.8), with 20 of them alcohol dependent (Table 6.9), during the 15-year period 1957–1972. The cumulative probability for any alcoholism was 19.3%; for alcohol dependence it was 8.6% (Öjesjö, Hagnell, & Lanke, 1982).

BACKGROUND FACTORS FOR MENTAL DISORDERS

We are currently conducting a study of background factors for alcoholism among men (Hagnell, Lanke, Rorsman, & Öhman, in press; Hagnell, Isberg, Lanke, Rorsman, & Öhman, in press). In this substudy, in contrast to material presented earlier in this chapter, we have used the 1957 cross-sectional study comprising every inhabitant in the official population register of the community of Lundby on July 1, 1957. One hundred and seven of the 1135 men were or had been alcoholics on or before that date. Of the 1228 nonalcoholics in 1957, 58 became alcoholics during the 15-year period 1957–1972. Forty-four of them were age 15 years or older. The final aim of the study is to do an integrated analysis of personality, social circumstances, and drinking patterns. So far we have only worked with personality and social background factors, about 300–400 altogether. Among these we have found certain single background factors with a prognostic value in the subsequent diagnosis of alcoholism (Table 6.10). If we look at background factors as single factors, using a logistic regression technique, "Temperance Board's registration," "Symptom neurosis," and "Psychopathy" have a precipitating influence on alcoholism with odds ratios of 10.1, 5.8, and 4.1, respectively.

If we look at single *or* combined background factors to find a prognostic value for the subsequent diagnosis of alcoholism, we get a somewhat different

Table 6.8. Incidence and Risk (± SD) of Developing Any Alcoholism among Males in the Lundby Community Cohort, 1957–1972

Age class	Observation years under risk	Cases	Annual incidence[a]	Cumulative probability
0–9	0	0		
10–19	1049.4	7	.0067 + .0025	.065 + .024
20 29	2421.0	14	.0058 ± .0015	.117 ± .026
30–39	2578.6	10	.0039 ± .0012	.151 ± .027
40–49	2281.1	5	.0022 ± .0010	.169 ± .028
50–59	2481.2	2	.0008 ± .0006	.176 ± .028
60–69	1904.1	2	.0011 ± .0007	.184 ± .028
70–79	995.6	1	.0010 ± .0010	.193 ± .029
80+	564.4	0	.0000 ± .0000	.193 ± .029
0+	14275.4	41		

[a]Age-standardized: .0030 ± .0005.
From Öjesjö *et al.*, 1983.

Table 6.9. Incidence and Risk (±SD) of Developing Alcohol Dependence among Males in the Lundby Community Cohort, 1957–1972

Age class	Observation years under risk	Cases	Annual incidence[a]	Cumulative probability
0–9	0	0		
10–19	1064.3	2	.0019 ± .0013	.019 ± .013
20–29	2527.0	10	.0040 ± .0013	.057 ± .017
30–39	2751.4	4	.0015 ± .0007	.070 ± .018
40–49	2434.5	3	.0012 ± .0007	.082 ± .019
50–59	2600.4	0	.0000 ± .0000	.082 ± .019
60–69	2033.6	1	.0005 ± .0005	.086 ± .020
70–79	1111.1	0	.0000 ± .0000	.086 ± .020
80+	597.0	0	.0000 ± .0000	.086 ± .020
0+	15119.3	20		

[a]Age-standardized: .0013 ± .0003.
From Öjesjö et al., 1983.

picture (Tables 6.11, 6.12). Symptom neurosis, which alone gives an odds ratio of 5.8, gives in combination with the Sjöbring variant "subsolidity" an odds ratio of 15.8 when "Temperance Board's registration" is included and 13.5 when it is not included. Protective are subvalidity according to Sjöbring in combination with psychosomatic symptoms (0.084) and cerebral lesion according to Sjöbring (= MBD etc.) (0.21).

Finally, we looked at single background factors of a social type (Table 6.13), although "alcoholism in first-degree relatives" might be consid-

Table 6.10. Single Background Factors with Prognostic Value for the Outcome of Alcoholism

"Known by Temperance Boards" included	
Background factors	Odds ratio
Precipitating:	
Temperance Boards' registration	10.1
Symptom neurosis	5.8
Psychopathy	4.1
Protective:	
Cerebral lesion, MBD, etc.	0.18
Personality traits: Tired, poor concentration, heavy, gloomy	0.23

Table 6.11. Single or Combined Background Factors with Prognostic Value for the Outcome of Alcoholism

"Known by Temperance Boards" included	
Background factors	Odds ratio
Precipitating:	
Sjöbring variant: Solidity below medio + symptom neurosis	15.8
Temperance Boards' registration	11.2
Personality traits: High consciousness, alertness + psychophysiological symptoms with evident psychiatric component	5.9
Psychopathy	3.7
Protective:	
Cerebral lesion, MBD, etc.	0.21

ered both social and genetic. All of these factors except "married" are precipitating.

Our next step will be to study the interactions among the various social factors and then to combine personality with social factors. We also want to include the drinking patterns.

At present we are also studying background factors for depressions, diseases of the senium, asthenic states, and panic anxiety, the findings of which we intend to present in forthcoming reports.

Table 6.12. Single or Combined Background Factors with Prognostic Value for the Outcome of Alcoholism

"Known by Temperance Boards" not included	
Background factors	Odds ratio
Precipitating:	
Sjöbring variant: Solidity below medio + symptom neurosis	13.5
Personality traits: High consciousness, alertness + psychophysiological symptoms with evident psychiatric component	5.5
Psychopathy	4.3
In- or outpatient (or other) psychiatric care	3.9
Protective:	
Sjöbring variant: Validity below medio + psychophysiological symptoms with evident psychiatric component	0.084
Personality traits: Tired, poor concentration, heavy, gloomy	0.21

Table 6.13. Selected Social Background Factors with
Prognostic Value for the Outcome of Alcoholism

Social background factors	Odds ratio
Precipitating:	
Proletarian environment	14.6
Abnormal family situation	4.85
Gang engagement	12.6
Crisis	10.1
Alcoholism in first-degree relatives	5.58
Craft occupation	2.77
Protective:	
Marital status: Married	0.568

ACKNOWLEDGMENTS

This study has been supported by Grant No. 71/2 from the Bank of Sweden Tercentenary
Foundation, Grant No. 3474 from the Swedish Medical Research Council, and Grant No. 81/
1189 from the Swedish Council for Planning and Coordination of Research.

REFERENCES

Essen-Möller, E., Larsson, H., Uddenberg, C., & White, G. (1956). Individual traits and
    morbidity in a Swedish rural population. *Acta Psychiatrica et Neurologica Scandinav-
    ica* (Supplement 100).
Essen-Möller, E., & Hagnell, O. (1975). 'Normal' and 'Lesional' traits of personality according
    to Sjöbring: Re-ratings and prognostic implications. The Lundby Project. *Neuropsy-
    chobiology, 1*, 146–154.
Hagnell, O. (1966). *A prospective study of the incidence of mental disorder*. Stockholm:
    Scandinavian University Books, Svenska Bokförlaget/Norstedts-Bonniers.
Hagnell, O. (1981). The Lundby Study on psychiatric morbidity (Sweden). In S. A. Mednick
    & A. E. Baert (Eds.), *Prospective longitudinal research; an empirical basis for the
    primary prevention of psychosocial disorders* (pp. 189–206). New York: Oxford Univer-
    sity Press.
Hagnell, O., & Tunving, K. (1972). Prevalence and nature of alcoholism in a total population.
    Social Psychiatry, 7, 190–201.
Hagnell, O., Lanke, J., Rorsman, B., & Öjesjö, L. (1982). Are we entering an age of melan-
    choly? Depressive illnesses in a prospective epidemiological study over 25 years, the
    Lundby Study, Sweden. *Psychological Medicine, 12*, 279–289.

Hagnell, O., Lanke, J., Rorsman, B., Öhman, R., & Öjesjö, L. (1983). Current trends in the incidence of senile and multi-infarct dementia. A prospective study of a total population followed over 25 years; the Lundby Study. *Archiv für Psychiatrie und Nervenkrankheiten, 233*, 423–438.

Hagnell, O., Lanke, J., Rorsman, B., & Öjesjö, L. (1986). A prospective longitudinal study of the incidence of mental disorders in a total population investigated in 1947, 1957, and 1972. The Lundby Study.

Hagnell, O., Isberg, P.-E., Lanke, J., Rorsman, B., & Öhman, R. (in press). Predictors of alcoholism in the Lundby Study: III. Social risk factors for alcoholism. *European Archives of Psychiatry and Neurological Sciences.*

Hagnell, O., Lanke, J., Rorsman, B., & Öhman, R. (in press). Predictors of alcoholism in the Lundby Study: II. Personality traits as risk factors for alcoholism. *European Archives of Psychiatry and Neurological Sciences.*

Öjesjö, L., Hagnell, O., & Lanke, J. (1982). Incidence of alcoholism among men in the Lundby community cohort, Sweden, 1947–1972. *Journal of Studies on Alcohol, 43*(11), 1190–1198.

Sjöbring, H. (1973). Personality structure and development: A model and its application. *Acta Psychiatrica Scandinavica* (Supplement 244).

DISCUSSION

C. R. Cloninger: Do subsolidity and anxiety features predict alcoholism even before there are temperance-board registrations, or any other evidence of alcohol abuse? Are these really antecedent, or could the individuals have already started abusing alcohol?

Hagnell: There was no alcohol abuse before; these factors preceded it.

Ernest Gruenberg: I would like to compliment you on an enormous data base and your attempt to weave your way through it. My question is this: You have a few dozen cases that develop alcoholism, and you have 1000 background characteristics; how are you going to decide which ones are worth paying attention to? You are bound to get some correlations just by chance because you have so many background variables. How are you handling that problem in your complicated analysis?

Hagnell: We did not consider all of the background characteristics, but only about 300. Of these, many were rare, and others were so remote from alcoholism that we did not use them. That left about 100, and, using a cross-tabulation procedure, we eliminated a lot of combinations. We then divided our population into three groups, and applied a linear log regression procedure.

I am afraid I have not given an adequate explanation of our method, but it would take a good deal of time to explain it fully.

Robert Spitzer: I would like to ask Dr. Hagnell about the cohort effect that he found with depression. One possibility is that subjects in different time periods have different concepts to explain their experiences. Could he say more about the process of the interview, the possibility that either the subjects or the interviewer had a different way of explaining or conceptualizing the same experience?

Hagnell: With respect to the interviewers, we have all had about the same amount of experience in diagnosing depressions. We have had the same training at the same medical center (Lund). I was trained by and worked with Essen-Möller; and Leif Öjesjö, who did the 1972 interviews, was trained by me. So I think what we diagnosed as depression, and how we conceptualized it, remained the same during the 25 years of the study.

Also, diagnosis was not based only on our impression, but on additional information: extensive information from local doctors, from psychiatric hospitals, and from what we call the social assurance company, which is special for Sweden and involves a very thorough investigation. We had such information not just for those who remained in Lundby, but for all wherever they were in Sweden. The use of this data in arriving at our diagnoses should have leveled out any individual differences we might have had.

7

The Initial Frame of Reference of the Stirling County Study: Main Questions Asked and Reasons for Them

ALEXANDER H. LEIGHTON
Dalhousie University

INTRODUCTION

The Stirling County Study had its origin, in part at least, some 40 years ago as a reaction to the hermaphrodite state of psychiatric theory—half metaphysics and half science.

Forty years ago in America Kraepelinian psychiatry and Meyer's commonsense psychiatry were being overrun by psychoanalysis and succeeding waves of neopsychoanalysis. As a result, the concepts of "mental" and "illness" lacked consensus; intuition was often employed as a test of validity; the products of speculation were treated as ascertained truths; and there was in the relationship between hypotheses and systematic data a looseness not tolerated elsewhere in the life sciences. Because of these unfettering conditions, the growth rate in psychiatric theories was out of hand and on the road to becoming a source of danger to the discipline—like the horns of the Irish elk, which paleontologists say got so voluminous, many-pointed, and heavy that they exterminated the animal.

Because of these conditions, a number of people began to think that it would be worthwhile to put emphasis on searching for what Karl Jaspers (1963, p. 858) described as "substantial, valid, and enduring" fact. If sufficient anchor points in systematic data could be found, it appeared likely that they would serve as a basis for sorting the more from the less likely theories. This might be done, it seemed to me, in a series of steps constituting successive approximations that would move progressively toward ever greater clarification and validity.

Such an idea was somewhat at variance with prevailing views among research psychologists who, following laboratory models, were inclined to think that in science every maneuver must consist in the testing of a specific hypothesis. My training in natural history as well as in clinical work inclined me to believe that accumulating banks of descriptive data might prove useful.

The point of departure selected was the general problem of whether social and cultural factors played a part in the origin, course, and outcome of psychiatric disorders (Leighton, 1959, pp. 3–4). Considering how to cope with this led to three somewhat more specific subquestions:

1. How many people have mental illnesses? That is, what is the actual frequency of these disorders in a population, both treated and untreated? It seemed evident that both figures would have to be available as baseline information if one were to examine the effects of social and cultural factors.

There was much talk in those days about treated cases being the "tip of the iceberg." As a consequence, I sometimes thought that a major part of the problem was discovering the dimensions of that portion of the iceberg that was hidden from sight.

2. What are the kinds of disorders that people have? That is, how do the total figures break down in terms of different clinical categories?

3. How are these disorders distributed in populations? That is, do there appear to be associations between the frequencies of psychiatric disorders and the presence of particular social or cultural factors?

Quantitative thinking of the kind represented in these questions, though informal, was by no means alien to clinicians. Our teachers and peers in residency training frequently employed such words as "common," "rare," "sometimes," "always," "never," "exceptional," "more than," and "when you see such and such you can be sure that. . . ." The problem was the lack of specificity in these expressions. Much of what was said might be true, but there was little basis for knowing.

Further contemplation of the three questions—How many? What kinds? and How distributed?—made it evident that they contained concepts that would have to be more clearly stated. Attempting this led to developing the frame of reference which I shall now outline. It is the product of many advisors and colleagues who participated in the Stirling County Study; and it is to them I refer when I use the pronoun "we."

HOW MANY PEOPLE WITH MENTAL DISORDERS ARE THERE?

This question embodies the notion of *population*. We defined a population for our purposes as all the people occupying a geographic space and living for the most part under conditions that could be considered characteristic of the human species rather than exceptional. In other words, collectivities such as refugee camps were excluded.

Because the individuals who make up a population move about geographically and have birth-to-death life-arcs, any statement about a population must, to be valid, take account of this time-change dimension. New individuals are always flowing into a population through immigration and through birth, while others are disappearing through emigration and death. We likened the population of Stirling County, therefore, to a river, and ourselves to observers standing at a spot past which it flowed. Always there, it was nevertheless always different in its components at whatever time-one, time-two, time-three, and so on, one might choose.

Also embodied in this "How much?" question is the notion of *frequency*. This refers not only to the individuals who make up a population, but also to various properties possessed by these individuals. As a consequence, emergence, duration, and disappearance are characteristic of these properties in a double sense: they come, last, and go as individuals come, last, and go, but in addition they may come, last, and go within the life-arc of an individual. This is true whether the properties in question be mental disorder, baldness, influenza, diabetes, or good looks. The notion of frequency in a population, therefore, has to be broken down into the component notions of *prevalence* and *incidence*.

It seemed to us at the beginning that a fairly good estimate of mental illness prevalence could be obtained for any given time-one. Incidence, however, was more problematic. In a first survey, it could only be estimated from retrospective accounts given by individuals, and these would be variable in their accuracy. If we made later surveys of the population, however, at time-two, time-three, and so on, it might be possible to obtain more dependable incidence data by using the first survey as a baseline. For a start, therefore, we decided to concentrate on prevalence and to develop as much knowledge as possible about this dimension at a selected time-one. This date turned out to be May 1, 1952. Our hope was that by securing prevalence facts for that date, we could later, through follow-up investigations, move into the study of incidence.

Finally, also involved in the first question was the notion of *mental disorders*, the phenomena we wished to identify and count. In the beginning the main problem appeared to be securing that cooperation from the population which would be essential for acquiring the necessary systematic data.

I had some optimism about this, because of previous experience in gathering life histories from Navahos, Eskimos, and Japanese. The readiness that people had shown to talk about their lives led me to think that it would be feasible to carry out successful case-finding in a population.

When we turned to the matter of identifying instances of mental illnesses through such data, the question of "What is a case?" was immediately upon us. Inasmuch as the many difficulties and facets of this problem, both real and unreal, are well known and have been discussed by numerous authors, I shall not attempt to resummarize them here, but shall go directly to a short description of how we undertook to deal with the issue.

Having had some experience during the war with the operational approach to problem solving, it seemed to me that we would be well advised to employ this orientation, given the state of psychiatric theory and the lack of clarity and consistency in its terminology. The fact that we wanted to measure the hidden portion of an iceberg made it seem appropriate to use the phenomena displayed in the visible portion as the basis for constructing definitions. A first step was to look at the diagnostic process as commonly practiced in hospitals and outpatient clinics and to begin by breaking it down into operational components. When we did this we discovered that a major component—the assignment of cause—could not be operationalized in any reliable way except in some of those cases in which the etiology was organic. Today, the assignment of psychological cause is not considered a necessary part of diagnosis, but at midcentury a psychiatric diagnosis was generally regarded as defective if it lacked a statement about etiology. This was particularly true with regard to the psychoneuroses.

A second reason for rejecting the use of definitions based on psychological etiology was the likelihood that they would run the risk of building spurious correlations into our findings—spurious because they would be part of the definitions employed. The diagnostic categories of "exogenous," "endogenous," and "transient situational disturbance" illustrate the possibility for this kind of error.

The appearance of the first *Diagnostic and Statistical Manual of Mental Disorders* (American Psychiatric Association, 1952) aided our deliberations by providing a somewhat more consistent technical language. Otherwise, however, it helped little because it remained grounded in the idea that the identification of etiology was the basis of diagnosis.

Considering what to do led to looking at the epistemology of definitions and getting much help from Kroeber and Kluckhohn's (1952) scholarly monograph on the definition of the word "culture." As a result, I was attracted by the concept of *ostensive definition*, and to its appropriateness given our focus on the tip of the iceberg. An ostensive definition consists in examples of what is meant rather than causal ideas, and it is grounded in the observable. If you ask me what I mean by a red tie, and if instead of talking about light-wave frequency, I reply by showing you a red tie, that is an ostensive definition. By sacrificing hermeneutics, ostensive definitions remove all the operational problems posed by unverifiable etiologies.

My colleagues and I, following this line of thought, decided that the ostensive definition for the Stirling County Study would consist in all that assortment of clinical phenomena commonly seen among inpatients and outpatients. While such a definition lacked elegance, it had the advantage of staying close to the observable and to clinical practice. It also involved classifying mental illness phenomena on the basis of similarities and dissimilarities of behavior and expressed feelings. Such categories are, of course, in keeping with the traditions originated by Sydenham.

The notion of syndrome, in short, replaced etiology as central in our diagnostic operations. Because of the close association at this time between the word diagnosis and the assignment of etiology, however, we gave up using "diagnosis" and spoke in terms of identifying symptoms and syndromes. Quite often we used the term "symptom pattern."

Our use of syndromes, based as it was on phenomena at the tip of the clinical iceberg, was encouraged by two old and well-known models each occurring in a very different research field. One consisted in the way taxonomists distinguish species of plants and animals by means of morphologic patterns. The other was in the way pathologists distinguish among pathological tissues and between the pathological and the normal. In the latter model, as every medical student knows, microscopic slides are selected as standards that exemplify different kinds of pathological and normal tissues. When an unknown tissue is encountered by a pathologist its pattern is compared with those shown in the standard slides; and it is categorized by judging which one of the standards it most closely resembles.

It was not, of course, possible for us to keep a drawer full of live patients, the way the taxonomist and the pathologist can keep dead exemplars. We could, however, approximate this by converting our ostensive definitions into descriptive definitions and using them as standards of reference (Leighton, 1959, pp. 93–115).

Having ablated psychological etiology and moved symptom and syndrome to a central position, our further analysis of the diagnostic operation focused on the concept of work *impairment* and on the *duration* attributable to syndromes (Leighton, Harding, Macklin, Macmillan, & Leighton, 1963, pp. 52–54, 73–75). These were both handled by establishing systems for making estimates.

A fourth component was something we termed "confidence." By this is meant the degree of assurance felt by an evaluator who, when looking at the data about an individual, discovers that he or she is indeed dealing with something that very closely approximates one or more of our descriptive definitions. The scale for the confidence rating had four points: A, B, C, and D, with A being high confidence and D meaning not a case (Leighton, Harding, Macklin, Macmillan, & Leighton, 1963, pp. 119–120).

It is evident that confidence is an estimate of probability, but it is the clinical evaluator's psychological sense in the matter rather than statistical probability. It seemed to us that this formed an important component in the diagnostic process virtually everywhere in clinical medicine. Depending on the information available, any particular diagnosis was conceived as falling into one of three categories: high, medium, and low confidence that a disorder is present.

The dimension of confidence, we thought, would be helpful later in the analysis of correlations. For example, a group of subjects labeled ill with high confidence could be expected to contain very few false positives, but the

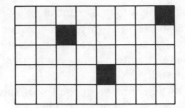

Legend : Each space represents a possible
              psychiatric symptom

■ = presence of symptom

Figure 7.1. Nominal scale: presence or
absence of symptoms with psychiatric
significance.

residual might contain numerous false negatives. On the other hand a group labeled ill with low confidence might contain many false positives while the residual would contain very few false negatives. Today these notions would be expressed more ably in terms of sensitivity and specificity.

The upshot of our analysis of the diagnostic process therefore consisted in five scales for use in identifying and classifying instances of mental illness in the population at large: individual symptoms, syndromes, impairment, duration, and confidence. As can be seen in Figures 7.1–7.6, the first two of these are nominal or categorical scales, two are ordinal scales, and one (duration) is an interval scale.

It must be admitted that at this stage in the development of our methods, the criteria for positioning an individual on these scales were highly subjective, involving much clinical judgment. Greater objectivity and specificity of criteria came later in successive steps. Nevertheless, the ratings on these scales for each individual were recorded separately. This has made it possible in recent years for Murphy, Neff, Sobol, Rice, and Olivier (1985) to operationalize the criteria that underlay the clinical judgments.

Partly to explain our choice, and partly to enable the reader to make other choices if desired, we published separate tabulations of symptoms, syndromes, impairment, and confidence as well as their synthesis in a typol-

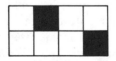

Figure 7.2. Nominal scale: presence or
absence of psychiatric syndromes.

Legend : Each space represents a possible
              psychiatric syndrome

■ = presence of syndrome

Figure 7.3. Ordinal scale: impairment.

ogy we called "need for psychiatric attention." The latter constituted our main way of summarizing the prevalence rates (Leighton, Harding, Macklin, Hughes, & Leighton, 1963; Leighton, Harding, Macklin, Macmillan, & Leighton, 1963).

Presenting our data in these several modes was confusing to a number of readers, especially social scientists, who at times treated our symptom tabulations as if they were case counts. Among clinicians, too, the fact that we had chopped out etiological criteria and had separated diagnosis into descriptive components made for difficulties. Some, indeed, went so far as to say that if psychodynamic etiology were being omitted, the results could not be other than trivial. John Whitehorne, for instance, Head of the Department of Psychiatry at Johns Hopkins Medical School, following Meyer, told me that he thought we were tabulating "human miseries" rather than anything that had real clinical significance. Others who were less focused on psychoanalytic etiology nevertheless reached similar conclusion through overlooking the attention we actually gave to impairment and duration.

Our own best estimate of the iceberg, taking into account the part above as well as below the surface, came to 20% for the adult population (Leighton, Harding, Macklin, Hughes, & Leighton, 1963, pp. 139–170, 253–279; Leighton, Lambo, Hughes, Leighton, Murphy, & Macklin, 1963).

WHAT ARE THE RATES FOR THE DIFFERENT KINDS OF DISORDERS?

The frame of reference of the Stirling County Study embraced the notion that mental illnesses are an exceedingly heterogeneous lot. We did not subscribe to the unitary concept advocated by Karl Menninger (1959, pp. 516–528) or to the vaguer ideas along the same line that permeated the outlook of many of

Figure 7.4. Interval scale: duration in months or years.

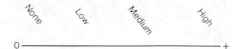

0 ——————————————————————— +   Figure 7.5. Ordinal scale: confidence.

the social scientists who entered psychiatric epidemiology. We thought in terms of multiple etiologies, multiple manifestations, and very imperfect knowledge regarding the relationships between the two.

We did, however, conduct a state-of-the-art assessment of likelihood with regard to the relative influence of genetic, organic, psychological, and sociocultural factors in relation to each of the major syndromes (Leighton, 1959, pp. 115–124). As a result, it seemed probable to us that genetics might be the most influential in schizophrenia, postconception organic factors in some forms of mental retardation, psychosocial factors in the various disorders called at that time psychoneurosis, and so on.

Given that mental illnesses were regarded as multiple in their origins and in their patterns of expression, a decision had to be made as to whether we should try to identify and count all kinds of disorders in the population or limit ourselves to one or two. The choice was made in favor of all varieties for the following reasons.

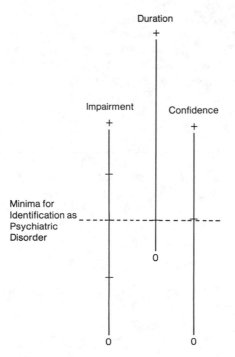

Figure 7.6. Criteria for identification given the presence of symptoms and syndromes.

First, there seemed to be some general orienting value in getting a picture of relative prevalence rates.

Second, if, as we suspected, some syndromes were more apt to be influenced by environmental factors than others, this could only be revealed by having data that would permit comparisons.

Third, it appeared advisable to take account of a widespread view in clinical psychiatry to the effect that at least some symptom patterns were substitutable for one another. The basis for this was the theory that a particular underlying psychopathological process could produce alternative syndromes, and further that these syndromes could change from one into another without alteration in the underlying pathological condition (Browning & Houseworth, 1953; Hafner, 1979; Thomas, Stern, & Lilienfeld, 1956). The belief in this notion was encouraged by the fact that in organic medicine a malady such as tuberculosis, syphilis, or streptococcal infection could wear several very different faces. In psychiatry, a common idea was that peptic ulcers and overt anxiety states were alternative and substitutable, one for the other.

Having decided to try to count all the syndromes that occurred in the members of the population, the question arose as to what to do if an individual displayed more than one syndrome. Should we follow the common clinical practice of assigning a main diagnosis and avoiding where possible secondary diagnoses?

We decided that it would be less distorting and better for the later analyses if we recorded symptoms and syndromes as we found them. Should it be deemed necessary to collapse and combine categories, this could always be done subsequently, whereas it would not be possible to separate entities that had been lumped together at the time of initial recording. Our aim was to prevent as much as possible the predetermining of correlations by either theoretical conviction or operational convention.

From this decision came additional problems in communicating with those clinicians and social scientists who thought in terms of a unitary mental illness process rather than in terms of syndromes, impairment, duration, and clinical confidence. We were urged by Tsung-y Lin and others to translate our tables into something that would approximate customary diagnostic categories. We were, however, too preoccupied to attempt this at the time, and to some extent it seemed to us that it would be undoing and contradicting what we thought we had accomplished. I believe now that Lin gave wise advice and I wish that I had acted on it.

With regard to data-gathering methods, we considered a number of alternatives and experimented with some of them. Eventually, however, we settled on the structured questionnaire interview backed up by other sources of information.

The decision to rely on the questionnaire interview was influenced by the methodological developments achieved by sociologists and psychologists in the United States Army during World War II. Leading figures in this field were Leonard Cottrell, Paul Lazersfeld, Shirley Star, Edward Suchman, and Robin Williams. In particular, the Army's experience with its Neuropsychiatric Screening Adjunct (drawn to our attention by Suchman) and the preliminary experiments by Allister Macmillan (1957) from our own group, led us to think it likely that a questionnaire interview could play an important role, at least in detecting psychoneurotic types of disorders.

It is difficult to appreciate today how strong and widespread was the belief among psychiatrists that nothing of any real clinical significance could be obtained through a questionnaire, especially when administered by a nonphysician. The view was that an adequate appraisal could only be made by a well-trained psychiatrist interacting directly with the patient. It was believed that the psychiatrist must be able to observe comportment and be free to follow up on the hints and leads in the patient's responses.

On the other hand, numbers of social scientists thought so exclusively in terms of dimensions that syndrome categories had very little meaning. As a result, they ignored the limitations imposed by the word "psychoneurotic" attached to Macmillan's Health Opinion Survey questionnaire (1957), and tried to use and evaluate the instrument as if it were a general measure of mental morbidity (Tousignant, Denis, & Lachapelle, 1974). Consequently, quite erroneous conclusions were drawn.

Through experimentation with its use, my colleagues and I came to respect the questionnaire's ability to indicate what would now be called affective, dysthymic, and anxiety patterns of disorder, but we doubted its usefulness with schizophrenia, brain syndrome, mental retardation, and personality disorders. Today it seems likely that our doubts were misplaced and that we would have been better off had we made a bolder thrust.

As it was, we turned instead to other sources of information such as general practitioners, clergy, police, and teachers. Of these, the general practitioners proved the most informative and relevant, and we therefore adopted the plan of interviewing all of them about each individual in our samples. The fact that the population was rural made this feasible in a way that does not obtain in a city. Out of our first sample of about 1098 drawn in 1952 only 50 individuals were unknown to any physician while most were known to two and some to three or more. Much of the information so obtained fitted quite well with that gathered in the questionnaires and in addition supplied evidence regarding brain syndromes, psychoses, and other conditions which our questionnaire was not designed to pick up.

After the initial baseline survey in 1952 and the spread it showed of different symptoms and syndromes, together with rates of impairment, duration, degrees of confidence, and need for psychiatric attention, we turned to ascertaining the validity of the data so obtained. By "validity" I mean the degree to which the individuals identified as cases in our prevalence count approximated the phenomena making up the visible part of the iceberg, as they were supposed to do. It is important to mention that the problem at this stage was not construct validity. Nor was it, obviously, a matter of validity based on etiology. The problem was whether the 200+ individuals who made up the 20% mentally ill in our sample really were close approximations to the patients seen in mental hospitals and outpatient services. Perhaps it is appropriate to refer to this as "ostensive validity."

There were several reasons for this concern. One was uncertainty regarding our data-gathering and evaluation methods. Despite some experimentation in advance we felt that we really did not know whether these would work, and believed that, following the first survey, they should be thoroughly cross-checked.

An additional reason for concern with validity was the high prevalence rates we had obtained. While these were not so high as believed by those who mistook our symptom tabulations for case counts, nevertheless, they were high enough to warrant investigation.

The checking on validity was both intensive and extensive for some years and involved qualitative as well as quantitative assessments. These included establishing an outpatient service in the population whereby a set of clinically identified psychiatric cases from the same population was made available as a base for comparisons with survey identified cases and noncases. Also included were examinations of subsamples of the population by clinical psychiatrists (Beiser, 1971; Leighton, Leighton, & Danley, 1966). Studies using the same concepts and methods were conducted in other populations within Nova Scotia, in the United States (Benfari, Beiser, Leighton, Murphy, & Mertens, 1974) and overseas (Leighton, Lambo, Hughes, Leighton, Murphy, & Macklin, 1963; Leighton, 1974) so that differences and similarities in results could be compared. One comparison with another method, that of Professor Essen-Möller, was also made. Using both methods, subsamples from Sweden and Stirling County were compared (Leighton, Leighton, Hagnell, Harding, Kellert, & Danley, 1971). Currently, Jane Murphy is working on a 17-year cohort study of outcome in an attempt to illuminate the predictive validity of the ratings made at the time of the original survey in 1952.

HOW ARE THE PREVALENCE RATES OF
DIFFERENT KINDS OF PSYCHIATRIC DISORDERS
DISTRIBUTED IN THE POPULATION?

A population has, of course, manifold characteristics and so approaching this question requires that one specify which particular properties one would expect to find associated with the distribution of which kinds of mental disorders—in other words, distribution of what in relation to what?

The problems of defining and operationalizing population characteristics were as large as, and in some ways parallel to, those encountered regarding mental illnesses. The limitations of space, however, make it necessary to treat them here in a more sketchy fashion.

As background it is perhaps helpful to recall that the Great Depression of the 1930s followed by World War II had brought the phenomena of distressing social conditions to the foreground of both public and professional awareness. Like many others, my training and research during these years involved working with people who were suffering greatly from the effects of both chronically and acutely depriving conditions. My research ranged from observing poverty-stricken Navajos at the depth of the depression to interviewing survivors in Hiroshima some 3 months after the bomb.

Clinical researches by others during this time, such as those of Grinker and Spiegel (1945) and Sargant and Slater (1940), pointed out that acutely stressful conditions could precipitate, if not originate, instances of mental disorder. Evidence with regard to chronic conditions was less clear, but it seemed plausible that this might also lead to mental illness, even if in a more gradual, subtle, and less dramatic way.

Our task, therefore, in contemplating the population of Stirling County, was to plan in such a way as to identify varying degrees and durations of depriving social conditions wherever they existed. It seemed appropriate, therefore, to look to the sciences of anthropology and sociology for relevant theories and methods.

Considering anthropology first, those theories that concerned culture and personality seemed most germane as well as the most interesting and lively. A central notion was that culture shaped personality and that the patterning of personality could make an individual resistant or prone to developing mental illnesses. The field, however, like psychiatry, was in an uproar of conflicting theories and ill-defined terms, so that it was rather difficult to form rejectable hypotheses. The writings of Margaret Mead, Ruth Benedict, Harry Stack Sullivan, Abram Kardiner, Karen Horney, Weston Labarre, Geoffry Gorer, and others were exceedingly interesting, but difficult to construe in a way that would permit scientific investigation of a population.

The one thing that virtually all authors agreed on was that difference in culture must make a difference in personality formation and, therefore, in rates and types of mental illnesses. Thus it came about that in choosing Stirling County, a major factor was that half of the population was French-speaking and the other half English-speaking.

An extensive anthropological field study of these cultural moieties was conducted, but the only hypothesis rejectable by epidemiologic methods that we were able to generate was that a major difference in prevalence rates would be found (Leighton, 1959, pp. 280–286). In other words, we were not able to construct a satisfactory theoretical basis for predicting which group would have the higher rates of what disorders. The closest we could come to this was predicting that those subsets of the population that were on the fringe of both groups, and so not clearly identified with either French or English, would be the most exposed, diachronically and synchronically, to psychological stresses and would therefore have higher rates.

In looking to sociology, we found ideas pertaining to societal disintegration to be the most relevant. Stemming originally from Emile Durkheim, these were, in the postwar period, being developed theoretically and methodologically by Robert Merton, Paul Lazersfeld, Edward Suchman, Talcott Parsons, and others. The root notion visualizes society as a system that under normal circumstances displays patterning, function, and adaptation to changing conditions in the interests of its own survival. Under some conditions, however, the patterning (called "structure" in sociology) and functioning deteriorate, and adaptive capacity becomes impaired, constituting a state of societal disintegration. A society so disintegrating is in danger of extinction if repair processes do not emerge and succeed, although such a society may rock along for some time in a chronic malfunctional rather than moribund state.

This "structural-functional" orientation complemented my background in biological and evolutionary theory. Further, I believed that I had seen societal disintegration among Navajos, Eskimos, and Japanese, and had seen it impose a considerable load of psychological distress on most of the men, women and children subjected to it. One could hypothesize, therefore, that if psychological distress is an important influence in the appearance of mental illnesses, there should be higher than normal rates of disorders in socioculturally disintegrated populations (Leighton, 1959, pp. 286–351, 1974).

Pilot studies in Stirling County suggested that it was a suitable place in which to explore these ideas. The 20,000 people were distributed in over 90 settlements that were geographically distinguishable and at various levels of integration and disintegration. It seemed feasible to reject the prediction that the most disintegrated settlements would have the highest prevalence rates, the best integrated would have the lowest, and that most of the county would have rates that were in between.

Starting with this general framework of cultural and social theory, we proceeded to operationalize it by hammering out descriptive definitions applicable to this particular county, and criteria for identifying varying degrees of cultural identity and social integration in the settlements. Some examples of the kinds of criteria employed are ethnic self-perception, economic sufficiency, intrasettlement leadership, and family unity.

It is possible to liken what we were trying to do to someone's taking a beehive as the focus of attention and attempting to discover how variations in the adaptation of the hive as a whole to differing circumstances had impact on the health of individual bees.

In addition to these gleanings from the social sciences, we were aware that the public health tradition puts emphasis on describing populations in terms of age, sex, marital status, ethnic grouping, and socioeconomic levels. Our data collecting was arranged so as to permit breakdowns of this kind.

CONCLUSIONS

In this chapter I use "frame of reference" rather than the word "theory." As a result of a long string of efforts to conduct scientific studies, I harbor, like my teachers Aubrey Lewis and Adolf Meyer, a profound mistrust, amounting to disbelief, in either grand, overarching theories or thin, elegant ones. In my opinion, the greatest achievement of nineteenth-century organic medicine was the discovery that grand theories are treacherous and must be viewed with grave suspicion. Aping physics in this regard, as Ernst Mayr (1982, pp. 37–45) has shown, is not good for the life sciences. It leads to metaphysics. Neither psychiatry nor the social sciences have yet come to appreciate this fact adequately; and the consequences are, I believe, a severe drag on their scientific advance.

It is an illusion, of course, for any scientist to think that he can abandon all theory and proceed empirically. One is surrounded by what Karl Popper (1981, pp. 36–50) calls "World 3" containing a medley of hypotheses together with large, small, and middle-range theories. Two maneuvers, however, appear to be useful in coping with this: one is to organize all these ideas in some rough but relevant way in relation to the scientific problem that you propose to attack; and the second is to maintain an attitude of tentativeness with regard to belief in their validity. A frame of reference, therefore, differs from a theory in the preliminary nature of its factual structure and in its heavy emphasis on the suspension of credence.

The Stirling Study frame of reference in the years since it was originally developed has undergone considerable modification, largely as a result of confrontation with the data it generated. One example of this was the unexpectedly high rate of impairing syndromes.

Another confrontation came from the negation of our cultural hypothesis: We could find very little significant difference in prevalence rates between French and English speakers. We were led to suppose that this had occurred because the cultural contrast between these two moieties was not great enough, and as a result studies were conducted among Eskimos in Alaska and among Yorubas in Nigeria. As reported some years ago by Jane Murphy (1972), again the differences were considerably less than expected on the basis of our initial frame of reference.

These remarks should not be construed as meaning that we have now scrubbed all theories of cultural determinism in relation to all mental illnesses. We suspect that more refined data and more discriminating methods of analysis may well reveal some interesting and important relationships between some cultures and some kinds of mental illnesses. On the other hand, we think that the ideas about cultural determinism with which we started, which continue to be held by many people today, and which are often assumed in the media, are too simplistic and very apt to crowd out of consideration other etiologic processes, including some that are also social-environmental.

A third area of confrontation that led to modifying the initial frame of reference was discovering that the traditional public health variables of age and sex had very strong correlations with prevalence rates. As is now well known, women had higher rates than men in some disorders while the reverse was true in others. A curious and unexpected finding was that people over 70 had lower rates than those who were younger. These demographic variables have stimulated a considerable amount of speculation and new hypothesis formation.

Our expectations based on societal integration–disintegration theory are supported by strong positive correlations between disintegration and high prevalence rates. It appears that malfunction and maladaptation of a societal system is associated with the presence of many cases of clinically definable mental illnesses. What remains unknown is the direction and degree of the causal influences. Which is operating—social selection or psychological stress?

Such results have encouraged us to venture into experimental studies aimed at improving societal integration and then trying to see if this makes a difference in the prevalence rates. What is evident is that whether the etiology is social selection or psychological stress or both together, societal processes are involved, and that we therefore need more theory about these processes and more investigations if we are to improve our understanding of the origin, course and outcome of mental illnesses. For even if mental illnesses turn out to be more biologically determined than most psychiatrists have until recently supposed, it will still remain that many aspects of these illnesses are the product of cultural and social influences.

Frames of references are like scaffolding on which you stand while you build something better. When you get the better structure built, you climb onto it and use it in turn as scaffolding while you, or the next generation, build something still better.

ACKNOWLEDGMENTS

I should like to thank John Clausen and Ernst Gruenberg for numerous conferences during the early Stirling period that proved to be especially helpful. I should also like to express appreciation for the encouragement given these endeavors by the late Frank Boudreau, president of the Milbank Memorial Fund. Acknowledgment for early financial support is gratefully made to the Carnegie Corporation of New York, the Milbank Memorial Fund, and the Canadian Department of Health and Welfare; and to Dalhousie University for support in connection with preparing this chapter.

REFERENCES

American Psychiatric Association (1952). *Diagnostic and statistical manual, mental disorders.* Washington, DC: Author.

Beiser, M. (1971). A psychiatric follow-up study of "normal" adults. *American Journal of Psychiatry, 127*(11), 1464–1472.

Benfari, R. C., Beiser, M., Leighton, A. H., Murphy, J. M., & Mertens, C. (1974). The manifestation of types of psychological states in an urban sample. *Journal of Clinical Psychology, 30*, 471–483.

Browning, J. S., & Houseworth, J. H. (1953). Development of new symptoms following medical and surgical treatment for duodenal ulcer. *Psychosomatic Medicine, 15*(4), 328–366.

Grinker, R. R., & Spiegel, J. P. (1945). *Men under stress.* Philadelphia: Blakiston.

Hafner, R. J. (1979). Behaviour therapy as a test of psychoanalytic theory. *American Journal of Psychiatry, 136*(1), 88–90.

Jaspers, K. (1963). *General psychopathology.* Chicago: University of Chicago Press.

Kroeber, A. L., & Kluckhohn, C. (1952). Culture: A critical review of concepts and definitions. *Monographs of the Peabody Museum Papers, 47*(1). Cambridge: Harvard University.

Leighton, A. H. (1959). *My name is Legion: The Stirling County Study of psychiatric disorder and sociocultural environment* (Vol. 1). New York: Basic Books.

Leighton, A. H. (1974). The Erosion of Norms. *Australian and New Zealand Journal of Psychiatry, 8*, 223–227.

Leighton, D. C., Harding, J. S., Macklin, D. B., Macmillan, A. M., & Leighton, A. H. (1963). *The character of danger: The Stirling County Study* (Vol. 3). New York: Basic Books.

Leighton, D. C., Harding, J. S., Macklin, D. B., Hughes, C. C., & Leighton, A. H. (1963). Psychiatric findings of the Stirling County Study. *American Journal of Psychiatry, 119*, 1021–1026.

Leighton, A. H., Lambo, T. A., Hughes, C. C., Leighton, D. C., Murphy, J. M., & Macklin, D. B. (1963). *Psychiatric disorder among the Yoruba: A report from the Cornell-Aro Mental Health Reseach Project in the Western Region, Nigeria.* Ithaca, NY: Cornell University Press.

Leighton, A. H., Leighton, D. C., & Danley, R. A. (1966). Validity in mental health surveys. *Canadian Psychiatric Association Journal, 11*(3), 167–178.

Leighton, D. C., Leighton, A. H., Hagnell, O., Harding, J. S., Kellert, S. R., & Danley, R. A. (1971). Psychiatric disorder in a Swedish and a Canadian community: An exploratory study. *Social Science and Medicine, 5*, 189–209.

Macmillan, A. M. (1957). The health opinion survey: Technique for estimating prevalence of psychoneurotic and related types of disorder in communities. *Psychological Reports* (Monograph Supplement 7).

Mayr, E. (1982). *The growth of biological thought: Diversity, evolution and inheritance.* Cambridge: Harvard University Press.

Menninger, K. (1959). *A psychiatrist's world.* New York: Viking Press.

Murphy, J. M. (1972). A cross-cultural comparison of psychiatric disorder: Eskimos of Alaska, Yorubas of Nigeria and Nova Scotians of Canada. In W. P. Lebra (Ed.), *Transcultural research in mental health.* Honolulu: University Press of Hawaii.

Murphy, J. M., Neff, R. K., Sobol, A. M., Rice, J. X., Jr., & Olivier, D. C. (1985). Computer diagnosis of depression and anxiety: The Stirling County Study. *Psychological Medicine, 15,* 99–112.

Popper, K. R. (1981). The Worlds 1, 2 and 3. In K. R. Popper & J. C. Eccles, *The self and its brain* (pp. 36–50). Berlin: Springer International.

Sargant, W., & Slater, E. (1940). Acute war neuroses. *Lancet, 2,* 1–2.

Thomas, A., Stern, M., & Lilienfeld, A. (1956). Relationship of psychosis and psychosomatic disease. *The Journal of Nervous and Mental Disease, 123*(3), 249–256.

Tousignant, M., Denis, G., & Lachapelle, R. (1974). Some considerations concerning the validity and use of the Health Opinion Survey. *Journal of Health and Social Behaviour, 15,* 241–252.

DISCUSSION

Ernest Gruenberg: You said that you didn't have higher rates of mental disorders among the French-speaking than among the English-speaking people whom you studied. Did you study the syndromes? Do these two cultural groups have the same syndrome distributions?

Leighton: In gross terms they had the same kinds of syndromes and the same proportions. There was some indication that sociopathic or antisocial patterns were a little more common among the French-speaking and the psychosomatic disorders a little more common among the English-speaking, but these findings were not statistically significant. They were intriguing trends, but you had to winnow the data down to certain subpopulations before they would emerge, and they were very different in size from the age, sex, and social integration–disintegration findings. These latter leaped out from the data.

Robert Spitzer: You referred to a 20% prevalence. Is that lifetime prevalence or current prevalence?

Leighton: In the original Stirling County Study, the data from 1952 was reported. The term we used was "total reportable prevalence," which was meant to imply that we did not believe the respondent could remember everything, nor did we think the general practitioner whom we interviewed could remember everything. The aim was lifetime prevalence; what we got we thought of as the best approximation, and that was 20%.

More recently Jane Murphy has brought our way of reporting in line with DSM-III as closely as possible. In so doing she has included alcoholism, which we did not include before, and changed what constitutes "current." The net effect is to add a few cases and take away a few, so 20% is still very close to the total. What we lost in one direction we gained in another; the few percentage points of increase brought about by the alcoholics were compensated for by other minor changes.

I do not want to imply that this population was abnormally low on alcoholism. Most alcoholics, as you know, have other disorders, and many of the alcoholics were included originally not because of alcoholism but because they were depressed or otherwise symptomatic.

Spitzer: Is it possible for you to make any comparison between your findings and the more recent ECA findings, recognizing that different methods and terminology were employed?

Leighton: Jane Murphy did that to some extent with regard to the New Haven work in an article published in the *Archives of General Psychiatry.* She is now planning to do this further with ECA categories in several papers that are now in preparation.

Felton Earls: I would like to ask a question about the integration versus disintegration of a community. Over the 20 to 30 years of your study, were there communities that changed from integrated to disintegrated or vice versa, and were you able to detect any change in frequency of illness as a function of this general change? More specifically, do you know if being raised in a disintegrated community represents a vulnerability toward acquiring a mental illness as an adult, or vice versa, if growing up in an integrated community protects one as an adult?

Leighton: With regard to the first question on whether these communities have changed, yes, they have, and we have been trying to monitor the change. One in particular changed dramatically over a 10-year period, from being one of the most disintegrated to being about average for the county in this regard. We did a repeat epidemiologic survey and found that the rates had dropped somewhat. Our subjects constituted a very small settlement of about 120 people, and the amount of generalization you can make from such a sample is, of course, limited. It encourages you to go on and do more. We did try to instigate various community development operations designed to help disintegrated communities become more integrated. We took epidemiologic measures at two points in time to see if any change occurred, and we also had controls. Over a period of six years we did try to replicate the first experiment, but those data are still being analyzed, and we do not yet know the effect.

Earls: And what about childhood? Do you know whether the adults grew up in a disintegrated or an integrated community?

Leighton: We have data that can be analyzed that way, but we have not yet done so.

8

Prevalence and Outcome of Depression and Anxiety Disorders: Findings from the Stirling County Study

JANE M. MURPHY
Harvard Medical School and Massachusetts General Hospital

Psychiatric surveys of general populations can now be estimated to number well over a hundred when both diagnostic and general mental health studies are included (Dohrenwend, Dohrenwend, Gould, Link, Neugebauer, & Wunsch-Hitzig, 1980). These investigations have been carried out in many different geographic locations and at different points in time over a considerable number of years. Due to the fact, however, that standard methodologies are only now being used in multisite studies, important questions remain about the influence of place as well as time on rates of psychiatric disorders (Regier *et al.*, 1984). The focus of this chapter is the passage of time, holding place constant. The purpose is to review findings available thus far from a study designed to make use of longitudinal research strategies to provide some evidence on two epidemiologic issues (Murphy, Sobol, Neff, Olivier, & Leighton, 1984; Murphy, Neff, Sobol, Rice, & Olivier, 1985; Murphy, Olivier, Sobol, Monson, & Leighton, 1986).

One of the issues is whether *rates* of disorders that characterize *populations* of adults are changing over time. The strategy used to address this question is the repeated cross-sectional survey approach in which information about point prevalence is compared from two independent samples of a population, one sample having been selected early in the study period and the other sample having been selected more recently. The other issue concerns the natural history or *outcome* of disorders experienced by *individual* adults. The strategy for exploring this aspect is the cohort follow-up approach in which information gathered a second time from the same individuals is compared with their initial information.

The materials to be presented concern depression and generalized anxiety disorders. It is now generally accepted that these types of disorders are more common than is conveyed by reference to rates of treatment for them (Shapiro *et al.*, 1984). It is largely for this reason that general population epidemiology is considered to be a useful method for investigating both descriptive and theoretical questions about such disorders. There are, for example, theoretical bases for interest in whether rates of depression and anxiety are changing over time as well as whether such disorders have similar or different outcomes. If several longitudinal studies using the same methods and definitions consistently pointed to a fluctuating rate for one type of disorder and a stable rate for the other, etiologic hypotheses about the relative influence of social and genetic factors could usefully be generated for more particularized testing. The same would apply if several longitudinal studies indicated that one type of disorder was more often chronic than the other.

The existing longitudinal studies of community populations that deal with depression and anxiety are, however, few in number and methodologically different (Mednick & Baert, 1981). Firm comparisons across a large number of studies regarding the question of time's influence are not yet feasible. Binder and Angst (1981), for example, summarize the current state of knowledge by saying that "remarkably little is known about the normal course and outcome of less serious psychiatric disorders" (p. 157). Similarly, little is known about trends in the rates of depression and anxiety.

In view of these limitations, the results of a single study should be offered and interpreted mainly as a contribution to descriptive epidemiology. Such an orientation has guided this preliminary overview of the Stirling County Study as a longitudinal investigation. While a few comparisons to other longitudinal studies will be presented, the purpose of such comparisons is mainly to give context and to contribute to the growth of descriptive knowledge.

THE STIRLING COUNTY STUDY

The place of study is a county named for research purposes by the pseudonym Stirling. It is located in Atlantic Canada and is similar in many regards to shoreline counties in New England. The initial study that serves as a baseline was oriented to the year 1952 (Hughes, Tremblay, Rapoport, & Leighton, 1960; Leighton, 1959; Leighton, Harding, Macklin, Macmillan, & Leighton, 1963).

When the study began the population consisted of approximately 20,000 children and adults living in about 5000 households located in about 100 named communities of varying sizes. The county was rural, with the primary industries of fishing, lumbering, and farming providing the main economic support for half of the families. The span of historical time to which the longitudinal design is tied extends through a major part of the third quarter of the century with the year 1970 being the focus of the most recent wave of data gathering. Over this period, the occupational structure of the county underwent considerable alteration with only the fishing industry remaining a source of employment for a substantial portion of the population. An attendant change has been the growth of the service industries. Other changes are relevant to transportation, the mass media, education, and a rising standard of living.

While the population continued to number about 20,000 throughout the study, census information indicates that there were some changes in the age composition (Canada Dominion Bureau of Statistics, 1953; Statistics Canada, 1974). The older age categories increased while the category of those from 30 to 39 years of age decreased. Migration of young people into urban areas and the return of older people are factors that may have contributed to these changes. On the whole, however, Stirling County remained free of the population depletion that has characterized some rural areas and has, in contrast, taken on features of modern living that can be described as small-scale urbanization.

Before the study began, the psychiatric needs of this population were met by 11 general physicians who either provided care themselves, sometimes using the local general hospital, or referred cases to a provincial mental hospital. As part of the initial research endeavor, a community mental health center was established in the county (Leighton, 1982). Subsequently the center became part of a provincially administered network of such services. Throughout the study, the health services available to the county's population continued to include from 11 to 13 general physicians at any one time, a few specialists, as well as the psychiatric services of the local center.

Four types of data have been gathered for the purposes of psychiatric epidemiologic investigation. One of these involves the administration of a structured questionnaire interview with subjects selected to constitute probability samples as well as with those subjects followed up as cohort members. The other types of data derive from the health service sector and involve reports from general physicians about the subjects, records of psychiatric treatment and referral from the community mental health center, and death certificates for those who died. The study as a whole involves 2848 subjects, only a portion of whom figure in the analysis here. A complete description of the longitudinal design has been published elsewhere (Murphy, in press).

While the sampling frame and completion rates will be described below, the combination of repeated cross-sectional and cohort follow-up surveys used in this report is clarified by reference to the sample sizes. The two cross-sectional surveys involve 1003 adults for 1952 and 1094 adults for 1970. The cohort follow-up involves reinterviews in 1969 with survivors from the 1952 sample of 1003.

PSYCHIATRIC ASSESSMENT METHODS:
DEPRESSION AND ANXIETY

Although the final data gathering for this study occurred in the early 1970s, my colleagues and I were considerably delayed in beginning the analysis due to a study carried out in South Vietnam (Murphy *et al.*, 1974; Murphy, 1977). When able to return to the Stirling Study, a number of important advances for psychiatric epidemiology were taking place. The Schedule for Affective Disorders and Schizophrenia (SADS) (Endicott & Spitzer, 1978) had been successfully used in a community survey in New Haven (Weissman, Myers, & Harding, 1978). This demonstrated that a comprehensive diagnostic approach was feasible for general population studies. Robins (1978) and Weissman and Klerman (1978) had spelled out the need for a new trend in psychiatric epidemiology that would give more attention to reliable diagnostic assessment than had been true of many of the earlier studies. Prepublication copies of DSM-III were in circulation (American Psychiatric Association, 1980). The NIMH Epidemiologic Catchment Area Program (ECA) was being planned (Regier *et al.*, 1984), and a new instrument to be used in this program was under construction, the Diagnostic Interview Schedule (DIS) (Robins, Helzer, Croughan & Ratcliff, 1981). Across the Atlantic, the Present State Examination (PSE) was also being used and evaluated for community studies (Brown & Harris, 1978; Wing, Cooper, & Sartorius, 1974; Wing, Mann, Leff, & Nixon, 1978). Psychiatric epidemiology was clearly undergoing change and vitalization.

For those of us who were taking up the task of analyzing the data from the Stirling County Study, the late 1970s was a time for reflection. It seemed to us that the value of a longitudinal study depended on whether or not there was a reasonable degree of comparability with the type of information that was being produced in the new studies. It was impossible, however, to turn the clock back and redo the work in such a way that comparability could be confidently established. Faced with this actuality, we reviewed the kind of data gathered and our early methods of analyzing it in an effort to develop a systematic overview of relationships to the new approaches (Murphy, 1980).

One of the differences was that the rates reported for our early work combined the input of what subjects could tell about themselves in response to structured interviews with what general physicians could describe about these subjects in response to a semistructured interview with a psychiatrist. The subject–interview approach is by far the more common and evolving procedure. While we believe that the general physician data is valuable, one of our earliest decisions was to lay the foundation for reporting rates from the two perspectives separately. Another difference was that the structured interviews with subjects concerned only a portion of the spectrum of psychiatric disorders and were much less comprehensive than the new interview schedules like the PSE, SADS, and DIS. Insofar as comparability could be approached, it would need to be limited to analysis of symptoms in the domains of depression and anxiety.

For the baseline study, the subject interview information had been read and evaluated by psychiatrists using the principles described by Leighton in Chapter 7. Because these principles emphasize descriptive diagnosis, we viewed them as being compatible with the principles employed in DSM-III. To indicate the level of congruence perceived, Table 8.1 shows the relationships between the diagnostic algorithm used for depression in the Research Diagnostic Criteria (RDC) (Spitzer, Endicott, & Robins, 1975) and the plan of analysis originally outlined for use in the Stirling County Study.

In order to analyze the interview data in a consistent fashion, we decided to use these principles as a guide for constructing a computer program. If an adequate program could be designed, we planned to use it to reanalyze the baseline data and to analyze for the first time the information from the most recent waves of data gathering.

The interviews with subjects followed a questionnaire format administered by trained lay interviewers. The questionnaire contains a general health history with some open-ended questions as well as a medical checklist and questions about impaired functioning in the person's everyday work role. The questionnaire also contains the Health Opinion Survey (HOS), an inventory of twenty questions designed in the preparatory phase of the study as a means of gathering evidence about depressive and anxious symptomatology (Macmillan, 1957). The HOS questions ask for lifetime generalizations with many of them using the word "ever" to give orientation to this perspective. The response categories ask for an estimate of frequency in terms of "often," "sometimes," and "never."

We have described elsewhere the conceptual and operational aspects of using the Stirling diagnostic model to build a computer program (Murphy

Table 8.1. Comparison of Diagnostic Models

Research Diagnostic Criteria	Stirling County Study
1. Essential features of a syndrome.	1. Pattern of symptoms reflecting a syndrome.
2. Frequent occurrence of a minimum number of specified associated symptoms.	2. Symptoms intense and pattern complete.
3. Symptoms persist over minimum duration.	3. Symptoms interfere with normal everyday functioning.
4. Symptoms associated with impairment in role functioning, taking medicine, or seeking help.	4. Symptoms and impairment persist long enough to suggest that an episode of a disorder occurred.

Table 8.2. Analytic Components and Syndromes Used in DPAX

Analytic Components	Depression	Anxiety
Orienting features	Nervous trouble Nervous breakdown	Nervous trouble Nervous breakdown
Essential features	Poor spirits	Frightening dreams Palpitations Trembling
Associated symptoms	Sleep difficulty	Sweating Paresthesias
	Loss of appetite Food tasteless	Cold sweats Sick headaches Upset stomach
	Fatigue Many ailments	Bad taste in mouth
Impairment	Going easy on work	Going easy on work
Duration	At least one month	At least one month

Note. Adapted from Murphy, Sobol, Neff, Olivier, & Leighton, 1984, *Archives of General Psychiatry, 41*, p. 992, Copyright 1984, American Medical Association, and from Murphy, Olivier, Sobol, Monson, & Leighton, 1986, *Psychological Medicine, 16*, p. 119.

et al., 1985). The program is algorithmic in design. The different steps involve the application of discriminant function analyses as well as criteria for essential features, associated symptomatology, impairment, and duration. In light of the focus on *de*pression and *an*xiety, we named the program DPAX.

The "definition of a case" used in the baseline study referred to a Typology of Need for Psychiatric Attention. We refer to this definition as PSYATT in reference to the fact that *psy*chiatric *att*ention was part of the original name. The PSYATT typology combined ratings for confidence that a psychiatric syndrome was quite complete and intense, with ratings for disability and duration. By virtue of using a threshold demarcation within this typology, cases were identified for counting in a prevalence rate. The purpose of DPAX was to implement the PSYATT definition using the HOS and other parts of the health questionnaire. In this regard we perceived some conceptual correspondence between our task and the procedures developed by Wing *et al.* (1978). The latter involve the union of an instrument for gathering information, the PSE, a definition of disorder, the Index of Definition or ID, and a computer program, CATEGO.

The DPAX program does an adequate job of reproducing the original evaluations made by psychiatrists, as indicated by sensitivity of 92% and specificity of 98%. We plan to make further assessments of the program as work progresses. For purposes here, Table 8.2 shows the symptoms used to define the syndromes of depression and generalized anxiety as well as the overall criteria employed to identify disorders. The first component is labeled "orienting features" and refers to "nervous trouble" and "nervous breakdown." Eight out of ten persons identified by the program either volunteered in the open-ended section of the interview that they were bothered by "nerves" or responded positively to a structured question that they felt they might have a nervous breakdown. While such information is neither essential nor sufficient to the diagnostic model employed in DPAX, its commonness made us believe it deserved to be named.

DPAX makes five diagnostic differentiations: "severe depression," "moderate depression," "severe anxiety," "moderate anxiety," and a residual category called "mild mixed affective." The distinction between severe and moderate mainly refers to the number and frequency of associated symptoms. The residual category contains subjects who felt that they were going to have a nervous breakdown, for example, but whose remaining symptomatology was scattered across both syndromes fulfilling the complete criteria of neither.

The use of DPAX also indicates that a sizable proportion of cases that meet the full criteria for depression also meet the full criteria for generalized anxiety. The fact that complete profiles of more than one syndrome are often combined in a given disorder gave rise to the hierarchical principle of classification. Following modern conventions, DPAX arranges the diagnoses in a hierarchy in which depression takes priority over anxiety. In order to explore the relationships between the two syndromes, however, we designed DPAX so that it is flexible enough to indicate when a disorder is purely depression, purely anxiety, or involves a combination of both complete syndromes.

PREVALENCE

Using DPAX, we began the analysis of the longitudinal data by comparing point prevalence relevant to the 1952 sample with that for the 1970 sample (Murphy *et al.*, 1984). Each of the samples used here was selected as a probability sample of heads of households. The selection principles involved a sequence in which a male head of household (main breadwinner) was chosen in alternation with a female head of household (main preparer of food). Heads of single-sex households were accepted into the sample whenever they appeared in the selection without disrupting the alternation. The completion rates for these samples are shown in Table 8.3. Seventy-six individuals from the first sample were also selected for the second. This was occasioned by the fact that persons from the early sample who survived and continued to reside in Stirling County had an equal chance with all others in the population to be selected for the recent sample.

In 1970 we also selected a probability sample of persons who did not fill the position of a head of household. Analysis focused on the influence of position in household led to the conclusion that the findings for the recent period would not have been different if the sampling frame had included all adults (Murphy *et al.*, 1984).

Table 8.3. Information on Samples for Comparing Point
Prevalence: Stirling County Study

Year	Number Selected	Number Interviewed	Completion Rates
1952	1098	1003	91%
1970	1230	1094	89%

Note. Adapted from Murphy, Sobol, Neff, Olivier, &
Leighton, 1984, *Archives of General Psychiatry, 41*, p. 993, Copyright 1984, American Medical Association.

The results of applying DPAX indicated that the current aggregated prevalence of depression and generalized anxiety was remarkably similar for the 1952 and 1970 samples. As standardized rates, overall prevalence was 12.5% for the early sample and 12.7% for the recent sample. The rates for the separate diagnostic categories were also strikingly similar, as shown in Table 8.4. Log linear analysis (Bishop, Fienberg, & Holland, 1975; Olivier & Neff, 1976) indicated that there were no significant main effects associated with the year of study and that there were no significant interactive effects between year and age and sex.

There were some small changes, especially a diminished distance between the overall rates for women and men, that have attracted our interest for further research. Nevertheless, knowledge of the stability of prevalence as assessed at points in time that were 18 years apart provides anchor points around which subsequent investigation will be pursued.

It is important to note, however, that prevalence is only one way to assess what is going on in a population in terms of experiences with disorders of various types. It is of interest in this regard that the Lundby Study in

Table 8.4. Point Prevalence Rates per 100 Subjects:
Stirling County Study

Diagnostic Categories	1952	1970
Severe depression	1.4	1.5
Moderate depression	3.9	4.1
Severe anxiety	1.3	1.7
Moderate anxiety	3.7	2.9
Mild mixed affective	2.2	2.5
Aggregated categories	12.5	12.7

Note. Adapted from Murphy, Sobol, Neff, Olivier, &
Leighton, 1984, *Archives of General Psychiatry, 41*, p. 995, Copyright 1984, American Medical Association.

Sweden selected incidence as the rate for reporting its first findings about depression (Hagnell, Lanke, Rorsman, & Öjesjö, 1982).

There are several reasons for believing that comparison of findings from the Lundby and Stirling Studies would be valuable. Both studies took root in populations that at the beginning shared a number of similarities related to their rural character. The Lundby Study has also been concerned with about the same historical period of time as the Stirling Study. Both studies also used a diagnostic approach as outlined for the Lundby Study by Essen-Möller and Hagnell in this volume. In view of these similarities, it is useful to comment on the fact that the Lundby Study has reported a significant increase in the incidence of depression while we have reported a stable prevalence of depression. The Lundby and Stirling findings insofar as they solely concern depression are shown in Table 8.5.

Assuming that these findings are accurate representations of the incidence and prevalence, respectively, of depression in the two populations, questions can be raised about whether they suggest that the Lundby population is at greater risk than the Stirling population or, alternately, whether the findings reflect differences in research strategy and in the nature of incidence and prevalence.

The Lundby findings are based on following a total population as a cohort with psychiatric assessments having been made in 1947, 1957, and 1972. By the time of the final assessments, approximately 40% had moved out of Lundby and were residing in densely populated areas. The Lundby findings reflect the first occurrences of depression during the intervals between the assessments and do not in and of themselves indicate anything about the duration of the depressions enumerated. They are low in relation to prevalence rates, such as those for the two different Stirling samples, because prevalence incorporates all the disorders in evidence at one time with many of them having long durations.

It can be suggested that rising incidence is not necessarily a contradiction to steady prevalence, since prevalence varies as the product of incidence and average duration (MacMahon & Pugh, 1970). If the increase in incidence referred mainly to short-term nonrepeating episodes of depression, the influence on prevalence might be minimal. It would take an epidemic of such first

Table 8.5. Comparison of Prevalence and Incidence Findings Regarding Depression

Lundby Study		Stirling Study	
Average Annual Incidence		Point Prevalence	
1947–1957	1957–1972	1952	1970
.18%	.45%	5.3	5.6

depressions occurring at the time of a prevalence enumeration for the prevalence rate to change markedly. So also, if the increase in incidence referred, by some chance, to an exceedingly serious form of depression that carried a heavy risk for suicide, there would be little impact on subsequent prevalence because those who suffered the disorder would have died. Similarly, if the increase in incidence referred to people who were immediately and effectively treated, there would be little influence on prevalence because these persons would have recovered. If, on the other hand, the increase in incidence referred to depressions that tended to run a chronic course with relatively little threat to life, there would be undoubtedly an increase in prevalence, unless for some reason people who suffered chronic depression preferentially migrated out of the population being studied.

This sketch of possible relationships between incidence and prevalence is intended to underscore that more information is needed than now exists for interpreting evidence such as derived from the findings thus far available from the Lundby and Stirling studies. It is pertinent, however, that the Lundby researchers have indicated that, in their study, the risk of developing an "endogenous or global" depression was only half that of developing a depression of another type. This suggests that a substantial part of the increased incidence may have referred to reactive depressions of fairly short durations. In addition, it would be of interest to know if the incidence of depression was higher among those who moved into urban areas than among those who remained in Lundby. While this information has not yet, to my knowledge, been reported, it might throw light on the relationship between the Lundby and Stirling findings, since the latter refer to persons residing in one locale. The information might also illuminate findings from the current ECA studies that indicate a higher prevalence of major depression in urban areas compared to rural as reported by Blazer *et al.* in Chapter 3. Thus, while the Lundby Study has provided important evidence that the incidence of depression may be increasing, the Stirling Study suggests that, if so, the influence on prevalence may still be minimal.

OUTCOME

Turning to the part of the Stirling Study that involves a 17-year follow-up of the 1003 adults in the 1952 sample, we decided to focus first on the relationship between diagnosis and prognosis (Murphy *et al.*, 1986). This decision was influenced by the desire to see if the diagnostic algorithms used in DPAX had any predictive usefulness. Because of our interest in diagnosis and subsequent psychiatric morbidity, we were necessarily confined to analyzing information about those persons who were identified by DPAX on the basis of their responses to interviews in 1952 and who survived to the end of the cohort interval in 1969 and were reinterviewed at that time. These persons constituted a relatively small part of the total cohort.

In later reports we plan to present information on the total cohort in order to explore the relationships between prior psychiatric illness and mortality as well as to assess the influence of comorbidity and several social factors. These future plans emphasize that what is presented here is limited in scope. Nevertheless, the issue of what happens over time to cases identified in a general population study is important. Questions have been raised, for example, about "knock-on-door" psychiatric surveys as to whether the answers people give may simply reflect the transient circumstances of that particular day in their lives.

The application of DPAX to the interviews carried out in 1952 indicated that point prevalence was 12.5%. This rate reflects standardization for age, sex, and districts in which variable sampling ratios were used. The actual number of persons enumerated in the rate was 120. The overall goal of the follow-up effort was to determine the vital status in 1969 of each person in the total original sample, to gather death certificates for those who had died, and to reinterview the subjects who were living either in the local county and province or in neighboring areas of the United States and Canada. Our funding did not allow us to send interviewers to more distant locations. Because the completeness and representativeness of follow-up information is crucial to interpreting the results of an outcome study, Table 8.6 shows the follow-up effort in such a way that the 120 subjects enumerated in the prevalence rate at baseline can be compared with the rest of the sample.

Approximately 25% of the cohort as a whole died during the 17 years under investigation. There were proportionately more cases who died than noncases, but we do not yet know the meaning of this difference in terms of age of death. Among survivors we were able to reinterview similar proportions of cases and noncases. The cases and noncases are also quite similar in terms of the proportions who refused, had moved, or were unavailable at the time of final interviewing. The subjects in this outcome analysis are the 64 cases who survived and were reinterviewed. They constitute 81% of all the cases who survived.

As a main measure of outcome, we used the DPAX assessment of the final interviews. The DPAX results divide the subjects into those who reported a depression and/or anxiety disorder as occurring during the follow up period versus those who reported themselves to be free of such disorders during that period. The application of DPAX to the final interviews indicated that 56% of the cohort of cases had a poor outcome in these terms.

Over and above asking the same questions that are used by DPAX, the final interviews contained supplemental questions that were intended to enhance the clarity with which the course of illness could be described. The supplemental questions were asked if the subject responded positively to those questions that play a central role in the DPAX analysis, that is, being in poor spirits, feeling that one was going to have a nervous breakdown, or being bothered by nervousness. The subjects were asked to indicate the

Table 8.6. Results of Follow-up Effort: Stirling County Study

Sample at Baseline	Total	Decedents n (% of total)	Survivors n (% of total)	Reinterviewed n (% of survivors)	Refused n (% of survivors)	Moved[a] n (% of survivors)	Not Available[b] n (% of survivors)
Cases in 1952	120	41 (34.2)	79 (65.8)	64 (81.0)	4 (5.1)	8 (10.1)	3 (3.8)
Others	883	208 (24.0)	675 (76.0)	554 (82.1)	29 (4.3)	71 (10.5)	21 (3.1)
Total	1003	249 (24.8)	754 (75.2)	618 (81.9)	33 (4.4)	79 (10.5)	24 (3.2)

[a]Moved = Living as of December 31, 1969, but moved out of the searchable area.
[b]Not available = Living as of December 31, 1969 in the searchable area, but not located during field phase or too ill to be interviewed.

Note. From Murphy, Olivier, Sobol, Monson, & Leighton, 1986, *Psychological Medicine, 16,* p. 122.

period in their lives when these symptoms became noticeable and how long they persisted, as well as to make further ratings of intensity and frequency over and above those given in the basic responses to the HOS questions.

Bearing in mind that DPAX requires that a subject give evidence of when and how long he or she was "going easy on work," the supplemental questions also go beyond this to inquire about the duration of other types of disabilities as well, such as going to a hospital for a nervous condition. This supplemental information on duration indicated that the poor-outcome group contained 17 subjects who indicated that they were rarely free of either the central symptoms or the disability required by DPAX. Thus, for this cohort, we estimate that 26.5% should be considered long-term chronic cases.

Based on log linear analysis, age and sex were found to lack significance in predicting outcome. Findings on the relationships between initial diagnoses and poor outcome are given in Table 8.7. The proportions of cases in the poor-outcome group are sharply differentiated by the diagnoses. Among those who initially exhibited the complete syndromes of both depression and anxiety, about 80% had a poor outcome, while among those with the residual diagnosis of mixed affective disorder in which neither syndrome was completely represented, about 85% had a good outcome. A log linear analysis of the data shown here indicated that the main effect of diagnosis on prognosis was significant ($p = .005$) and that diagnosis did not interact with age or sex in its effect on outcome. An analysis dealing with the separate influences of depression and anxiety showed that the effect of depression controlled for anxiety was highly significant ($p = .00025$), while that of anxiety controlled for depression was not significant ($p = .37$).

The results of this effort to assess outcome indicated that over a 17-year period, 56% of the cases in the cohort had a poor outcome, with 26% being long-standing chronic cases. In order to compare these findings to those in other investigations, reference can be made to three community studies that reported on follow-up periods of 3 to 6 years (Beiser, 1971; Gillis & Stone, 1973; Schwab, Bell, Warheit, & Schwab, 1979). As shown in Table 8.8, these studies used different methods for gathering information and different defini-

Table 8.7. Effects of Initial Diagnosis on Prognosis: Stirling County Study

Categories	Subjects	Poor Outcome
Depression and anxiety	24	79.2%
Depression only	8	75.0%
Anxiety only	26	38.5%
Mixed affective	6	16.6%

Note. From Murphy, Olivier, Sobol, Monson, & Leighton, 1986, *Psychological Medicine, 16*, p. 124.

Table 8.8. Comparison of Outcome Studies

Study	Method	Cohort Interval	Chronic Cases
Schwab et al. (Florida Health Study, U.S.)	Cutting point for score based on responses to HOS	3 years	70%
Beiser (Stirling County Study, Canada)	Psychiatrists' annual face-to-face assessments	5 years	52%
Gillis & Stone (Cape Coloured community study, South Africa)	Psychiatrists' evaluations of questionnaire material similar to that in Stirling Study	6 years	56%
This study	DPAX results	17 years	26%

tions of cases. Most of the cases, however, were described as mainly involving depression and anxiety. Each study presented outcome in terms of the duration of the index episode by indicating the proportion of cases that remained cases throughout the follow-up period. Together these studies suggest that the number of continuously chronic cases may start as high as 70% for 3 years and drop to 26% for 17 years.

The 5-year study in Stirling County (Beiser, 1971) dealt with a selection of subjects different from those described here. The 5-year cohort consisted of approximately 60 cases and 60 noncases who were examined in an effort to assess the validity of the psychiatric evaluation procedures that DPAX was designed to reproduce. The fact that half of the cases were found to be chronic on the basis of annual assessments made face-to-face by psychiatrists lends support to the view that a sizable portion of cases identified in the general population have long durations.

Using a definition of poor outcome that included recurrent as well as continuous episodes, our main finding is that depression had a poorer long-term prognosis than did anxiety. Prognostic contrasts between depression and anxiety have not received as much attention as those between schizophrenia and major affective psychoses (Bland & Orn, 1978, 1982; Tsuang, Woolson, & Fleming, 1979). Recognition of the seriousness of depression has not been absent, however, especially as this has been suggested in clinical studies. Within the framework of the NIMH collaborative investigations of the psychobiology of depression, Klerman (1980) has reported that over four years only 40% of a group of neurotic depressive patients experienced a complete remission, even though they received treatment. Furthermore, the concept of "double depression" has been introduced to reflect that patients with major depression often resolve into long-term dysthymia (Keller & Shapiro, 1982). Added to this information on chronicity is the relationship between depression and suicide that the Lundby group, for example, has reported (Hagnell & Rorsman, 1978).

Only a few of the cases in the Stirling Study received care in psychiatric facilities. Nevertheless it seems appropriate to suggest that the 56% poor-outcome figure indicates that cases in the community share many similarities with cases identified because they have sought treatment from psychiatrists. The effort to relate diagnosis to prognosis indicated that depression carried an especially high risk for poor outcome. This leads us to believe that depression is serious not only because of its risk for suicide but also because of its risk for damaged life.

SUMMARY

Thus far two main findings are available from the longitudinal investigation in Stirling County. One is that the point prevalence of both depression and anxiety disorders remained stable as assessed by cross-sectional surveys of an early and a recent sample. The other is that, using a cohort follow-up strategy, depression was found to carry a higher risk for future psychiatric morbidity than anxiety. It has been suggested that the prevalence findings are not necessarily in contradiction to those from the Lundby Study that indicate that the incidence of depression is increasing. This is occasioned by the fact that incidence rates do not themselves contain information on duration. If future studies continue to indicate that the incidence of depression is rising and if a large part of that increase were to refer to the types of depressions that carry as heavy a risk for chronicity and recurrence as suggested in the Stirling study, it can be anticipated that prevalence will begin to show the dual influences of incidence and duration.

ACKNOWLEDGMENTS

This research has been supported by the U.S. National Institute of Mental Health Grant MII39576 and by National Health Research and Development Project No. 6603-1154-44, Health and Welfare Canada.

REFERENCES

American Psychiatric Association. (1980). *Diagnostic and statistical manual of mental disorders* (3rd ed.). Washington, DC: Author.

Beiser, M. (1971). A psychiatric follow-up study of "normal" adults. *American Journal of Psychiatry, 127,* 1464–1472.

Binder, J., & Angst, J. (1981). A prospective epidemiological study of depression, psychosomatic and neurotic disturbances (Switzerland). In S. A. Mednick & A. E. Baert (Eds.),

Prospective longitudinal research: An empirical basis for the primary prevention of psychosocial disorders (pp. 157–160). Oxford: Oxford University Press.

Bishop, Y. M. M., Fienberg, S. E., & Holland, P. (1975). *Discrete multivariate analysis: Theory and practice.* Cambridge: MIT Press.

Bland, R. C., & Orn, H. (1978). Fourteen year outcome in early schizophrenia. *Acta Psychiatrica Scandinavica, 58,* 327–338.

Bland, R. C., & Orn, H. (1982). Course and outcome in affective disorders. *Canadian Journal of Psychiatry, 27,* 573–578.

Brown, G. W., & Harris, T. (1978). *Social origins of depression: A study of psychiatric disorder in women.* New York: The Free Press.

Canada Dominion Bureau of Statistics (1953). *Ninth census of Canada, 1951.* Ottawa: Author.

Dohrenwend, B. P., Dohrenwend, B. S., Gould, M. S., Link, B., Neugebauer, R., & Wunsch-Hitzig, R. (1980). *Mental illness in the United States: Epidemiological estimates.* New York: Praeger.

Endicott, J., & Spitzer, R. L. (1978). A diagnostic interview: The schedule for affective disorders and schizophrenia. *Archives of General Psychiatry, 35,* 836–844.

Gillis, L. S., & Stone, G. L. (1973). A follow-up study of psychiatric disturbance in a Cape Coloured community. *British Journal of Psychiatry, 123,* 279–283.

Hagnell, O., & Rorsman, B. (1978). Suicide and endogenous depression with somatic symptoms in the Lundby Study. *Neuropsychobiology, 4,* 180–187.

Hagnell, O., Lanke, J., Rorsman, B., & Öjesjö, L. (1982). Are we entering an age of melancholy? Depressive illnesses in a prospective epidemiological study over 25 years: The Lundby Study, Sweden. *Psychological Medicine, 12,* 279–289.

Hughes, C. C., Tremblay, M. A., Rapoport, R. N., & Leighton, A. H. (1960). *People of cove and woodlot: The Stirling County Study* (Vol. 2). New York: Basic Books.

Keller, M. B., & Shapiro, R. W. (1982). "Double depression": Superimposition of acute depressive episodes on chronic depressive disorders. *American Journal of Psychiatry, 139,* 438–442.

Klerman, G. L. (1980). Long-term outcomes of neurotic depressions. In S. B. Sells, R. Crandall, M. Roff, J. S. Strauss, & W. Poulin (Eds.), *Human functioning in longitudinal perspective: Normal and psychopathic populations* (pp. 58–73). Agincourt, Ontario: Macmillan of Canada.

Leighton, A. H. (1959). *My name is legion: The Stirling County Study of psychiatric disorder and social environment* (Vol. 1). New York: Basic Books.

Leighton, A. H. (1982). *Caring for mentally ill people: Psychological and social barriers in historical context.* New York: Cambridge University Press.

Leighton, D. C., Harding, J. S., Macklin, D. B., Macmillan, A. M., & Leighton, A. H. (1963). *The character of danger: The Stirling County Study* (Vol. 3). New York: Basic Books.

MacMahon, B., & Pugh, T. F. (1970). *Epidemiology: Principles and methods.* Boston: Little, Brown.

Macmillan, A. M. (1957). The health opinion survey: Technique for estimating prevalence of psychoneurotic and related types of disorders in communities. *Psychological Reports, 3,* 325–339.

Mednick, S. A., & Baert, A. E. (Eds.) (1981). *Prospective longitudinal research: An empirical basis for primary prevention of psychosocial disorders.* Oxford: Oxford University Press.

Murphy, J. M. (1977). War stress and civilian Vietnamese: A study of psychological effects. *Acta Psychiatrica Scandinavica, 56,* 92–108.

Murphy, J. M. (1980). Continuities in community-based psychiatric epidemiology. *Archives of General Psychiatry, 37,* 1215–1223.

Murphy, J. M. (in press). The Stirling County Study. In M. M. Weissman, J. K. Myers, & C. Ross (Eds.), *Community surveys.* New Brunswick, NJ: Rutgers University Press.

Murphy, J. M., Murfin, G. D., Jamieson, N. L., Rambo, A. T., Glen, J. A., Jones, L. P., & Leighton, A. H. (1974). *Beliefs, attitudes, and behavior of the lowland Vietnamese: The effects of herbicides in South Vietnam.* Washington, DC: National Academy of Science.

Murphy, J. M., Neff, R. K., Sobol, A. M., Rice, J. X., & Olivier, D. C. (1985). Computer diagnosis of depression and anxiety: The Stirling County Study. *Psychological Medicine, 15*, 99–112.

Murphy, J. M., Olivier, D. C., Sobol, A. M., Monson, R. R., & Leighton, A. H. (1986). Diagnosis and outcome: Depression and anxiety disorders in a general population. *Psychological Medicine, 16*, 117–126.

Murphy, J. M., Sobol, A. M., Neff, R. K., Olivier, D. C., & Leighton, A. H. (1984). Stability of prevalence: Depression and anxiety disorders. *Archives of General Psychiatry, 41*, 990–997.

Olivier, D. C., & Neff, R. K. (1976). *LOGLIN 1.0 user's guide.* Boston: Harvard University School of Public Health.

Regier, D. A., Myers, J. K., Kramer, M., Robins, L. N., Blazer, D. G., Hough, R. L., Eaton, W. W., & Locke, B. Z. (1984). The NIMH epidemiologic catchment area program. *Archives of General Psychiatry, 41*, 934–941.

Robins, L. N. (1978). Psychiatric epidemiology. *Archives of General Psychiatry, 35*, 697–702.

Robins, L. N., Helzer, J. E., Croughan, J., & Ratcliff, K. S. (1981). National Institute of Mental Health diagnostic interview schedule: Its history, characteristics, and validity. *Archives of General Psychiatry, 38*, 381–389.

Schwab, J. J., Bell, R. A., Warheit, G. J., & Schwab, R. B. (1979). *Social order and mental health: The Florida Health Study.* New York: Brunner Mazel.

Shapiro, S., Skinner, E. A., Kessler, L. G., Von Korff, M., German, P. S., Tischler, G. L., Leaf, P. J., Benham, L., Cottier, L., & Regier, D. A. (1984). Utilization of health and mental health services. *Archives of General Psychiatry, 41*, 971–978.

Spitzer, R. L., Endicott, J., & Robins, E. (1975). *Research diagnostic criteria (RDC) for a selected group of functional disorders, Instrument No. 58, ed. 2.* New York: Biometrics Research, New York State Psychiatric Institute.

Statistics Canada (1974). *1971 census of Canada.* Ottawa: Author.

Tsuang, M. T., Woolson, R. F., & Fleming, J. A. (1979). Long-term outcome of major psychoses: I. Schizophrenia and affective disorders compared with psychiatrically symptom-free surgical conditions. *Archives of General Psychiatry, 39*, 1295–1301.

Weissman, M. M., & Klerman, G. L. (1978). Epidemiology of mental disorders: Emerging trends in the United States. *Archives of General Psychiatry, 35*, 705–712.

Weissman, M. M., Myers, J. K., & Harding, P. S. (1978). Psychiatric disorders in a U.S. urban community: 1975–1976. *American Journal of Psychiatry, 135*, 459–461.

Wing, J. K., Cooper, J. E., & Sartorius, N. (1974). *The measurement and classification of psychiatric symptoms.* Cambridge: Cambridge University Press.

Wing, J. K., Mann, S. A., Leff, J. P., & Nixon, J. M. (1978). The concept of a "case" in psychiatric population surveys. *Psychological Medicine, 8*, 203–217.

DISCUSSION

C. R. Cloninger: I was impressed by the difference in the prognosis of patients who had both a full syndrome of depression and a full syndrome of anxiety, and of patients who had mixed anxiety and depressive features but did not fulfill the criteria for either syndrome. How would patients with the mixed anxiety-depressive features be characterized clinically? Are these people with neuroses or with no illness?

Murphy: In the original analysis of the first survey in Stirling County, the diagnostic assessments were made by psychiatrists. It was those assessments that DPAX was constructed to reproduce. Most of the community subjects diagnosed by DPAX as mixed-affective had originally been designated by the psychiatrists as "psychoneurotic—other." This means that, while the psychiatrists rated these cases as definitely psychoneurotic, they did not see a sufficiently clear diagnostic picture to be able to place them in a particular category. Also, the mixed-affective group had fewer symptoms than those diagnosed as depressed or anxious. This was one of our reasons for calling them "mild" in contrast to the "moderate" or "severe" designations used for anxiety and depression. Thus they seem to be very close to the threshold for separating neurosis from absence of neurosis. Now, seeing the outcome results, it does seem as if the mild mixed-affective group is distinctive. Perhaps my conclusion that cases of depression and anxiety in the community are like patients should exempt the mixed-affectives, although I imagine that among outpatient and private patient groups there are some mild cases of this type.

Cloninger: I suppose that some of the people with a good outcome could still have been chronically tense. For example, the patients with anxiety syndrome could have had a chronic tension state but not much impairment.

Murphy: That is right. Only a few subjects in this cohort were free of symptoms at the end or said that they had symptoms for only a short duration. Many remained symptomatic but did not fulfill the criteria for impairment that we established for defining a case.

Cloninger: Did you look at whether they had depression or anxiety syndromes?

Murphy: I have not looked at it that way yet, but it is an interesting question and I will explore it.

Robert Spitzer: This is an exciting study and again shows the wisdom of not using diagnostic hierarchies, but looking at syndromes separately. In the revision of DSM-III we plan to suspend the diagnostic hierarchy that prevented the joint diagnosis of a major depressive episode and panic disorder during a single episode of illness.

Could you comment on the absence of a cohort effect in your findings, which were based on longitudinal data, and the major cohort effect in the ECA findings, which were based on retrospective DIS data?

Murphy: It is important to emphasize that our study concerns the period from 1950–1970. It is possible that in the subsequent decade something happened that would produce a cohort effect in our findings, had we been able to carry out another survey at the same time that the ECA studies were going on. With that as a general qualification, let me describe what I understand the cohort effect based on the DIS to be. I see it as having two components: high prevalence among the young and low prevalence among other groups. Because earlier clinical and epidemiologic studies have indicated a high prevalence among older people, we assume that the DIS data reflect an increase among the young over time and a decrease among the older.

In our findings, there were no significant interactions between year of study and age. Nor, for that matter, were there any significant interactions between time and sex. There were, however, some suggestive shifts especially noticeable in the aggregated rate for depression and anxiety. A three-way interaction between time, age, and sex was almost significant. It consisted of a drop in prevalence among older women over time and an increase in prevalence among younger men over time. Accompanying this was the fact that women in the age range 30–39 showed an increase over time. In the recent period, this particular group of relatively young women had a "peak" of prevalence that was quite visibly different from their prevalence rate earlier. Thus, against our background of overall stability of prevalence in our findings, we see suggestions that an increase among the young may have been in process by 1970.

Turning to the aspect of the effect that suggests a decrease among the elderly, it is quite interesting that in both of our study years, prevalence rises through age 69 and then drops. The drop occurs in both men and women. Because the drop occurred in both the 1950 and the 1970 samples, I do not believe that this is a cohort effect. I think it reflects selective mortality, or it may be a life-cycle effect. It is possible that those who survive beyond general life expectancy are not only sturdy but may also reach a serene phase of life that gives rise to few incidence cases of depression or anxiety.

Alexander Glassman: It bothers me a great deal that all of these survey studies fail to look at the issue of borderline personality disorder. Some people probably think the syndrome doesn't exist. Other people are convinced that it includes a larger number of people than those with depression or anxiety. Certainly there is an issue as to whether it exists, and here I am speaking of Kernberg's or Gunderson's concept of borderline, that group of people. The validity of that syndrome is reasonably open to question, but one of the problems that arises when we talk about "double depression," or about people with both anxiety and depression, is that we need better descriptors of that group of people. We clearly see cases who have an unremitting illness or unremitting difficulties where they are always seriously impaired. They clearly have affective flares that involve both anxiety and depression, but their condition is "stably unstable" over many years. It makes the interpretation of epidemiologic data difficult when we do not know how large a group borderlines are, or even if they exist as a valid entity. However, I think the possibility needs to be considered when we look at large populations and when we start to talk about cohort effects or double depressions. We need to know more about the nature of these populations.

Murphy: One can only agree. Perhaps in the ECA studies of the 1990s, DSM-IV will have the criteria for borderline personality sufficiently defined that information can be gathered by an instrument such as the DIS, permitting cases to be counted in general population studies.

Cloninger: Is there something special about Stirling County that has protected it from some of the increases in depression that we have recently seen from the Lundby study and other studies in the United States? How do you account for the differences in the cohort effect between studies?

Murphy: I do not believe it would be accurate to say that Stirling County is unusual. Most of the main social trends that have occurred elsewhere pertain there as well, except that Stirling County has not become a metropolitan conglomerate. While I have suggested that evidence of increasing incidence in Lundby is not necessarily incompatible with steady prevalence in Stirling County, I do think it is worth emphasizing that the two studies are different in design. The increase in depression incidence comes from following cohort members to wherever they came to live, and about 40% moved from rural Lundby to densely populated areas. The information on stable prevalence comes from two cross-sectional samples of the same area. It will be interesting to see if migration into a highly urbanized area is a risk factor for depression in the Lundby study. On the other hand, it seems to me that the probability of genetic factors in the etiology of some types of depressions would constrain marked increases. Both the profile of depressive symptomatology in our study and the evidence of poor outcome from our cohort follow-up suggest to me that the kind of depression we have identified may be more like what is sometimes called endogenous depression than is the case in other studies.

FINDINGS FROM OTHER EPIDEMIOLOGIC STUDIES: TREATMENT AND RISK FACTORS FOR SCHIZOPHRENIA

9

Long-Term Care in Schizophrenia: Contributions from Epidemiologic Studies in the United Kingdom

JOHN K. WING
Institute of Psychiatry, London

EPIDEMIOLOGY AND EVALUATIVE RESEARCH

J. N. Morris (1964) listed seven kinds of uses for epidemiology; study of historical trends, description of community health, operational analysis of health services, determination of individual risks, completion of the clinical picture, identification of syndromes, and discovery of causes. His inclusion of health services research is particularly relevant in a country like the United Kingdom which has a National Health Service (NHS) organized by geographic health districts, most of whose boundaries are contiguous with local government social services areas (boroughs, towns, or counties). The health and social services can therefore be based, at least in theory, on the three principles of geographic responsibility, comprehensive coverage, and integrated organization. Local planning, therefore, again at least in theory, can be informed by local epidemiologic knowledge.

All health districts collect information about mental hospital admissions and discharges, which are amalgamated into the national statistics for England, Northern Ireland, Scotland, and Wales. More comprehensive data are available from cumulative psychiatric case registers which cover the whole range of specialist service contacts and provide a useful sampling frame for intensive studies. There are six such registers in England, one in Scotland, and one in Wales. In addition, several substantial comparative investigations have been based on ad hoc registers, set up as sampling frames specifically for the purpose.

This chapter deals with the relatively new field of evaluative health services research, with particular reference to schizophrenia, as it has developed in the United Kingdom during the past 30 years. Inevitably, the decline in size of the large psychiatric hospitals will form the background to much of the discussion. Most of the studies quoted are British; the extensive American literature has not been considered because the culture and service organization are overtly so different. The principles, however, should hold good in whatever context they are applied. Many of the examples are taken from studies carried out in Camberwell, a working-class district in southeast London, now with a population of 130,000, where the Maudsley Hospital and Institute of Psychiatry are situated. A cumulative case register was set up there at the end of 1964 and has been used continuously since to monitor and evaluate the developing community service.

Ideally, the cycle of service planning and evaluation requires:

1. An epidemiological base, that is, a geographically defined catchment area with known socioeconomic characteristics.

2. Mechanisms for identifying people with problems due to psychiatric disease or disability, social disadvantage, or personal distress, the interaction of which gives rise to social disablement. These people are regarded as being in potential need of some form of help.

3. Investigation as to whether people in potential need are receiving those methods of care professionally regarded at any given time as appropriate to relieve their problems, that is, effective, acceptable, and economic. (The term "care" is used broadly, to include all forms of treatment, prevention, counsel, shelter, and welfare.)

4. Discovering whether the services delivering such care are efficient, acceptable, and economic and, if not, devising means of improving them.

A discipline of evaluative research with this kind of epidemiological base, informing what has become known as "bottom-up" planning, has yet to become firmly established, but many of the techniques are well developed and the potential advantages are substantial.

SOCIOECONOMIC INDICES

The calculation of incidence and prevalence rates relevant to needs for care raises all the problems generally familiar to epidemiologists, but some have special cogency. Health districts differ from each other in terms of sociodemographic characteristics (particularly age, ethnic composition, poverty, and social isolation), population movement, geographic features, and service patterns and traditions.

Age

Camberwell contains a high proportion of people over 75, and the proportion of this age group increased by 5.5% between 1971 and 1981 compared with 0.9% for England as a whole.

Ethnicity

In 1971, approximately 11% of the population were first- or second-generation immigrants, mainly from the West Indies but also from India and Pakistan (L. Wing, 1979). The proportion must have increased substantially since because of a differential birth rate (Kramer, 1978). By 1981, 12.1% were first-generation immigrants from these countries; information about the second and third generations was not collected in the census. First contact rates for schizophrenia are thought to be higher in this group, but difficulties in calculating the size of the denominator make comparisons problematic.

A definite elevation of the rate at which the triad of social impairments (loosely, autistic-type behaviors) occurred in the children of migrants from the West Indies compared with the native-born was found in a survey of the at-risk Camberwell population carried out in 1970 (L. Wing, 1979). All children of school age known to the health or social services or identified by schoolteachers as problematic were included. Most with the syndrome are mentally retarded but it can occur at all levels of ability. In the more intellectually able, the manifestations of autism, and of the related Asperger's syndrome, are frequently confused with those of schizophrenia, not necessarily at the time of the first contact when a variety of diagnostic labels may be applied, but later in the course (L. Wing, 1981). A more recent survey carried out in Salford confirms the relationship with ethnicity (Fryers, personal communication).

Poverty and Social Isolation

Camberwell is a comparatively poor but stable working-class district. For example, a much smaller proportion of houses are owner-occupied than elsewhere 25% compared with 58% for England as a whole, in 1981. The proportion of private householders with more than 1.5 persons per room, and the proportion of one-parent to total households (the latter probably reflecting ethnicity as well as poverty), were twice as high in Camberwell as the national average. Rateable values of property and occupational class composition tell the same story. The literature does not suggest that these indices are likely to be linked to a higher-than-average incidence rate of schizophrenia, but prevalence rates well may be affected.

Social isolation is not a feature of the district. The proportion of single-person households, for example, is 28% compared with 24% for England. There is, however, a floating population of homeless people because of the presence of a large night shelter in the center of Camberwell which, until recently, has catered for 8000 admissions a year. Some people remain as residents, others are settled in local homes, and a sizable proportion of both groups have previously been discharged from psychiatric hospitals.

Several surveys of severely socially disadvantaged people have been carried out, showing that the proportion who are physically and/or mentally disabled increases as the quality of accommodation diminishes. Such private hostel or "hotel" accommodation as is available to the very poor is highly selective. The Salvation Army noted that the "drunkards, disruptive influences, mentally ill, disreputable, verminous, out of work" are turned away. In the Salvation Army's own hostels, at least 15% of the men interviewed were afflicted by schizophrenia. In some extended-stay houses, the proportions are much higher, and they are highest of all among those sleeping "rough" on the streets (Leach & J. K. Wing, 1980).

. The movement of people with schizophrenia into areas where they can be socially isolated is well documented. In the United States, where poverty and social isolation often go together, it has sometimes been difficult to separate the two factors (Dunham, 1965; Faris & Dunham, 1939). In U.K. studies it is clear that social isolation has much the greater association (Hare, 1956; Stein, 1957). Though Camberwell is not socially isolated in terms of census indices, the influx of the "single homeless" does increase the size of the numerator representing severe mental disorder.

These problems are characteristic of inner conurban areas. Most epidemiologic surveys ignore them. Research concerned with needs for care cannot do so.

Changes in Population Size

A striking characteristic of Camberwell, shared with inner conurban areas in the United Kingdom more generally, is the decline in the size of its population, which has halved during the past 60 years. Figure 9.1 shows the relative changes in population size that have occurred in the areas covered by seven cumulative psychiatric registers in England and Wales (Gibbons, Jennings, & J. K. Wing, 1984). Areas like Oxford, which has doubled its population in the same period, and Worcester are highly attractive. The medium-sized industrial cities, like Cardiff, Nottingham, and Southampton, have increased slowly at about the national rate. Areas like Camberwell where the population has halved, and Salford, near the centers of large conurbations, are markedly declining.

These trends will affect the respective prevalence rates if a recent population count is used to estimate the denominator. Assuming that there is a differential movement of relatively healthy people into districts such as Oxford and Worcester and, on a smaller scale, a relative export of those who seek the anonymity of central-city areas, it would be expected that indices of hospital-bed occupancy and long-term service contact would be favorable compared with those elsewhere. On the other hand, districts such as Camberwell and Salford will not only lose part of the healthy population and attract

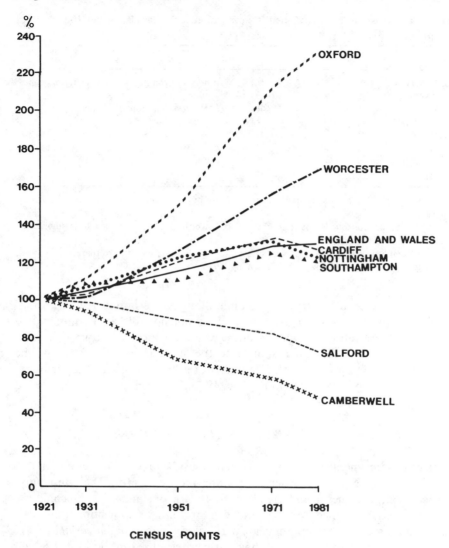

Figure 9.1. Psychiatric register areas, April 1981. 100%-June 1921. (From Gibbons, Jennings, & Wing, 1984).

some of the less healthy, but also long-stay residents in sheltered accommodation or long-term attendees at day hospitals and sheltered workshops are likely to be disproportionately represented among those who remain.

Table 9.1 shows the rates of occupancy of hospital beds in two length-of-stay categories—short-stay (under one year) and medium–long-stay (one

Table 9.1. Hospital Beds Occupied in Seven Register Areas (Rates per 100,000 total population, 31.12.81)

	Under 1 Year*	1–5 Years	
Camberwell	—**	56)	Inner conurban areas with declining popu-
Salford	70	58)	lation
Cardiff	74	46)	Medium-sized industrial cities with average
Nottingham	69	38)	population increase
Southampton	70	37)	
Oxford	36	16)	Attractive areas with increasing popula-
Worcester	41	20)	tions
England	57	37	

Note: The over-5-year group is omitted because population changes make rates noncomparable.

*For "short-stay" beds, the ratio of upper to lower limit is 2:1; for "new long-stay" beds, the ratio is 3:1.

**Camberwell short-stay beds are affected by special factors and are therefore omitted.

Source: Gibbons, Jennings, & J. K. Wing, 1984.

to five years). Even omitting the maximum long-stay group there are substantial differences between register areas. It is not possible at the moment to compare these rates by diagnosis but it would be surprising if specific rates for schizophrenia did not demonstrate the same range of variation. The national average proportion of people with schizophrenia in the medium-long-stay group is 44% (Mann & Cree, 1976).

DIAGNOSIS AND THE MEASUREMENT OF CHRONICITY

The usual idiosyncracies of diagnostic style must be taken into account, in the British Isles as elsewhere, when calculating the numerator. The latest published example comes from Ireland, where the use of standardized techniques of diagnosis has failed to substantiate a prevailing supposition that first admission rates for schizophrenia are particularly high (Nuallain *et al.*, 1984). The generally narrower range of diagnostic criteria used in the United Kingdom (which do not, however, specify a particular length of history for inclusion in the diagnosis, as does DSM-III) compared with countries outside Europe, is well known (Cooper *et al.*, 1972; WHO, 1973; J. K. Wing, Cooper, & Sartorius, 1974). First-admission rates for schizophrenia used to provide a fairly accurate estimate of the incidence in countries with a well-developed health care system (Ødegård, 1952). Now that increasing numbers of people with schizophrenia are not admitted to hospitals but receive treatment and care in other ways, the "first-ever contact" rate with a range of psychiatric services provides a more accurate estimate. Table 9.2 shows the age–sex profile derived from data collected in the Camberwell Register (J. K. Wing & Der, 1984; J. K. Wing & Hailey, 1972) between 1964 and 1982. The overall rate has remained steady at about 14 per 100,000 per year, much the same as the national first-admission rate used to be. (It is now about 9 per 100,000 per year.) Shields (1978) calculated the cumulative lifetime risk to age 55 from Camberwell Register data as 0.86%. To age 65 the risk was 0.90.

However, so far as needs for long-term care are concerned, a major and even more difficult problem is the identification and measurement of chronic disabilities. There are three main components in "social disablement" (the final expression in social deficit): (1) impairments that may be hypothe-sized to be specific to a particular diagnosis, (2) social disadvantages that can hamper optimum social performance even in a well person but that can also amplify the effects of impairments, and (3) self-attitudes of despair and demoralization that may persist even when the underlying causes for them have been removed. All three components tend to interact to blur any initial diagnostic distinctions. This is particularly true of the so-called "negative" schizophrenic syndrome, which is unsafe to use as the sole criterion for diagnosis.

In the 1930s, when only a third of patients first admitted to hospitals with a diagnosis of schizophrenia were discharged within the subsequent two years, the remainder being likely to remain residents until they died, length of stay was taken as a criterion of chronicity and, through a process of circular reasoning, as an indication of needs for care (Brown, 1960). By the early 1950s it was clear that this was unsatisfactory. Many long-stay residents were not severely disabled. In a number of pioneering hospitals the length of stay at first admission was being substantially reduced and long-stay patients were being discharged following "rehabilitation."

Table 9.2. First-ever Contact Rates for Schizophrenia, Camberwell 1964–1982

Age	Males	Females	Total
15–24	32.7	22.6	27.6
25–34	36.5	25.8	31.1
35–44	13.9	16.7	15.4
45–54	11.1	11.5	11.3
55–64	5.5	9.8	7.7
65–74	8.9	17.5	13.9
75+	8.3	17.8	15.2
Population, 15+	19.1	17.5	18.3
Total	14.6	13.9	14.2

Source: Wing & Der, 1984.

The subsequent decline in the numbers of beds occupied in psychiatric hospitals is well documented. In England, the peak rate of bed occupancy was 344 per 100,000 persons in 1954. Figure 9.2 shows part of the more recent trend, within three length-of-stay groups. Short-stay (under 1 year) residents occupy about 60 beds per 100,000, and there is only a slow, if any, decline. The size of the medium–long-stay group (one to five years) is also fairly steady at about 40 per 100,000. Only the maximum long-stay group (over 5 years) is still declining, and this decrease is now largely due to death rather than discharge.

Figure 9.2. Resident inpatients on 31 December 1971–1981 by length of stay. English psychiatric hospitals rates per 100,000 total population. (From the Department of Health and Social Security, 1984.)

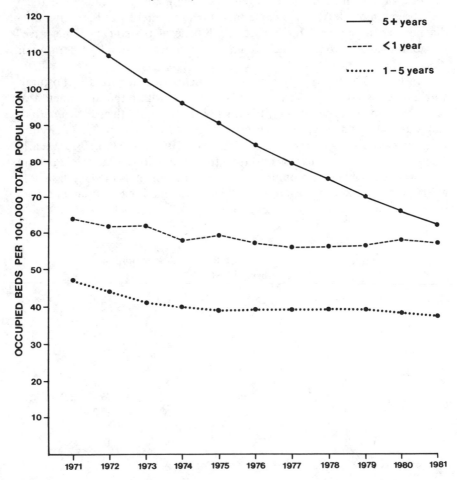

New techniques therefore have to be developed to identify and measure the problems that arise in people with schizophrenia and that indicate a potential need for the best available forms of care. It will be convenient to consider these problems initially in terms of the three length-of-stay groups shown in Figure 9.2.

THE "OLD" LONG STAY

We can begin with a number of studies, carried out in the 1950s and 1960s, into the relationship between the environments provided by psychiatric hospitals and the disabilities and attitudes of schizophrenic patients who lived in them (J. K. Wing, 1961, 1962; J. K. Wing & Brown, 1961, 1970). In the most detailed of these studies, each of the three hospitals concerned was responsible for a geographic district within the NHS and provided virtually the whole of the local psychiatric service, private provision being minimal. First-admission rates were comparable, as were the socioeconomic characteristics of hospital inpatients. All female residents over two years and under age 65, who had a diagnosis of schizophrenia confirmed by the investigators, were interviewed, as were the nurses looking after them. Independent ratings were made of symptoms occurring at interview and behavior observed in the ward. Measurements were made of the quality of environment experienced by the individuals concerned (personal possessions, contacts with the outside, nurses' attitudes, time budget, ward restrictiveness). The survey was repeated in 1960, 1962, 1964, and, in less detail, in 1968, and note was made of any discharges or deaths during the 8-year period.

There were marked social differences among the three hospitals which could be summarized in terms of the degree of environmental poverty characterizing them. The time budget proved particularly crucial. At the first hospital (Netherne), the time spent by patients doing absolutely nothing was, on average, 2 hours 48 minutes per patient per day. At the third (Severalls) it was 5 hours 39 minutes on average. The second (Mapperley) came in between. All the indices used showed equivalent differences. Figure 9.3 shows, for example, the proportions of patients in the three hospitals who owned various items of personal clothing or equipment.

The clinical ratings of blunting of affect, poverty of speech, incoherence, and coherently expressed delusions were classified using predetermined rules, into the categories shown in Figure 9.4, which also revealed large differences among the hospitals.

When correlating the social and clinical indices together, however, the length of time doing nothing proved most highly related to the negative impairments in schizophrenia. This was not only true across hospitals in each of the three main surveys, but within hospitals and over time. Where the

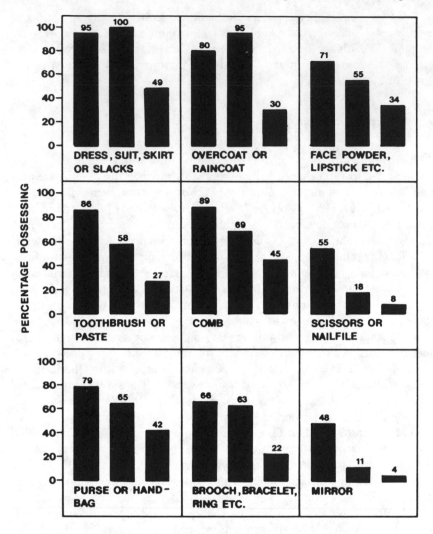

IN EACH CELL THE BLOCKS REPRESENT HOSPITALS A,B
C IN THAT ORDER

Figure 9.3. Personal possessions (supplied privately or by the hospital) of long-stay female schizophrenic patients. (From J. K. Wing & Brown, 1970. Reprinted by permission.)

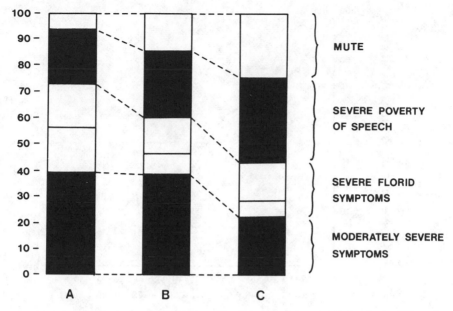

Figure 9.4. Hospitals by clinical classification of patients. (From J. K. Wing & Brown, 1970. Reprinted by permission.)

environment became more socially stimulating, negative impairments decreased, and vice versa. A subsequent controlled experiment demonstrated an immediate response to social stimulation and relapse when the stimulus was withdrawn (J. K. Wing & Freudenberg, 1961).

The other environmental indices were also measures of social disadvantage but were more related to self-attitudes than to symptoms. However, the most substantial factor influencing such attitudes, among those measured, was length of stay in a hospital. For example, the longer a patient had been a resident, irrespective of severity of clinical condition, the more likely he or she was to be indifferent to discharge or to actively wish to stay (Fig. 9.5). This gradual acceptance of the way of life of the hospital in people who could have been more independent was labeled "institutionalism." It is an extreme example of the overprovision mentioned earlier.

All three factors—severity of negative impairment, social disadvantage, and adverse self-attitudes—were related to probability of discharge during the 8-year study period. Most of those who left the hospital had been only moderately impaired originally, although, in the second half of the period, some of those who had improved clinically were also discharged. Several

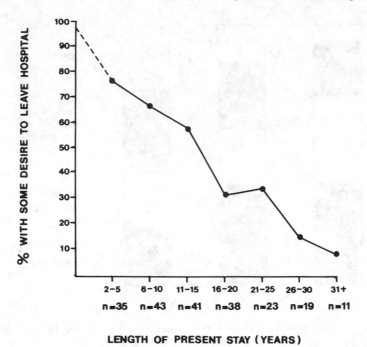

Figure 9.5. Attitudes to discharge of 210 long-stay schizophrenic women in 3 mental hospitals: by length of stay (63 patients who were mute or incoherent omitted). (From J. K. Wing & Brown, 1970. Reprinted by permission.)

rehabilitation experiments confirmed these findings (J. K. Wing, 1960, 1963; J. K. Wing, Bennett, & Denham, 1964). Negative impairments were the most central factor in social disablement since, although environmental amplification was reversible, such impairments could only be reduced to a minimum level that varied between individual patients, and they would readily deteriorate if social poverty again increased. Some of the most severely impaired patients were impervious to social influences. Medication did not, on the whole (there were exceptions), much influence the results in long-stay patients.

The conclusions drawn from this study were cautious. It was certainly possible to improve the mental hospital environment, which would probably lead to some clinical improvement, to a decrease in social disadvantages and a boost to self-esteem. This would not, however, cure schizophrenia. Many people remained chronically handicapped even in a good social environment. The question remaining was: What is the best way to help them, not only to minimize disablement but also to maintain it at the lowest possible level while preserving a decent quality of life? These conclusions, particularly the qualifications, were not well understood at the time, and the results did not much influence service policy.

THE EARLY-DISCHARGE POLICY

A 5-year follow-up study of schizophrenic patients admitted to the same three hospitals in 1956 was being carried out at the same time as the inpatient survey. The outcome for patients first admitted in 1956 to Mapperley and Severalls hospitals is shown in Figure 9.6 (Brown, Bone, Dalison, & J. K. Wing, 1966).

Few admissions, even to the Severalls hospital, lasted as long as one year. Almost all first admissions were discharged within a few months, even in 1956. The policy pursued by the second hospital, Mapperley, is clearly evident. Frequent brief admissions were interspersed with contacts with outpatient clinics and home visits by social workers, nurses, or psychiatrists. Day care was also more common than in the other two districts.

Nevertheless, the clinical course and outcome was much the same in all three districts, as was the social and employment record. The pattern of care adopted in Nottingham (Mapperley) did not prevent morbidity compared with the other districts, but relatives did mention more problems arising from

Figure 9.6. Summary charts of contacts with services during five years after first admission to Mapperley and Severalls hospitals in 1956 with diagnosis of schizophrenia. (From Brown, Bone, Dalison, & Wing, 1966. Reprinted by permission.)

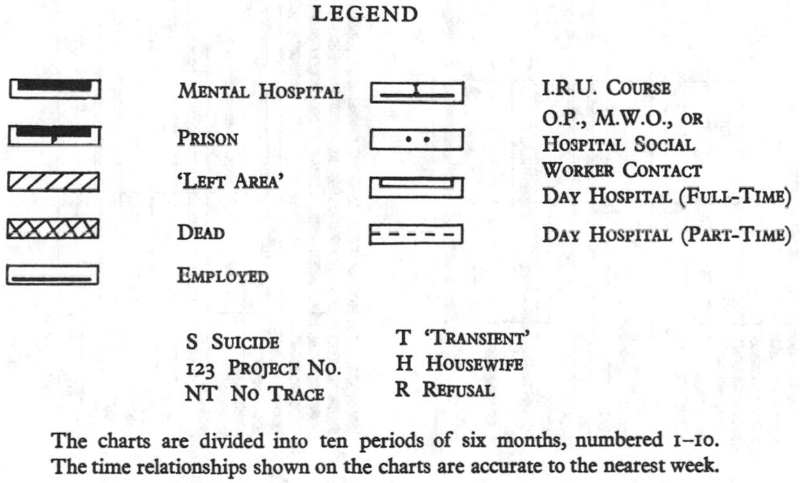

LEGEND

▭	MENTAL HOSPITAL	▭	I.R.U. COURSE
▭	PRISON	▭	O.P., M.W.O., OR HOSPITAL SOCIAL WORKER CONTACT
▨	'LEFT AREA'	▭	DAY HOSPITAL (FULL-TIME)
▨	DEAD	▭	DAY HOSPITAL (PART-TIME)
▭	EMPLOYED		

S SUICIDE   T 'TRANSIENT'
123 PROJECT NO.   H HOUSEWIFE
NT NO TRACE   R REFUSAL

The charts are divided into ten periods of six months, numbered 1–10.
The time relationships shown on the charts are accurate to the nearest week.

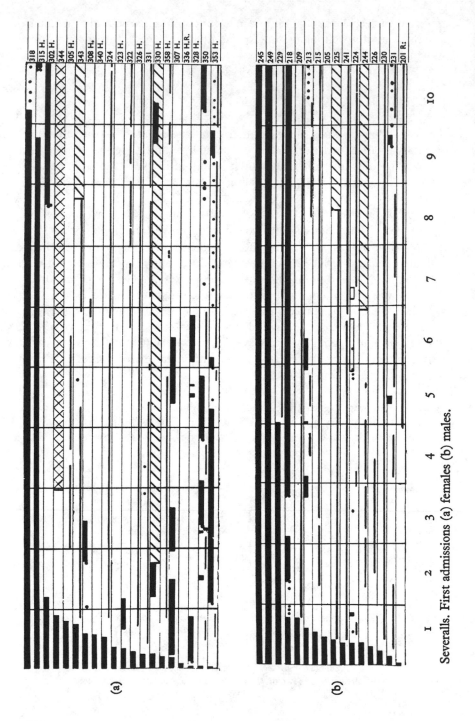

Severalls. First admissions (a) females (b) males.

164

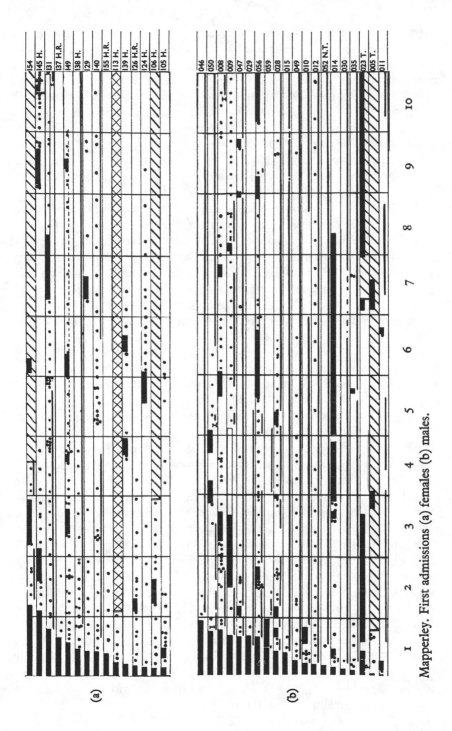

Mapperley. First admissions (a) females (b) males.

165

the longer period spent at home. They did not, however, actually complain more even when it appeared that they did have something to complain about. The higher frequency of contacts with "community services" in Nottingham might have been expected to lower morbidity. The fact that it did not appeared due to the fact that frequency of contact was not particularly associated with severity of disability or disturbance. The amount of medication used was calculated in each study. Patients at Mapperley received the highest doses and those at Netherne, the lowest.

The overall course of schizophrenia, as determined by this study in clinical as well as social terms, is shown in Figure 9.7. Two earlier studies are included for comparison. There may have been some improvement over the years, although it is not as striking as might have been hoped. Three recent European follow-up studies have suggested that some 20–25% of schizophrenic disorders clear up relatively quickly, although the short-term course can be stormy, while a similar proportion result in severe long-term disability. Manfred Bleuler (1978) has argued that these proportions have probably not changed much, following the introduction of modern methods of social and pharmacological treatment, but that the other 50–60% of cases that run a fluctuating course might well have been influenced by medication and by factors in the social environment.

There is evidence from a number of studies, albeit not epidemiologically based, that this contention contains a measure of truth. Preventive medication (Hirsch, Gaind, Rohde, Stevens, & J. K. Wing, 1973; Leff, 1973; Leff & J. K. Wing, 1971; Stevens, 1973), life events (Brown & Birley, 1968), over-vigorous rehabilitation (J. K. Wing et al., 1964), and management problems within the family (Brown, Birley, & J. K. Wing, 1972; Leff, Hirsch, Gaind, Rohde, & Stevens, 1973; Vaughn & Leff, 1976), interact to help determine relapse rates. Intervention based on this knowledge can often be successful (Leff, Kuipers, Berkowitz, Eberlein-Vries, & Sturgeon, 1982). An epidemiological base is required in order to identify and count the patients and families who can benefit from such procedures. So far as a high degree of emotional expressiveness (EE) in relatives is concerned, most studies have been restricted to patients within a few years of first florid onset and only 40–50% of these have relatives with high EE. It is not clear how far the results can be generalized to the large majority of patients now living outside hospitals. Moreover, longer-term research is required in order to discover whether family breakdown can be prevented using these techniques. The theory that social overstimulation leads to breakdown with florid symptoms while social understimulation exacerbates negative impairments (J. K. Wing, 1975, 1977; J. K. Wing & Brown, 1970), so that the person afflicted by schizophrenia has to walk a tightrope with different kinds of danger on each side, could be tested by using naturally occurring variations in service combined with an epidemiological approach.

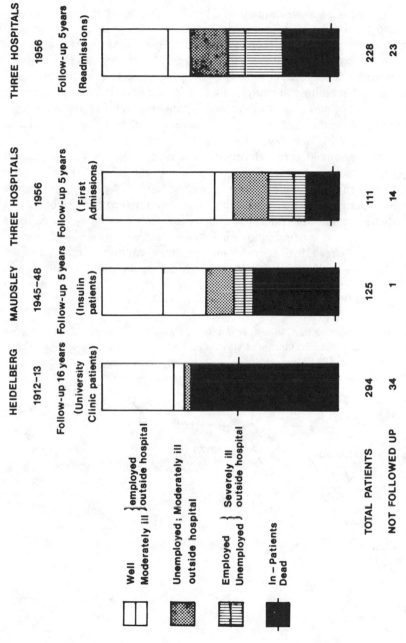

Figure 9.7. Social and clinical outcome in schizophrenia, 1912–1956. (From Brown *et al.*, 1970.)

167

THE "NEW" LONG STAY

The medium–long-stay accumulation shown in Figure 9.2 is of particular interest to those who wish to anticipate needs for care in the future. The dynamics of the process are more evident from Figure 9.8, where successive quinquennial census days, on which existing old-long-stay (over one year) residents are excluded, are taken as the origin for successive annual counts of people newly becoming long-stay residents. By the end of 1981 it looked as though a figure of about 100 Camberwell inpatients would represent the total of people needing the kind of long-term care offered by a local psychiatric hospital (J. K. Wing and Der, 1984).

Of these, about 40 were suffering from dementia. Only 36 had been given a diagnosis of schizophrenia. This compares with the proportion, estimated at about two-thirds, commonly found among long-stay patients in former times. Such statistics, although valuable for describing the practices of a given health district, cannot be translated directly into needs for care. They can be used, however, as a starting point for more intensive study of local needs.

Mann and Cree (1976) selected one hospital at random from each of the Health Regions of England and Wales and, during 1972–1973, interviewed samples of patients who had been residents between one and three years and

Figure 9.8. Build-up of 'new' long-stay numbers, Camberwell (nonresident > 1 year on quinquennial census days but long-stay on subsequent annual census days. (From J. K. Wing & Der, 1984.)

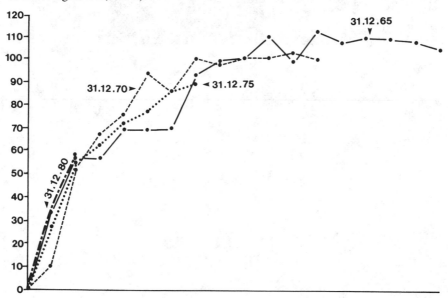

were under age 65. Of the 400 patients in the series, 44.4% were given a diagnosis of schizophrenia. Patients were substantially less clinically impaired than those in the comparative study of J. K. Wing and Brown (1961). For example, in their sample 56.4% of the schizophrenic patients in residence from 2–10 years had severe symptoms (coherent delusions, incoherence of speech, poverty of speech, or muteness). The equivalent figure in the later series was 24.3%.

However, the social characteristics of the sample were not advantageous. Residents were predominantly middle-aged to elderly (the men younger than the women), unmarried or separated from their spouses, with poor employment records and few social supports. Significant physical disability, such as loss of a limb, blindness, or cancer was present in 16% of cases. One-third had been admitted on seven or more occasions. One-fourth had spent more than 5 years in a hospital before the current admission.

An interesting comparison between the two hospital investigations concerns attitude to discharge. In the three-hospital study, 42% of patients in residence between two and ten years definitely wanted to leave, while among the schizophrenic patients in Mann and Cree's (1976) study, the equivalent proportion was 29%, although the length of stay was much shorter.

On the basis of systematically collected information from patients, nurses, social workers, and psychiatrists, a judgment was made by the research workers as to the residential accommodation that would be most suitable. The proportions in each category are shown in Table 9.3, separately for the schizophrenic and nonschizophrenic patients. Apart from the category of special needs for people with chronic brain syndromes, mental retardation, alcoholism, sensory deficits, or physical handicaps, there is little difference between the needs identified for the two diagnostic groups. Only 10% were thought to be able to live independently, but new ideas about sheltered housing were urgently needed. These judgments were necessarily subjective although based on systematic data. A more operational procedure is required.

The results were checked against the local needs of equivalent Camberwell patients, who were seen at about the same time (Mann & Sproule, 1972) and were found to be very similar. In this local study, relatives were also interviewed. Patients and relatives were asked about the degree of welcome patients would receive if they returned home from the hospital. As shown in Table 9.4, patients regarded themselves as considerably more welcome than was justified by the relatives' response. (A similar finding was recorded by J. K. Wing, Monck, Brown, & Carstairs, 1964.)

Many of the large psychiatric hospitals that serve conurbations like London are situated miles away from their catchment areas. This is true for Camberwell but the policy of the Maudsley hospital, which is located in the district, has been since the mid-1960s to focus all psychiatric services locally.

Table 9.3. Residential Accommodation Recommended for Sample of Patients in Hospitals between 1 and 3 Years (15 hospitals in England, 1972/3)

Accommodation Recommended	Schizophrenia	Other Diagnoses	Total
Further hospital care	77	58	135
Supervised hostel	52	36	88
Less supervised accommodations	14	24	38
Unsupervised accommodations	13	8	21
Specialized accommodations	11	90	101
(Extended leave)	9	8	17
Total	176	224	400

Source: Mann & Cree, 1976.

Since that time, only patients with dementia have been transferred to a distant mental hospital and this practice, too, will be stopped eventually. For a postgraduate teaching hospital to take responsibility for a catchment area was a serious decision. A particular problem was the calculation of the likely future accumulation of long-stay patients. The view was taken that estimates based on recent statistical trends would not be satisfactory since the assumption underlying such projections had to be that the trends would necessarily continue, at least approximately, as before (Robertson, 1981).

It was decided that any Camberwell patient under age 65, with a diagnosis other than progressive brain disease, who stayed in the hospital as long as a year, should ideally live in a house, not a ward, and that an experimental "hospital hostel" should be established to test the feasibility of the idea (J. K. Wing, 1972).

The rationale, so far as schizophrenic patients, who would constitute the largest single diagnostic group, were concerned was that shelter should be provided in order to mitigate the stresses that everyday life poses for the vulnerable and that often lead to relapse, but that a structured environment

Table 9.4. Estimate of the Welcome Likely if a Patient Returned Home (Camberwell patients in residence for 6 months to 3 years)

Degree of Welcome	Patient's Estimate	Relative's Estimate
Definite	20	12
Doubtful	12	6
None	10	24
Not known or not applicable	20	20

Source: Mann & Sproule, 1972.

with carefully graduated exposure to an ordinary form of life would provide an adequate level of social stimulation, thus minimizing the development of secondary amplification of negative symptoms. A suitable house (hostel ward) on the Maudsley site was modified, and patients who had been residents between 1 and 7 years as of December 31, 1977, were selected.

The evaluation of this innovation was epidemiologically based in the sense that the names of all candidates meeting the criteria laid down for entry to the hostel ward were taken from the Camberwell Register, and all were interviewed and followed up, whether or not they were transferred. A random control design was not used, however, since a group of patients in the large psychiatric hospital could not be considered for entry and were included only for purposes of comparison. Nevertheless, this combination of epidemiological base, comparative design, and follow-up assessment is well suited to health services research. (For a more complete example, see L. Wing, J. K. Wing, Stevens, & Griffiths, 1972).

Twenty-nine patients (20 of them men) were included in the sample. All but six had been given a hospital diagnosis of schizophrenia. Two were in special forensic hospitals and two in remote noncatchment hospitals. These four were not regarded as candidates. Eight were in the catchment mental hospital; they were included but not considered for the hostel ward. Of the remaining 17 patients, 13 were transferred to the hostel from acute wards, 3 were discharged, and only one was considered unsuitable, because of severe behavior disturbance.

The ward was a large Victorian house on the grounds of the Maudsley hospital but facing the main road. The setting was homelike and not clinical. Patients were expected to attend day units during working hours. All the residents transferred had been socially disabled for years. The most common behavior problems were slowness, underactivity, poor self-care, lack of motivation, and social withdrawal. There were few differences initially between those who entered and those who remained in hospital wards. Staff in the hostel were able to attempt more rehabilitative procedures, and residents improved in social behavior compared with the rest. None of the patients had to be transferred back to conventional wards. Relatives, although initially wary, were very pleased with the change.

The costs of the hostel were higher than those of a large hospital ward, mainly due to a higher staff-to-patient ratio. Within the English system, however, in which it is planned to phase out the large hospitals altogether in due course, these patients will be accumulating on acute wards if no other provision is made. In that context, the higher costs are not unwarrantable (Wykes, 1982).

Three years after the hostel ward was opened, 6 of the residents had improved sufficiently in self-care and general social performance to be transferred to a house a few miles away in Camberwell. Each has a bed–sitting room and there is a shared kitchen. The hostel-ward staff visit daily to ensure that residents are looking after themselves and attend a day center or day hospital. Some patients were unable to cope with the increased responsibility and had to return to a more protected environment, but in general this innovation, too, has proved successful. It has resulted in a lowering of costs because the same staff look after 20 rather than 14 people (Wykes, 1983).

Similar hostel wards have since been opened in Manchester and Southampton. The first of these is being experimentally as well as epidemiologically evaluated.

The question now arises as to how many such hostels and associated homes are required to cater for all the people in Camberwell who need them. It will be answered by continuing to monitor the process of accumulation in acute wards and by providing new forms of care as the need arises. This seems a better way of planning than making statistical projections on the basis of dubious assumptions about the stability of recent trends. However, all such provision must be considered within the total context of hospital and community services for the long-term psychiatrically disabled in the local geographic area.

LONG-TERM COMMUNITY CARE IN CAMBERWELL

The concept of need for services is notoriously resistant to definition in terms that are replicable, even across health districts in England, let alone internationally. Comparability is best achieved if there is good sampling and standardized assessment. The latter should be based ideally on three levels of data. First, there are the clinical symptoms or impairments, the social disadvantages, and the self-attitudes of afflicted individuals. Second, there are the methods of treatment, rehabilitation, care, counsel, and welfare that best professional practice would recommend in each case. Third, there are the services required to deliver these methods of help. Good clinical practice takes all these aspects into account, but the process of reaching each decision is substantially subjective and contains many elements that are not specified.

Apart from being based on systematic data and guided by some specified rules, all the needs assessments so far considered have been essentially clinical in nature. In the following studies, some more explicit rules were introduced as a means of discovering whether a more standardized needs assessment was feasible.

In the first instance, an exploratory survey was designed in order to make a preliminary estimate of the service needs of people in prolonged (over 1 year) contact with high-dependency community services in Camberwell; that is, including a stay in day or residential care but excluding those in a hospital for more than a year (Wykes, Creer, & Sturt, 1982). This group is one that would formerly have been at high risk of a prolonged hospital stay.

Anyone living in Camberwell, age 18 or older, who was a resident in or attending one of the community psychiatric day or residential units as of June 30, 1979, and who had been in contact with some psychiatric service (including outpatient clinics) for a year or more was eligible for inclusion in the survey. Those who had been continuously in a hospital, without a break of over 30 days, for more than one year on the census day, were excluded. Outpatient stays of contact were regarded as continuous if there were no gaps longer than 90 days.

The maximum degree of contact, therefore, would be just under 1 year in a hospital or a year or longer in a nonhospital residential unit or in a day unit. The minimum amount would be one day (the census day) in a residential or day unit, preceded by four single outpatient contacts at 90-day intervals. In fact, no one in the series had only this minimal level; most were closer to the maximum.

Table 9.5, taken from the Camberwell Register, shows the number of people attending day or residential units on census day, divided according to whether or not they met the further criterion of one year in contact. A total of 334 people were in day care, in a hospital for less than 1 year, or in nonhospital residential care, out of approximately 130,000 Camberwell rsidents—a 1-day rate of 257 per 100,000. Of these, 181 (54% or 139 per 100,000) had been in an episode of contact with some psychiatric service for at least 1 year.

Table 9.6 shows the day and residential settings used by the 181 people in the census. Nearly all those in residential units had some occupation in a day

Table 9.5. Camberwell Residents in Contact with the Psychiatric Services as of June 30, 1979, by Length-of-Service Episode

Day or Residential Setting on June 10, 1979*	In Contact with Psychiatric Services During the Previous Year without a Break of 3 Months or More	Less than One Year's Previous Contact	Total
Long-stay inpatient (one year or more without a break of 30 days or more)	208	—	208
Short-stay inpatient (less than one year)	50**	118	168
Day hospital	41	27	68
Day center or sheltered workshop	68	—	68
Nonhospital residential unit only	22	8	30
Total	389	153	542

*Settings are arranged hierarchically; those in units higher in the order may also be attending units lower down, but are only counted once.
**The total figures indicate the patients who were eligible for the study ($N = 181$).
Source: Wykes *et al.*, 1982.

Table 9.6. Setting on Census Day for Camberwell Residents Eligible for Inclusion in the High-Contact Survey

Day Settings	Residential Settings				
	Hospital Wards	Supervised Hostels	Unstaffed Homes	No Residential Care	Total
Hospital wards (inpatients)	47	—	—	—	47
Day hospitals	3	4	5	32	44
Day centers	—	12	1	34	47
Sheltered workshops	—	2	2	17	21
Daytime occupation in hostel	—	6	—	—	6
No daytime care or occupation	—	8	8	—	16
Total	50	32	16	83	181

Source: Wykes *et al.*, 1982.

unit. Almost half of those attending day units were living with relatives, friends, or in their own rooms. Twenty-three persons had to be excluded (either because the Register was not up to date or because permission to interview was refused), leaving 158 for assessment.

The results of the survey were analyzed by diagnosis in order to ascertain whether there were any characteristics specific to schizophrenia, which accounted for 47% of the total. People with this condition tended to be less often married and more often immigrant, and to have had a longer contact with services, beginning at a younger age, than others. Diagnosis did not appear relevant to service distribution or to the profile of needs. In general, characteristics were much the same as for new long-stay inpatients, though clinical impairments were less severe. The following summary is based on results for the total sample.

The assessment included a description of the social milieu and practices of all units, contacts with public amenities, characteristics of social behavior, and relatives' opinions. The research team, comprised of a clinical psychologist, a social worker, and a statistician, considered the data collected for each individual and made a judgment concerning the type of care required in each case. Table 9.7 shows the results, in terms of needs met and unmet and of overprovision. About one-third of the series had at least one unmet need.

Needs for care were also considered in terms of needs for service. In general, it was thought that settings tended to offer too few of the stresses of everyday living rather than too many. More could have provided opportunities for self-help, both domestically and occupationally. There was, however, an important minority of the series who seemed to require more supervision and protection than they were receiving.

These conclusions were not intended to be taken at face value since the study was as much an exercise in feasibility as an evaluative research. Moreover, because the development of the Camberwell services has been heavily influenced by earlier research (J. K. Wing & Hailey, 1972), and because of the unique contributions that the Maudsley hospital, with its expertise and its endowment funds, and the Institute of Psychiatry have made to local developments, it can be hypothesized that needs are markedly greater in other districts with comparable sociodemographic characteristics. Such assumptions can only be tested by the development of better assessment techniques.

A study now under way is intended to replicate the main features of this survey, using a more detailed and more clinical assessment procedure that is designed to be usable in comparative research and, in simpler form, to be useful clinically. For example, a range of clinical, social, and personal problems are defined in terms of ratings of items in interview schedules and case records. If any of these are above a threshold point a "need for care" is potentially present. For each item-group a range of forms of care is specified. Whether these are being given or have been offered in recent times is noted. Overprovision, in terms of care given when the equivalent problems are not present, is also recorded. Needs for care, whether met or unmet, are then translated into needs for service, including "minimum therapeutic agents" and any particular kind of environmental setting required. The problems of relatives and their level of "emotional expression" are also rated.

The detailed clinical workup, based on a draft of the tenth edition of the Present State Examination (for the ninth, see Wing *et al.*, 1974) and including ratings of clinical impairments and course, will provide an answer, which

Table 9.7. Summary of Needs of 158 People in the High-Contact Series

Type of Service	No Need and No Service	No Need but Service Given	Need Met	Need Unmet	Need Not Clear
Security	134	1	18	1	4
Administration of medication or medical assessment	9	11	116	22	—
Training in domestic skills	138	—	5	7	8
Self-care	112	—	38	3	5
Behavior modification	141	—	8	4	5
Counseling	108	1	27	16	6
Social activities	128	1	10	12	7
At least one of these needs	9	—	94	55	—

Source: Wykes *et al.*, 1982.

the pilot study did not, to the question whether differential types of care are needed for different groups of people in long-term contact with services. It is already clear, for example, that problems of living with chronic schizophrenic symptoms or impairments are not catered to by a specific form of counseling. Symptom profiles and frequencies will also be available. For example, one clinical result likely to emerge is the presence of a significant subgroup of people with a condition resembling Asperger's syndrome whose needs for care seem rather different from those of people with chronic schizophrenia. If successful, and current experience is promising, it may be possible to undertake international studies in the field of health services research that are more detailed and more comparable than any accomplished so far.

Mention should be made of a small study of the views of relatives of people with schizophrenia about the services they have experienced (Creer & J. K. Wing, 1974). Two samples were drawn. In February 1973, 157 individuals suffering from schizophrenia were known to the National Schizophrenia Fellowship (a charitable organization devoted to the welfare of afflicted people) because their relatives were members. Three-fourths of the patients were men and three-fourths were under age 40; most, in fact, were between age 20 and 30. Members of the fellowship were usually parents rather than other kin and most lived in the southeastern section of the country (18% in London and 38% from the rest of the southeast). Very few lived in Wales or Scotland and none in Northern Ireland. (There has been a large expansion in membership throughout the United Kingdom since then.) It was decided to interview a sample from London and as many as possible from the Midlands and the North, in order to collect a group of about 50 interviews with people who had experienced a wide range of services.

By way of contrast, a sample was drawn from the Camberwell Register. All schizophrenic patients who were in touch with psychiatric services at the beginning of July 1972, who were in contact with relatives, had not recently been inpatients, and were not suffering from some chronic physical condition as well, were included in the initial sample. Four who had recently been interviewed in other research projects and five whose spouses were also mentally ill were excluded. This left 59 patients. In 18 cases the consulting psychiatrist concerned thought that it would be unwise, for various reasons, for the patient or relative to be approached. The remaining 41 patients were asked for permission to see their relatives, and if this was granted an interview was solicited. A further 11 refusals from patients or relatives reduced the number of relatives completing the interview to 30. It is possible that this group is biased because of the exclusion of certain patients with more difficult behavior or whose relatives were particularly distraught. Four of the patients who refused were married women with children, who did not want their husbands to be interviewed. In one case it was the husband of the patient who objected. In another 4 cases, refusal was due to a feeling that nothing useful would come out of the study. One further refusal was due to ill health in the relative and in one case the reason was unclear.

The behavioral characteristics of patients that were found problematic by relatives are summarized in Table 9.8. "Social Withdrawal" and "Socially Embarrassing Behavior" are categories of items that can be summed to give reliable scores. As would be expected from the sampling, relatives who joined the charitable organization, the National Schizophrenia Fellowship (NSF), described more difficult problems. Similar differences between the two groups are apparent throughout the whole range of clinical, social, and personal measurement. The services experienced by Camberwell relatives were regarded as substantially more satisfactory (50% fully satisfied) than those described by NSF members (10% fully satisfied).

The data from this study have been used to help improve methods of family intervention (Berkowitz, Eberlein-Vries, Kuipers, & Leff, 1984).

Even in a comparatively well-serviced area such as Camberwell many chronically disabled people are not receiving the care they need. In an earlier epidemiological, experimental, and follow-up study, people with psychosis, age 18–54, had been in contact with services during 1965–1967 but not in 1968, and had been unemployed for at least 1 year, were considered for the study (L. Wing *et al.*, 1972). The object was to offer the facilities of a newly established rehabilitation workshop to a group selected at random from the total of those both eligible and suitable. Seventy-five people were included in the study, and all were followed up 2 years after the date of inclusion. At that time one person was known to be in a shelter for destitute men and another

Table 9.8. Severity of Behavior Disorders in Two Samples of People with Schizophrenia

	National Schizophrenia Fellowship	Camberwell	Total (%)
Social withdrawal, etc.			
None or slight	4	4	10
Moderate	29	20	61
Marked	17	6	29
Socially embarrassing behavior			
None or slight	11	16	34
Moderate	26	12	48
Marked	12	2	18
Not known	1	—	1
	($N = 50$)	($N = 30$)	($N = 80$)

Source: Creer & J. K. Wing, 1974.

was in a common lodging house and could easily have become destitute. If only one psychiatrically disabled person from each area the size of Camberwell became destitute each year, the numbers would soon accumulate sufficiently to account for all of those known to be living rough or in night shelters in the United Kingdom. Moreover, even without becoming destitute, it is easier for people to cease attending day centers than for long-stay residents to leave the hospital.

Finally, an estimate can be made of the overall prevalence of chronic psychiatric disablement in Camberwell (excluding mental retardation). At the end of 1982 there were 149 long-stay hospital inpatients from Camberwell per 100,000 of the population. (This is higher than the national average, 114 per 100,000, because of the depopulation factor mentioned earlier.) In addition, the unduplicated rate for Camberwell people in other residential care (i.e., short-stay inpatients, hostel and group-home residents), or in day hospitals or day centres, who had been in contact with psychiatric services of some kind for at least one year, was 139 per 100,000. If the two figures are added together, the resulting rate of people utilizing hospital and community services over a long period—288 per 100,000, about half of whom are schizophrenic—can be used as an approximate estimate of the numbers with disorders of the kind that used to result in long-term hospitalization. This estimate is minimal. Even so, it represents 85% of the peak (1954) bed-occupancy rate for England, which was 344 per 100,000.

SUMMARY

The epidemiological method is particularly well adapted for use in evaluative studies of health and social services. These services are intended to minimize and maintain at a low level all the components of social disablement—disease, disability, disadvantage, and distress. It is particularly opportune to study such matters in a country like the United Kingdom where services are geographically based on more or less contiguous health and social services districts and where a substantial and well-documented decline in hospital-bed occupancy has occurred during the past 30 years, so much so that the eventual closure of all the large psychiatric hospitals is contemplated. Schizophrenia, which accounted for two-thirds of all the long-stay accumulation in these hospitals at the point of peak occupancy (344 per 100,000) in 1954 is at the heart of these changes.

Studies of long-stay schizophrenic patients in the 1950s and 1960s demonstrated that part of the "negative" symptomatology could be accounted for by lack of social stimulation, to which they seemed very vulnerable. Time spent doing nothing was a particularly sensitive indicator. Social disadvantages such as pauperism, segregation, few social supports, and restricted opportunities to practice the ordinary activities of daily living led, in many cases, even when negative impairments were not severe, to an attitude of acceptance of the institutional regime and inability to cope with any other way of life (institutionalism). Making the social environment more socially rich led to a decrease in negative symptoms, to an extent that varied from individual to individual. Rehabilitation techniques systematized this approach and were, for a time, very successful. Schizophrenia was not cured, however, and many people remained severely disabled even in a good environment.

Follow-up studies at the same time showed that the length of stay of newly admitted patients was being markedly shortened but that the services available after discharge varied as widely as those of long-stay inpatients. It was less easy, however, to demonstrate differences in outcome, perhaps because the after-care contacts made in areas with much community activity were not necessarily concentrated on those who particularly needed them. New environmental hazards, this time in the shape of social overstimulation, were shown to result in a high rate of relapse with positive symptoms, and readmission.

Meanwhile a new long-stay group was building up, composed of people who quickly became institutionalized after a long experience of severe disability, disadvantage, and distress. Surveys suggested that most could live in more domestic, though still supervised, accommodations, and experiments demonstrated this.

Surveys of long-term attendees or residents in services that provided alternatives to prolonged hospital care, such as day centers and hostels, indicated substantial unmet needs even in districts where services were relatively plentiful. (The features of districts likely to show high needs are outlined.) It seemed that there were as many cases of chronic schizophrenia as ever, although generally less severe, because of less secondary amplification. Since that time, knowledge has gradually been acquired of how to help afflicted people and their families, if any, to live with chronic schizophrenia, not only through the use of medication, shelter, and welfare provision but through practical health education. A practical, systematic, and regularly repeated needs assessment procedure, combined with a local at-risk register, in order to ensure that needs are identified and met, now seems most necessary.

REFERENCES

Berkowitz, R., Eberlein-Vries, R., Kuipers, L., & Leff, J. (1984). Educating relatives about schizophrenia. *Schizophrenia Bulletin, 10*, 418–428.

Bleuler, M. (1978). *The Schizophrenic disorders: Long-term patient and family studies.* (S. M. Clemens, Trans.) New Haven: Yale University Press.

Brown, G. W. (1960). Length of hospital stay and schizophrenia: A review of statistical studies. *Acta Psychiatrica Neurologica Scandinavica, 35,* 414–430.

Brown, G. W. & Birley, J. L. T. (1968). Crisis and life changes and the onset of schizophrenia. *Journal of Health and Human Behavior, 9,* 203–214.

Brown, G. W., Birley, J. L. T., & Wing, J. K. (1972). Influence of family life on the course of schizophrenic disorders: A replication. *British Journal of Psychiatry, 121,* 241–258.

Brown, G. W., Bone, M., Dalison, B., & Wing, J. K. (1966): *Schizophrenia and Social Care.* Maudsley Monograph No. 17. London: Oxford University Press.

Cooper, J. E., Kendell, R. E., Gurland, B. J., Sharpe, L., Copeland, J. R. M., & Simon, R. (1972). *Psychiatric diagnosis in New York and London.* Maudsley Monograph No. 20. London: Oxford University Press.

Creer, C., & Wing, J. K. (1974). *Schizophrenia at home.* National Schizophrenia Fellowship, 79, Victoria Road, Surbiton, Surrey, KT6 4JT.

Dunham, H. W. (1965). *Community and schizophrenia: An epidemiological analysis.* Detroit: Wayne State University Press.

Faris, R. E. L., & Dunham, H. W. (1939). *Mental disorders in urban areas.* Chicago: Häfner.

Gibbons, J., Jennings, C., & Wing, J. K. (Eds.). (1984). *Psychiatric care in eight register areas, 1976–1981.* Psychiatric Case Register, Knowle Hospital, Fareham, Hants, P017 5NA.

Hare, E. H. (1956). Mental illness and social conditions in Bristol. *Journal of Mental Science, 102,* 349–357.

Hirsch, S. R., Gaind, R., Rohde, P. D., Stevens, B. C., & Wing, J. K. (1973). Out-patient maintenance of chronic schizophrenic patients with long-acting fluphenazine: Double blind placebo trial. *British Medical Journal, 1,* 633–637.

Kramer, M. (1978). Population changes and schizophrenia. In L. C. Wynne, R. L. Cromwell, & S. Matthysse (Eds.), *The nature of schizophrenia* (pp. 545–571). New York: Wiley.

Leach, J., & Wing, J. K. (1980). *Helping destitute men.* London: Tavistock.

Leff, J. P. (1973). Influence of selection of patients on results of clinical trials. *British Medical Journal, IV,* 156–158.

Leff, J. P., Hirsch, S. R., Gaind, R., Rohde, P. D., & Stevens, B. C. (1973). Life events and maintenance therapy in schizophrenic relapse. *British Journal of Psychiatry, 123,* 659–660.

Leff, J. P., Kuipers, L., Berkowitz, R., Eberlein-Vries, R., & Sturgeon, D. (1982). A controlled trial of social intervention in the families of schizophrenic patients. *British Journal of Psychiatry, 141,* 121–134.

Leff, J. P., & Wing, J. K. (1971). Trial of maintenance therapy in schizophrenia. *British Medical Journal, 3,* 599–604.

Mann, S., & Cree, W. (1976). 'New' long-stay psychiatric patients: A national sample of 15 mental hospitals in England and Wales 1972/3. *Psychological Medicine, 6,* 603–16.

Mann, S., & Sproule, J. (1972). Reasons for a six-month stay. In J. K. Wing & A. M. Hailey (Eds.), *Evaluating a Community Psychiatric Service.* London: O.U.P.

Morris, J. N. (1964). *Uses of epidemiology* (2nd ed.). London: Livingstone.

Nuallain, M. N., O'Hare, A., Walsh, D., Blake, B., Halpenny, J. V., & O'Brien, P. F. (1984). The incidence of mental illness in Ireland. Patients contacting psychiatric services in three Irish counties. *Irish Journal of Psychiatry, 5,* 23–29.

Ødegård, Ø. (1952). The incidence of mental diseases as measured by census investigations versus admission statistics. *Psychiatric Quarterly, 26,* 212.

Robertson, G. (1981). *The provision of in-patient facilities for the mentally ill: A paper to assist National Health Service planners.* London: Department of Health and Social Service.

Shields, J. (1978). Genetics. In J. K. Wing (Ed.), *Schizophrenia: Towards a new synthesis* (pp. 53–87). New York: Grune & Stratton.

Stein, L. (1957). "Social class" gradient in schizophrenia. *Brit. J. prev. soc. Med., 11,* 181–195.

Stevens, B. (1973). Role of fluphenazine decanoate in lessening the burden of chronic schizophrenics on the community. *Psychol. Med., 3,* 141–158.

Vaughn, C. E., & Leff, J. P. (1976). The influence of family and social factors on the course of psychiatric illness. *British Journal of Psychiatry, 129,* 125–137.

Wing, J. K. (1960). A pilot experiment on the rehabilitation of long-hospitalised male schizophrenic patients. *Brit. J. prev. soc. med., 14,* 173–180.

Wing, J. K. (1961). A simple and reliable sub-classification of chronic schizophrenia. *J. ment. Sci., 107,* 862.

Wing, J. K. (1962). Institutionalism in mental hospitals. *Brit. J. clin. soc. Psychol., 1,* 38–51.

Wing, J. K. (1963). Rehabilitation of psychiatric patients. *British Journal Psychiatry, 109,* 635–641.

Wing, J. K. (1972). Planning services for the mentally ill in Camberwell. In J. K. Wing & A. M. Hailey, *Evaluating a community psychiatric service* (pp. 343–358). London: Oxford University Press.

Wing, J. K. (1975). Impairments in schizophrenia: A rational basis for social treatment. In R. D. Wirt, G. Winokur, & M. Roff (Eds.), *Life history research in psychopathology* (Vol. 4). Minneapolis: University of Minnesota Press.

Wing, J. K. (1977). The management of schizophrenia in the community. In G. Usdin (Ed.), *Psychiatric medicine.* New York: Brunner/Mazel.

Wing, J. K., Bennett, D. H., & Denham, J. (1964). *The industrial rehabilitation of long-stay schizophrenic patients.* Medical Research Council Memo. No. 42. London: Her Majesty's Stationery Office.

Wing, J. K., & Brown, G. W. (1961). Social treatment of chronic schizophrenia: A comparative survey of three mental hospitals. *J. ment. Sci., 107,* 847–861.

Wing, J. K., & Brown, G. W. (1970). *Institutionalism and schizophrenia.* London: Cambridge University Press.

Wing, J. K., Cooper, J. E., & Sartorius, N. (1974). *The description and classification of psychiatric symptoms: An instruction manual for the PSE and CATEGO system.* London: Cambridge University Press.

Wing, J. K., & Der, G. (1984). *Report of the Camberwell Psychiatric Register, 1964–1983.* MRC Social Psychiatry Unit, London, SE5 8AF.

Wing, J. K., & Freudenberg, R. K. (1961). The response of severely ill chronic schizophrenic patients to social stimulation. *American Journal of Psychiatry, 118,* 311–322.

Wing, J. K., & Hailey, A. M. (Eds.) (1972). *Evaluating a community psychiatric service: The Camberwell Register, 1964–1971.* London: Oxford University Press.

Wing, J. K., Monck, E., Brown, G. W., & Carstairs, G. M. (1964). Morbidity in the community of schizophrenic patients discharged from London mental hospitals in 1959. *British Journal of Psychiatry, 110,* 10–21.

Wing, L. (1979). Mentally retarded children in Camberwell. In H. Hafner (Ed.), *Estimating needs for mental health care* (pp. 107–112). Heidelberg: Springer-Verlag.

Wing, L. (1981). Asperger's syndrome: A clinical account. *Psychological Medicine, 11,* 115–129.

Wing, L., Wing, J. K., Stevens, B., & Griffiths, D. (1972). An epidemiological and experimental evaluation of chronic psychotic patients in the community. In J. K. Wing & A. M. Hailey (Eds.), *Evaluating a community psychiatric service: The Camberwell Register 1964–71* (pp. 283–308). London: Oxford University Press.

World Health Organization (1973). *The international pilot study of schizophrenia.* Geneva: Author.

Wykes, T. (1982). A hostel-ward for 'new' long-stay patients. In J. K. Wing (Ed.), *Long-term community care. Psychological Medicine* (Suppl. No. 2), 57–97.
Wykes, T. (1983). Brief communication: A follow-up of 'new' long-stay patients in Camberwell, 1977–82. *Psychological Medicine, 13*, 659–662.
Wykes, T., Creer, C., & Sturt, E. (1982). Needs and deployment of services. In J. K. Wing (Ed.), *Long-term community care: Experiences in a London borough. Psychol. Med.* (Monograph Suppl. No. 2).

DISCUSSION

Ernest Gruenberg: No one should think that only in Camberwell do people conduct community surveys to find unmet treatment needs. Psychiatric examinations were carried out on a probability sample of people in eastern Baltimore, and two of my colleagues, Alan Romanoski and Jerry Nestadt, have reported what they and their colleagues thought, as clinicians, that these people needed in the way of treatment. One of the uses of epidemiology is to go beyond the clinical horizon, which necessarily is limited to psychiatric registers. There is a vast group outside the clinical horizon, and they also need some treatment.

Wing: Let me address Dr. Gruenberg's point. I introduced Chapter 9 with a reference to Ødegaard's statement that most people with schizophrenia do, in fact, come into contact with services. If you have a case register you know about them, and I think there are few people in Camberwell with schizophrenia of whom we are not aware.

Gruenberg: Nobody knows whether this is true. You have never done a survey.

Wing: We have done three community surveys in Camberwell. We don't, of course, pick up very many in the community survey. You don't expect to find very many, but the ones we do pick up, we know about.

Joseph Zubin: Your demonstration of the results in those three hospitals, and the fact that you can reduce the negative symptoms to a minimum, are, of course, very exciting. They certainly fit into the general questions that are facing our own work in this country about the basic nature of negative symptoms: How do they come about? What is their significance? Are they indigenous to the illness? Your work has demonstrated that many of them are artifacts due to iatrogenic, ecogenic, and nosocomial factors.

I wonder about that irreducible minimum that you mentioned. Can you theorize as to whether that is really germane to schizophrenia? Might it be a residue of the premorbid personality, or due to some other factor, rather than a genuine aspect of schizophrenia?

Wing: Dr. Zubin has put his finger on an important question, as usual. First of all, I don't think one should make a diagnosis of schizophrenia solely on the negative symptoms; that is bad clinical practice. The people with severe negative symptoms who don't seem to respond to any kind of treatment and who have never manifested positive symptoms have in several studies been shown to have abnormal CT scans, for example, perhaps with no genetic loading. There may be environmental causes, but many of these cases are so long term that it is very difficult now to determine whether a positive diagnosis of schizophrenia could ever have been made.

Making a diagnosis solely on negative symptoms is opening a ragbag, into which go a number of cases that get called "schizophrenic" that might better be allocated to some other category. One such condition is adult autistic psychopathy, or Asperger's syndrome. Asperger published his monograph on this subject at the same time that Kanner published on infantile autism, but he published it in German, which a contemporary of mine wrongly called a dead language for psychiatry. That was in the mid-1940s. What Asperger was describing was a condition which many people would call simple schizophrenia or schizoid personality, but it is more closely related to autism than to schizophrenia. That is just one possibility out of a very wide range of conditions which Ben Pasamanick has called "the continuum of reproductive causality."

If you look at the people with the fluctuating conditions that Manfred Bleuler talked about (and they fluctuate during a long-term stay in the hospital as well as in the community, though less so), what you see is the positive symptoms emerging from time to time within the context of the chronic negative symptoms, and I think you can have no doubt about the diagnosis in that group, at least. But there are also cases that manifest only the positive symptoms without the negative.

Zubin: Can you say more about the positive symptoms?

Wing: The easiest way to study them is to look at acute episodes of schizophrenia (where, of course, negative symptoms can also increase temporarily). Then you see the characteristic primary experiences and secondary elaborations and explanations that are usually called positive symptoms. These, too, are heavily influenced by environmental events. There is no doubt, for example, that they can be induced in a group of vulnerable people by exposing them to too-intensive rehabilitation. Similarly, life events or an adverse family situation (which is by no means uncommon) can precipitate a relapse. There is a very large descriptive literature in this area.

10

Overview and Initial Results from a Risk-Factor Study of Depression and Schizophrenia

BRUCE P. DOHRENWEND, PATRICK E. SHROUT, BRUCE G. LINK,
JOHN L. MARTIN, AND ANDREW E. SKODOL
New York State Psychiatric Institute and Columbia University

Our central question is: Is environmentally induced stress a causal factor in the occurrence of episodes of major depression and of schizophrenic disorder? If so, what are the processes involved?

The most direct evidence on this question comes from a handful of retrospective case-control studies of stressful life events and these two types of disorder. We will review what we regard as the most important studies before reporting results from our own research on 122 major depressives, 65 persons with schizophrenia or schizophrenia-like disorders ("schizophrenic disorder") and 197 well controls.

REVIEW OF THE EVIDENCE

Since our concern is with two types of disorders that are quite rare in the general population, we must perforce become interested in case-control studies. Our primary interest is in the role of stress factors in onset rather than course. For this reason, the case-control studies are retrospective in nature. Without exact knowledge in advance of the risk factors involving stress, prospective studies based on selection of cohorts of those exposed to the stress factors and followed through the risk period for developing the disorders have not yet been conducted.

Various investigators have listed criteria for adequate retrospective case-control studies of the role of environmentally induced stress in various types of psychopathology. We have been influenced by Brown (1974) and Hudgens (1974), for example, in developing the list shown in Table 10.1. These criteria are probably essential for a study to yield decisive findings.

However, several of the criteria are extremely difficult to meet. Consider by way of illustration, the problems that would be involved with two of the

Table 10.1. Ideal Criteria for a Case-Control Study of Life Events and Episodes of Various Types of Psychopathology

The cases should consist of a representative sample of individuals from the population being studied who have recently developed the episodes for the first time.

The procedures for collecting the symptom data and the rules for combining these data into diagnoses of cases should be explicit and replicable.

The controls should consist of a representative sample of the demographic counterparts of the cases in the population being studied.

There should be similarly selected comparison groups of cases with other types of symptomatology.

Data on life events should be gathered systematically from the subjects and their informants on fully enumerated lists of events rather than from patient charts where recording of the relevant information tends to be fragmented.

Both the occurrence of the events and the occurrence of onsets and/or recurrences of the episodes should be dated accurately with respect to one another.

Events that are likely to occur as consequences of the individual's mental state and behavior must be distinguished from events that occur independently of such personality factors.

Data on alternative or complementary dispositional or risk factors should be secured.

Repeated follow-ups should be conducted at suitable intervals of time to test whether the circumstances preceding recurrence are the same as the circumstances preceding onset, and whether they can be made to differ in meaningful ways with the occurrence of intervening factors such as type and duration of treatment.

criteria in a case-control study of schizophrenia. In an analysis of results from epidemiological studies of true prevalence, Link and Dohrenwend (1980) have found that perhaps a fifth of the diagnosed schizophrenics on the average have never been in inpatient or outpatient treatment. To obtain a representative sample of persons who develop schizophrenic episodes, therefore, we must be able not only to agree upon and identify the important characteristics of these episodes but also draw samples of those showing such characteristics—whether these individuals have been officially recognized (e.g., by admission to a mental hospital) or not. And while it is clear that some fateful events such as death of a loved one are very likely to occur independently of the individual's mental condition or behavior, and others such as being convicted of a crime are not, most events are between these two extremes and require considerable additional information about the context in which they occur before such a determination can even begin to be made. The most widely used checklist approaches to measuring life events make no provision for doing this.

It should not be surprising, therefore, that there is no single case-control study of life stress and schizophrenia that meets all of the above criteria. Very few of the retrospective case-control studies of life stress and episodes of either major depression or schizophrenia in the literature even came close. We have to relax the criteria to get even a handful of studies to examine, keeping this question about the role of environmentally induced stress in mind.

We will consider for the most part only those studies that come reasonably near to meeting four of the criteria set forth in Table 10.1. These constitute the irreducible minimum for providing useful results bearing on the problem of whether life events play a causal role, and they consist of adequate controls, replicable diagnostic criteria, attention to assessing which events occur independently of the subjects' prior mental state, and careful attention to dating of the occurrence of events in relation to the occurrence of the episodes of psychopathology. Failure to attend to these problems makes much of the published research difficult to interpret. With particular reference to life events, methodological problems, especially those related to the question of independence, have been particularly serious (cf. Dohrenwend, Dohrenwend, Dodson, & Shrout, 1984).

Schizophrenia

A variety of definitions of schizophrenia have been used in case-control studies to date. We will discuss the occurrence of acute psychotic episodes rather than of schizophrenia as defined, for example, by DSM-III since operationally this is more nearly what was investigated in these studies.

Two case-control studies have shown that the number of life events reported by schizophrenics before onset of an episode was significantly greater than the number reported by controls for a comparable period. One of these, by Jacobs and Myers (1976) in New Haven, focused on a survey of 62 first admissions; the other, by Brown and Birley (1968) in London, was concerned with 50 patients admitted for acute episodes of schizophrenia. Although the consistent finding of these two studies was that there was a significantly higher rate of life events in their reporting periods, 1 year in the former and 3 months in the latter study, for patients compared with community controls, this excess was due mainly to events that could be dependent on the patient's mental condition. It is of considerable interest, therefore, that Brown and Birley, who dated the occurrence of events within 1-week periods, found that events that were independent of a person's psychiatric condition occurred more frequently in the 3-week period preceding episodes of schizophrenia than in a comparable period in the lives of their controls. Forty-six percent of the patients but only 12% of the controls experienced at least one independent event in this 3-week period. This difference was not found in earlier 3-week periods. Moreover, this finding is not an isolated one, since Leff and his colleagues (Leff, Hirsch, Gaind, Rohde, & Stevens, 1973) found a relatively high frequency of events in the period just prior to relapse in a sample of schizophrenics being treated with phenothiazines in the community. In addition, Brown and Birley (1968) showed that their results held regardless of first-admission versus readmission status of the patient, and also for patients experiencing first episodes versus those experiencing relapses.

How severe were the events that preceded the onset of schizophrenic episodes? It is possible to envision a set of events that, when they occur close together in a brief period of time, could approximate the conditions of extreme situations such as combat (B. P. Dohrenwend, 1979). These consist of fateful loss events such as death of loved ones that occur outside the person's control; events that exhaust the individual physically, especially those involving physical illness or injury that is life threatening; and, finally, events not previously classified in these two categories that are likely to disrupt social supports, events such as a move from one community to another, a change of job, or a marital separation. When several events of these three types occur in a brief period of time, we have the presence of what we hypothesize to be a pathogenic triad approximating the stress conditions of extreme situations. Fortunately, Brown and Birley (1968) provide information on the actual events experienced in the 13-week period prior to onset or relapse. It is clear from this material that not one of the cases experienced events from all three elements of our hypothesized pathogenic triad. However, Brown, Harris, and Peto (1973) reported with regard to the same study that about 16% of the cases experienced events that the investigators judged to be markedly severe and that, moreover, this was three times the rate of such events among the controls.

Rogler and Hollingshead (1965) have provided additional relevant data from a study of 20 couples, at least one of whom was diagnosed as schizophrenic following their first contact with a mental health agency. They are compared to very carefully selected matched controls from a slum section in San Juan, Puerto Rico. The particular result of interest is that the death of a child was a frequent antecedent to the onset of disorder. Of 12 child deaths in the 40 San Juan families, 11 were concentrated in 7 of the families containing one or more schizophrenic parents.

We read the evidence from these studies as indicating that severely stressful life events play a causal role in the onset of some acute schizophrenic disorder. How large a role relative to other risk factors cannot be determined since other risk factors were not tested in these studies.

Depression

To date, case-control studies of depression have not been designed with current DSM-III, Feighner, or RDC criteria explicitly in mind. There are ambiguities about the best of the studies purporting to investigate depression, that by Brown and Harris (1978), centering on the problem of what the investigators are measuring as "depression." Critics have, in fact, engaged Brown and Harris in a controversy about the extent to which clinical depression against some form of lesser distress has been identified in the community cases counted by Brown and his colleagues (Brown & Harris, 1982; Wing, Mann, Leff, & Nixon, 1978).

On the basis of current evidence, we really do not know very much about the relation of nonspecific distress or demoralization to major depression. There is no question that scores on scales of such distress vary with the occurrence of life events (e.g., Myers, Lindenthal, & Pepper, 1974). The role of life events in major depression, as currently defined by DSM-III criteria, however, is unclear. In turning to previous studies, we must speculate about the relation between depression as diagnosed in these studies and major depression as currently defined by DSM-III. It seems likely to us that a majority of the patient cases of depression studied by such researchers as Paykel (1974) and also included in the studies of Brown and his colleagues would meet criteria for major depression.

In his case-control studies of life events and clinical depression, Paykel (1974) found that undesirable events, but not desirable events, were reported in excess in the 6 months prior to the onset of depression. He also identified a class of events that he labeled "exits," in which a person leaves the social field of the subject. The events which Paykel included in this category were death of close family member, marital separation, divorce, family member leaving home, child getting married, and son being drafted. Paykel found that the presence of one or more of these events was strongly associated with onsets of depression. While only 5% of controls reported one or more exits in the 6-month reporting period, 25% of the depressed patients reported at least one such event.

Brown and Harris (1978) also reported a difference in recent life events between depressed women, whether treated or untreated, and nondepressed community controls. They found that depressed women had experienced an excess of a class of events that Brown and Harris labeled "severe" in the period, on the average, of 38 weeks before the onset of depression. Specifically, 61% of patient cases and 68% of community cases, but only 28% of community controls, had experienced at least one such event.

In general, comparisons with the results for schizophrenia suggest that life events play a considerably larger role in depression (Brown and Harris, 1978); however, considerably less attention has been given by Brown and his colleagues and by Paykel to the problem of independence of the life events than in the studies of schizophrenia. Nevertheless, there are replications and related studies of this work that do pay attention to this problem.

For example, in an exploratory study of the difference in recent life events experienced by 34 diagnosed acute neurotic cases found in general practices and which probably included a substantial number of depressives, and in matched general-practice patients free of psychiatric disturbance, Cooper and Sylph (1973) adopted Brown and Harris's procedure for identifying severe events by means of ratings of long-term contextual threat. They found that 47% of their neurotic patients but only 6% of their controls had experienced at least one severe event during the 3-month comparison period. Adopting another classification employed by Brown in his study of schizo-phrenics, but not in his study of depressed women, they did not find a significant difference in the number of events experienced by cases and controls that were independent of the illness. This statistical result may be a function of the small number of subjects in the study, since 53% of the cases and only 26% of controls reported at least one independent event. Brown has stated (although the data are not provided) that the results of the London study hold for independent events (cf. Brown and Harris, 1978; Lloyd, 1980).

Moreover, there is evidence from the Brown and Harris (1978) study that other factors in the ongoing situation such as number of young children in the home are additional sources of stress that increase the risk of developing a depressive episode and still others such as the availability of social support from a close confidant that decrease it.

THE STUDY

We conceive of the life-stress process as consisting of three main structural components. The first is *recent events* that occur within a relatively brief time interval (usually a few months to a year). These events can range from extreme situations, such as combat and natural disasters, to the more usual life events that most of us experience at one time or another such as birth of a child, marriage, death of a loved one, getting a new job, losing a job, and so on. For some purposes, especially when it is possible to take multiple mea-surements at brief intervals over time, they can include smaller events such as some of those that Lazarus and his colleagues associate with daily "hassles" (Kanner, Coyne, Schaefer, & Lazarus, 1981).

The second major component is the *ongoing social situation*. Here, the origins of the various elements of the situation antedate the observation period for recent events, but have an impact within the period—a current impact. Under this heading we include the presence or absence of what we call supportive social networks, a noxious or hazardous work environment, the presence of a chronically ill relative in the home, and so on. We also include what Brown and Harris (1978) refer to as ongoing difficulties and what Pearlin and Lieberman (1979) refer to as role strains.

The third component consists of *personal dispositions*. Under this head-ing we include genetic vulnerabilities, insofar as we can measure them (the only way we know at the moment is to find the rates of disorder in first-degree relatives), and the residues of remote events such as early childhood bereavement. With regard to the latter, although we do not know what the current dispositional residue of a remote event such as childhood bereavement might be, we would measure whether there was bereavement and we would assume that if it has a current impact it would have it via personal dispositions since its effects long since would have been internalized. We would also include personal assets in the form of physical stamina, health, intelligence, and personal liabilities such as blindness, deafness, a game leg, and so on. We consider of central importance a set of normal personality variables that range from attitudes of mastery to helplessness, and include locus of control, Type A behavior pattern, masculinity-femininity (especially with regard to depression), and denial.

In the present retrospective case-control study, we have been studying variables in each of these three components of the life-stress process as possible risk factors for episodes of major depression and episodes of schizophrenic disorder. The research setting is the Washington Heights section of New York City surrounding the Columbia Presbyterian Medical Center.

Method

The cases of DSM-III major depression and "schizophrenic disorder" (including mainly DSM-III schizophrenia, schizophreniform disorder, brief reactive psychosis, schizo-affective psychosis, and atypical psychosis) were recruited and received initial diagnoses mainly from psychiatric facilities. An additional small sample of cases of major depression were located in a general population sample from which the well controls were also selected.

Prior to their recruitment into the risk-factor study, both patient and community samples had been interviewed about mental health complaints as part of a methodological study of psychiatric symptom inventories including screening scales from the Psychiatric Epidemiology Research Interview (PERI) (B. P. Dohrenwend, Shrout, Egri, & Mendelsohn, 1980). We will call this first interview the "methods" interview. A subsample of community residents scoring high on a screening scale measure of nonspecific distress (B. P. Dohrenwend et al., 1980) were then given a diagnostic interview using a modification of the Diagnostic Interview Schedule (DIS) of Robins, Helzer, Croughan, and Ratcliff (1981).

In the original methods study sample, households were enumerated and contacted to determine if an eligible respondent between 19 and 59 years of age lived there. In 93% of the households screening information was provided and 68% of these contained one or more respondents. Of the 943 eligible respondents, 55% (514) were successfully interviewed in the methods study. Since these respondents provided the relevant demographic contrasts required for the initial essentially methodological study, intensive efforts to pin down "hard to schedule" respondents and to convert refusals were not undertaken.

Later, when the second wave of interviewing, which involved substantive hypotheses, was conceived and implemented for the present risk-factor study, provision was made to check on a subsample of hard-to-interview subjects ($N = 48$). This group included 33 individuals who initially refused but were converted with intensive effort, 12 who failed to keep two appointments (our usual cutoff as a lost case), but were obtained on a third or later appointment, and 3 respondents who could not be reached by telephone after eight attempts at varied times of the day (our usual cutoff as a lost case) but were reached on a ninth or subsequent attempt. Our major concern was that this hard-to-get sample might differ markedly by having higher levels of psychopathology. In this regard it was found that hard-to-reach respondents were likely to have slightly less pathology, scoring lower on scales measuring nonspecific distress, false beliefs and perceptions, schizoid personality, and problems due to drinking (see B. P. Dohrenwend *et al.*, 1980, for descriptions and psychometric properties of the scales).

Moreover, considerable attention was paid to ensuring an adequate reinterview rate. As a result, 83% of the initial sample (429) for the methods interview were located and reinterviewed with the risk-factor instrument. This group included the 197 community respondents who became the well controls for the substantive case-control study and also 24 persons who were added to the cases of major depressions secured from treatment facilities.

The patient samples were selected from outpatient clinics and inpatient facilities in the same general area of New York City. The goal was to select patients in two diagnostic categories, major depression and schizophrenia and schizophrenia-like psychotic disorders. In addition, considerable effort was made to locate cases in their first episodes of each of these types of disorders. As we have emphasized, it was extremely difficult to locate first-episode cases, but in the end we interviewed 164 patients consisting of 50 first-episode major depression, 21 first-episode schizophrenic disorder, 48 repeat major depression and 43 repeat schizophrenic disorder.

The psychiatric status of the patients was independently assessed in the form of DSM-III diagnoses. These were either made or supervised by members of the biometrics unit at New York State Psychiatric Institute under the direction of Robert Spitzer, using clinical records and unstructured clinical interviews. In a study on supervising intake diagnosis (Spitzer, Skodol, Williams, Gibbon, & Kass, 1982) the four-member biometrics team (Robert Spitzer, Andrew Skodol, Janet Williams, and Mimi Gibbon) had demonstrated agreement between pairs of members on the diagnostic class of patients' principal diagnoses in 21 of the 24 (87%) cases that were jointly interviewed. In comparison, the rate of agreement between a biometrics rater and a clinic rater was only 66% over 50 cases. Since the biometrics rater's diagnosis was more frequently in agreement with final consensus diagnoses based on all available information, the biometrics group had established that they used DSM-III reliably and that the validity of their judgments exceeded those of the clinicians who made the intake diagnoses.

In a study of the process of second-hand supervision (Skodol, Williams, Spitzer, Gibbon, & Kass, 1984) used to check a substantial proportion (approximately 50%) of the patients' diagnoses in this study, the biometrics group found a 9% rate of change (i.e., from one major diagnostic class to another) on Axis I ($N = 200$). In both the Spitzer *et al.* (1982) and the Skodol *et al.* (1984) studies of supervision, there were high proportions of changes involving the affective disorders class. Each study, however, documented that, in the case of major depression, diagnostic errors involved the underdiagnosis of episodes of depression rather than their overdiagnosis. It is likely then, that the case group of major depressives recruited for this study is a conservative one, leaving us fairly certain that it does not contain many false-positive diagnoses.

The psychiatric status of a sample of community respondents was assessed using a modified DIS protocol. This interview was administered to all persons in the community sample who reported high levels of nonspecific distress (B. P. Dohrenwend *et al.*, 1980) at the time of the risk-factor interview. In addition, the DIS was administered to a random sample of persons without high distress in order to keep the DIS interviewers and evaluators blind to psychiatric status as determined by PERI. The modifications to the DIS, made by Janet Williams, one of the original authors of the DIS, consisted of the elimination of several diagnoses not of interest to the study such as tobacco-use disorder and anorexia nervosa that were not needed to diagnose depressive or schizophrenic disorders, and the inclusion of additional questions to allow diagnosis of dysthymic disorder and the melancholic subtype of major depression.

These diagnostic interviews in the community were conducted by social workers who had at least a Master's degree and several years of clinical experience and who were specially trained by Dr. Williams. The resulting DSM-III diagnoses represent a consensus between the interviewers and Williams and Gibbon from biometrics who supervised them.

On the basis of the screening and diagnostic results, three major groups were defined: (1) subjects who had a datable episode of major depression within the year preceding the risk-factor interview; (2) subjects who had a datable episode of a schizophrenic disorder within the year preceding the risk-factor interview; (3) and subjects who had no major psychiatric disorder and who did not score high on nonspecific distress at the time of the risk-factor interview. The first two groups can be further subdivided with regard to whether the index episode of the disorder was their first or a repetition of one or more previous episodes, and whether they were selected from the community or patient populations. The details of the operational definitions of these groups are provided in Table 10.2.

Table 10.2. Definitions of Case and Comparison Groups for Risk-Factor Study (*N*s are shown in parentheses)

Group	Patient Characteristics	Community Characteristics
A. Major depression (*N* = 122)	DSM-III diagnoses of 296.22, 296.23, 296.24, 296.32, 296.33, 296.34. (*N* = 98)	DIS (modified) diagnoses of 296.32, 296.33, 296.34 with episode onset within 10 months of RF interview. (*N* = 24)
	First-episode cases: DSM-III diagnoses of 296.22, 296.23, 296.24. (*N* = 50 out of 98)	No case with DIS (modified) diagnoses of 296.22, 296.23, 296.24 and with recent onset.
B. Schizophrenic disorder (*N* = 65)	DSM-III diagnoses of 295.XX, 297.10, 298.30, 297.90, 295.40, 298.80, 295.70, 298.90. (*N* = 64)	DIS (modified) diagnoses of (as at left) with episode onset within 10 months of RF interview. (*N* = 1)
	First episode cases: No episode reported previously. (*N* = 21 out of 64)	No case with first episode within 10 months of RF interview.
C. No major disorder, not demoralized (*N* = 197)	(*N* = 0)*	Not screened as possible case by PERI: if given DIS, no current disorder; not high on RF demoralization (below 2.3 for men, below 2.6 for women). (*N* = 197)**

*Patients with these characteristics were not recruited explicity.

**In several cases there were discrepancies between the DIS (modified) and the PERI screen; in these cases, both interviews were reviewed by two psychiatrists and a judgment was made whether a disorder was present.

We have included the bereaved (DSM-III diagnosis, V62.82) with the major depressed since the only distinguishing clinical characteristic is the presence of a specified social situation. In fact, only two of the 122 in Group A were bereaved.

The definition of Group C is the most complicated, since different amounts of information were available for different respondents. Community respondents were categorically eliminated from this group if they were high on the measure of nonspecific distress (B. P. Dohrenwend *et al.*, 1980) included in the risk-factor interview, or if they had reported during the methods interview that they had been hospitalized for a nervous or mental disorder. The cutoff points we used for high distress differed by gender; within each sex, about 30% were characterized as demoralized. Community members were also eliminated from this "psychologically well" group if either they were classified as possible cases as a result of their responses to the PERI symptom items in the methods interview, or they were classified as having a present disorder as a result of responses to the modified DIS. The case screening rule for the symptom items was developed using logistic regression (see Shrout, B. P. Dohrenwend, & Levav, in press, for a description of the method and an application using data from a study in Israel), based on a linear function of the following symptom scales: Nonspecific Distress or Demoralization (measured during the methods interview), Suicidal Ideation and Behavior, Somatic Problems, Insomnia, False Beliefs and Perceptions, and Drinking Problems. Respondents with high levels of symptoms on one or more of these scales would be classified by the rule as possibly having a current disorder at the time of the methods interview.

In the risk-factor interview, information was obtained from the subjects about their current social circumstances, social network, recent life events, remote landmark events, and family history of illness as well as personality characteristics and recent feelings of demoralization. As in the other field operations, the interview was given by a trained, experienced interviewer. Most questions were asked verbally, although some paper-and-pencil measures were filled out by the respondent in the presence of the interviewer. Events were probed for date of occurrence and qualitative descriptive information was obtained about what actually happened and the circumstances under which the event occurred. More information about and references to published sources on the measures is contained in the results section below.

While there are weaknesses in this design, especially in the representativeness of the case samples which are composed largely of patients, our case-control study of stress and disorder has unique strong points that are missing from previous investigations of this kind. For example, the previous studies have compared one type of case with controls or two types of cases without controls. In the present study, the two different types of cases together with a community control group are compared in the same design, and personality variables as well as recent life events and important aspects of the ongoing situation are investigated at the same time. Moreover, the cases are diagnosed according to DSM-III criteria and the controls are screened to exclude the types of cases in which we are interested and other types of severe mental disorder. Until we are able to study truly representative samples of untreated as well as treated cases from the community supplemented by treatment sources, it will probably not be possible to improve very much on the design of the present retrospective case-control study.

RESULTS OF INITIAL ANALYSES: CONTINUOUS VARIABLES

The first analyses that we will report consist of comparisons of the depressed and schizophrenic disorder case groups to the group of nondemoralized noncases from the community on continuous variables. These risk-factor variables are well constructed as they stand but can be further refined on the basis of detailed qualitative data that we have secured on the life events and tests of convergent and discriminant validity with regard to the personality variables. As reported here the life-event variables are simple counts of self-reported events that occurred in the year prior to the episode of disorder for which the cases were selected and the year prior to the interview for controls. The life-events section of PERI was used for this purpose (B. S. Dohrenwend, Krasnoff, Askenasy, & B. P. Dohrenwend, 1978). The network variables are adapted from the work of Claude Fischer and his colleagues (Fischer *et al.*, 1977). The personal disposition variables are self-report measures developed and/or tested in the course of this project and include such well-known scales as Rotter's (1966) measure of locus of control and the Jenkins Activity checklist (Jenkins, Rosenman, & Friedman, 1967).

In this analysis, the group contrast for each of the risk-factor variables is assessed after statistically controlling for factors that may have resulted in spurious associations. As shown in Table 10.3, the case groups differed from the comparison group on a variety of demographic variables that may have been a result of sampling and recruitment. Besides the examination of bivariate (unconditional) associations between the case-group variable and demographic variables, we conducted a series of logistic regression analyses

Table 10.3. Demographic Characteristics of Case and Control Groups

		Major Depression ($n = 122$)	Schizophrenic Disorder ($n = 65$)	Nondemoralized Noncase ($n = 197$)
Sex	Male	30 (25%)	32 (49%)	98 (50%)
	Female	92 (75%)	33 (51%)	99 (50%)
Ethnicity	Hispanic	35 (29%)	12 (19%)	44 (22%)
	Black	38 (31%)	28 (43%)	56 (28%)
	Other	49 (40%)	25 (38%)	97 (49%)
Marital status	Married	37 (30%)	6 (9%)	113 (57%)
	Separated or divorced	45 (37%)	25 (39%)	36 (18%)
	Single or widowed	40 (33%)	34 (52%)	48 (24%)
Education	Not high school grad	35 (29%)	25 (39%)	38 (19%)
	High school grad	59 (48%)	32 (49%)	92 (47%)
	College grad	28 (23%)	8 (12%)	67 (34%)
Family income	Less than $7,000	41 (34%)	31 (48%)	23 (12%)
	$7,000–$15,000	44 (36%)	26 (40%)	57 (29%)
	$15,000–$25,000	25 (20%)	5 (8%)	69 (35%)
	Over $25,000	12 (10%)	3 (4%)	48 (24%)
Mean age (standard deviation)		36.8 (11.9)	34.2 (12.7)	40.8 (12.2)
Mean father's occupational prestige (standard deviation)		42.7 (14.8)	37.4 (11.6)	43.0 (13.6)

(with each case group compared with the control group on the dependent variable) to identify demographic variables that needed to be controlled because of conditional associations, and to test the effectiveness of various functional forms of the control variables.

As a result of these analyses, we decided to control for the following variables in every case-control comparison: sex, ethnicity (black, Hispanic, other), education (less than high school, high school graduate, college graduate), marital status (never married, divorced or separated, married), age (as a continuous variable), income (in four categories) and the respondent's father's occupational prestige (also continuous). Although the respondent's occupational prestige was different in the case and comparison groups in Table 10.3, no difference remained when education, income, and father's occupational prestige were controlled. Through the preliminary multivariate analyses we also discovered that an interaction between ethnicity and father's occupational prestige should be controlled to make the case and comparison groups comparable. Not surprisingly, father's occupational prestige had a different effect for Hispanics, many of whom were immigrants.

Table 10.4 shows results from a comparison of the depressed and schizophrenic disorder case groups and the group of community "wells." In the first six columns are the overall means and sample sizes for each group before statistical adjustments are made for the control variables discussed above. In the last seven columns are the results of the analysis of covariance which adjusted for the control variables. Besides the overall significance of the difference between the three groups, the table shows planned contrast between the three groups.

Recent Life Events

Consider first a comparison of recent life events in the 1-year period prior to the episode of disorder for the depressive cases and the schizophrenia disorder cases by contrast with the 1-year period prior to interview for the well controls. We will focus especially on events in each of the three elements of the pathogenic triad described earlier, starting with fateful loss events.

Fateful Loss Events. The events that we judged on a priori grounds likely to involve fateful loss that occurred directly to the subject and that were included in the list our interviewers presented to respondents are shown in Table 10.5. We have probed each of these and other events to elicit more details about what actually occurred. It is possible that we will subtract some of the events that turn out not to be fateful or do not involve substantial loss, and add events from elsewhere that turn out, on probing, to be fateful.

Based on a simple count of whether the subjects said the events in Table 10.5 were present or absent, and with controls on the demographic variables included above, Table 10.4 shows a higher rate of fateful-loss events for the major depressives than for both the schizophrenic disorder cases and the controls. Those with schizophrenic disorders did not differ significantly from the controls over the period of a year; we have not yet checked to see if these events nevertheless tended to build up in the 3-5 weeks prior to the psychotic episode, as occurred with independent events in the Brown and Birley (1968) and Leff *et al.* (1973) studies.

Physical Illness and Injury. The second component of the pathogenic triad consists of events that exhaust the individual physically—especially when they are life threatening. Among these we expect physical illness and injury to be especially prominent. We will know more about these matters when we analyze the detailed information elicited about each event. Up to now we have looked simply at the number of physical illnesses and injuries reported and these are significantly higher in both major depressives and schizophrenic disorder cases than in controls with the relevant demographic variables controlled.

Other Events That Are Likely to Disrupt Usual Social Supports. The third and last element of the pathogenic triad consists of events, other than those involving fateful loss and serious physical illness or injury, that are highly likely to disrupt usual social supports. Table 10.6 shows the events we put in this category on a priori grounds; that is, prior to examining the detailed information elicited about each event. A higher rate of these events was reported by both major depressives and those with schizophrenia-like disorders than by well controls, relevant demographic variables remaining constant.

By and large, the differences in Table 10.4 on fateful loss, physical illness and injury, and other events likely to disrupt social supports held for both first-episode and repeat-episode cases. Thus, the results have implications for both onset and recurrences of the two types of disorders. The relationships were evident for these three classifications of events in the pathogenic triad only, not with total number of events.

Social Networks and Social Support

As noted earlier, we followed the procedure developed by Claude Fischer and his colleagues (1977), for eliciting the members of the social networks of our cases and controls. Briefly, this involved asking each person in the study to name those individuals with whom he or she had or could have had supportive exchanges during the past year in nine areas of activity such as care of children, watching the house while he or she was away, discussion of decisions at work, discussion of personal problems, borrowing money, and social/recreational activities. From this information, we constructed such network variables as size and extensiveness (the number and density of coverage of the areas of activity) listed in Table 10.4. With relevant demo-

Table 10.4. Comparison of Risk-Factor Means across Depressed, "Schizophrenic," and Well Groups

Risk-Factor Variable	Unadjusted Means (Ns)			Significance of Overall F	Adjusted Differences Between Groups		
	A Depressed	B "Schizophrenic"	C Well		A vs. C	B vs. C	A vs. B
Count of fateful loss events to R	.79 (122)	.38 (65)	.46 (197)	.03	.37*	.02	.36†
Count of physical illness or injury events to R	.30 (122)	.25 (65)	.11 (197)	.001	.21***	.14*	.07
Count of social network loss events to R	.69 (122)	.77 (65)	.24 (197)	.001	.36***	.40***	−.03
Size of social network	8.23 (122)	5.86 (65)	10.26 (197)	.01	−.98†	−2.4**	1.37†
Number of confidants	3.42 (122)	2.37 (65)	3.20 (197)	.17	.32	−.34	.66†
Number of social companions	4.03 (122)	2.74 (65)	5.19 (197)	.002	−1.27**	−2.13**	.86
Number of instrumental	5.09 (122)	3.43 (65)	6.00 (197)	.013	−.26	−1.41**	1.16**
Extensiveness of network	9.33 (122)	8.08 (65)	10.02 (197)	.001	−.38†	−1.14***	.76**
Multiplexity of network	54.72 (122)	45.60 (65)	43.45 (197)	.004	5.32*	−5.42	10.74***
Density of network	.38 (109)	.47 (53)	.46 (191)	.004	−.12**	−.02	−.10*
Instrumental support	.485 (114)	.387 (48)	.552 (155)	.28	−.04	−.12	.08
Emotional support for change	.410 (114)	.420 (48)	.615 (155)	.005	−.20***	−.15†	−.05
Emotional support for event occurrence	.484 (115)	.488 (58)	.698 (178)	.001	−.23***	−.17*	−.05
Similarity of view of event change	.535 (114)	.461 (48)	.633 (155)	.08	−.09†	−.13*	.04

Similarity of view of event occurrence	.677 (115)	.589 (58)	.778 (177)	.01	−.08*	−.14**	.06
Levenson Internal-external locus of control	3.16 (121)	3.38 (63)	2.69 (197)	.001	.41***	.56***	−.15
Rotter Internal-external locus of control	1.48 (120)	1.46 (64)	1.37 (192)	.001	.08***	.05†	.03
Jenkins Speed and impatience factors Type A behavior pattern	.42 (120)	.35 (58)	.34 (196)	.001	.11***	.05†	.06*
Spence–Helmreich Selected positive masculinity items—Mastery	3.15 (121)	3.28 (62)	3.74 (197)	.001	−.55***	−.48***	−.07
Negative keyed negative items selected from Marlowe–Crowne, Fenz–Epstein—Denial	1.46 (122)	1.42 (62)	1.35 (197)	.001	.11***	.06*	.05†
Spence–Helmreich Selected negative femininity items	3.74 (122)	3.45 (61)	3.18 (197)	.001	.44***	.13	.31*

*p < .05.
**p < .01.
***p < .001.
†p < .10.

Table 10.5. Fateful Loss

	MAG Score
Child died	1036
Spouse died	821
Unable to get treatment for an illness or injury	611
Lost a home through fire, flood or other disaster	580
Found out that cannot have children	518
Family member other than spouse or child died	463
Miscarriage or stillbirth	457
Close friend died	457
Took a cut in wage or salary without a demotion	396
Assaulted	383
Did not get an expected wage or salary increase	343
Laid off	325

graphic variables statistically controlled, we have found so far, as Table 10.4 shows, the following differences:

1. The networks of the schizophrenic disorder cases are significantly smaller, less extensive and have fewer instrumental supporters than either the depressives or the controls. The differences are especially marked for repeat episode schizophrenic disorder cases.

2. Both the schizophrenic disorder and depressive cases have fewer social companions than the controls.

3. The networks of the depressives are less dense and more multiplex than those of either the schizophrenic disorder cases or the controls.

Table 10.6. Objective Loss in Social Network

	MAG Score
Divorce	633
Went to jail	566
Marital infidelity	558
Married couple separated	515
Retired	461
Stopped working (not retirement) for an extended period	456
Fired	407
Broke up with a friend	328
Person moved out of the household	333
Engagement was broken	309

Some of these differences are undoubtedly a function of the personal characteristics and behaviors of the cases. We are conducting further analyses to see which network characteristics accompany differences in social and cultural variables and are, hence, more likely to be environmental in origin.

One of our purposes in eliciting the social networks of our respondents was to investigate how the networks were activated, for good or ill, when the respondents experienced stressful events. To this end we asked respondents which persons from the network and from outside the network were involved in some of the recent stressful events they experienced and the major changes associated with these events. Of those involved, we then asked which ones (up to three) were most involved. For each of the most involved others, the subject was asked a series of questions that enabled us to construct further indices of whether the other actually was perceived as helping or hindering in three ways: by evaluating the event and changes the same way the subject did ("view concordance"), by providing instrumental support, and by providing emotional support.

The core questions that form the basis of these measures are asked for each of several events, starting with the largest negative event the respondent experienced. These responses are combined across each person's set of events, and the resulting support score can be interpreted as a probability of having a particular type of support. The mean number of events on which change-related support scores are calculated is three for controls, depressives, and schizophrenic disorder cases (ranging from one to eleven). For event-related support scores, the mean number of events is three for the control group, and four for the two patient groups.

Controlling for the previously described demographic variables, Table 10.4 shows:

1. The amount of perceived instrumental support does not differ significantly among the patient groups and the control group.

2. Emotional support for event-precipitated change is significantly lower among depressives compared with well controls.

3. Emotional support for event occurrence itself is significantly lower among both patient groups compared with well controls.

4. View concordance regarding event-precipitated change is lower (at the .10 level) in both patient groups compared with controls.

5. View concordance regarding the event itself is significantly lower in both patient groups compared with controls.

6. There are no significant differences between the two patient groups on any of the five measures of support.

Overall, these findings are consistent with our expectations that lower levels of perceived social support would be found among patient groups compared with controls. Although the strongest differences appear for support measures focused on the occurrence of the event as compared to those focused on event-precipitated change, some of this difference is due to greater statistical power associated with tests on variables in the former category. We were surprised at the lack of group differences on our measure of instrumental support, and this result requires further examination. If it holds up it indicates that the lack of getting actual help is a less important risk factor for severe psychopathology than the lack of getting emotional support and having views about events that are disparate from those in the social network.

Personality Variables

Under the general heading of personal dispositions as the third major component of life stress processes, we are investigating a set of variations in normal personality ranging from attitudes of mastery at one pole to helplessness at the other. This basic dimension can be seen to have interesting variants at each extreme, some of them leading to poor coping in certain stress situations. At the mastery end, for example, one can put extreme Type A personality reactions that may well lead to problems in coping (Matthews & Glass, 1983). At the helplessness end, we might consider denial that, under some circumstances, could be functional (Lazarus, 1983). And it is interesting to consider how closely attitudes of mastery appear to coincide with masculine personality characteristics and helplessness with feminine ones as measured, for example, by the Spence-Helmreich scales (1978). This particular variant of the mastery–helplessness dimension may have implications for the development of depression, a disorder that is far more prevalent in women than in men.

With this introduction, our choice of some of the personality measures listed in Table 10.4 should come as no surprise. They include the measures of locus of control developed by Rotter (1966) and Levenson (1973), Jenkins's measure of Type A behavior (Jenkins *et al.*, 1967) and a set of items that we are calling "Mastery Orientation" from Spence-Helmreich (1978). They also include a scale of denial that we constructed from various sources such as Crowne and Marlowe (1960) and Epstein and Fenz (1967). Controlling the same demographic variables as in the analyses of recent life events and network characteristics, we have found some strong differences, as Table 10.4 shows:

1. On the Rotter (1966) and Levenson (1973) scales, both depressive and schizophrenic disorder cases show greater external locus-of-control orientation than do controls.

2. Depressives score higher than both schizophrenic disorder cases and controls on items from Jenkins *et al.* (1967) that measure the Type A behavior pattern.

3. Both depressives and schizophrenic disorder cases endorse fewer positive items that we have selected from the Spence–Helmreich masculinity scale to indicate an orientation characterized by mastery.

4. Especially the depressives but also the schizophrenic disorder cases show more denial than controls on a subset of Crowne–Marlowe (1960) negative items and nonsymptomlike items from Epstein–Fenz (1967) that we selected to measure this variable.

5. Depressives endorse more negative femininity items on the Spence–Helmreich masculinity–femininity measure than schizophrenic disorder cases or controls. Examples of these negative femininity items are "very emotional," "highly needful of others' approval," "feelings easily hurt," and "cries very easily." Much more than the other personality scales, however, this one contains items that could be symptoms of depressive disorder.

While the differences between the case and comparison groups shown in Table 10.4 are of interest, one cannot tell from the analysis of covariance if the effects of the risk-factor variables are redundant; that is, if the same cases are causing several variables to be significant. We therefore wanted to examine whether certain of the life events measures, the more objective network variables (excluding the less antecedent measures of perceived support), and the personality variables (excluding the symptomlike scale of negative feminine characteristics), had distinct effects. In Table 10.7, accordingly, results are shown from a set of logistic regression analyses that tested whether each risk factor contributed an effect above and beyond the effects of the other risk factors. Two separate sets of analyses were done, one comparing the depression group to the noncases, and the other comparing the schizophrenic disorder group to the noncases. Stepwise logistic regression (Harrell, 1980) was performed with the log-odds of the grouping variable regressed on the control and risk-factor variables that were not significant, holding the other variables constant; the control variables were kept in the equations because of their importance for ruling out spuriousness.

Table 10.7 shows that a number of risk factors seem to contribute distinct effects for depression. We found to our gratification that, while total number of events in the past year made no difference, elements of the "pathogenic triad" (B. P. Dohrenwend, 1979) tended to be positively associated with depression: number of fateful loss events to the respondent, number of physical illness events to the respondent, and number of nonfateful losses to respondent's social network. Among the social network variables, several were associated in a direction that is consistent with a lack of protective factors: network extensiveness, number of social contacts, and density. An increase in the percent multiplexity of network ties was positively associated with depression, as was the overall network size (not including household members). This result on network size appears puzzling until we

Table 10.7. Logistic Regression Coefficients (Standard Errors) for Risk-Factor Variables with Independent Effects on Caseness†

	Outcome	
Risk-Factor Variable	Major Depression (N = 105) vs. Noncase (N = 186)	Schizophrenic Disorders (N = 48) vs. Noncase (N = 186)
Number of fateful loss events	.52** (.19)	.46 (.55)
Number of physical illness events	.87+ (.54)	1.25 (.94)
Number of network loss events	.59* (.29)	1.35* (.60)
Size social network	.31*** (.08)	-.40++ (.24)
Number of social companions	-.43*** (.11)	-.49* (.22)
Extensiveness of network	-.44** (.16)	.12 (.29)
Social network multiplexity	.04** (.01)	-.01 (.02)
Social network density	-1.88** (.83)	-2.18** (1.30)
Type A personality	3.89*** (1.24)	.11 (2.60)
Mastery	-1.94*** (.43)	-2.06** (.79)
Denial	3.22 (1.57)	1.57 (2.33)
Locus of control (Rotter)	2.00 (1.31)	6.70** (2.65)

†Maximum-likelihood estimates of logistic regression parameters in models that included terms for sex, education, ethnic group, income, paternal occupational prestige, marital status, and ethnic by paternal prestige interactions.
+$p < .11$.
++$p < .10$.
*$p < .05$.
**$p < .01$.
***$p < .001$.

note that it is a conditional effect, with number of social contacts held constant; only if more than a quarter of the social network are not social companions is the overall size of the network likely to be related to depression. Among the personal disposition variables that we considered as risk factors, our measures of Type A and Denial were positively associated with depression, while our measure of Mastery was negatively associated.

Fewer risk factors for schizophrenic disorder emerged from the logistic regression analysis than for depression—partly because, with a smaller *n* than for the depressives, there is less power to detect them. The event measure, number of network loss events, was significant, as were three social network variables, total size of network, number of social companions, and density of network. All of these differences show the schizophrenic cases at a disadvantage. Of the personal disposition measures, two were associated with schizophrenic disorder: Mastery was negatively associated and external locus of control was positively associated. The question yet to be answered is whether these patterns of results for major depression and schizophrenic disorder are truly different. In order to statistically test the specificity of the effects we will have to employ multinomial logistic regression (Levin & Shrout, 1981) rather than the binomial logistic regression model available in SAS (Harrell, 1983) and BMDP (Dixon & Brown, 1979). The multinomial model takes into account the fact that the same control group is used in both case-control comparisons.

RESULTS OF INITIAL ANALYSES: A CATEGORICAL VARIABLE

The second analysis that we will report focuses on a categorical rather than continuous risk-factor variable. It is offered diffidently since it is still more preliminary than the previous analyses of continuous variables. In it we utilize self-reports of the respondents about the psychiatric problems of their first-degree relatives rather than direct interviews with the relatives themselves. (The questions we asked are a far cry from a diagnostic interview.)

Each respondent was asked whether each of his or her first-degree relatives had ever had "serious mental or emotional problems such as problems with depression, suicide attempts, odd or violent behavior, or difficulties with drugs or alcohol." If answering in the affirmative, the respondent was further asked to name "the specific mental or emotional problem(s) that the relative(s) had," and whether the relative was "ever in a hospital" for the specific problem. If outpatient treatment was mentioned, this was also recorded.

A 7-point scale was constructed to represent a measure of certainty regarding the reports of a positive family history. The scale consisted of two dimensions: diagnostic specificity and treatment history. Four different degrees of diagnostic specificity were distinguished: 1) problem behavior not necessarily indicative of a mental disorder; 2) unspecified psychiatric problem or psychiatric problem mentioned only in general terms; 3) specific psychiatric problem or syndrome; and 4) specific psychiatric diagnosis. Psychiatric treatment was either mentioned or not mentioned. These two dimensions were combined as indicated in Table 10.8.

According to this scale, a score of *1* indicates a minimal suggestion of the presence of a mental disorder, *2* denotes a low degree of certainty regarding a mental disorder in a family member, and so on, up to a score of *7*, indicating the highest degree of certainty. A rating of *0* stands for no history reported, or a determination that a disease or problem was nonpsychiatric. Based on the assumption that a precise psychiatric diagnosis usually indicates contact with a mental health professional, this category is rated higher than a psychiatric syndrome for which treatment was specifically mentioned.

Let us illustrate how the ratings were made with some actual examples of each: "A speech problem due to deafness" was an example of a rating of *0*. "He's keeping everything in" was an example of *1*. "A nervous condition or breakdown" was a *2*. "Psychotic behavior" or "depression" was a *3*. "She had a nervous breakdown when she had her first baby and has been in and out of a hospital often since then" was a *4*. "She had depression and shock treatment" was a *5*. "Chronic paranoid schizophrenia" was a *6*. "Schizophrenia, she was committed" was a *7*. Approximately five examples of each rating were identified and provided to two experienced psychiatrist raters for a test of the reliability of the ratings.

Using this scale, the two psychiatrists independently rated 393 verbatim reports of mental illness in first-degree relatives. A kappa of .71 was achieved; there were 89 disagreements. A consensus rating was made for all family history reports for which there had been a disagreement.

For a preliminary analysis of the family history variable, a dichotomous rating of family history present or absent was made, dividing the scale between a rating of 2 or less versus 3 or more. This means that unspecified psychiatric problems or psychiatric problems described only in general terms

Table 10.8. Certainty of Family History Scale

Diagnostic Specificity	Psychiatric Treatment	
	Not Mentioned	Mentioned
Problem behavior not necessarily indicative of a mental disorder	1	1
Unspecified psychiatric problem	2	4
Specific psychiatric problem	3	5
Specific psychiatric diagnosis	6	7

were not considered evidence of a positive family history, unless accompanied by mention of treatment for the problems. Both patient and community samples were examined for presence of family history of mental disorder. The patient sample was divided into the diagnostic groups of major depression ($N = 98$) and schizophrenia ($N = 64$) and the community sample was divided into major depression ($N = 24$), and noncases ($N = 197$).

The results indicate that for individuals with major depression the rate of positive family history (i.e., one or more first-degree relatives with a score of 3 or more) is high and strikingly consistent between patient and community case samples. The percentage of patients with major depression who received a positive rating was 62.2%, and 62.5% of the community major depressives were rated family history positive. In the schizophrenic disorder group, 53.1% had positive family histories. These are in contrast to a family history positive rate of 25.9% among the community wells. These differences remain large and statistically significant with controls on the demographic variables that we held constant in the preceding analyses.

CONCLUSIONS

These initial results do not demonstrate but are consistent with the following picture of risk factors for episodes of major depression and episodes of schizophrenic disorder. This picture is one of an excess of recent environmentally induced stress impinging on persons with problematic personality characteristics and possible genetic vulnerability in the context of relatively weak networks of potential social support. Thus, prior to the episode of disorder for which they were chosen, both groups of cases had an excess of recent, nonfateful negative events that were likely to disrupt usual social supports and an excess of physical illness or injury; both groups had weaker social networks than the well controls and perceived less emotional support from these networks when confronted by stressful events; both groups showed higher external locus of control, scored higher on a scale of denial, and lower on a scale measuring an attitude of mastery; in addition, individuals in both case groups were far more likely than the well controls to have one or more first-degree relatives with a probable psychiatric disorder.

While the two groups of cases were similar on the above factors, they also differed markedly from each other on several others. There was an excess of recent fateful loss events for the major depressives but not for the schizophrenic disorder cases; the networks of the schizophrenic disorder cases were less extensive and showed fewer instrumental supporters than did the networks of the major depressives as well as the controls; the major depressives were more likely to show Type A behavior than the schizophrenic disorder group or the controls; and it was the major depressives who tended to score high on a scale of negative feminine characteristics by contrast with both the schizophrenic disorder group and the well controls.

We are in the process of examining a number of additional potential risk factors including childhood bereavement, the noisome characteristics of occupations, and domestic arrangements. We expect to have some sharp contrasts to report on these factors as well.

We think that these sets of differences reported so far are vivid and interesting. As yet, however, they do not demonstrate the importance of environmentally induced stress in the causation of these episodes of disorder. There are a number of additional tests that will have to be passed before any such claim can plausibly be made on the basis of a retrospective case-control study of this kind. We will need to investigate much further how firm the social and psychological variables that differentiate the groups are when viewed as possible causal risk factors.

For example, it may be that some of these possible risk factors are state dependent; that is, are themselves a function of the episode of psychopathology for which the cases were selected rather than antecedents to the episode. This is especially important with regard to the personality variables. To test the matter further, it will be necessary to follow up cases into episode-free periods to see whether the personality differences persist or are reversed in the absence of an episode (cf. Hirschfeld *et al.*, 1983).

Of all the factors we have investigated, fateful-loss events that are dated with reference to the episodes of disorder and, as a rule, occur outside the control of the respondent, have the firmest claim to causal status. Even with them, however, there are ambiguities. The main reason is that a straight checklist approach contains a large amount of error. This is reduced when the checklist is administered, as in the present study, in an interview. We have found, nevertheless, that the error is still substantial. For example, a respondent may say that he or she is "laid off" when, on more intensive inquiry, it turns out that "laid off" was a euphemism for being fired. Accordingly, we made provisions in the interview to obtain additional information about each event and the circumstances under which it occurred. We also secured a variety of appraisals of the events by the respondents that should give us an indication of whether the respondents tend to distort their perceptions and reactions to the events on the basis of their personality characteristics, including prior episodes of disorder or dispositions to disorder. With regard to networks, we plan to examine the extent to which different network variables are a function of environmental differences related to demographic factors such as gender, class, and ethnic background and which are functions of dispositional variables, including prior episodes of disorder.

Once we have learned more about these variables from tests of their firmness as risk factors of the kinds just described, we will use them in investigations of five alternative theoretical models of how the three sets of components of the life stress process (recent events, the ongoing situation, and personal dispositions) are related to each other and to episodes of major depression and schizophrenic disorder. The five models were formulated on the basis of analysis of the literature by the late Barbara Dohrenwend and by Bruce Dohrenwend and have been set forth in several publications with Barbara Dohrenwend as senior author (e.g., Dohrenwend & Dohrenwend, 1981). They are summarized in Figure 10.1.

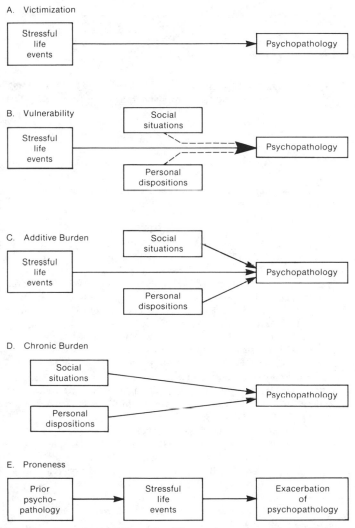

Figure 10.1. Five hypotheses about the life stress process. (From Dohrenwend & Dohrenwend, 1981.)

These models are not mutually exclusive. They include the possibility, especially in the model that we call "proneness," that the directions of the relationships among the variables we have been investigating are quite different from the ones we prefer. Our preference-based prediction, however, is that the models shown in Figure 10.1 will evolve on the basis of results from this and other studies into a more complex set in which environmentally induced stress will be accurately portrayed as a prominent causal factor in these types of disorders.

ACKNOWLEDGMENTS

This work has been supported by U.S. National Institute of Mental Health Grant MH36208 and U.S. National Institute of Mental Health Research Scientist Award K05-MH14663.

REFERENCES

Brown, G. W. (1974). Meaning, measurement, and stressful life events. In B. S. Dohrenwend & B. P. Dohrenwend (Eds.), *Stressful life events: Their nature and effects* (pp. 217–243). New York: Wiley.

Brown, G. W., & Birley, J. L. T. (1968). Crises and life changes and the onset of schizophrenia. *Journal of Health and Social Behavior, 9,* 203–214.

Brown, G. W., & Harris, T. (1978). *Social origins of depression: A study of psychiatric disorder in women.* New York: The Free Press.

Brown, G. W., Harris, T. O., & Peto, J. (1973). Life events and psychiatric disorders. Part 2: Nature of the causal link. *Psychological Medicine, 3,* 159–176.

Cooper, B., & Sylph, J. (1973). Life events and the onset of neurotic illness: An investigation in general practice. *Psychological Medicine, 3,* 421–435.

Crowne, D. P., & Marlowe, D. (1960). A new scale of social desirability independent of psychopathology. *Journal of Consulting Psychology, 24,* 349–354.

Dixon, W. J., & Brown, M. B. (1979). The BMOP biomedical computer programs—P series. Berkeley: University of California Press.

Dohrenwend, B. P. (1979). Stressful life events and psychopathology: Some issues of theory and method. In J. F. Barrett, R. M. Rose, & G. L. Klerman (Eds.), *Stress and mental disorder* (pp. 1–16). New York: Raven Press.

Dohrenwend, B. P., Shrout, P. E., Egri, G., & Mendelsohn, F. S. (1980). Measures of nonspecific psychological distress and other dimensions of psychopathology in the general population. *Archives of General Psychiatry, 37,* 1229–1236.

Dohrenwend, B. S., & Dohrenwend, B. P. (1981). Life stress and psychopathology. In D. A. Regier & G. Allen (Eds.), *Risk factor research in the major mental disorders.* National Institute of Mental Health (DDHS Publication No. ADM 81-1068, pp. 131–141). Washington, DC: U.S. Government Printing Office.

Dohrenwend, B. S., Dohrenwend, B. P., Dodson, M., & Shrout, P. E. (1984). Symptoms, hassles, social supports, and life events: Problem of confounded measures. *Journal of Abnormal Psychology, 93*(2), 222–230.

Dohrenwend, B. S., Krasnoff, L., Askenasy, A. R., & Dohrenwend, B. P. (1978). Exemplification of a method for scaling life events: The PERI life events scale. *Journal of Health and Social Behavior, 19*, 205–229.

Epstein, S., & Fenz, W. D. (1967). The detection of areas of emotional stress through variations in perceptual threshold and physiological arousal. *Journal of Experimental Research on Personality, 2*, 191–199.

Fischer, C. S., Jackson, R. M., Stueve, C. A., Gerson, K., Jones, L. M., & Baldassare, M. (1977). *Networks and places: Social relations in the urban setting.* New York: The Free Press.

Harrell, F. (1983). *SAS-supplemental library user's guide.* Cary, N.C.: SAS Institute.

Hirschfeld, R. M. A., Klerman, G. L., Clayton, P. J., Keller, M. B., McDonald-Scott, P., & Larkin, B. H. (1983). Assessing personality: Effects of the depressive state on trait measurement. *American Journal of Psychiatry, 140*, 695–699.

Hudgens, R. W. (1974). Personal catastrophe and depression: A consideration of the subject with respect to medically ill adolescents, and a requiem for retrospective life event studies. In B. S. Dohrenwend & B. P. Dohrenwend (Eds.), *Stressful life events: Their nature and effects* (pp. 110–134). New York: Wiley.

Jacobs, S., & Myers, J. (1976). Recent life events and schizophrenic psychosis: A controlled study. *Journal of Nervous and Mental Disease, 162*, 75–87.

Jenkins, C. D., Rosenman, R. H., & Friedman, M. (1967). Development of an objective psychological test for the determination of the coronary-prone behavior pattern. *Journal of Chronic Diseases, 20*, 371–379.

Kanner, A. D., Coyne, J. C., Schaefer, C., & Lazarus, R. S. (1981). Comparison of two modes of stress measurement: Daily hassles and uplifts versus major life events. *Journal of Behavioral Medicine, 4*, 1–39.

Lazarus, R. S. (1983). The costs and benefits of denial. In B. S. Dohrenwend & B. P. Dohrenwend (Eds.), *Stressful life events and their contexts* (pp. 131–156). New Brunswick, NJ: Rutgers University Press. (Original work published 1981 by Neale Watson).

Leff, J. P., Hirsch, S. R., Gaind, R., Rohde, P. D., & Stevens, B. S. (1973). Life events and maintenance therapy in schizophrenic relapse. *British Journal of Psychiatry, 123*, 659–660.

Levenson, H. (1973). Multidimensional locus of control in psychiatric patients. *Journal of Consulting and Clinical Psychology, 41*, 397–404.

Levin, B., & Shrout, P. E. (1981). On extending Bock's model of logistic regression. *Communications in Statistics, A10*, 125–147.

Link, B., & Dohrenwend, B. P. (1980). Formulation of hypotheses about the true prevalence of demoralization in the United States. In B. P. Dohrenwend, B. S. Dohrenwend, M. S. Gould, B. Link, R. Neugebauer, & R. Wunsch-Hitzig (Eds.), *Mental illness in the United States: Epidemiological estimates.* New York: Praeger.

Lloyd, C. (1980). Life events and depressive disorder reviewed: II. Events as precipitating factors. *Archives of General Psychiatry, 37*, 541–548.

Matthews, K. A., & Glass, D. C. (1983). Type A behavior, stressful life events, and coronary heart disease. In B. S. Dohrenwend & B. P. Dohrenwend (Eds.), *Stressful life events and their contexts* (pp. 167–177). New Brunswick, NJ: Rutgers University Press. (Original work published 1981 by Neale Watson).

Myers, J., Lindenthal, J. J., & Pepper, M. P. (1974). Social class, life events and psychiatric symptoms: A longitudinal study. In B. S. Dohrenwend & B. P. Dohrenwend (Eds.), *Stressful life events: Their nature and effects* (pp. 191–205). New York: Wiley.

Paykel, E. S. (1974). Life stress and psychiatric disorder: Applications of the clinical approach. In B. S. Dohrenwend & B. P. Dohrenwend (Eds.), *Stressful life events: Their nature and effects* (pp. 119–134). New York: Wiley.

Pearlin, L. I., & Lieberman, M. A. (1979). Social sources of emotional distress. In R. G. Simmons (Ed.), *Research in community and mental health* (Vol. I) (pp. 217–247). Greenwich, CT: JAI Press.

Robins, L., Helzer, J. E., Croughan, J., & Ratcliff, R. S. (1981). National Institute of Mental Health Diagnostic Interview Schedule: Its history, characteristics and validity. *Archives of General Psychiatry, 38*, 381–389.

Rogler, L. H., & Hollingshead, A. B. (1965). *Trapped: Families and schizophrenia.* New York: Wiley.

Rotter, J. B. (1966). Generalized expectancies of internal versus external control of reinforcement. *Psychological Monographs, 80* (609).

Shrout, P. E., Dohrenwend, B. P., & Levav, I. (in press). A discriminant rule for screening cases of diverse diagnostic types: Preliminary Results. Journal of Consulting and Clinical Psychology.

Skodol, A. E., Williams, J. B. W., Spitzer, R. L., Gibbon, M., & Kass, F. (1984). Identifying common errors in the use of DSM-III through diagnostic supervision. *Hospital and Community Psychiatry, 35*, 251–255.

Spence, J. T., & Helmreich, R. (1978). *Masculinity and femininity: Their psychological dimensions, correlates and antecedents.* Austin: University of Texas Press.

Spitzer, R. L., Skodol, A. E., Williams, J. B. W., Gibbon, M., & Kass, F. (1982). Supervising intake diagnosis: A psychiatric "Rashomon." *Archives of General Psychiatry, 136*, 815–817.

Wing, J. K., Mann, S. A., Leff, J. P., & Nixon, M. M. (1978). The concept of a 'case' in psychiatric population surveys. *Psychological Medicine, 8*, 203–217.

DISCUSSION

C. R. Cloninger: Could you comment on the rationale for your choice of focus on the 1-year life event period as opposed to a shorter or longer period?

Dohrenwend: We picked a 1-year period because that is about as far back as you can go without getting into even more severe problems of recall than you face with a 1-year period. We don't get a great fall-off in event reporting in, say, a 6-month period as compared with a 12-month period. The findings of Brown and his colleagues in their study of depression suggest that you would miss important information by taking a shorter period.

Cloninger: In some of your analyses, have you tried making the distinction of 6 months versus 1 year?

Dohrenwend: Not yet, but we shall, and we have included some additional checks on the reliability.

Robert Rose: Did you apply to some of these analyses your strategy for clarifying the differences among life events, separating those that were perhaps caused by the clinical phenomenon from those independent of it?

Dohrenwend: Yes, that is central.

Rose: In your listing of fateful losses and nonfateful loss events, not all of these are beyond control. Did you break these out and do a separate analysis on them?

Dohrenwend: Most of those that we call "fateful" are outside the control of the subject. Some portion of those that we call "nonfateful" will be within the control of the subject, and some portion will be outside his or her control. We won't know which until we analyze our quantitative data on that group of events, but some of the events are undoubtedly brought on by the subjects.

Rose: In terms of the fateful versus nonfateful, or within the control concept, is that isomorphic or the same to exclude those that might be part of the illness process itself?

Dohrenwend: I don't think you exclude the events that are possibly confounded with the illness process, but rather you analyze them with that possibility explicitly stated; for example, they could be tremendously important in testing a proneness model. Moreover, we would not interpret nonfateful events as having an environmental impact if they are a function of dispositional variables that involve normal personality variations rather than a prior psychiatric disorder or its insidious onset. So, the problem is not to exclude nonfateful events. The problem is to learn what they are and analyze them appropriately.

Ann Pulver: You mentioned that you used a modified DIS. Could you comment on how it was modified, and why?

Dohrenwend: I would like Dr. Williams to answer that, because she did the modification.

Janet Williams: What we needed was a clinician-administered interview to make DSM-III diagnoses, and the DIS was the only interview available at the time that made DSM-III diagnoses at all. I modified it to include the specific criteria for the DSM-III diagnosis of dysthymic disorder in more detail than is currently in the DIS, and I also included the criteria for melancholia.

We then trained the clinicians to follow the general structure of the DIS, including the probe flowchart, but encouraged them, particularly in the psychosis section and wherever else symptoms were acknowledged, to add any clinical questions that might help clarify the presence or absence of a symptom. Finally, the diagnoses were actually made by the clinicians rather than by a computer algorithm.

Dohrenwend: There was also one other modification. We needed to be able to date episodes—to date their onset—and there was no provision in the regular DIS for doing that. This study depends on the dating of onset, which is a very difficult thing to do. So we had to introduce modifications for that purpose as well.

Nan Lin: In your scoring of the nonfateful life events, did you use the magnitude of the scores or just the number of the events?

Dohrenwend: We summed the unit scores, and the means are the averages of the unit scores—not the weighted scores, just the unit scores.

Lin: Two of the social network and social support variables are positively associated with depression. Do you have any speculations as to why?

Dohrenwend: I will let Dr. Shrout answer that one.

Shrout: Those two positive associations are from the data in Table 10.7. This is easier to explain, since the unconditional results in Table 10.4 are consistent with the conditional results in Table 10.7. The multiplexity variable was created by John Martin at Columbia to refer to the percentage of the network members that fulfill more than one support function. A low value means that many members of the network were named in response to one and only one support question. Not surprisingly, the well group has a lower value than the depressed group. The cases apparently have fewer supporters, but these help in more than one way.

It is more surprising that size of network has a positive association with depression in Table 10.7, especially when the means in Table 10.4 suggest that noncases have larger networks than cases with depression. But the coefficients in Table 10.7 are interpreted as partial regression coefficients. The effects of all the other variables in the equation are held constant when the coefficient for network size is estimated. Since the equation includes the variable "number of social companions," the conditional interpretation of network size is "number in network who are nonsocial companions." We speculate that the cases with depression may have more noncompanions in their network as a result of help-seeking, and we are attempting to verify this speculation using qualitative information collected during the interview.

Seymour Kety: The large number of factors that differentiate depressed or schizophrenic individuals from well individuals is very impressive, but one is also impressed with the rather few factors that differentiate the schizophrenic from the affective disorders. I wonder to what extent that is the result of your having included in the schizophrenic group the schizophreniform psychosis, which, from much of the evidence all the way back to Bleuler, does not really seem to be part of the schizophrenic syndrome. Have you had occasion to separate the schizophreniforms, and perhaps the schizoaffectives, many of which may be more truly affective disorders, and then deal with the DSM-III schizophrenics?

Dohrenwend: We have not done that yet. We plan to do it, but I would like to mention that even though we have not done it, there are some striking contrasts in the factors that differentiate the "schizophrenic disorder" group and those that differentiate the depressives from the controls. The role of fateful loss for the depressives is much greater than for the schizophrenics. The Type A behavior pattern characterizes the depressives but not the schizophrenic disorder group. The networks of the schizophrenic disorder group differ from those of the depressives as well as from the well controls. These contrasts between the depressives and the schizophrenic disorder group will be investigated further in analyses of subtypes both within the schizophrenic disorder group and within the group of major depressives. The results reported here are from our initial analyses. I am glad you are calling for analyses of the subtypes of disorder; they are necessary and will be done.

Shep Kellam: In the research of Dr. Dohrenwend and his colleagues, the idea of putting together models that include internal environmental (psychological and biological predispositions) as well as external environmental conditions is elegant. What about the possibility of an additional potential model that would begin with internal predispositions which then, under certain social situations, lead to psychopathology? This model moves the internal predisposition to an exogenous earlier role, and it ties temperament measures in childhood to early behavioral response measures in childhood that are not necessarily pathology per se but are predispositions to later pathology.

Dohrenwend: One possibility is that what you are mentioning could be accommodated in the existing models through an expansion of the personal dispositions component. They would be handled similarly to our handling of remote events, such as childhood bereavement. We think loss of a parent during childhood is a dispositional variable for adults because it is no longer disruptive of usual activities; if it has an effect, it is through current dispositional variables, especially personality characteristics. So we measure childhood bereavement, even though we do not know what consequences of the early experience have been incorporated into the personality. It would be harder to measure childhood temperament retrospectively and get its reflection in a current disposition.

Kellam: The studies of Norman Watts, Felton Earls, Lee Robins, and ourselves all find early aggression leading to long-term outcomes, mediated through social situations. The model I am suggesting is that these early behavioral responses may derive from genetics or learning or both, but they are not necessarily themselves psychopathology. They are behavioral predispositions. For example, if you take a schizophreniform symptom, such as shyness, do those people have a vulnerability in social situations to a later disorder?

Dohrenwend: In a comprehensive model they should be added in.

Kellam: It may be that those earlier behavioral and temperament variables, rather than the later disorder, are carried by the genetic structures.

Dohrenwend: They should be added into the theoretical model, whether one can measure them or not. I have others that I list under "personal disposition" that we haven't included in the present study. It would be nice if we had I.Q. It should be there. It would be very nice if we had reliable measures of physical appearance and stamina. They should be there, and so should those that you mentioned. It is well to be reminded that we have not measured all that we should be measuring.

METHODOLOGIC ISSUES FOR EPIDEMIOLOGIC STUDIES: THE PROBLEM OF CASE IDENTIFICATION

11

Presidential Address

Case Identification for Category Validation:
The Challenge of Disorder-Specific Assessment

JAMES BARRETT
Dartmouth Medical School

Case identification is a central issue for epidemiologic research. In the past decade substantial progress has been made in developing reliable instruments to assess psychopathology. The Diagnostic Interview Schedule (DIS) (Robins, Helzer, Croughan, & Ratcliff, 1981), The Schedule for Affective Disorders and Schizophrenia (SADS) (Endicott & Spitzer, 1978), and The Psychiatric State Evaluation (PSE) (Wing, Cooper, & Sartorius, 1974) are representative of these modern assessment methods. All have been used as case identification instruments in large-scale population surveys. In such studies the focus is on the individual and on the characteristics of groups of individuals who have particular disorders.

Case identification, when the focus of study is the disorder (not the individual), is a related but separate topic, one of increasing importance for psychiatry in the 1980s. Examples would include the validation work necessary to establish the usefulness of the proposed categories under DSM-III, treatment response studies, or studies on naturalistic outcome. I will focus here on case identification issues when a goal is "category validation"—the validation of individual proposed diagnostic categories.

Historically, going back to Kraepelin and to Meyer, course of illness has been a principal means of validation for psychiatric disorders. Indeed, for many disorders it was the only method of validation. Robins and Guze (1970), in a discussion of validation issues for psychiatric disorders, emphasized the importance of a clear, describable clinical picture coupled with a predictable course over time as the major components which establish that a given proposed disorder is a valid entity. I will begin my remarks by presenting data from a recent longitudinal study with which I was involved, a study that sought to obtain natural history data on outcome for patients with outpatient disorders, primarily depressive or anxiety disorders (Barrett, 1981,

1984). A principal focus of this study was validation of the disorders using course as a criterion. The results from that study will serve as a point of departure for addressing issues of case identification for category validation.

A FOLLOW-UP STUDY OF NEUROTIC DISORDERS: OBSERVATIONS RELEVANT TO DIAGNOSTIC CATEGORIZATION

Description of the Study

Individuals with outpatient psychiatric disorders were recruited using the "symptomatic volunteer" method. That method involves advertising, usually in newspapers or on the radio, for subjects with particular symptoms. Those who reply are then screened further to identify properly those who truly have the disorder in question, using whatever criteria the investigators have decided to use. Criteria for acceptance into this study was presence of a depressive or anxiety disorder according to Research Diagnostic Criteria (RDC) (Spitzer, Endicott, & Robins, 1975). We examined eight RDC categories, but I will present data for only depressive disorder categories. These categories are Major Depressive Disorder, subsequently abbreviated as major depression (MD); Episodic Minor Depressive Disorder (ED); and Chronic Intermittent Minor Depressive Disorder, which I will shorten to chronic depression (CD). The fourth disorder is Labile Personality Disorder (LP), a condition that often presents with dramatic depressive symptomatology, and so it was included as a depressive disorder. Conceptually the first two disorders, major depression and episodic minor depression, are episodic, while the other two, chronic depression and labile personality, are long-standing, or character, disorders.

Individuals who responded to the newspaper advertisement underwent further screening, eventually receiving a clinical interview designed to establish the presence or absence of the RDC disorders under examination. The study was begun in 1976, before the structured interview for making RDC diagnoses, the SADS, was available for general use. However, in the years just before beginning this work, I had been one of the interviewers in the developmental work for the SADS. I thus was intimately familiar with the procedures and questions of that instrument, and I taught a similar methodology to my clinical interviewers. The interview included questions about particular symptoms, using SADS probes when appropriate. The probe questions were followed by other clarifying questions, usually open-ended. The interviewers were expected to know the concept of the symptom each probe question was after and were to ask whatever additional questions were necessary to establish to their satisfaction whether or not that symptom was truly there.

I would describe this case identification method as a semistructured interview to establish particular RDC diagnoses, carried out on subjects preselected by self-report instruments to have significant depressive symptoms, and conducted by specially trained interviewers with clinical experience in diagnosis and psychopathology. The study design called for four 6-month follow-up assessments which provided follow-up data over a 2-year period. At each 6-month follow-up examination, a similar semistructured interview was used to establish if any of the targeted RDC disorders were present, then or during the past 6 months (Barrett, 1984). I personally conducted many of these follow-up interviews, and my remarks in this address are based on that experience as well as on the data that emerged.

Diagnostic Outcome of Subjects Grouped by the Initial Diagnostic Categorization

I first want to examine course—the diagnostic outcome at 2 years—of subjects grouped by their initial diagnostic categorization. Figures 11.1–11.4 present a summary of these data. In the figures the initial RDC assessment, the "principal" diagnosis assigned to the patient at screen, is on the left, while the right side of the figure shows what happened to subjects over the 2-year period, how each would best be categorized diagnostically when information from the five points in time was considered.

Episodic Minor Depressive Disorder. Figure 11.1 presents this information for those initially diagnosed as Episodic Minor Depressive Disorder. In this group of subjects, when one examined course over time a subset of individuals, a large group of subjects who emerged quite clearly, remained true to the original episodic minor depression conceptualization. These were individuals who generally had been functioning well prior to the onset of their depressive symptoms. There was a reasonably clear time of onset for their symptoms, and, when in an episode, the subjects easily described themselves as being different from their usual selves. The duration of symptoms varied,

Figure 11.1. Episodic minor depressive disorder: 2-year outcome.

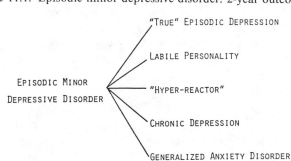

but typically these subjects continued to experience symptoms for weeks or months, up to several months. They improved, usually gradually, over several weeks' time, although in some cases the improvement was quite dramatic and took place in a few days. Improvement was characterized by returning to their usual selves and to a level of successful functioning. Their condition did not change into anything else, at least during the 2-year observation period.

There was another group of subjects in this group initially diagnosed as episodic minor depression who had quite a different course. They were "up and down" throughout the 2 years, presenting themselves as having periods when they were "very depressed" and other periods when they felt perfectly well. Their "usual selves," although including periods when they seemed to function adequately, were characterized by many ups and downs, often presented in a somewhat dramatic fashion. It was also characteristic that at subsequent visits—for example, the final visit two years later—when they were asked to recall the symptoms which brought them into the study, they had trouble remembering them. It was as if their lives were full of periods when they were "depressed," alternating with periods when they were not. There was nothing particularly distinctive about each of these periods, with the most recent one being what was remembered with any detail. This was in striking contrast with the first group, who could clearly describe what they had experienced 2 years earlier, recalling it as a period when they were not their usual selves. It appeared, with course as a variable, that individuals in this second group more appropriately belonged in the labile personality group, and they are so recorded in Figure 11.1.

Still within the episodic minor depressives, with course as a variable, there was a third group. These I will call "hyper-reactors." They were subjects who readily admitted to many symptoms, but these symptoms seldom produced any real interference with functioning. Further, at clinical interview they just did not seem that symptomatic. It was as if they were reporting a high level of symptomatology but with a rather low level of distress, in contrast to both the preceding groups whose members were symptomatic, distressed, and looked it. This "hyper-reactor" group of patients did have some similarities to labile personality in that they reported a wide range of symptoms, but, in contrast to the "true" labile personalities, their lives were not stormy or disordered, but were generally unremarkable and rather stable. They were similar to the first group, the "true" episodic depressives, in that their level of functioning was generally high and their degree of impairment low when they were their usual selves. This, however, was also the case when they were "in episodes," in contrast to the "true" episodic depressives who showed more impairment at those times.

There was another group of subjects whose members were virtually always depressed, at a rather low level, when seen at each of the five follow-up visits, and indeed throughout the 2-year period. With course as a variable, individuals in this group appeared conceptually similar to the Chronic Inter-mittent Depressive Disorder category. Their feeling virtually always de-pressed, but with some variation in the level of that depression, was quite striking.

Finally, for a very few subjects initially characterized as episodic minor depression, at subsequent visits anxiety was a more striking symptom, with their condition at that time consistent with a diagnosis of Generalized Anx-iety Disorder. This was a group of subjects characterized by a high level of both depression and anxiety when they were in an episode, and the category to which they were assigned seemed to depend on the relative predominance of one type of symptomatology over the other, although both were virtually always present. Under the RDC definitions, there was a hierarchical rule which stated that if both anxiety and depression were present, the patient should be called a depressive disorder. For this group of subjects, it appeared that mixed anxiety-depression was characteristic, but with the depression sufficiently minimal at later visits that they were called, appropriately I think, Generalized Anxiety Disorder.

What this material showed is that, when these subjects initially charac-terized as having the same diagnosis, episodic minor depression, were fol-lowed over time, discrete subgroups emerged, depending on the course. One group, a very large group fortunately, the one I have called "true" episodic depression, emerged which appeared very similar to the original conceptuali-zation of Episodic Minor Depressive Disorder as outlined in that RDC category description. However, a single-point-in-time assessment also in-cluded other conditions which, with data available on course, appeared to be quite different. For some, such as the hyper-reactor group, there was no existing diagnostic category into which the subjects fitted easily. For others, existing categories such as Labile Personality or Generalized Anxiety Dis-order appeared appropriate when the picture over two years was examined. Obviously one issue is: Were these subjects misdiagnosed initially, or were they correctly diagnosed, but the disorder turned into something else at a later date? I will return to this issue after presenting data for the other depressive disorder categories.

Major Depressive Disorder. Figure 11.2 presents material for Major Depressive Disorder. When we examined what happened over time for individuals initially categorized as having this disorder, the types of outcomes showed considerable similarity to those observed with the episodic minor depressives. There was one group of subjects who appeared very similar to the "true" episodic depression group, although when seen initially they were experiencing more severe symptomatology than the episodic minor depres-sives. The subsequent course of this group was recovery from their disorder characterized by returning to their usual selves and usually functioning well. This group also could vividly recall being in an episode, and could accurately

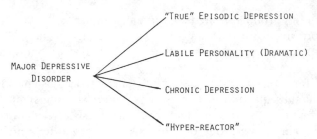

Figure 11.2. Major depressive disorder: 2-year outcome.

describe a beginning and an ending to the episode. One cluster of subjects in this group consisted of younger people who had experienced a major loss, such as the death of a child, while another cluster included subjects who were older and whose symptoms were more severe, lasted longer, and were of the more endogenous type.

As with the episodic minor depressives, with course as a variable, within the major depressives there emerged a group which seemed to be more accurately categorized as labile personality, and a third group which seemed appropriately to fit the conceptualization of chronic depression. In addition, a very small group of subjects fitted the description of the group I have called hyper-reactors.

Summarizing this material, Episodic Minor Depressive Disorder and Major Depressive Disorder contained "true" episodic groups of patients, by far the larger groups in both disorders, who had a reasonably consistent and describable course. Also in both diagnostic groups were individuals who, when seen over time, were more accurately categorized as having a different disorder, usually a character disorder, or as not fitting clearly into any of the categories of the RDC classification as conceptualized in the category descriptions.

Chronic Intermittent Minor Depressive Disorder. Figure 11.3 presents findings for those initially diagnosed as having Chronic Intermittent Minor Depressive Disorder. Individuals in this category indeed appeared qualitatively different from those in the preceding "true episodic" groups. Most striking was the relatively unchanging nature of the depressive symptoms for a large group of subjects in this category. They were brooders, chronically unhappy with their lot in life, negativistic about many things, and they seldom experienced pleasure in the usual sense of the word. They also tended to have high levels of anxiety, but of the worrying type. As might be expected, it was difficult to define an episode for individuals in this group. They virtually always had some symptomatology, although these symptoms would wax and wane, and at periods of increased symptomatology they might be classified as having an episodic disorder. In general they did not get dramati-

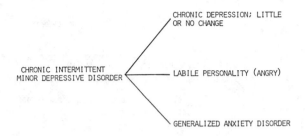

Figure 11.3. Chronic depressive disorder: 2-year outcome.

cally better as was the case with most individuals with major or minor depression, although some did report some improvement. They were chronic complainers, and they were not much fun to be around.

Within the chronic depressives, there was a second group which emerged when course was examined. It consisted of subjects who had periods of more dramatic symptomatology and who experienced swings from periods of depression to periods of anxiety. Individuals in this group were also complainers, but their complaining had more of an angry, demanding quality to it. They appeared to more closely approximate the conceptualization of Labile Personality Disorder in that there were periods when they denied depression. As with the labile personality group described earlier, they had difficulty dating the beginning and end of periods when they were very depressed, presenting themselves as "depressed all my life" if interviewed at a down time, but not presenting such a description when interviewed at times when they were feeling better.

Finally, within the group initially classified as chronic depressives there was a small number of subjects who consistently reported primarily worry and tension during the 2-year observation period. Their clinical picture, with course as a variable, was consistent with Generalized Anxiety Disorder, but of a chronic type.

Labile Personality Disorder. The range of outcomes for the fourth depressive disorder category, Labile Personality Disorder, is shown in Figure 11.4. Many subjects stayed the same, with continuing ups and downs. Others cycled with superimposed episodic depression, usually minor but occasionally major, whereas others had periods of superimposed anxiety and probably would have received the diagnosis of Generalized Anxiety Disorder if seen at that time. There was a small group of subjects who seemed to cycle with chronic depressive disorder, receiving that diagnosis at some of the follow-up assessments. There was another small group which improved, and rather dramatically, appearing to really change during the 2-year period.

As described in the earlier data, some individuals initially categorized as major depression or as episodic minor depression appeared to appropriately

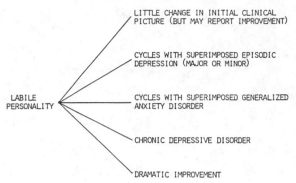

Figure 11.4. Labile personality: 2-year outcome.

belong in the labile personality category. Those individuals, and a large subset of individuals initially characterized as labile personality, did form a coherent group which appeared qualitatively different from those depressed individuals who did not show such a character structure, those I have called the "true" episodic depressives. As in the RDC category conceptualization, this group was characterized by dramatic swings in their moods, often related to what was going on around them. Many were rather dramatic, suggestible, and the lives of some were often stormy. Some had trouble with impulsiveness. In terms of other personality traits, they frequently showed many more dependency needs, appeared to be looking for others to care for them, and to see themselves as relatively powerless.

With the availability of clinical information over time, it was clear that subjects with Labile Personality Disorder presented a problem in classification when seen only once because their symptomatology of the moment tended to color their history. When they were down, they were very down, and gave sufficient depressive symptomatology to meet criteria for either Episodic Minor or Major Depressive Disorder, although often they would not have met the 2-week-duration criterion if it had been possible to obtain a fully accurate history.

The Effect of a Characterologic Disorder on Outcome at 2 Years

Another aspect of this data is the effect of a characterologic diagnosis on outcome at 2 years. The original thrust of the study had been to characterize each individual by a "primary diagnosis," obtained at the initial interview, which was then used as a predictor variable for subsequent analyses. Table 11.1 shows improvement at 2 years with subjects classified by the "primary diagnosis" approach, where no attention was paid to the presence

Table 11.1. Self-Rating of Improvement after Two Years for Outpatient Depressive Disorders (Combined Categories)

RDC Diagnostic Group	N	Improved		No Change or Worse	
		N	%	N	%
Episodic minor depressive disorder	99	82	83	17	17
Major depressive disorder	25	18	72	7	28
Labile personality disorder	18	10	56	8	44
Chronic minor depressive disorder	27	10	37	17	63
Total	169	120	71	49	29

Chi square = 24.0; $p < .000$.

or absence of a simultaneous character disorder, or "double diagnosis." Overall, 71% of the subjects reported an improvement in their condition over the 2-year period. Twenty-nine percent reported that there was no change in their condition or that they were worse. The category with the highest rate of improvement, 83%, was episodic minor depression. The category with the next highest rate of improvement, 72%, was major depression. Labile personality showed an improvement rate of 56%. The category with the lowest rate of improvement, 37%, was chronic depression. These differences in improvement rates were significant by chi square.

Table 11.2 shows what happened when attention was paid to double diagnosis. In the table the preceding four diagnostic groupings are expanded into eight by keeping separate those subjects who had an episodic depressive disorder superimposed upon a character disorder. There is a ninth category, the hyper-reactor group discussed earlier. The table is rank-ordered by improvement rates, and now there are two groups which showed 100% improvement by self-report at 2 years. One group was those who had major depression only, and the other group was the hyper-reactor group. Episodic minor depression only, with 87% improvement, was next. Labile personality with a superimposed major depression also showed a high improvement rate, 86%. Somewhat lower, but still showing a high improvement rate, was chronic depression with a superimposed episodic minor depression (75%) and labile personality with a superimposed episodic minor depression (73% improvement). Next, with 56% improvement, is "labile personality only," followed by "chronic depression only," with 37% improvement. These are the same groups that were shown in Table 11.1. Last, however, was a group that showed no improvement over the 2-year period—chronic depression with a superimposed major depression.

Table 11.2. Self-Rating of Improvement after Two Years for Specific Depressive
Disorder Categories

		Improved		No Change or Worse	
	N	N	%	N	%
Major depressive disorder only	10	10	100	0	0
"Hyper-reactor" with a superimposed MD or ED	15	15	100	0	0
Episodic minor depressive disorder only	45	39	87	6	13
LP with a superimposed MD	7	6	86	1	14
CD with a superimposed ED	8	6	75	2	25
LP with a superimposed ED	33	24	73	9	27
Labile personality disorder only	18	10	56	8	44
Chronic depressive disorder only	27	10	37	17	63
CD with a superimposed MD	6	0	0	6	100
Total	169	120	71	49	29

Chi square $= 48.3$; $p < .0000$.

What does all this mean? One obvious observation is that different
patterns of outcome emerge when one pays attention to double diagnosis.
Table 11.3 groups subjects into the original "primary diagnosis" groups (left
side of the table) and shows the effect of "double diagnosis" on improvement
at 2 years (right side of the table). Major depression, for example, when
secondary diagnoses were ignored, showed only a 72% improvement rate.
This improvement rate rose to 100% when those with a double diagnosis—
chronic depression or labile personality—were removed. Clearly double diagnosis, for major depressives at least, does have an effect on outcome. These
findings emphasize the importance of identifying a personality disorder when
examining outcome, a point I will return to later in this address.

ACCURATE CASE IDENTIFICATION FOR CATEGORY
VALIDATION: ISSUES AND CONCERNS

The Need for Longitudinal Assessment

The preceding data came from a study concerned with validation of individual diagnostic categories, and they focus attention on several areas of concern
relevant to such category validation. One principal finding was that assessment at several points in time can result in different diagnostic categorizations at those times. But what is the meaning of those changes? Figure 11.5

presents the possibilities for the situation, a real one in the data just presented, of a patient assessed, at one point in time, as having a major depressive disorder and, at a second point in time 6 months later, as having labile personality disorder. One possible meaning of this change is that major depression "changed" to labile personality. Implied here is that both are the same disorder with different phases, as, to use a medical example, syphilis changing to tertiary lues. Another possibility is that both disorders were present independently—the major depression ended, and labile personality subsequently began. A third possibility is that the diagnosis of major depression at the first assessment was "wrong," and the "correct" diagnosis of labile personality was established at the second assessment. A fourth possibility is the reverse—the first assessment diagnosis was correct and the second was wrong.

Which of these possibilities is selected will depend on the conceptualization of the disorders in question. In this example, possibilities 1 and 2 are unlikely because labile personality is conceptualized as an enduring condition, one present constantly over many years. The choice then is between 3 and 4. I favor 3 in this example, because conceptually those with labile personality can and do show a great deal of depressive symptomatology on occasion. If the initial assessment happened to take place at one of those times, and it was the only assessment, it would be easy to see the depressive symptoms and hard to recognize the underlying character structure. The reverse situation is not true, as major depressive disorder is conceptualized, and thus 4 is unlikely.

A major point here, and it is one made in the clinical data just presented, is that the passage of time allowed the clinical picture to reveal itself. A second subsequent assessment permitted the "correct," on conceptual

Table 11.3. "Primary Diagnosis" Approach Contrasted with "Double Diagnosis" Approach: Improvement at Two Years

"Primary Diagnosis" Approach		"Double Diagnosis" Approach	
MD (25):	72%	MD only (10):	100%
		"Hyper-reactor" (2):	100%
		LP-MD (7):	86%
		CD-MD (6):	0%
ED (99):	83%	"Hyper-reactor" (13):	100%
		ED only (45):	87%
		CD-ED (8):	75%
		LP-ED (33):	73%
LP only (18):	56%		56%
CD only (27):	37%		37%

POSSIBILITIES:

    1. MD CHANGED TO LP (SAME DISORDER AT DIFFERENT PHASES)

    2. EACH OCCURRED INDEPENDENTLY (MD ENDED; SUBSEQUENTLY LP BEGAN)

    3. MD WAS "WRONG"; LP WAS "RIGHT" ("ERROR" IN INITIAL ASSESSMENT)

    4. MD WAS "RIGHT"; LP WAS "WRONG" ("ERROR" IN SECOND ASSESSMENT)

Figure 11.5. Possible meanings of a change in diagnostic categorization between two assessments separated by time.

grounds, diagnosis to be made. It is important to emphasize that the first assessment was not necessarily a "bad" assessment. Assume that it was a careful assessment, and that it was reliable—two raters, using present methodology, entirely agreed that major depressive disorder was present. The problem is that it was based on limited information, or at least insufficient information for a characterologic condition to be detected.

There is strong evidence from earlier studies that multiple assessments are needed to identify accurately character disorders. To give one example, in a study carried out in England, Giel, Knox, & Carstairs (1964) examined naturalistic outcome at 5 years for a group of neurotic outpatients. The initial assessment was a full evaluation by experienced psychiatrists. Since the focus of the study was on outcome for neurotics, all patients with a character disorder were specifically excluded. Yet, at follow-up assessment 5 years later, 22% of the patients were found to have a personality disorder. The investigators had not been able to detect the personality disorder at the initial assessment, causing them to comment that "during the episode of decompensation, symptoms of neurosis are most in evidence, and only after recovery from the neurosis are the enduring peculiarities of personality again apparent."

The point I wish to emphasize is that longitudinal information was required to establish the character disorder diagnosis. For a considerable number of patients (22%) the accurate diagnosis of a personality disorder could not be made by experienced clinicians even when they were trying to do so.

Variables Related to the Quality (Validity) of Information Needed for Accurate Case Categorization

What other variables relate to the quality of information obtained and thus the accuracy of a diagnostic categorization? A list of variables I consider important is presented in Table 11.4. Since the assessments obtained from community surveys may be used as the baseline diagnoses for category validation, I have included in the table a summary evaluation of how well instruments used in recent surveys do on each of these variables. I included the DIS because of its use in the ECA studies and because it has rapidly become an assessment "standard." The SADS was used in the recent New Haven Community Survey (Weissman & Myers, 1978). The PSE has been used in community surveys in England and in Europe (Bebbington, Hurry, Tennant, Sturt, & Wing, 1981; Wing, 1980).

Quality of rapport is the first variable listed. (The order of variables is arbitrary, but more or less follows the usual sequence for a diagnostic assessment.) Rapport relates to accuracy of information obtained. It is essential to obtain information that the respondent might be reluctant to admit, such as material that was socially undesirable, or embarrassing. Rapport is presumed to improve with repeated contact, assuming that the initial contact was positive.

Survey methodologies all have limitations with respect to establishing rapport as I am defining it here. An interviewer must approach a chosen respondent, introduce himself or herself, and obtain cooperation with the goals and procedures of the study. By definition respondents are community members, most of whom will not have labeled themselves as sick. The

Table 11.4. Case Categorization: Variables Related to Quality (Validity) of Data Obtained

Variable	DIS	SADS	PSE
1. *Quality of rapport:* Presumed to improve with repeated contact, assuming initial contact was positive.	++	++	++
2. *Time available:* Accuracy of data assumed to improve with more time available, and with return visit.	++	++	++
3. *Standardized information gathered:* Quality of data assumed to improve when same information is asked of all.	++++	+++	+++
4. *Special interviewer knowledge required* to assess certain items. Accuracy of some items assumed to improve when trained rater is part of the rating process.	No	Yes	Yes
5. *Reliability of item information* should be clearly established.	+++	+++	+++
6. *Use of other informants* or of record data. Assumed to improve accuracy of some types of data.	No (±)	No (±)	No
7. *Number of assessments required* for initial categorization data. Accuracy of data needed to categorize some disorders assumed to improve with longitudinal assessments.	One	One	One

+ Poor.
++ Fair.
+++ Good.
++++ Excellent.

interviewer's task then is to obtain the information on the interview schedule, with the hope and expectation that honest and accurate answers will be obtained to all the questions asked. Knowing someone over time, and the development of trust about how sensitive or embarrassing information will be handled, is generally not possible. I thus rate each of the methodologies shown as variable, and on the average as "fair," with respect to rapport.

The amount of time available to collect the information is the next variable listed. More time available allows both a more careful appraisal of individual items of information and more information itself to be gathered. But if an interview is too long, other considerations can affect quality of the information, such as subject fatigue, and "nay-saying" to get rid of the interviewer. Having a flexible time, with the interviewer able to return on other days as often as necessary, is desirable. Here again accuracy of information obtained is the issue, with accuracy expected to improve with more time available and with repeat visits.

I would rate each of the methodologies shown as fair on this variable also. The time available is limited, usually two hours or so, and subject fatigue can be a problem. Return visits are theoretically possible, but they are a nuisance and seldom done as a routine in community surveys.

Obtaining standardized information—asking the same questions to all respondents—is another variable. It permits a consistent evaluation, improving the quality of information obtained, particularly when large numbers of respondents are being assessed.

The DIS scores highest on this variable. One of the major achievements of the DIS is that the same questions are asked in the same way of all respondents. The other instruments listed also score high on this variable; all are structured clinical interviews. The accuracy of the data obtained, however, would be expected to be affected by the two variables already discussed—rapport and time available—and by the next one, "special interviewer knowledge required" to obtain certain information.

The accuracy for various items of psychopathology, panic anxiety, for example, is expected to improve when the interviewer has special training or experience and thus is able to ask pertinent clarifying questions about symptom material elicited. Such an interviewer does not just record responses but is an integral part of the process of determining the presence or absence of items of psychopathology.

The PSE and the SADS specifically require interviewers who are fully knowledgeable about items of psychopathology and psychiatric syndromes. The DIS does not.

Reliability—in the scientific sense—of the item information obtained is another variable. All these instruments have high established item reliability. But it is worth noting that item reliability is not item validity. Interviewers can agree that a respondent answered "no" to a symptom, and yet that symptom may still be there but not revealed by the respondent. Quality of rapport and social desirability of an item again play a role here.

Use of other informants, which can include searching other records as well as talking to others expected to have the desired information, is another assessment method variable. It obviously has great usefulness for improving the accuracy of certain types of information, such as details of previous hospitalizations or treatments. It has great utility in assessing the presence of any character disorder. It is virtually required when the respondent is considered a poor informant because of dementia or forgetfulness.

Seeking other informants or record material is time consuming and a nuisance and thus is seldom done as a routine in community survey assessment, although its use in selected cases would greatly enhance the accuracy of diagnostic data obtained. Use of other informants was not part of DIS, SADS, or PSE assessment as routinely conducted on community members.

The final assessment method variable in Table 11.4 has already been discussed: the number of assessments required for the initial diagnostic categorization. In practice the DIS uses only one, and, as commonly used in community surveys, the same is true for the SADS and the PSE. Thus none of these assessment methodologies specifically call for repeat assessments separated in time as a requirement for any initial diagnostic categorizations.

Characteristics of Case Categorization from Survey Assessments

In this overview of currently used survey case identification instruments on variables expected to influence the accuracy of the data obtained, and thus of the diagnostic categorization, at least two points can be made. First, the instruments vary, with some presumed "better" than others for particular types of information. Second, as used in survey methodology, none is ideal for category validation for some disorders. This should not come as a surprise, as of necessity there are constraints on such an assessment. Repeating those constraints, the interviewer's task is to make initial contact with a stranger and establish sufficient rapport to obtain honest and accurate responses to all questions asked. The assessment must take place in a reasonable period of time, usually one to two hours. The entire source of information is usually the respondent alone. The assessment is at a single point in time, and information obtained is thus limited to how a particular respondent presents himself or herself on that day.

Keep in mind that the goal of such an assessment is to provide "best estimates" for presence or absence of the disorder in question. There will be false positives, such as labile personality being called major depression, and there will be false negatives, particularly those who, for whatever reason, deny symptoms they know to be there. The expectation is that these will cancel each other out. As an estimate of prevalence of specific disorders, DIS diagnoses in the ECA studies must be seen as major advance, since they derive from a standardized assessment linked to an operationally defined nosology.

But these diagnoses are estimates. The accuracy of the estimates will vary with each disorder. Different issues are involved when validation of hypothesized diagnostic entities—category validation—is the goal. Here false negatives and false positives are to be avoided if at all possible. To use an analogy from general medicine, one could imagine a study to determine the prevalence of myocardial infarction which used a very careful history as the diagnostic assessment—quality of the pain, radiation to the left arm, a crushing sensation in the chest, and so on. I would accept that such a diagnostic categorization would provide reasonably accurate estimates of the prevalence of the condition. There would be some false positives, as those with other conditions with pain radiation to the left arm, and there would be false negatives, such as those who do not experience the pain or who experience it in an atypical location. But the overall estimates would be useful.

If instead the focus is on the condition itself, on myocardial infarction as a diagnostic entity, as would be the case in determining the efficacy of a particular treatment, it becomes essential to exclude all those who do not truly have a myocardial infarction. More time would be allowed for the assessment, and the patient would receive other tests, such as an electrocardiogram. For the initial assessment one would use whatever methodology was currently available to determine the presence or absence of a myocardial infarction as that disorder was then understood and conceptualized.

The same issues hold for psychiatric disorders. In case identification for category validation, the major issue should be to choose the ideal method for determining the presence or absence of the particular disorder under study, given its current conceptualization. A related issue is the degree of accuracy that can be expected for a particular disorder from a particular type of assessment. Case identification from community survey techniques unavoidably has certain constraints and limitations, and these limitations are more important for particular diagnostic categories than for others. When category validation is the issue, it is important that the assessment method be linked to the disorder in question.

Misuse of Standardized Interviews and Diagnostic Systems

An additional current concern with respect to accurate diagnostic categorization is what I call "pseudo-comparability of diagnosis" or of assessment. With the availability of standardized assessment instruments such as the DIS or the SADS has come an explosion in their use as the diagnostic categorization instrument for a host of studies. On the surface this would appear fine, given the careful work that has gone into these instruments, and the proven reliability at the item level. But that reliability assumes proper use, and it is the increasing improper use of the instruments that is worrisome. To cite one example, I was approached recently by a group of investigators to comment on a diagnostic study they had conducted. They indicated that they had used the RDC system and the SADS to make their assessments, and their results had been so reported in an article to be published. None of the investigators had received formal training in the use of the SADS or of the RDC system. What they had done was read the SADS interview and discuss it together. They then cut it up into sections, deleted questions of low interest to them, and added a few others. This assessment instrument was then provided to different psychiatric residents, at first- and second-year levels, rotating through the inpatient service. Each resident used it as a question-and-answer instrument to establish the presence or absence of particular disorders.

Obviously this SADS assessment is not comparable to the standardized one advocated by its authors, Endicott and Spitzer. But the physicians using it were not being devious—they were acting in good faith, and saw themselves as using improved, modern methodology. This example was not an isolated one in my experience, but was all too common, or at least common enough to cause me to raise it as a concern.

Another example comes from a recent experience of serving on the NIMH Initial Review Group concerned with reviewing epidemiologic studies. In grants coming through that committee, there was near universal proposed use of the DIS or the SADS as a case categorization measure, particularly the DIS because it used lay interviewers and therefore was less expensive. In several instances it was reasonably clear that the applicant had little knowledge of the instrument but had included it as "latest technology" or as a "gold standard." There was more than one study that proposed the use of the DIS to diagnose a particular disorder, and yet the applicant was not aware that the DIS did not cover the disorder in question. That the DIS does not make all DSM-III diagnoses was a common misunderstanding.

Besides unfamiliarity with what the instrument assessed, unfamiliarity with the training required to properly use the instrument was also evident and not a rare event. More worrisome was the suggestion that the user did not particularly care—it was as if some investigators were under great pressure to seize this new technology, with the result that it was applied uncritically. The problem is that it is hard to tell, when reading a journal article, about the quality of assessment. Such unexciting method details are usually the first to go when journal editors reduce the length of an article.

But the problem is not trivial. Pseudo-comparability of diagnosis is real and very much with us. I can see the potential for as much confusion in knowing what the diagnosis really was in clinical studies using SADS or DIS as formerly existed in studies using DSM-II. Without some enforced quality control, and a way of communicating it to journal readers, we run the danger of having replaced the old DSM-II form of diagnostic ambiguity—the same labels used, but with different defining criteria—with a new form of ambiguity—the same labels used, but with varying and unclear methods of assessment, masquerading as "standardized," and "reliable." To quote, or rather paraphrase, Joseph Zubin in his Hoch Award address last year, "Today's progress is tomorrow's problem." There is no doubt that RDC, DSM-III, SADS, and DIS represent substantial progress in case categorization. The challenge is to have these advances not be tomorrow's problems.

Obviously one solution would be to have some sort of quality control required in the training and use of these instruments. Indeed, quality control measures were and are used in studies such as the ECA and the NIMH Collaborative Study on Depression. The authors of the DIS stress the importance of proper training. In a recent issue of the *DIS Newsletter* (1984) are the following statements: "Since the results of a study depend on the quality of the data collected, the role of the interviewer in this process becomes of paramount importance, and we take our responsibility as trainers very seriously. In our training, we constantly stress supervision and quality control in the use of the interview and recommend that users have periodic retraining sessions to prevent slippage and to keep interviewing standards at a maximum."

This is sound advice. But the problem is that there is no formal method to ensure quality control in the use of the DIS or SADS outside of these large collaborative studies. And so pseudo-comparability of diagnosis is with us, and it may become tomorrow's problem.

THE IMPORTANCE OF THE CHARACTEROLOGIC AXIS

Earlier in this address I commented on the significance of the characterologic axis. The results from the naturalistic outcome study showed that it was important to pay attention to specific diagnosis in considering outcome, and in particular that it was important to identify a character disorder when one was present. Although the earlier literature usually does not report results by an axial system (e.g., it does not pay attention to "double diagnosis"), there is great consistency about the effect of "chronic" symptoms on outcome. Kedward (1969), in a British study which investigated psychiatric disorders in a general practice, reported, "One of the most striking findings of the prevalence study [of psychiatric disorders] was the very high proportion of chronic cases, over 50% in both sexes" (p. 2). In that study the outcome at three years of "new cases"—episodic cases—was 72–75% improved, whereas the 3-year improvement rate for "chronic" cases was 41–50%. Kedward went on to state that these data suggested the existence of two subgroups of neurotic disorders in general practice, one with a good prognosis, and the other running a refractory course that continued longer than 3 years. He concluded that "duration of illness is a most important factor when a psychiatric patient presents and when his progress is reviewed" (p. 4). Eitinger (1955), in a 10-year follow-up study of Norwegian patients hospitalized with neurotic disorders, reported that a short duration of illness seemed "to be directly in proportion to the tendency towards improvement, both in the case of the immediate results [discharge from hospital] and the later results" (p. 41). Hornstra and Klassen (1977), in a 1-year follow-up study of U.S. depressive patients identified in a community survey, reported a "striking finding" that in certain patients depressive mood lasted from year to year and was not related to life events. Lambert (1976) summarized the results of several outcome studies by stating that "the longer the duration of the illness, the fewer the patients who were found to have recovered" (p. 111) and that "future work should attempt to specify clearly the nature of the sample being studied and to give special attention to the past histories of patients in regard to the onset and duration of their disturbance."

These investigators drew attention to duration or chronicity of symptoms as a predictor of outcome. I am suggesting that duration may have been an indicator of the presence of a characterologic condition. These earlier studies did not discuss directly this possibility. Some investigators did hypothesize "personality defects," a concept close to the one of a characterologic diagnosis, to explain this relationship of duration of symptoms to outcome. I mentioned the work of Giel *et al.* (1964) when discussing the need for a longitudinal assessment to properly identify those with character disorders. In that study a short duration of illness before consultation related to a favorable outcome, and those with a less favorable outcome had a high frequency of "abnormal personality characteristics," in other words, a personality or character disorder.

Cooper, Fry, and Kalton (1969), in another study of general-practice patients in England, examined a 5-year outcome of neurotic patients. They found two subgroups of depressives, one with a psychiatric diagnosis in only one of 5 years and with a good outcome, and another, a "distinct subgroup," with psychiatric illness in at least four of the 5 years and with poor outcome. They hypothesized that "the former group comprised chiefly situational reactions in relatively stable individuals, while the latter represented some form of constitutional vulnerability"—that is, a personality or character problem. Hoehn-Saric, Frank, Stone, and Imber (1969), in a 10-year follow-up study of treated neurotics in the United States, reported that "high improvement was significantly related to a favorable premorbid personality," and concluded that the most important criterion for predicting improvement was not diagnosis but the patient's personality. Eitinger (1955), in the Norwegian 10-year follow-up, also emphasized the effect of personality on outcome, commenting that, although the premorbid personality (which was categorized as "deviating" versus "nondeviating") played a comparatively subordinate part for the immediate prognosis (release from hospital), it played a very decisive part in the later prognosis (outcome at 10 years).

In a recent study, a 1-year follow-up of treated patients, Keller and Shapiro (1982) found that those patients with a major depressive disorder and an underlying chronic depressive disorder, a phenomenon they called "double depression," had a lower recovery rate than those patients who had only a major depressive disorder. They stated that "the distinction between patients with and without such so-called double depression may be an extremely important one to make in terms of outcome assessment" (p. 441). They further commented, "Researchers have largely ignored the phenomenon of double depression in describing samples" and that "conclusions about course and outcome of a sizable number of patients included in both naturalistic and drug studies of affective disorders may be difficult to interpret because it is not clear what proportion of those patients had double depressions" (p. 441). I strongly agree with this last statement.

DSM-III, as one of its innovations, is an axial system. Axis II, the characterologic axis of DSM-III, may turn out to be a major predictor of outcome. It has not received the attention it deserves, either with respect to careful operational definitions of the individual categories, or with respect to establishing and improving the methodology to assess those categories.

CONCLUDING REMARKS

Category validation has been a principal focus of this address. Of those diagnoses we are currently using, which is a "true" entity—which diagnoses are "real" in nature? The definition of "disease" or "disorder" is not a simple question and could easily be the topic of another paper. But it is worth remembering some points made by Robert Kendell several years ago, in his discussion of reliability and validity issues in relation to psychiatric diagnosis. Kendell (1975) pointed out that reliability is concerned with the defining characteristics of a disorder, whereas validity is concerned with the correlates of that disorder once it has been defined. Much of recent methodologic work in diagnosis has been concerned with reliability issues, with category definition, and quite properly, given the problem of DSM-II, with its loosely defined categories which permitted the same clinical picture to be legitimately diagnosed under several different categories. Clearly reliability does have to precede validity. But now the pendulum has swung too far in the other direction, where reliability in the sense of interrater agreement at a cross-sectional assessment is taken as a gold standard for the true presence of a symptom or of a disorder. Considering the symptom level, two raters can agree that a patient said he is not impulsive, does not steal, and gets along well with people, but does that agreement make those symptom items "true" for that patient? I think not.

Similarly, at the diagnostic category level, that kappas of 0.6 to 0.8 can be obtained for particular disorders at cross-sectional assessments, as has been demonstrated with current methods, is important. But suppose it could be demonstrated that those kappas became 0.8 to 0.9 when information from repeat assessments was available. I do not believe this would be the outcome in every case, but my point is that the determination of the diagnostic reliability using longitudinal assessments needs to be done, for some disorders at least. In earlier diagnostic reliability studies, kappas of 0.3 to 0.5 were common for neurotic disorders, and lower values, 0.2 to 0.4, were usual for character disorders. These results were taken as evidence that those disorders were vague, could not be defined, and thus possibly were not real entities. In the field trial data for DSM-III, the results were only slightly better. The kappa for Axis II disorders as a group was reported as 0.54 (Spitzer, Forman, & Nee, 1979), and other studies have reported kappas for many of the individual Axis II disorders to be quite low (Mellsop, Varghese, Joshua, & Hicks, 1982). Yet these diagnostic reliability studies used a cross-sectional assessment.

Finally, some personal observations, and then I will conclude with two pleas concerning studies where diagnosis is a variable. In psychiatry we are currently in an era where improved tools are available to assess the validity of proposed diagnostic entities, be they DSM-III, RDC, or the current ICD. Reviewing my own career, in the 1960s I was trained as a PSE/PSS interviewer as part of my participation in the United States–United Kingdom diagnostic project (Cooper, Kendell, Gurland, Sharpe, Copeland, & Simon, 1972). In the 1970s I was involved in the development of and was trained in the SADS interview. I was not directly involved with the DIS, but I followed with interest the successful evolution of that instrument.

Concurrent with these new assessment techniques, I have lived through and witnessed the evolution of improved diagnostic systems, with careful category definitions, including specified inclusion and exclusion criteria, as in the RDC and DSM-III.

With these advances, both in assessment techniques and in precision of conceptualization of diagnostic categories, we are quite rightly in a period of concern with category validation. DSM-IV is to follow DSM-III. Which categories are real—have useful correlates, in Kendell's terms—and should be retained, and which should be modified and dropped, are questions under study.

And this leads me to the first plea, one that is obvious, and yet somehow needs repeating. For any study where diagnosis is a predictor variable, and here I include all clinical studies, not just category validation studies, tailor the method of assessment to the disorder under examination. Do not just use what assessment method is handy, whether it be the DIS or the SADS, but use what is best for the disorder under examination, given present knowledge and how that disorder is conceptualized.

My final plea deals with category validation studies for character disorders. For such studies, include a longitudinal assessment as an integral part of the initial categorization. And consider, for certain disorders, requiring information from a second informant. DSM-III's Axis II deserves careful examination, with appropriate attention to accurate assessment techniques for each of its categories. Only then can the correlates of the individual disorders be properly established.

ACKNOWLEDGMENTS

Portions of the material reported, the 2-year follow-up data on outpatient depressive disorders, were from an investigation supported by Grant MH-27865 from The National Institute of Mental Health.

REFERENCES

Barrett, J. E. (1981). Psychiatric diagnoses (Research Diagnostic Criteria) in symptomatic volunteers. *Archives of General Psychiatry, 38*, 153–157.

Barrett, J. E. (1984). Naturalistic change after 2 years in neurotic depressive disorders (RDC categories). *Comprehensive Psychiatry, 25*, 404–418.

Bebbington, P., Hurry, J., Tennant, C., Sturt, E., & Wing, J. K. (1981). Epidemiology of mental disorders in Camberwell. *Psychological Medicine, 11*, 561–579.

Cooper, B., Fry, J., & Kalton, G. (1969). A longitudinal study of psychiatric morbidity in a general population. *British Journal of Preventive and Social Medicine, 23*, 210–217.

Cooper, J. E., Kendell, R. E., Gurland, B. J., Sharpe, L., Copeland, J. R. M., & Simon, R. (1972). *Psychiatric diagnosis in New York and London*. London: Oxford University Press.

DIS Newsletter (1984). E. Goldring (Ed.), Vol. 1, No. 1, pp. 4–5.

Eitinger, L. (1955). Studies in neuroses. *Acta Psychiatrica et Neurologica Scandinavica* (Supplement 101).

Endicott, J., & Spitzer, R. L. (1978). A diagnostic interview: The Schedule for Affective Disorders and Schizophrenia. *Archives of General Psychiatry, 35*, 837–844.

Giel, R., Knox, R. S., & Carstairs, G. M. (1964). A five year follow-up of 100 neurotic outpatients. *British Medical Journal, 2*, 160–163.

Hoehn-Saric, R., Frank, J. D., Stone, A. R., & Imber, S. D. (1969). Progress in psychoneurotic patients. *American Journal of Psychotherapy, 23*, 252–259.

Hornstra, R. K., & Klassen, D. (1977). The course of depression. *Comprehensive Psychiatry, 18*, 119–125.

Kedward, H. (1969). The outcome of neurotic illness in the community. *Social Psychiatry, 4*, 1–4.

Keller, M. B., & Shapiro, R. W. (1982). Double depression: Superimposition of acute depressive episodes on chronic depressive disorders. *American Journal of Psychiatry, 139*, 438–442.

Kendell, R. E. (1975). *The role of diagnosis in psychiatry.* Oxford: Blackwell Scientific Publications.

Lambert, M. J. (1976). Spontaneous remission in adult neurotic disorders: A revision and summary. *Psychological Bulletin, 83*, 107–119.

Leighton, A. H. (1959). *My name is Legion: The Stirling County study of psychiatric disorder and social environment.* New York: Basic Books.

Mellsop, G., Varghese, F., Joshua, S., & Hicks, A. (1982). The reliability of Axis II of DSM-III. *American Journal of Psychiatry, 139*, 1360–1361.

Robins, E., & Guze, S. B. (1970). Establishment of diagnostic validity in psychiatric illness: Its application to schizophrenia. *American Journal of Psychiatry, 126*, 983–987.

Robins, L. N., Helzer, J. E., Croughan, J., & Ratcliff, J. S. (1981). National Institute of Mental Health Diagnostic Interview Schedule: Its history, characteristics, and validity. *Archives of General Psychiatry, 38*, 381–389.

Spitzer, R. S., Endicott, J., & Robins, E. (1975). *Research diagnostic criteria for a selected group of functional disorders* (2nd ed.). New York: Biometrics Research, New York State Psychiatric Institute.

Spitzer, R. L., Forman, J. B. W., & Nee, X. (1979). DSM-III field trials: 1. Initial inter-rater diagnostic reliability. *American Journal of Psychiatry, 136*, 815–817.

Weissman, M. M., & Myers, J. K. (1978). Affective disorders in a U.S. urban community: The use of Research Diagnostic Criteria in an epidemiological survey. *Archives of General Psychiatry, 35*, 1304–1311.

Wing, J. K. (1980). The use of the present state examination in general population surveys. *Acta Psychiatrica Scandinavica* (Supplement 285).

Wing, J. K., Cooper, J. E., & Sartorius, N. (1974). The measurement and classification of psychiatric systems. Cambridge, UK: Cambridge University Press.

DISCUSSION

Robert Spitzer: I would like to share the concern that you expressed about pseudocomparability. There is a tendency now for everybody to say that they used the DSM-III system, but if one investigates what they did, often they have not used the DSM-III criteria at all, only the DSM-III terminology.

I have a question about your use of the term "characterologic" to refer to chronic depression. The DSM-III category that corresponds to chronic depression is dysthymic disorder, which is an Axis I disorder. There is a controversy about whether dysthymic disorder should be considered a personality disorder, an Axis II disorder. One reason it is not on Axis II was our feeling that, in a sizable number of cases of dysthymia, the onset was not that early. It might have been going on for five years or so, but often it would not have had an onset in adolescence or early adult life, which would be necessary to justify referring to it as a personality disorder. What are your thoughts on this?

Barrett: That is a good question. In the study I reported, we used the RDC category chronic intermittent minor depressive disorder, which required only a 2-year duration criterion. However, many of the people whom we saw reported having the depressive symptoms all their lives, which would be consistent with a personality disorder. I understand why you put DSM-III dysthymic disorder on Axis I, to be able to include, as you described, those with depressions which were not lifelong, presumably unrecovered episodic depression. And yet, over the years the literature has consistently reported on categories such as "depressive character," usually described as lifelong. There were many such individuals in our naturalistic study.

So I think depressive character is a disorder and should be included as a category under Axis II. I fully agree that there may be episodic depression that does not improve and goes on for more than two years, but I think at this stage it is worth trying to keep those people separate, in terms of validation studies, from those who give a history of depression that is lifelong.

Jean Endicott: I think that one of our problems is that we don't know how best to categorize those with less-than-full syndromes, and that they definitely do need a prolonged longitudinal study with multiple sources of information. The patients do not read the textbooks. And patients change; for example, you can have a patient who, with confirmation from relatives, sounds labile, then goes into a period of cyclothymia, then settles into a period of dysthymia, and then looks anxious. What we may decide is that the less-than-full syndromes share certain features, and that they are not disorders in the same sense as some of the full-syndrome conditions.

Barrett: I agree. Again, what I tried to show in these data is that when you follow people over time, some do keep a consistent symptom picture and give a consistent history. I am arguing for keeping those groups separate. Others show a changing history with varying symptomatology, and for these people I think it is desirable to have a catch-all category such as the RDC "other psychiatric disorder." In validation studies, they should not be combined with those who show a clinical picture consistent with the diagnostic category as conceptualized.

12

Informant Variance in the Diagnostic Assessment of Hyperactive Children as Young Adults

SALVATORE MANNUZZA AND RACHEL GITTELMAN
New York State Psychiatric Institute and Long Island Jewish-Hillside Medical Center

This chapter represents an opportunistic investigation in that it takes advantage of a longitudinal study of hyperactive children (Attention Deficit Disorder with Hyperactivity, or ADDH) and matched controls to examine some methodological issues pertinent to the assessment of psychiatric disorders in adolescents and young adults.

One aspect of psychiatric assessment that is of concern, especially to those studying young populations, is the source to be used to obtain diagnostic information. The use of multiple informants is costly, and should be relied upon only if it offers clear advantages. The nature and extent of subject–informant discordance are important to the study of the rate of psychiatric disorders in all age groups, but especially to the study of children and adolescents. The psychiatric literature on parents and their offspring, in general, has indicated poor agreement between parent and child on the reporting of symptoms, and consequently of psychiatric disorders. For example, Kashani, Orvaschel, Burk, and Reid (1985) interviewed adults with major affective disorder and their offspring (age 7–17) and reported low parent–child agreement for the presence of a psychiatric diagnosis in the child (kappa = .22). In a study by Cohen, O'Connor, Lewis, Puig-Antich, and Malachowski (1984) in which randomly selected adults and their offspring (age 9–13) were interviewed, the correlation between diagnoses based on parent and child reports was also poor ($r = .24$). Other investigators have examined agreement on specific discrete behaviors, rather than diagnostic assignments, and they too have found that information varies depending on the source. Stewart, Mendelson, and Johnson (1973), who interviewed hyperactive youngsters and their parents, found that significantly more parents than children reported symptoms of ADDH, but significantly more children than parents reported playing hookey. Herjanic and Reich (1982) interviewed children (age 6–16) referred to a child psychiatry service and their parents. Of

168 interview questions, 122 (73%) yielded kappas of less than .30. Children reported significantly more subjective distress (e.g., anxiety and depression), somatic symptoms, antisocial behavior, and psychotic symptoms than their parents; parents reported significantly more problematic behaviors (particularly in school) and personality problems (e.g., difficult temperament) than their children.

In the absence of external validating criteria, the investigator is left in a quandary as to which source of information to trust, and as to whether differential weightings are appropriate for the child's, as opposed to the parent's, version.

To assess the relative merits of the reports of parents and adolescents who had been diagnosed as hyperactive in childhood, we examined whether either source differentiated former patients from controls when information obtained from the other informant was accounted for. Essentially, the question we address is whether the parent interviews contribute to the distinction between hyperactive children grown up and controls, above and beyond the information provided by the youngsters, and vice versa; that is, whether the youngsters add to group contrasts already provided by the parents.

A second methodological issue concerns the means for assessing psychiatric disorders in adolescents. Several structured interviews have been devised for evaluating psychopathology in adults (see Endicott & Spitzer, 1980) and children (Costello, Edelbrock, Kalas, Kessler, & Klaric, 1982; Herjanic, Herjanic, Brown, & Wheatt, 1975; Kovacs, Feinberg, Crouse-Novak, Paulauskas, & Finkelstein, 1984; Puig-Antich, 1982). However, there is no established interview schedule that has been specifically devised for use with adolescents. We report on our experience using the Diagnostic Interview Schedule (DIS) (Robins, Helzer, Croughan, & Ratcliff, 1981; Robins, Helzer, Ratcliff, & Seyfried, 1982), an adult interview, in individuals from 16 to 23 years of age.

METHOD

The design of the current study has been presented elsewhere (Gittelman, Mannuzza, Shenker, & Bonagura, 1985) and is reviewed here only briefly.

Subjects

Probands consisted of 103 white male adolescents, age 16 and older, who had been diagnosed as pervasively hyperactive between ages 6 and 12. All had been rated hyperactive by both teachers *and* parents or clinic staff. Additional childhood criteria included: school referral because of behavior problems; WISC IQ of 85 or greater; no psychosis or neurological disorder; family speaks English and has a telephone. Information at follow-up was obtained on 101 cases (98%) of the targeted group.

Controls were white adolescent males who had been treated in a clinic of the Department of Adolescent Medicine at the same medical center, mostly for routine physical exams. Those who were injured in accidents or had chronic illnesses were excluded. The parents of prospective controls were telephoned and asked whether elementary school teachers had ever complained about their child's behavior. If not, the subject was recruited. A total of 100 male controls were evaluated at follow-up.

Follow-up intervals ranged from 5.7 to 11.3 years, with a mean of 9.0 years ($SD = 1.09$). The mean ages at follow-up for probands and controls, respectively, were 18.3 ($SD = 1.5$) and 18.9 ($SD = 1.5$). Controls were significantly older than probands ($p < .004$), but the absolute difference is small, and age at follow-up was not correlated with psychiatric status in either group. Probands and controls had identical mean SESs, 3.1 ($SD = 1.0$ for both groups).

Follow-up Diagnostic Instruments

Adolescents were interviewed with the *Teenager or Young Adult Schedule* (TOYS), a 470-item semistructured interview that was derived, for this study, from the *Diagnostic Interview Schedule* (DIS) (Robins *et al.*, 1981, 1982). The DIS was expanded to provide inquiry about aspects of behavior not strictly relevant to the formulation of DSM-III diagnoses, such as friendship and dating patterns, conflict in the home, etc., as well as to provide the information necessary to diagnose Conduct Disorder and Attention Deficit Disorder with and without Hyperactivity. Otherwise, the text of the DIS was preserved unchanged.

Parents of subjects (usually the mother) were interviewed with the *Parent Interview* (PARI), a 181-item informant interview in which parents were questioned about their adolescent offspring. The PARI is made up of a subset of items from the TOYS. Areas of function unlikely to be known to parents (e.g., obsessions) were omitted.

DSM-III Diagnoses

Prior to assessment, the recruiting social worker explained the study to participants and obtained signed consents. She noted the necessity for maintaining the blind, and explicitly requested that no mention be made of any biographical information about the youngster's first 13 years. Accordingly, questioning on the TOYS and PARI was restricted to functioning since age 13 only, and questions pertaining to elementary school years were systematically avoided.

All interviews were conducted by psychologists who were trained in clinical assessments. They were required to formulate DSM-III diagnoses and to justify each diagnosis by indicating, in a narrative summary, the criteria fulfilled. All narratives and diagnoses were blindly and independently checked (by S.M.), and questionable cases were reviewed with the project director (R.G.). Based on the concurrent, independent diagnoses of two psychologists who observed 27 interviews, an overall diagnostic agreement of 88% (kappa = .78) was obtained.

RESULTS

Diagnoses Based on Adolescents' (TOYS) and Parents' (PARI) Reports

Eighty-six probands (85%) and 95 parents of probands (94%) were interviewed; and in 80 cases (79%) both were interviewed. All 100 controls and 98 of their parents were interviewed; consequently, both informants were available for 98% of the control group.

Using both self- and parent reports (i.e., identifying the disorder as present if either informant reported symptoms), the full ADDH syndrome persisted in about one-third of probands. Also, Conduct Disorder and Substance Use Disorder (primarily marijuana abuse) were significantly more prevalent in probands. (For further details, see Gittelman et al., 1985).

Parent-Offspring Agreement. Table 12.1 shows the diagnostic agreement between the subjects and their parents, as indexed by kappa. For the proband and control groups, concordance and discordance are shown for the presence of any DSM-III disorder, and for each of the three most prevalent disorders and those that differentiated the probands and controls significantly: ADDH, Conduct/Antisocial Disorders, and Substance Use Disorder. Among the probands, agreement is somewhat improved when ADDH is not included as a mental disorder. The marked discordance between probands and their parents for ADDH (kappa = .19) is due to the relative excess of parental reports for this disorder. Conversely, the poor agreement for the diagnosis of Substance Use Disorder (kappa = .14) is accounted for by the fact that adolescents reported it more frequently than their parents.

With one exception, the kappa values for the control group are low, primarily because the base rates of disorders are so low that it is very difficult to exceed the very high chance prevalence of "no disorder." (Although such a situation yields low kappas that estimate how much the two sources agree controlling for chance agreement, it yields misleadingly high percentage agreement that capitalize on chance agreement.)

Discriminant Validity. To determine whether the two types of informants (parents and subjects) provided independent discrimination between

Table 12.1. Agreement between Adolescent Subjects and Their Parents on the Presence of DSM-III disorders at Follow-up in Probands and Controls

	Subject/Parent-Based Diagnoses					
	Yes/No $N(\%)$	*No/Yes* $N(\%)$	*Yes/Yes* $N(\%)$	*No/No* $N(\%)$	Percent Agreement	Kappa
Probands ($N = 80$)						
Any DSM-III						
Including ADD	3(4)	15(19)	25(31)	37(46)	77	.55
Excluding ADD	5(6)	5(6)	18(23)	52(65)	88	.69
ADDH*	4(5)	17(21)	5(6)	54(68)	74	.19
Conduct disorder	5(6)	4(5)	15(19)	56(70)	89	.69
Substance use disorder	10(13)	5(5)	2(2)	64(80)	82	.14
Controls ($N = 98$)						
Any DSM-III						
Including ADD	10(10)	5(5)	5(5)	78(80)	85	.32
Excluding ADD	10(10)	4(4)	4(4)	80(82)	86	.29
ADDH*	0	3(3)	0	95(97)	97	.00
Conduct disorder	5(5)	0	3(3)	90(92)	95	.52
Substance use disorder	5(5)	1(1)	1(1)	91(93)	94	.23

*Attention Deficit Disorder with Hyperactivity.

probands and controls, analyses of variance for proportions with arcsin transformation were applied to the diagnostic data for subjects who had an adolescent and parent interview ($n = 80$ and 98 for probands and controls, respectively). The results of these analyses are presented in Tables 12.2–12.5.

After controlling for the diagnoses based on the self-reports, the parents provided significant discrimination between the probands and controls for the presence of any DSM-III diagnosis ($\chi^2 = 28.73, p = .000$; see Table 12.2). Similar significant group discrimination was obtained from parent reports for ADDH ($\chi^2 = 19.60$, $p = .000$; see Table 12.3) and Conduct Disorder ($\chi^2 = 10.01, p = .007$; see Table 12.4). In the case of Substance Use Disorder, parents did not contribute independent discrimination to the group contrasts ($\chi^2 = 3.25$, NS; see Table 12.5).

Controlling for parental reports, the adolescents did not significantly discriminate between probands and controls for the presence of a DSM-III diagnosis ($\chi^2 = 1.00$, NS), Conduct Disorder ($\chi^2 = 0.88$, NS), or Substance Use Disorder ($\chi^2 = 3.80$, NS). However, the youngsters, independent of the parental reports, provided significant discrimination between cases and controls for the prevalence of ADDH ($\chi^2 = 7.51, p = .02$).

Odds ratios were calculated for each diagnostic group and compared for probands and controls. The odds ratio indicates the probability that a subject will be given a diagnosis based on self-report, if he is considered to have the diagnosis on the basis of parental report, and vice versa (Fleiss, 1973). An

Table 12.2. Pattern of Paired Agreement between Adolescents and Their Parents in 80 Probands and 98 Controls: DSM-III Diagnoses

		Parent Reports	
		Diagnosed	Not Diagnosed
Adolescent	Diagnosed	25/5 (83%)	3/10 (23%)
Reports	Not diagnosed	15/5 (75%)	37/78 (32%)

Numerator values are probands, denominator values are controls.

Numbers in parentheses represent the percentage of probands in that cell.

Parent reports, $\chi^2 = 28.73$, 2 DF, $p = .0000$ (controlled for adolescent reports).

Adolescent reports, $\chi^2 = 1.00$, 2 DF, NS (controlled for parent reports).

Table 12.3. Pattern of Paired Agreement between Adolescents and Their Parents in 80 Probands and 98 Controls: Attention Deficit Disorder

		Parent Reports	
		Diagnosed	Not Diagnosed
Adolescent	Diagnosed	5/0 (100%)	4/0 (100%)
Reports	Not diagnosed	17/3 (85%)	54/95 (36%)

Numerator values are probands, denominator values are controls.

Numbers in parentheses represent the percentage of probands in that cell.

Parent reports, $\chi^2 = 19.60$, 2 DF, $p = .0000$ (controlled for adolescent reports).

Adolescent reports, $\chi^2 = 7.51$, 2 DF, $p = .02$ (controlled for parent reports).

Table 12.4. Pattern of Paired Agreement between Adolescents and Their Parents in 80 Probands and 98 Controls: Conduct/ Antisocial Disorders

		Parent Reports	
		Diagnosed	Not Diagnosed
Adolescent Reports	Diagnosed	15/3 (83%)	5/5 (50%)
	Not diagnosed	4/0 (100%)	56/90 (38%)

Numerator values are probands, denominator values are controls.

Numbers in parentheses represent the percentage of probands in that cell.

Parent reports, $\chi^2 = 10.01$, 2 DF, $p = .007$ (controlled for adolescent reports).

Adolescent reports, $\chi^2 = 0.88$, 2 DF, NS (controlled for parent reports).

Table 12.5. Pattern of Paired Agreement between Adolescents and Their Parents in 80 Probands and 98 Controls: Substance Use Disorders

		Parent Reports	
		Diagnosed	Not Diagnosed
Adolescent Reports	Diagnosed	2/1 (67%)	10/5 (67%)
	Not diagnosed	4/1 (80%)	64/91 (38%)

Numerator values are probands, denominator values are controls.

Numbers in parentheses represent the percentage of probands in that cell.

Parent reports, $\chi^2 = 3.25$, 2 DF, NS. (controlled for adolescent reports).

Adolescent reports, $\chi^2 = 3.80$, 2 DF, NS. (controlled for parent reports).

Table 12.6. Relationship between Adolescent and Parent Diagnoses for Probands and Controls

	Odds Ratio			
Disorder	Probands	Controls	χ^2	p
Any disorder				
Including ADD	20.6	7.8	0.99	NS
Excluding ADD	37.4	8.0	2.22	NS
ADDH	4.0	27.3	0.74	NS
Conduct disorder	42.0	115.2	0.55	NS
Substance use disorder	3.2	18.2	0.96	NS

Note: The χ^2 values were computed for a log-linear model with maximum-likelihood estimations (Bishop, Feinberg, & Holland, 1975), and were used to test the significance of a group $\times$ adolescent $\times$ parent interaction.

odds ratio of 1 indicates chance agreement or equivalent likelihood for each informant source. As is shown in Table 12.6, there were no significant differences in odds ratios between subject groups, suggesting that the relationship between parent and adolescent reporting, regarding the risk for being diagnosed, was not different for probands and controls.

The DIS in the Assessment of Adolescents

All interviewers had experience administering the DIS to adolescents, and to adults, because the study included a DIS interview with the parents. Therefore, we were able to appreciate whether difficulties in assessment differed among younger and older individuals. Over 100 of the probands and controls were below age 18, and many had recently reached their sixteenth birthday.

We encountered no practical problems in using an expanded version of the DIS for assessing adolescent subjects. The wording of the DIS was not difficult for them to understand, and the instrument was very well accepted.

DISCUSSION

In the current study, parents and their adolescent offspring achieved good agreement on the diagnosis of Conduct Disorder. Unlike Herjanic and Reich (1982), we did not find that antisocial behavior was reported significantly more frequently by children than by parents. However, these investigators presented data on discrete antisocial *acts*, whereas we assessed the reliability of antisocial *disorders*. These would be expected to covary, but would not necessarily be identical.

Different from Conduct Disorder, reliability of ADDH was poor, showing a fourfold difference between the parent and self-reports of probands. This finding is consistent with Stewart *et al.*'s (1973) report that mothers reported more ADDH symptoms.

The above observations bear on reliability, or parent–offspring agreement, but do not address the issue of accuracy of reporting, or validity. Our findings on discriminant validity show that, for the full ADDH syndrome, both parent reports and self-reports discriminated between probands and controls even after controlling for diagnoses based on the other informant (parent or self). However, for Antisocial Disorder, parent diagnoses, but not self-diagnoses, significantly differentiated former patients and controls. These results suggest that, if group discrimination is taken as an index of validity, parent reports appear to have greater sensitivity for Antisocial Disorder than adolescent reports. Inspection of the data presented in Table 12.1 supports this conclusion. Although there was acceptable general agreement between parents and adolescents on the diagnosis of Antisocial Disorder (kappas = .69 and .52 for probands and controls, respectively), the diagnosis was given to four probands but *no* control on the basis of parent reports; in contrast, five probands and five controls were diagnosed as having an Antisocial Disorder on the basis of self-reports, exclusively.

Although there was very poor agreement between the probands and their parents for the diagnosis of ADDH, it cannot be concluded that positive reports of ADDH from adolescents are uninformative. Indeed, it is worth pointing out that the four cases of ADDH who were diagnosed exclusively on the basis of self-reports were all probands. Therefore, self-reports of ADDH in adolescents appear to have high specificity since the subjects given this diagnosis exclusively on the basis of self-reports were all from the affected group.

A word of caution is in order. The ability to discriminate between clinical and control groups is only one method of assessing validity. However, if parents of probands tended to report symptoms known to have occurred in their children's early years, this bias in reporting would be expected to increase subject group contrasts and, consequently, spuriously suggest that discriminant validity was demonstrated. Future investigators should obtain measures of other forms of validity as well, to establish that accuracy is being evaluated. We are presently assessing the relationship between Antisocial Disorder and criminal records to determine whether parent or self-reports are better indicators of concurrent validity (arrests during the follow-up interval), as well as predictive validity (arrests after evaluation).

Regarding epidemiological studies of mental disorder, the current research indicates that it is feasible to evaluate adolescents using an interview schedule designed for adults. Judging from our observation that questions seemed to pose no difficulty and were understood by adolescents, our general impression is that the DIS can be used effectively to diagnose individuals in this age group.

ACKNOWLEDGMENTS

This research was supported by USPHS Grant MH-18579 and MHCRC Grant MH-30906.
  The authors would like to thank Donald F. Klein and Mark Davies, for their helpful comments and suggestions concerning data analyses.

REFERENCES

Bishop, Y. M. M., Feinberg, S. E., & Holland, P. W. (1975). *Discrete multivariate analysis.* Cambridge: MIT Press.

Cohen, P., O'Connor, P., Lewis, S., Puig-Antich, J., & Malachowski, B. (1984, October). *A comparison of lay and clinician administered psychiatric diagnostic interviews of an epidemiological sample of children.* Paper presented at the annual meeting of the American Academy of Child Psychiatry, Toronto.

Costello, A. J., Edelbrock, C. S., Kalas, R., Kessler, M., & Klaric, S. A. (1982). *NIMH Diagnostic Interview Schedule for Children.* Pittsburgh: Western Psychiatric Institute.

Endicott, J., & Spitzer, R. L. (1980). Psychiatric rating scales. In H. I. Kaplan, A. M. Freedman, & B. J. Sadock (Eds.), *Comprehensive textbook of psychiatry.* Vol. 3 (3rd ed.; pp. 2391–2409). Baltimore: Williams & Wilkins.

Fleiss, J. (1973). *Statistical methods for rates and proportions.* New York: Wiley.

Gittelman, R., Mannuzza, S., Shenker, R., & Bonagura, N. (1985). Hyperactive boys almost grown up: I. Psychiatric status. *Archives of General Psychiatry, 42,* 937–947.

Herjanic, B., Herjanic, M., Brown, F., & Wheatt, T. (1975). Are children reliable reporters? *Journal of Abnormal Child Psychology, 3,* 41–48.

Herjanic, B., & Reich, W. (1982). Development of a structured psychiatric interview for children: Agreement between child and parent on individual symptoms. *Journal of Abnormal Child Psychology, 10,* 307–324.

Kashani, J. H., Orvaschel, H., Burk, J. P., & Reid, J. C. (1985). Informant variance: The issue of parent-child disagreement. *Journal of the American Academy of Child Psychiatry, 24,* 413–428.

Kovacs, M., Feinberg, T. L., Crouse-Novak, M. A., Paulauskas, S. L., & Finkelstein, R. (1984). Depressive disorders in childhood. *Archives of General Psychiatry, 41,* 229–237.

Puig-Antich, J. (1982). The use of RDC criteria for major depressive disorder in children and adolescents. *Journal of the American Academy of Child Psychiatry, 21,* 291–293.

Robins, L. N., Helzer, J. E., Croughan, J., & Ratcliff, K. S. (1981). National Institute of Mental Health Diagnostic Interview Schedule. *Archives of General Psychiatry, 38,* 381–389.

Robins, L. N., Helzer, J. E., Ratcliff, K. S., & Seyfried, W. (1982). Validity of the Diagnostic Interview Schedule, version II: DSM-III diagnoses. *Psychological Medicine, 12*, 855–870.

Stewart, M. A., Mendelson, W. B., & Johnson, N. E. (1973). Hyperactive children as adolescent: How they describe themselves. *Child Psychiatry and Human Development, 4*, 3–11.

DISCUSSION

Brigitte Prusoff: Did you say that the mothers were more important in assessing substance abuse and that the children did not know when they were abusing substances?

Gittelman: I did not say that. I indicated that if you control for parental reports of substance-abuse disorders, and if you use discriminant validity as your measure of accuracy, the parent and self-reports were redundant in the sense that neither contributed significantly to the distinction between former patients and controls. This applies once you control for the other source of information.

Prusoff: But if your validating criteria were adequate in this particular case, why should you assume that probands actually had more substance abuse?

Gittelman: I don't assume it; they do.

John Helzer: In the data you showed, there were 16 cases of substance abuse. In 10 of these the adolescent reported it. In 2 cases both parent and adolescent reported it, and in 4 cases only the parent reported it.

Gittelman: I did not intend to imply that you should not ask youngsters about substance-abuse disorder.

Helzer: In fact, it seemed just the opposite. They were the ones who know about it and who for the most part reported it.

Gittelman: True, but they did not give discrimination above and beyond what the parents reported.

Janet Williams: You said you did psychiatric assessments of the parents as well. Did you look at the differential validity of the reports from those parents who had significant psychopathology compared with the reports from those who were normal?

Gittelman: We did not, because we obtained no differences between the probands and controls in parental psychopathology.

Fay Stetner: Has anybody looked at it the other way around, by examining how many people with antisocial personality and substance abuse have histories of Attention Deficit Disorder (ADD)?

Gittelman: Yes, but retrospectively. That is a very risky exercise because we do not know the accuracy of the information obtained, unless we have contemporary records or confirmation from other sources. Perhaps others could address this question, since I do not have much experience with adult antisocial personality disorders with regard to what they report in their early histories.

Hans Huessy: Using a questionnaire that we validated on adult patients with ADD, we found that 45% of adult male alcoholics gave answers that were consistent with a childhood ADD history. Paul Wender, with a more limited instrument, came up with 35%.

13

Diagnostic Categorization by the
Diagnostic Interview Schedule (DIS):
A Comparison with Other Methods of Assessment

JACK D. BURKE, JR.
National Institute of Mental Health

INTRODUCTION

This chapter reviews studies that have assessed performance of the Diagnostic Interview Schedule (DIS) in assigning diagnoses to patients and community residents. The background for this topic has already been established in Chapter 12 by James Barrett, who discussed the issue of validating diagnostic categories, and in Chapter 5 by Gerald Klerman who made an important distinction between that task and the validation of diagnostic instruments.

Also relevant to this latter point is a major paper by Dr. Robert Spitzer (1983), who discussed the problem of validating diagnostic assessments in a review of the development of standardized diagnostic interviews and the impact of the DIS. Since I am picking up the same topic, it seems appropriate to begin by quoting him: "The DIS has put the proverbial ball in the clinician's court and the score is 40–love in favor of the DIS."

Let me hasten to say, as someone who has great respect for both the DIS and clinical interviews like the SCID, I think the sides are more evenly matched than that early score indicates. In fact, I wonder if Spitzer may have called the score at that point just to take advantage of the fact that at tennis matches in New York everyone cheers for the underdog!

This chapter considers a series of studies evaluating the performance of the DIS in assigning diagnoses to patients and community residents. These studies are important in understanding how to interpret findings from the Epidemiologic Catchment Area program (ECA), which relied on the DIS to generate diagnostic information on nearly 20,000 subjects (Eaton *et al.*, 1984; Myers *et al.*, 1984; Regier *et al.*, 1984; Robins *et al.*, 1984; Shapiro *et al.*, 1984). They are also important in a broader sense, to help understand the nature of diagnostic assessments and the types of discrepancies that arise when different techniques are used to apply the same diagnostic criteria.

An epidemiologic survey as large and ambitious as the ECA program could not have been undertaken before formulation of explicit diagnostic criteria in a system like the DSM-III (APA, 1980). A major concern of contemporary epidemiologic investigations has been the question, What is a case? (Wing, Bebbington, & Robins, 1980). With DSM-III's explicit statement of the minimum requirements for a diagnostic assignment, it was possible for Lee Robins, John Helzer, and their colleagues to write an interview schedule, the DIS, which applied these criteria. By building on the semistructured Renard Diagnostic Interview (Helzer, Robins, Croughan, & Welner, 1981), the authors of the DIS were able to write a set of completely specified questions to inquire about a subject's experience with the phenomena required by DSM-III. That approach made it seem feasible to use nonclinicians for the data collection, and to use a computer program to score the interview data and generate diagnostic output.

When the DIS was introduced for the ECA program, there was an immediate rush to use it by a multitude of other investigators as well, and it achieved a remarkable prominence almost by default, since it was the only well-known instrument suitable for DSM-III diagnoses. At the same time, it generated a certain skepticism: almost before it was used, some investigators questioned the lack of clinical judgment allowed the interviewer, the apparent unyielding rigidity of the probe system, and the details of how interview questions had been tailored to fit DSM-III criteria (Endicott, 1981; Ganguli & Saul, 1982; Robins & Helzer, 1981, 1982; Van Korff, Anthony, & Kramer, 1982). Now that some studies have conducted and reported about how the DIS performs, a tentative perspective can be gained on the usefulness of diagnostic output from the DIS. Just as important, by examining the nature of any discrepancies between the DIS and other assessment procedures, it may be possible to gain a clearer understanding of the problematic areas in diagnostic assessments in general.

METHODOLOGIC ISSUES

Categorization of Studies

The clearest way to categorize reports about a new diagnostic instrument would be to group them as studying either reliability or validity. So far, in terms of reliability, interrater agreement has been the focus in studies of the DIS. The large body of work on establishing reliability of psychiatric diagnoses, which in many ways led to development of explicit diagnostic criteria like the DSM-III, has produced guidelines for how interrater reliability should be established. Test-retest designs, with small intervals between the two administrations of the interview, have been preferred over exercises that rely on videotape or joint ratings of a single interview (Carey & Gottesman,

1978; Grove, Andreasen, McDonald-Scott, Keller, Shapiro, 1981; Klerman, 1983).

With the DIS, this test-retest design has been used, but there has been a complication because some of these studies have examined two issues at once—both the consistency across raters and the comparison of nonclinician and clinician interviewers. For example, in a preliminary study of the DIS conducted before the ECA began, Robins and her colleagues (Robins, Helzer, Croughan, & Ratcliff, 1981; Robins, Helzer, Ratcliff, & Seyfried, 1982) tested the DIS administered by a nonclinician versus the DIS administered by a clinician. That design was more than a test-retest study with two equivalent raters. As a result, some of these test-retest studies, which compared a nonclinician's DIS with a clinician's DIS, have been designated studies of "procedural validity," a term developed by Spitzer and Williams (1984) for testing the process of making a diagnosis.

Another problem has arisen in determining what an appropriate validity standard for a diagnostic instrument would be. Spitzer (1983) has addressed the issue by noting that there is no "gold standard" in psychiatry; similarly, in discussions among ECA investigators, Helzer has said that there are no "pure" DSM-III diagnoses separate from the method being used to apply the criteria.

So, a single cross-sectional comparison of any two instruments may not offer an adequate test of validity of the diagnostic assignment. For this reason, Dohrenwend and Shrout (1981) have proposed a "multimethod" strategy that uses more than just two independent instruments to assess the accuracy of an epidemiologic case-finding instrument. More generally, the work by Robins and Guze (1970) on criteria for diagnostic validity, as discussed by Akiskal (1980), Klerman (1983), and Barrett (Chapter 11), has suggested that a rigorous test of validity requires longitudinal investigation of both internal psychopathologic criteria and of external criteria like biological markers and response to treatment. Spitzer (1983) introduced the LEAD standard as a possible way of testing the validity of diagnostic assessments. This approach entails a *l*ongitudinal assessment by *e*xperts of *a*ll the *d*ata about a subject to formulate a best estimate or summary diagnosis to use as a standard of comparison. This proposal is important because it demonstrates how a test based on external validity criteria can be implemented in evaluating diagnostic instruments, assuming that appropriate criteria can be selected for the disorders in question. Since the studies so far reported have used only a single cross-sectional comparison to a single criterion measure, they may not meet the standards for a true test of "validity" of the DIS. As a result, these data appear at best suggestive until tests of predictive validity can be undertaken, such as implied in the proposal for the LEAD standard.

For these reasons, to avoid introducing any extra misclassification errors, it may be best to assume a conservative stance and refrain from classifying the existing studies of the DIS as "reliability" or "validity" studies.

Instead, they will be classified here as *test-retest* designs, when they compare the DIS with itself, or as *clinical comparisons*, when they compare the DIS with a psychiatrist's diagnosis made in some different way than with readministration of the DIS.

Data Reviewed

Cohen (1960), Bartko and Carpenter (1976), and Fleiss and his colleagues (Fleiss, 1981; Spitzer & Fleiss, 1974) have demonstrated the importance of using a statistic with appropriate properties when measuring agreement. As a result, most of the authors have presented their findings in terms of kappa; that uniformity is a happy finding for a reviewer, and it will be convenient to concentrate on those values in this chapter. Guidelines for interpreting values of kappa have been proposed; values above .75 can be interpreted to indicate excellent agreement, values between .40 and .75 indicate good agreement, and values below .40 indicate poor agreement beyond chance (Landis & Koch, 1977). At the same time, kappa does present one difficulty for any study of rare conditions. As Grove *et al.* (1981) have pointed out, for a fixed sensitivity and specificity, kappa is attenuated by a low base rate of the condition being studied (see Table 13.1).

As a consequence, they recommended caution in reporting kappa with low base rates of the condition being studied, and themselves decided not to report kappa when the base rate was below 5%.

To overcome this attenuation, Helzer and Spitznagel (1985) have proposed the use of another statistic, Yule's *Y*, a measure of association related to the odds ratio. Yule's *Y* may have other difficulties; for example, like the odds ratio, it may vary when the number of disagreements is constant but take on different patterns along the alternate diagonal of a two-way table (J. Fleiss, personal communication, June 1984; Bishop, Feinberg, & Holland, 1975). But one useful point is that it seems to indicate the approximate value that

Table 13.1. Effect of Low Prevalence Rates on Kappa

Prevalence Rate	Maximum Kappa
50%	.81
25%	.76
1%	.14

Assume: Sensitivity = .95; specificity = .95.
Source: Grove *et al.*, 1981.

Table 13.2. Variations among DIS Studies

1. Nature of comparison
   DIS vs. DIS, or
   DIS vs. a psychiatrist's diagnosis?
2. Type of subjects
   Clinic or community?
3. Time frame of diagnosis
   Lifetime or one month?

kappa would take if the prevalence rate in the sample were 50%. I will present values for Yule's *Y* when they are reported by the authors or when they can be calculated from the data presented (Bishop *et al.*, 1975).

Studies Included

To my knowledge, 10 studies have been published or will soon be published that address characteristics of the DIS in terms of specific DSM-III disorders. In addition, at least two other studies are relevant to this topic but are still preliminary. The authors of these two studies have generously provided some indication of their results, which will be mentioned but in less detail. However, all of the studies reported have had somewhat different designs; they also have different levels of quality. Although they will be treated equally in any summary display of findings, some of their strengths and weaknesses may become clear in this comparative review.

Each of the studies has reported on disorders covered by the DIS, but sometimes on only a subset of those. To provide as much comparability as possible, and to restrict the scope of information presented here, we concentrate on four disorders: Major depression (Major Depressive Episode); panic disorder; alcohol abuse and dependence; and schizophrenia. Two of these (depression and alcohol abuse) are common and illustrate interesting problems of how to construct a diagnosis; panic disorder presents special difficulties in timing episodes, and it has generally given the poorest results of any disorder; schizophrenia is difficult to study because it is so rare in a general population, but two special studies provide supplementary information about it (Pulver & Carpenter, 1983; Escobar, Randolph, Asamen, & Karno, in press).

To organize this material, three key features of the various studies will be used to provide a framework for discussion: these are the nature of the comparison made; the type of sample used; and the time frame of the diagnosis assigned (see Table 13.2). The first feature to consider is the type of comparison. As noted, some of the studies compared the diagnosis from one

DIS to the diagnosis from a second DIS. Depending on the study design, these could have been administered by two nonclinicians only, by two clinicians only, or by one clinician and one nonclinician. Comparisons in the second group of studies were made between a DIS diagnosis and a diagnosis based on examinations by a psychiatrist; these psychiatric diagnoses ranged from routine chart diagnoses to independent research interviews by an alternative instrument.

The second feature is the type of sample. It has often been argued that case-finding in the community is made difficult by several problems: the pathology may not be so severe or so prototypic as in clinical samples, and the subjects may be harder to interview because there is no presenting complaint and there may be no willingness or experience with the process of diagnostic interviewing. For these reasons, it has been suggested that findings in clinical samples may not carry over to community samples. It should also be noted that if baseline rates are low in the community, the attenuation of kappa with rare conditions may pose more of a problem in community samples.

A third feature is the time period of diagnosis. Most of the studies have reported findings based on the subject's lifetime, but at least one has concentrated on disorders present in the one month prior to interview. Studies dealing with lifetime diagnoses may suffer problems of poor subject recall; those dealing with current diagnoses may suffer problems about how to determine whether a disorder with recent activity should be judged present in a predetermined time period.

REVIEW OF FINDINGS

DIS versus DIS

Four studies have used a test-retest design to compare the DIS against itself (see Table 13.3). The first of these, conducted in St. Louis, used a sample composed mainly of psychiatric patients or ex-patients, for a total of 217 subjects (Robins *et al.*, 1981; Robins *et al.*, 1982) (see Table 13.4).

Lifetime diagnoses were compared for a DIS administered by a nonclinician and a second administered by a clinician, in random order. This study was the first to highlight the fact that a simple dichotomy of reliability and validity could not be applied to these DIS studies. After some consideration, this study design was designated as being "intermediate," offering something more than a test-retest of equivalent raters, but something less than comparison with an independent clinical diagnosis as a criterion. In this study, the findings were excellent for alcohol disorders (kappa = .86), good for major depression (kappa = .63) and schizophrenia (kappa = .60), and the base

Table 13.3. Summary of Study Features

	Comparison Measure		Subjects	
	DIS vs. DIS	DIS vs. MD	Clinic	Community
Robins	x		x	
Burnam	x		x	
Helzer	x			x
Wittchen	x			x
Hesselbrock		x	x	
Hendricks		x	x	
Anthony		x		x
Helzer		x		x
Wittchen		x	x	x

rates were high enough to use kappa with some confidence. For panic disorder, kappa was only fair (kappa = .40). As a result of this study, some refinements were made to the DIS and a new version (3) was produced for the use of ECA sites. (Yale began its first wave of surveys with the same DIS used in this study.) Early on, objection was made that it may be risky to draw too much reassurance from the findings of this study if community subjects are different and more difficult to assess than a clinical sample.

Another study conducted as part of preliminary fieldwork for the ECA program was reported by Burnam and colleagues (Burnam, Karno, Hough, Escobar, & Forsythe, 1983) at UCLA, who developed a Spanish translation of the DIS for use with Hispanic subjects there (see Table 13.4).

In that study, 151 monolingual and bilingual Spanish-speaking CMHC patients were given the DIS in a test-retest design by nonclinician interview-

Table 13.4. DIS versus DIS Comparison Studies: DSM-III Disorders

	Clinic samples		Community samples	
	Robins	Burnam	Helzer	Wittchen
Major Depression	0.63	0.56	0.33 (0.58)	0.76
Panic disorder	0.40	0.42	0.28 (0.67)	0.47
Alcohol disorders	0.86	0.76	0.68 (0.76)	
Schizophrenia	0.60	0.56		

Note. Values refer to kappa and (Yule's *Y*).

ers; bilingual patients took one DIS in English and the other in Spanish. The results for lifetime DSM-III diagnoses in the combined sample, of Spanish–Spanish and Spanish–English comparisons, were nearly as good as those obtained in the St. Louis study by Robins; again, there was excellent agreement for alcohol disorders (kappa = .76), good agreement for depression (kappa = .56) and schizophrenia (kappa = .56), and fair for panic disorder (kappa = .42).

A third study was performed by Helzer and colleagues (Helzer *et al.*, 1985) in St. Louis as part of the initial ECA community survey there (see Table 13.4). Three hundred ninety-four community residents were selected from designated diagnostic categories based on DIS results and were reinterviewed by a psychiatrist. One instrument used in this reinterview was the DIS administered by a psychiatrist. For lifetime diagnoses on the DIS, agreement for three of the disorders being considered here was lower than in the two clinical studies above. Agreement measured by kappa ranged from good (kappa = .68) for alcohol disorders to poor (kappa = .33 for major depression and kappa = .28 for panic.) However, the authors suggest that at least part of the reduction in kappa values could be caused by the very much lower prevalence of these disorders in the general population than in the sample of patients. That suggestion seems to be confirmed by the much higher values of Yule's Y, which the authors suggest indicate the value that kappa would reach in this sample if the prevalence rate were close to the 50% where kappa is at its maximum. In this case, the values for Y are excellent ($Y = .76$ for alcohol) and good ($Y = .67$ for panic, and $Y = .58$ for depression) (see Table 13.4).

The fourth study was conducted in Munich, Germany by H.-U. Wittchen and colleagues (Wittchen & Semler, 1984) as part of a longitudinal study of community residents and ex-patients followed over 7 years. In a study using a total of 62 subjects, including 42 from the community sample, 10 healthy subjects, and only 10 from the patient sample, they demonstrated in a test-retest study that agreement for depression (kappa = .76) and panic disorder (kappa = .47) was even better than in the two clinical samples studied in St. Louis and Los Angeles. Alcohol disorders were not assessed, and only one case of schizophrenia was found, but both times the DIS interviewer found it. In this study, the interviewers were doctoral level clinicians, including clinical psychologists and psychiatrists at the Max Planck Institute.

Preliminary findings from a similar study in Puerto Rico by Canino, Bird, & Shrout (in preparation) are also available. Using the Spanish translation of the DIS and a mixed sample of 60 community residents and 129 outpatients, they first conducted a procedural validity test with nonclinicians and psychiatrists as the two interviewers. Their findings showed that kappa for major depression and for panic disorder was about .6 in each case; and for schizophrenia it was about .45.

In the past, there has been some concern that in the rush to test whether the DIS is "valid," the basic question of its interrater reliability has been overlooked. Because these studies used such different designs, and the comparisons were complicated by a mix of interviewers and by foreign-language translations, they may not yield definitive conclusions, but they do suggest that interrater reliability is adequate for disorders like alcohol abuse and major depression. To judge from the study in Germany and from the Yule's *Y* values in the St. Louis ECA substudy, the interrater agreement in a community population may be similar to that demonstrated in a clinical sample.

DIS versus Diagnosis by a Psychiatrist

Although the interpretation of the test-retest studies was complicated, it is even more difficult to sort out the studies that used a psychiatrist's diagnosis as a criterion for the DIS. There was a wide variation in the sampling designs of these studies, and in some instances little information is provided about the nature of the clinical assessment procedure that was used to generate the psychiatrist's diagnosis.

Several of the studies that used a test-retest design also reported some comparisons to clinical diagnoses independent of the DIS. The first study, by Robins (Robins *et al.*, 1981; Robins *et al.*, 1982), compared DIS diagnoses with routine chart diagnoses; although these comparisons were favorable, the authors cautioned that using routine diagnoses from a teaching hospital from a time before DSM-III was in use was of questionable value in understanding any new diagnostic interview. The study from UCLA by Burnam *et al.* (1983) also compared DIS diagnoses to those made by mental health clinicians after unstructured interviews. However, these were not doctoral level clinicians, and little information is provided about how standardized the clinical assessments were. These comparisons were overall less favorable to the DIS than the results from other studies. Also, the study by Canino and colleagues in Puerto Rico compared the nonclinician DIS diagnoses with those made by the psychiatrists who had given the DIS but made independent judgments; in this case, the kappa values for major depression and schizophrenia were about .26–.29, but for panic disorder, kappa = .49.

The earliest study published with a careful comparison of the DIS with a research diagnostic assessment performed by psychiatrists was conducted by Hesselbrock and colleagues (Hesselbrock, Stabeneau, Hesselbrock, Mirkin, & Meyer, 1982) on an alcohol treatment unit (see Table 13.5). With 42 patients in this specialized unit, a mix of clinicians and nonclinicians administered the DIS and psychiatrists administered the lifetime version of the Schedule for Affective Disorders and Schizophrenia (SADS-L). For both present and past disorders, there was remarkably high agreement on RDC diagnoses of major depression (kappa = .72 present and kappa = .74 past) and alcohol disorder (kappa = 1.0 for both present and past diagnoses). The only other diagnoses reported were drug abuse and antisocial personality, which were also high. Note that the agreement values for alcohol disorders were not trivial, since not all patients qualified for the diagnosis.

Using 46 adult black patients in three diagnostic categories, Hendricks *et al.* (1983) studied performance of the DIS against routine chart diagnoses (see Table 13.5). The DIS interviewers were medical students and mental health clinicians in training; their own training on the DIS was not specified. The nature of the chart diagnoses used as a standard is not clear from this report; whether these were recent, whether they were reviewed independently to see if DSM-III criteria had been documented to justify the diagnosis, and whether the DIS interviewers were blind to the clinical diagnosis are relevant questions not answered in their article. As a result, the findings may be viewed at best as being suggestive. In this study, agreement for major depression was perfect (kappa = 1.0) and was good for alcohol (kappa = 0.50) and poor for schizophrenia (kappa = 0.24).

In the study previously described with 394 community residents from the ECA survey, Helzer *et al.* (1985) also had the psychiatrists complete a check-list of DSM-III criteria while they were readministering the DIS to subjects (see Table 13.5). At the conclusion of that interview, the psychiatrists probed any doubtful information and formulated their own clinical diagnoses. This procedure is very interesting, because it allows an item-by-item review of DIS questions to see which ones may have produced the most discrepancy in the DIS rating versus the psychiatrist's judgment. One difficulty is that it considers only lifetime symptoms; additional concerns about the timing of symptoms cannot be assessed so easily from these checklist data.

Table 13.5. DIS versus Psychiatrist's Diagnosis: DSM-III Disorders

	Hesselbrock (Clinic)	Hendricks (Clinic)	Anthony (Community)	Helzer (Community)	Wittchen (Clinic)	Wittchen (Community)
Major Depression	0.72	1.0	0.25 (0.71)	0.28 (0.58)	0.84	0.72
Panic disorders				0.32 (0.70)	0.45	0.30
Alcohol disorders	1.0	0.50	0.35 (0.65)	0.63 (0.73)		
Schizophrenia		0.24	0.19 (0.76)		0.44	0.53[a]

Note. Values represent kappa and (Yule's *Y*).
*Results refer to RDC Schizophrenia.

For alcohol disorders, the kappa value (kappa = .63) is consistent with the values from the other studies; however, kappa for major depression (kappa = .28) is lower than in other studies, and in fact is lower than for panic disorder (kappa = .32) in this study. To some extent, these findings may reflect the very low prevalence rates; lifetime prevalence for alcohol at St. Louis was 15.7%, for example, but for panic it was 1.5%, and for depression, 5.5%. This low prevalence is reflected in the comparatively higher rates calculated for Yule's Y than for kappa; for panic the value for Yule's Y ($Y = .70$) is above the range set by other studies, and for depression ($Y = .58$) it is close to the value of kappa in the prior studies.

The next study, conducted at Baltimore and reported by Anthony *et al.* (1985), is the largest, the most sophisticated in sampling, and the most ambitious in its effort to formulate clinically meaningful diagnoses. A total of 810 community residents were sampled on a probability basis from the ECA survey; four psychiatrists who had been kept completely blind to the DIS administered an independent examination, often in the subject's home, and formulated diagnoses according to DSM-III, ICD-9, and the Johns Hopkins classification systems; they also conducted brief neurological examinations and dictated case formulations and treatment recommendations. The principal guide to the examination was the Standardized Psychiatric Examination, a protocol developed by Drs. Romanoski and Chahal. At its core, the SPE is based on the one-month time frame of the Present State Examination, ninth edition, but in addition to covering the past month also covers past psychiatric and social history; to demonstrate the effort involved, 1209 items were added to the 140 items in the PSE to provide coverage of every diagnosis included in either the DSM-III or ICD systems (Folstein *et al.*, 1985).

Such a massive effort is admirable. It was clearly imaginative, and clearly relied on the dedication of the psychiatric interviewers throughout the study. Confronted with such a mammoth undertaking, though, other investigators almost cannot resist asking questions about the methodology. Two of the basic questions are worth raising here for their general relevance to this chapter, although I will try to outline them rather than adjudicate them:

First, could such a lengthy and demanding examination have been given with acceptable levels of reliability, comparable for example to those reported in the four DIS test-retest studies? No test-retest study has been done on the SPE, but the investigators at Baltimore report that group ratings of 35 videotaped interviews that were recorded during the course of the study provided acceptable agreement. Also, a portion of the sample was assigned to the four raters at random, and there was no significant variation in diagnostic rates among the examining psychiatrists for this group of subjects.

Second, what does such a comparison mean? The SPE has even on the surface enough differences with the DIS approach to cause some confusion about how to interpret any level of agreement or disagreement. For example, the need to find a way to integrate assessments of past history into the one-month framework borrowed from the PSE, the irreversible application of DSM-III exclusions which are not used in the ECA findings, and primary reliance on a one-month framework even for diagnoses like panic disorder or major depression, whose episodes may be hard to specify, all suggest major differences with interviews like the DIS, or even the SADS-L. One point used to illustrate the difference is the variation in prevalence rates found by the two methods. To cite the disorder with the greatest difference, the estimated one-month prevalence of phobias in Baltimore, by the DIS, was 11.2%; by the SPE, it was 21.3%.

I believe the response of the Baltimore investigators to this second point is that it was considered appropriate to use a blind, independent clinical assessment method for comparison, rather than simply accepting the DIS approach as setting the terms for comparison; the choice of the PSE as a framework was made because of its clinical relevance and its demonstrated reliability in other studies; and the nature of any resulting discrepancies between the two procedures can be studied (see Table 13.5).

The kappa values for three of the four disorders considered here are quite low, in the same range as found in the St. Louis study of community residents: major depression, kappa = .25; alcohol, kappa = .35; schizophrenia, kappa = .19. However, the prevalence rates are also low, and since the authors have reported the cross-product or odds ratio, it is possible to calculate Yule's Y for their data. If these estimates of agreement are accepted (for major depression, $Y = .71$, for alcohol, $Y = .65$, for schizophrenia, $Y = .76$), the values for Yule's Y suggest that agreement as measured by kappa appears low because of the low prevalence, but the strong association demonstrated by Y suggests that agreement may improve in samples with higher base rates. Interpretation of such findings will likely rest on whether a convincing argument has been made (cf. Helzer & Spitznagel, 1985) that a measure like Yule's Y is an adequate supplement to kappa when the sample being studied has a low base rate of the condition of interest.

Finally, another important study of the DIS has been performed in Munich by Wittchen, Semler, & von Zerssen (1985) (see Table 13.5). As part of the 7-year follow-up study of community residents and ex-patients, which provided subjects for the test-retest study of the German-language DIS, Wittchen and colleagues compared the DIS, as administered by psychologists and psychiatrists, to independent clinical assessments made on follow-up by psychiatrists who made ICD-8 diagnoses. For 130 subjects in the general population sample with a DIS diagnosis, high agreement was found between lifetime DSM-III diagnoses on the DIS and ICD-8 principal diagnoses for most disorders: for major depression, kappa = .72; for RDC schizophrenia, kappa = .53; and for panic disorder, kappa = .30. Not surprisingly, the agreement was at least as high when the cases found among the community residents were combined with cases found in the sample of ex-patients. However, these calculations are based on a sample of 130 that omits 42 subjects who were given ICD diagnoses that are not covered on the DIS, like personality disorders.

Another important study is being prepared for publication, and the investigators have provided some preliminary findings for this review. From the Yale ECA team, Myrna Weissman and Phil Leaf have conducted a study of an expanded SADS-L given by psychiatrists in comparison to the DIS diagnoses on 139 community residents from the ECA. In their study, they indicate that kappa values for affective disorders and for substance-use disorders are about .60, and Yule's Y values are about .70 or higher (M. Weissman, personal communication, 1985).

Another study published recently has compared the DIS to the Psychiatric Diagnostic Interview, a clinical interview for DSM-III developed by Othmer and colleagues in Kansas (Weller, Penick, Powell, Othmer, Rice, & Kent, 1985). Overall agreements with syndromes and symptoms were reported to be high, but data for specific DSM-III disorders have not yet been published.

Summary by Disorder

For major depression and alcohol disorders, the values for kappa have been relatively high, and generally acceptable. Schizophrenia is inconsistent, but considering values for Yule's Y to compensate for low prevalence, it may be that values for this disorder are acceptable. However, for panic disorder, the highest values obtained are usually at a marginal level of acceptability, and using Yule's Y does not provide much reassurance.

In reference to schizophrenia, two other studies of interest have been performed. A study by Pulver and Carpenter (1983) reported findings from their effort to administer the DIS to 43 subjects from the original cohort of 68 followed for five years in the Washington Center of the IPSS. Looking at lifetime symptom reports, they found that the DIS was able to detect 85.7% of delusions and 64% of hallucinations that had been present on one of the previous examinations of the sample, using the PSE. The authors expressed some disappointment at this evidence of apparently low sensitivity for past symptoms, and were concerned that surveys like the ECA would seriously undercount psychotic individuals. However, several interested investigators from the ECA have questioned details of that study design and have suggested that the figures were not so low, compared with what might have been expected in a group of psychotic patients (Carpenter & Pulver, 1984; Helzer & Robins, 1984; Karno, Burnam, Escobar, & Timbers, 1984; Pulver & Carpenter, 1984). A second study by Escobar *et al.* (in press) at UCLA examined performance of the DIS in a sample of 82 schizophrenics from a

VA hospital. In that study, 77% of the subjects were correctly diagnosed as schizophrenic by the DIS; those who were missed, though, were often missed because of negative information about the criterion for deterioration, not from lack of information about psychotic symptoms. The authors interpreted their study as providing reassurance about the DIS findings, but one concern is that the study design may be criticized; for example, the possible influence on the DIS interviewers of knowing the clinical diagnosis of all 82 subjects is an especially important question in this case.

Another concern about the findings is that the Pulver and Carpenter report raises a new question about the DIS and the way it is being used; DSM-III Criterion A has some redundancy built in, with multiple items counting toward the diagnostic threshold, so diagnosis may still be accurate even if some symptoms are missed. But by examining the quality of symptom information, Pulver and Carpenter (1983) challenged the suitability of using the DIS, administered by nonclinicians, for nosologic research based on community surveys.

DISCUSSION

Remarkably, in a few of these studies the kappa values for agreement reached a perfect 1.0. The range of other kappa values, and their companion values for Yule's Y, were in a midrange, though. A tentative conclusion based on this admittedly incomplete data base is that the findings are good enough in most studies to suggest that the DIS performs adequately as a case-finding instrument for disorders like alcohol disorders and major depression; its performance in panic disorder seems questionable; and its performance in schizophrenia is subject to concern about false-negative answers. Even the favorable results for most disorders are not so high as to prove that point definitively or to stop the search for improved methods. In that case, they probably serve as a type of projective test depending on the investigator's own sympathies. To declare my own bias, the values for most disorders are generally "good enough," at least in the context of a large, baseline survey of the community population.

It seems to me the argument cannot be pursued easily beyond the point of these tentative judgments until more definitive tests applying the Longitudinal, Expert, and All Data (LEAD) standard (Spitzer, 1983) or something like it have been done. Rather than pursuing that argument about how good the DIS is, then, I will suggest that it is more productive to examine the possible reasons for discrepancies between the DIS and a clinical instrument. Many of these points have been discussed by the authors in their original papers, and they have also been the focus of prolonged discussions in the DIS Workgroup of ECA investigators. In a previous paper (Burke & Regier, 1983) we attempted a comprehensive listing of reasons for differences between interview instruments; at this point it may be helpful to outline some basic issues that may apply to these DIS studies (see Table 13.6).

Nature of Discrepancies

Nature of Examination. One hypothesis that was proposed early on, and that still has vocal adherents, is that a clinical interview is inherently better than a completely structured instrument administered by a nonclinician. This argument suggests that the ability of a clinician to probe and confirm answers, or to explore the subject's contradictions, places the DIS in an inherently weak position, so it is certain to be inferior to any assessment that uses an intrinsically more powerful method. A response to this argument is that a clinical assessment *may* have this advantage, but the question arises whether that potential is realized in practice. Research showing the unreliability of routine clinical diagnoses led to development of explicit criteria; since then, new interviews for diagnostic assessment have been expected to demonstrate that raters can be trained to administer them reliably. If the merits of any particular clinical examination are taken as an empirical question rather than assumed on an a priori basis, the differences between the DIS and a clinical examination procedure can be explored without prejudging where the problems are. It may be useful in this context to remember the studies of computer-based assessments of suicidal patients that indicated better coverage than in clinical examinations (Greist *et al.*, 1973); another study of computer-based psychiatric histories conducted at the Maudsley Hospital demonstrated that, with an independent review of discrepancies between the computer and the clinical record, the "error" rate was about equally split between computer and clinician (Carr, Ghosh, & Ancill, 1983). In some cases, the advantage of a clinician's flexibility and judgment may be offset by an assessment procedure that is consistent, systematic, and comprehensive.

Table 13.6. Differences in Diagnostic Assessments

---

1. Nature of examination
2. Marginal cases
3. Subject variance over time
4. Criterion variance—assessment of inclusion items
5. Criterion variance—application of exclusion rules
6. Clustering and timing of symptoms or episodes
7. Differential diagnosis—misallocation into specific categories
8. Inherent unreliability of assessments

Marginal Cases. An important source of disagreement between the nonclinician's DIS and a clinical judgment has been examined carefully by Helzer and colleagues (1985) in their studies. They have demonstrated that for given disorders like alcohol abuse and dependence, agreement is remarkably high for subjects with few symptoms of a disorder or for those with many symptoms, who are definite cases. Most disagreements occur when the subject has reported experiencing some of the symptoms, especially when the number reported is just at the diagnostic threshold set by DSM-III; with alcohol disorders, for example, the worst agreement on the diagnosis is reached when the subject has reported three symptoms as positive. In these instances, it may not be clear whether to accept the clinician's determination of "caseness," or what is typically the more conservative judgment of the DIS that a marginal subject is not a case. The importance of these marginal subjects is that they may indicate the need for reconsidering the minimum threshold set in DSM-III, or they may be early or variant cases of the illness in question.

Subject Variance over Time. One problem for any study is that the interval between two interviews can allow substantial clinical change in subjects. This problem of change in the interim may be especially difficult with examination procedures that are keyed to a recent time period, like the 1-month period of the PSE. Ideally, the change may not be so troublesome in interviews based on a lifetime perspective; in practice, though, there has been speculation in some studies that the subject's current clinical state may influence reports of lifetime symptoms. Dr. Robins and others in the ECA program are investigating the stability of lifetime diagnosis, from the first DIS interview to the second one about a year later; my understanding is that Evelyn Bromet and colleagues at Pittsburgh are also preparing findings indicating that lifetime reports of depression on the SADS-L are unreliable, with some change depending on whether the subject is currently ill or has recently been ill at the time of the second interview (Bromet, personal communication, February, 1985).

In the three major studies comparing a DIS diagnosis to a psychiatrist's examination with community samples, there was considerable variation in time intervals between the two interviews. In the Munich study by Wittchen *et al.* (1985), 100% of the psychiatric reinterviews of the general population subjects were completed within 1 month of the DIS interview. In Baltimore 75% of the psychiatric reexaminations were completed within 1 month and 93% within 3 months. In St. Louis, 50% were completed in 6 weeks, and 85% were completed within 3 months. One intriguing question is whether the results from Munich show higher agreement because of this shorter interval between assessments. It may be worth noting that an unexamined effect in all three studies was the unvarying order; the DIS interview was always given first. Whether this fixed sequence had an effect on the subsequent psychiatric examination is unknown, but Robins *et al.* (1982) have noted that some evidence suggests that agreement may be higher when the nonclinician interviewer is first; however, overall agreement did not show an order effect in their early clinical study.

Criterion Variance: Assessment of Inclusion Items. At one time, there seems to have been a vague hope that with publication of DSM-III, criterion variance would be eliminated. This problem was shown most clearly in relation to the various interpretations that could be given to DSM-II categories. In a study of the multiple meanings of neurotic depression in DSM-II, Klerman, Endicott, Spitzer, & Hirschfeld (1979) demonstrated that different groups of subjects could be given the diagnosis depending on how the criteria were interpreted. Although the approach of DSM-III in making criteria explicit has reduced this problem, it has not eliminated it. Instead, it has taken new shape, as discussed by Helzer and Coryell (1983) in their editorial on the limits of precision in diagnostic criteria in the context of biological tests; similar arguments have been made by others (e.g., Chang & Bidder, 1985).

However concrete the criteria for a disorder like major depression may seem, there can be surprising variation in the way even insomnia is defined, for example. One interview may inquire about "difficulty falling asleep, waking up, or waking too early" every day for 2 weeks; guidelines for another assessment may specify at least 1 hour of unusually delayed sleep onset for more than half the time in the past month. It may be difficult to say whether one of these is "more accurate" in applying the intention of DSM-III; for symptoms like insomnia or weight loss, it is possible for two independent applications of DSM-III to identify different subjects as having the symptom, depending on the approach used to define the terms. This kind of variation, where both approaches may be within the limits set by the classification system but still be different from each other, may potentially occur in DSM-III. That possibility has led some investigators in the ECA to suggest that it could be misleading to calculate kappa values for agreement between two instruments that are basically dissimilar in their interpretations of DSM-III.

Criterion Variance: Application of Exclusion Rules. The statement of exclusions in DSM-III has led to disagreement about how to apply them, in the DIS or in clinical practice. In initial reports from the ECA studies, the DIS is being scored without attempting to apply the exclusion rules. Some of the assessment instruments used in these comparison studies with the DIS are consistent with this approach; for example, the SADS-L permits multiple diagnoses to be made. However, routine clinical diagnoses presumably apply the exclusion rules according to the judgment of the individual clinician; the psychiatrists using the SPE in Baltimore also applied the DSM-III exclusions in a way that cannot be reversed. These differences may also account for apparent disagreements about diagnostic assignments.

Clustering and Timing of Symptoms and Episodes. From both St. Louis and Munich, John Helzer and Uli Wittchen have presented evidence that one source of instability on all these assessments, whether in test-retest designs of the DIS or comparisons to clinical diagnoses, comes from the need to determine if the required symptoms occurred together in a "cluster," as with major depression. The subjects might report the presence of symptoms consistently from one examination to another, but they might report inconsistently whether these all occurred at the same time.

Another related problem is determining the most recent occurrence of a disorder, and this problem may account for discrepancies in studies of "current disorders," even if they are hard to identify. For example, even within the framework of the DIS, at least three different methods can be used to date the most recent episode. The "standard" ECA approach reflected in the first set of publications has used summary questions; those subjects who have met the lifetime criteria for a condition are generally asked, "When is the last time you had [e.g., the mood disturbance of depression and some of the other symptoms of depression endorsed in the interview]?" Another approach is to use symptom-specific "recency" questions for each positive symptom and to use the most recent of these item-specific dates as the determinant for most recent occurrence of the disorder.

Some preliminary evidence comparing these two methods in German samples indicates that they give different results, and suggests that the "symptom-specific" approach, which some expect to be more accurate, may be less reliable.

A third approach based on the symptom-specific recency data has also been described; rather than using the most recent single symptom to determine the last occurrence of a depressive episode, von Korff and Anthony (1982) required that at least four of the Criterion B symptoms be present in the past month, in a strict application of DSM-III criteria. They found that only 54% of the subjects designated as having had major depression in the past month by the "standard" ECA method met this more stringent requirement for diagnosis in the past month.

Differential Diagnosis: Misallocation into Specific Categories. There has been an interest among the ECA investigators to determine whether more comprehensive approaches, like the SADS-L or SPE, may permit more precise differential assessment of some subjects. For example, a subject with significant depression and anxiety, or with an affective psychosis, may undergo a detailed inquiry to determine whether one particular diagnosis is of major importance clinically; on the DIS, though, such probing is less intense. Further work at Yale on the study using the DIS and an extended SADS-L may permit a better understanding of how this problem may contribute to the disagreements.

In the meantime, it is reassuring to have specialized studies like the one by Hesselbrock that indicate good agreement between the SADS-L and DIS on which alcoholic patients also qualified for a diagnosis of major depression.

Inherent Unreliability of Assessments. It can be argued that reasonable evidence exists for interrater reliability of the DIS, in studies with equivalent raters and in studies with community residents. It can also be asserted that the research assessments by psychiatrists may be as reliable. Even granting both those points, some ECA investigators like Ernest Gruenberg (personal communication, May, 1984) have suggested that the reliability is still not high enough to rule out instability in administering an assessment instrument as a major cause of disagreement. In that sense, the unreliability of each of the two instruments being compared sets a low ceiling on the value of agreement that can be obtained in such studies, and we have come full circle back to the problem of determining whether interrater reliability is high enough for any of these instruments to support their claims to being useful, if not "valid." This argument may gain further support from the study by Bromet and colleagues in Pittsburgh; in that investigation, the test-retest reliability of the SADS-L, which uses the lifetime framework applied in the DIS, was very low over an 18-month period. With more work to determine interrater and long-interval test-retest reliability, it is possible that this argument will gain increasing force. It should be noted, though, that previous work from the collaborative study on depression and from other studies, using the SADS-L, shows that test-retest reliability for lifetime diagnoses is adequate at least for 6-month intervals (Andreasen *et al.*, 1981; Keller *et al.*, 1981; Leckman, Sholomskas, Thompson, Belanger, & Weissman, 1982).

Implications for the DIS

In regard to the DIS and its performance as a case-finding instrument for epidemiologic surveys, some conclusions may be reasonable, even though they are not definitive:

1. Available evidence suggests that adequate levels of interrater reliability can be obtained with clinical samples and community residents, although there is variation by disorder and possibly by length of the interval between test and retest.

2. From the data presented so far, agreement between the DIS and a diagnostic examination using psychiatrists is generally fair to good. Interpretation of the findings depends on the observer's judgment about comparing dissimilar approaches with DSM-III, and about the use of statistical measures that are not affected by low prevalence rates in a community population. However, even with the most favorable evidence of the studies by Helzer, Anthony, and Wittchen in community residents, several areas of assessment by the DIS are not well understood. These include the impact of different methods of determining whether symptoms cluster together,

whether a disorder has been active in the past month, and whether a related disorder not covered on the DIS may be a more appropriate diagnostic assignment.

3. At the same time, it can be stated that discrepancies between the DIS and a clinical examination are not always due to "errors" in one of the instruments. Examination of the source of discrepancies may lead to improvement in some problematic areas of assessment, including the capacity to assess subject variation over time, and to determine ways to clarify diagnostic criteria.

Further analytic work may take two directions. These agreement values may represent an overly simplistic approach, because they test agreement between instruments on each disorder taken one at a time. With the shift in DSM-III to allow multiple diagnoses to be assigned, and with that tendency reinforced by the decision not to apply exclusion rules in the DIS algorithms, subjects are likely to receive more than one diagnosis. Mezzich, Kraemer, Worthington, & Coffman (1981) have presented several strategies for assessing agreement as measured by a form of kappa when two instruments yield multiple diagnoses. Similarly, Kalter, Feinberg, & Carroll (1983) have recently suggested methods of combining data from several studies that assess performance of a diagnostic test; whether this approach is suitable to the DIS studies is not clear, in view of their tremendous differences in design and sampling, but some better way to draw conclusions from an accumulation of studies will be needed as this literature expands. With expanding literature, it may also be possible to categorize the studies more narrowly, and to discount studies based on inadequate methodologies, such as using unconfirmed chart diagnoses as a criterion measure.

Another important analytic issue has been raised by Myrna Weissman and her colleagues at Yale. If the instruments are identifying similar kinds of cases, even though not the same ones, it is worth asking if the two groups of cases would generate the same risk factors for the illness. So far, some preliminary work at Yale would tend to suggest that the DIS and SADS-L give similar information about psychosocial risk factors for some disorders.

The preliminary work on sources of discrepancy needs to be pursued, especially to assess the status of marginal cases. In some cases, like the ECA, the use of data from the second wave of interviews may be useful, but this analysis may also require additional data from longitudinal studies of the subjects.

At this point it is tempting to say that these studies point the way to improvements in the DIS. Optimistically, this improvement can be achieved easily: for example, by extending the information collected about timing of symptoms, by adding more relevant diagnostic categories to the interview to expand its scope, and by adding items intended to assess related features important in other systems. The production of a new interview merging the

DIS and elements of the PSE has been undertaken under sponsorship of ADAMHA and the World Health Organization. This new instrument is called the Composite International Diagnostic Interview (CIDI).

There is a counterargument, however. There have been suggestions that the foundation of the DIS, however elegant it may be for its original intent, is not sturdy enough to support this kind of expansion. Could a nonclinician interviewer manage much more complexity than already exists in the DIS? Probably the best answer to that will come from a trial, not from a hunch.

Future Research

These early studies have probably generated enough controversy to stimulate even more research to assess the performance of diagnostic interviews. By seeing now what we have available as evidence, it is possible to know more clearly what we wish had been done in the past. Two types of studies seem to be needed, regardless of the instrument under development: first, studies of reliability, using both short-interval and long-interval test-retest designs in the population where the instrument will be used; and second, longitudinal studies of the test and comparison instruments, to determine how the initial diagnostic assignments relate to some external criteria, such as subsequent course, response to treatment, relationship to familial pathology, and so forth. Any study assessing these external criteria, reviewed by Klerman (1983), may also be able to apply the LEAD standard proposed by Spitzer (1983).

CONCLUSIONS

Enough studies have been performed to show that the DIS performs reasonably well for most of the disorders it covers in terms of a test-retest comparison, and in terms of comparisons with several clinical diagnostic assessments. However, none of these has provided an adequate test of validity, which will probably require a longitudinal study and comparison with external criteria of validity. Presumably, such studies could be performed with both the DIS and a clinical interview, like the SCID, in the LEAD standard approach proposed by Spitzer.

ACKNOWLEDGMENTS

The Epidemiologic Catchment Area Program (ECA) is a series of five epidemiologic research studies performed by independent research teams in collaboration with staff of the Division of Biometry and Epidemiology (DBE) of the National Institute of Mental Health (NIMH). The NIMH principal collaborators are: Darrel A. Regier, Ben Z. Locke, and Jack D. Burke, Jr.;

the NIMH project officer is Carl A. Taube. The principal investigators and coinvestigators from the five sites are: Yale University, UOl MH334224—Jerome K. Myers, Myrna M. Weissman, and Gary L. Tischler; Johns Hopkins University, UOl MH33870—Morton Kramer and Sam Shapiro; Washington University, St. Louis, UOl MH33883—Lee N. Robins and John Helzer; Duke University UOl MH35386—Dan Blazer and Linda George; University of California, Los Angeles, UOl MH35865—Marvin Karno, Richard Hough, Javier Escobar, M. Audrey Burnam, and Dianne M. Timbers.

This chapter has benefited from extensive discussions held in the DIS Workgroup for the past 3 years. The core members of this Workgroup are: Yale University—Myrna Weissman and Phil Leaf; Johns Hopkins University—Alan Romanoski and Gerald Nestadt; Washington University at St. Louis—John Helzer; Duke University—Dan Blazer; UCLA—Marvin Karno and Javier Escobar; NIMH—Darrel A. Regier and Jack D. Burke, Jr. Helpful comments during these discussions have also been made by Ben Locke, Jeffrey Boyd, John Bartko, Hans-Ulrich Wittchen, Lee Robins, Ernest Gruenberg, Morton Kramer, Paul McHugh, Sheppard Kellam, Dianne Timbers, and Audrey Burnam.

REFERENCES

Akiskal, H. S. (1980). External validating criteria for psychiatric diagnosis: Their application in affective disorders. *Journal of Clinical Psychiatry, 41*(Dec. Suppl.), 6–15.

American Psychiatric Association. (1980). *Diagnostic and Statistical Manual of Mental Disorders* (3rd ed.). Washington, DC: Author.

Andreasen, N. C., Grove, W. M., Shapiro, R. W., Keller, M. B., Hirschfeld, R. M. A., & McDonald-Scott, P. (1981). Reliability of lifetime diagnosis: A multicenter collaborative perspective. *Archives of General Psychiatry, 38,* 400–405.

Anthony, J. C., Folstein, M., Romanoski, A. J., von Korff, M. R., Nestadt, G. N., Chahal, R., Merchant, A., Brown, C. H., Shapiro, S., Kramer, M., & Gruenberg, E. M. (1985). Comparison of lay D.I.S. and a standardized psychiatric diagnosis: Experience in eastern Baltimore. *Archives of General Psychiatry, 42,* 667–675.

Bartko, J. J., & Carpenter, W. T. (1976). On the methods and theory of reliability. *Journal of Nervous and Mental Disorders, 163,* 307–317.

Bishop, Y. M. M., Feinberg, S. E., & Holland, P. W. (1975). *Discrete multivariate analysis: Theory and practice.* Cambridge, MA: MIT Press.

Burke, J. D., & Regier, D. A. (1983, July). *Implications of an operational approach to psychiatric diagnosis.* Paper presented at the Symposium on Classification and Nosology, VIIth World Congress of Psychiatry, Vienna, Austria.

Burnam, M. A., Karno, M., Hough, R. L., Escobar, J. I., & Forsythe, A. B. (1983). The Spanish Diagnostic Interview Schedule: Reliability and comparison with clinical diagnoses. *Archives of General Psychiatry, 40,* 1189–1196.

Canino, G., Bird, H. R., & Shrout, P. (in preparation). The DIS: Reliability and concordance with clinical diagnoses in Puerto Rico.

Carey, G., & Gottesman, I. I. (1978). Reliability and validity in binary ratings: Areas of common misunderstanding in diagnosis and symptom ratings. *Archives of General Psychiatry, 35,* 1454–1459.

Carpenter, W. T., & Pulver, A. E. (1984). Reply to Letter to the Editor. *Schizophrenia Bulletin, 10,* 154–156.

Carr, A. C., Ghosh, A., & Ancill, R. J. (1983). Can a computer take a psychiatric history? *Psychological Medicine, 13,* 151–158.

Chang, M. M., & Bidder, T. G. (1985). Noncomparability of research results that are related to psychiatric diagnoses. *Comprehensive Psychiatry, 26,* 195–207.

Cohen, J. (1960). A coefficient of agreement for nominal scales. *Educational Psychological Measurement, 20,* 37–46.

Dohrenwend, B. P., & Shrout, P. E. (1981). Toward the development of a two-stage procedure for case identification and classification in psychiatric epidemiology. In R. G. Simmons (Ed.), *Research in community and mental health* (Vol. 2). Greenwich, CT: JAI Press.

Eaton, W. W., Holzer, C. E., von Korff, M., Anthony, J. C., Helzer, J. E., George, L., Burnam, M. A., Boyd, J. H., Kessler, L. G., & Locke, B. Z. (1984). The design of the Epidemiologic Catchment Area surveys: The control and measurement of error. *Archives of General Psychiatry, 41,* 942–948.

Endicott, J. (1981). Diagnostic Interview Schedule (Letter to the Editor). *Archives of General Psychiatry, 38,* 1300.

Escobar, J. I., Randolph, E. T., Asamen, J., & Karno, M. (in press). The NIMH-DIS in the assessment of DSM-III schizophrenic disorder. *Schizophrenia Bulletin, XX,* 000–000.

Fleiss, J. L. (1981). *Statistical methods for rates and proportions* (2nd ed.). New York: Wiley.

Folstein, M. F., Romanoski, A. J., Chahal, R., Anthony, J. C., von Korff, M., Nestadt, G., Merchant, A., Gruenberg, E. M., & Kramer, M. (1985). Eastern Baltimore mental health survey clinical reappraisal. In W. W. Eaton & L. G. Kessler (Eds.), *Epidemiologic field methods in psychiatry.* New York: Academic Press.

Ganguli, M., & Saul, M. C. (1982). Diagnostic Interview Schedule (Letter to the Editor). *Archives of General Psychiatry, 39,* 1442–1443.

Grove, W. M., Andreasen, N. C., McDonald-Scott, P., Keller, M. B., & Shapiro, R. W. (1981). Reliability of psychiatric studies of psychiatric diagnosis: Theory and practice. *Archives of General Psychiatry, 38,* 408–413.

Greist, J. H., Gustafson, D. H., Stauss, F. F., Rowse, G. L., Laughren, T. P., & Chiles, J. A. (1973). A computer interview for suicide risk prediction. *American Journal of Psychiatry, 130,* 1327–1332.

Helzer, J. E., & Coryell, W. (1983). How consistent are precise criteria? (Editorial). *Biological Psychiatry, 18,* 1201–1202.

Helzer, J. E., & Robins, L. N. (1984). Lifetime psychotic symptoms assessed with the DIS (Letter to the Editor). *Schizophrenia Bulletin, 10,* 5 7.

Helzer, J. E., Robins, L. N., Croughan, J., & Welner, A. (1981). Renard Diagnostic Interview. *Archives of General Psychiatry, 38,* 393–398.

Helzer, J. E., & Spitznagel, E. (1985). A proposed solution to problems in the kappa statistic for the calculation of interrater agreement. *Archives of General Psychiatry, 42,* 657–666.

Helzer, J. E., McEvoy, L. T., Robins, L. N., Spitznagel, E., Stoltsman, R. K., Farmer, A., & Brockington, I. F. (1985). Results of the St. Louis ECA physician re-examination study of the DIS interview. *Archives of General Psychiatry, 42,* 657–666.

Hendricks, L. E., Bayton, J. A., Collins, J. L., Mathura, C. B., Macmillan, S. R., & Montgomery, T. A. (1983). The NIMH Diagnostic Interview Schedule: A test of its validity in a population of black adults. *Journal of the National Medical Association, 75,* 667–671.

Hesselbrock, V., Stabenau, J., Hesselbrock, M., Mirkin, P., & Meyer, R. (1982). A comparison of two interview schedules: The Schedule for Affective Disorders and Schizophrenic-Lifetime and the NIMH Diagnostic Interview Schedule. *Archives of General Psychiatry, 39,* 674–677.

Kalter, N., Feinberg, M., & Carroll, B. J. (1983). Inferential statistical methods for strengthening the interpretation of laboratory test results. *Psychiatry Research, 10,* 207–216.

Karno, M., Burnam, M. A., Escobar, J., & Timbers, D. (1984). Lifetime psychotic symptoms assessed with the DIS (Letter to the Editor). *Schizophrenia Bulletin, 10,* 154–156.

Keller, M. B., Lavori, P. W., McDonald-Scott, P., Scheftner, W. A., Andreasen, N. C., Shapiro, R. W., & Croughan, J. (1981). Reliability of lifetime psychiatric diagnoses and symptoms in patients with a current psychiatric disorder. *Journal of Psychiatric Research*, *16*, 229–240.

Klerman, G. L. (1983, October). *The evaluation of diagnostic classes: The approach of the NIMH Collaborative Study*. Paper presented to the APA Invitational Workshop, DSM-III: An Interim Appraisal, Washington, DC.

Klerman, G. L., Endicott, J., Spitzer, R. L., & Hirschfeld, R. M. A. (1979). Neurotic depression: A systematic analysis of multiple criteria and meanings. *American Journal of Psychiatry*, *136*, 57–61.

Landis, J. R., & Koch, G. G. (1977). The measurement of observer agreement for categorical data. *Biometrics*, *33*, 671–679.

Leckman, J. F., Sholomskas, D., Thompson, W. D., Bellanger, A., & Weissman, M. M. (1982). Best estimate of lifetime psychiatric diagnosis: A methodologic study. *Archives of General Psychiatry*, *39*, 879–883.

Mezzich, J. E., Kraemer, H. C., Worthington, D. R. L., & Coffman, G. A. (1981). Assessment of agreement among several raters formulating multiple diagnoses. *Journal of Psychiatric Research*, *16*, 29–39.

Myers, J. K., Weissman, M. M., Tischler, G. L., Holzer, C. E., Leaf, P. J., Orvaschel, H., Anthony, J. C., Boyd, J. H., Burke, J. D., Kramer, M., & Stoltzman, R. (1984). Six-month prevalence of psychiatric disorders in three communities. *Archives of General Psychiatry*, *41*, 949–958.

Pulver, A. E., & Carpenter, W. T. (1983). Lifetime psychotic symptoms assessed with the DIS. *Schizophrenia Bulletin*, *9*, 377–382.

Regier, D. A., Myers, J. K., Kramer, M., Robins, L. N., Blazer, D. G., Hough, R. L., Eaton, W. W., & Locke, B. Z. (1984). The NIMH Epidemiologic Catchment Area Program. *Archives of General Psychiatry*, *41*, 934–941.

Robins, L. N., & Helzer, J. E. (1981). Reply to Letter to the Editor. *Archives of General Psychiatry*, *38*, 1300–1301.

Robins, L. N., & Helzer, J. E. (1982). Reply to Letter to the Editor. *Archives of General Psychiatry*, *39*, 1443–1445.

Robins, L. N., Helzer, J. E., Croughan, J., & Ratcliff, K. S. (1981). National Institute of Mental Health Diagnostic Interview Schedule: Its history, characteristics, and validity. *Archives of General Psychiatry*, *38*, 381–389.

Robins, L. N., Helzer, J. E., Ratcliff, K. S., & Seyfried, W. (1982). Validity of the Diagnostic Interview Schedule, Version II: DSM-III diagnoses. *Psychological Medicine*, *12*, 855–870.

Robins, L. N., Helzer, J. E., Weissman, M. M., Orvaschel, H., Gruenberg, E. M., Burke, J. D., & Regier, D. A. (1984). Lifetime prevalence of specific psychiatric disorders in three sites. *Archives of General Psychiatry*, *41*, 949–958.

Shapiro, S. S., Skinner, E. A., Kessler, L. G., von Korff, M., German, P. S., Tischler, G. L., Leaf, P. J., Benham, L., Cottler, L., & Regier, D. A. (1984). Utilization of health and mental health services. *Archives of General Psychiatry*, *41*, 971–978.

Spitzer, R. L., & Fleiss, J. L. (1974). A re-analysis of the reliability of psychiatric diagnosis. *British Journal of Psychiatry*, *125*, 341–347.

Spitzer, R. L. (1983). Are clinicians still necessary? *Comprehensive Psychiatry*, *24*, 399–411.

Spitzer, R. L., & Williams, J. B. W. (1984). Classification of mental disorders. In H. Kaplan & B. Sadock (Eds.), *Comprehensive textbook of psychiatry* (4th ed.). Baltimore: Williams & Wilkins.

von Korff, M. R., & Anthony, J. C. (1982). The NIMH Diagnostic Interview Schedule modified to record current symptom status. *Journal of Affective Disorders*, *4*, 365–371.

von Korff, M., Anthony, J. C., & Kramer, M. (1982). Diagnostic Interview Schedule (Letter to the Editor). *Archives of General Psychiatry*, *39*, 1443.

Weller, R. A., Penick, E. C., Powell, B. J., Othmer, E., Rice, A. S., & Kent, T. A. (1985). Agreement between two structured psychiatric diagnostic interviews: DIS and the PDI. *Comprehensive Psychiatry, 26,* 157–163.

Wing, J., Bebbington, P., & Robins, L. N. (1980). *What is a case?* London: Grant McIntyre.

Wittchen, H., & Semler, G. (1984). *Reliability of the German DIS, version 2. Final report.* Unpublished Manuscript (NIMH Internal Document).

Wittchen, H. U., Semler, G., & von Zerssen, D. (1985). Comparing ICD diagnoses with DSM-III and RDC using the Diagnostic Interview Schedule (Version II). *Archives of General Psychiatry, 42,* 677–684.

DISCUSSION

James Barrett: You are to be congratulated for a very thoughtful and careful presentation about a complex subject. In the considerable controversy around that subject what is needed is less heat and more light. Your review is a step in that direction.

Since at one point you quoted my concerns about the accuracy of a single-point-in-time diagnostic assessment, I want to make very clear what I was trying to say. I was not saying that a single-point-in-time assessment was always inadequate, but rather that it is important early on to determine for which disorders a single-point-in-time assessment is inadequate and for which disorders it may be entirely adequate. Your chapter does a very nice job of showing us that, for alcoholism and major depression, the single-point-in-time assessment by DIS was quite accurate and acceptable. For other disorders, such as panic disorder, there were problems.

Separate from the number of assessments, the type of assessment—by lay interviewer or by skilled clinician—may have contributed to the relatively poor agreement which you reported for the diagnosis of panic disorder. For panic disorder an assessment by a skilled clinician, such as a PSE-type assessment, could have given you better reliability and clinical validity. I say this because in my study with symptomatic volunteers, it was fairly common to have people saying "Yes" to specific panic-anxiety symptom questions. However, if you asked about these symptoms in a more open-ended way, such as initially asking, "Have you had a time when you experienced anxiety?" and then, if you got a positive answer, going on to ask, "What was it like?" some people would say, "Boy, Doc, that was the worst thing I ever experienced—I hope that never happens again," and then go on to spontaneously describe racing heartbeat, sweaty palms, and so on. This kind of response was striking and convincing that panic anxiety was present. In contrast, some people (particularly those with labile personality who tend to say "Yes" to everything), if asked about symptoms in this open-ended way, would not give a very convincing picture of panic anxiety. One is comfortable saying that panic anxiety disorder was not present in those patients. So panic anxiety may be one example of a condition where a different sort of assessment will give you both more reliable and more valid information.

Burke: I certainly agree with you that an improvement in assessment is needed for panic disorder. The studies I have reviewed today are a fair reflection of the state of the field right now, but there are other studies in preparation, and I am concerned about how we would interpret the data if, in fact, major depression and alcoholism did not do as well in those studies as they have in these. Even for those disorders it is not clear that we have a large enough body of evidence to decide that a single-point-in-time assessment was adequate for them. So I would not want to eliminate those disorders from longitudinal studies.

Alan Romanoski: I have been closely involved with the Clinical Reappraisal study of the DIS, also referred to as the Baltimore study. I wish to clarify several issues raised by Dr. Burke. In his presentation he listed a summary table of possible reasons for the discrepancies between the DIS and other diagnostic assessments. While some of these imputed reasons for disagreement between DIS diagnoses and those of clinical psychiatrists remain speculative and deserve further research, analyses of data at the Hopkins site have permitted us to lay many of the speculations to rest. I feel that it is important to make these points clearly at this time because the results of the Baltimore study have undergone extraordinary scrutiny—both from without and within the ECA—for a variety of reasons.

My first point concerns the nature of the clinical examination that we used in Baltimore, the Standardized Psychiatric Examination (SPE). The SPE includes all 140 items of the Present State Examination (PSE-9), and we added over 1000 other items.

Two hundred ninety-six of our SPE items assess the examinee's present mental state: 140 PSE-9 items and 156 additional items. Eighty-one of these remaining 156 items are a combination of review-of-systems and somatization disorder checklist with such questions as "Do you ever get chest pain?" "Do you ever have trouble with constipation?" and so on. Thirty-three of these 156 items are a cognitive battery, including the Mini-Mental Status Examination. Thirty-two of the items concern substance abuse. Many of the items can, of course, be skipped if the subject does not use certain substances. Of the additional items we created, only approximately 50 utilize the PSE-9-type format.

The other 900 items on the SPE, those not directly concerned with the present mental state, include 128 ratings of diagnoses and treatment recommendations which are made *after* termination of the examination. They include a 100-item "quickie" neurological examination which takes less than 10 minutes to do, and whose results are also recorded after completion of the interview session. Most of the other 900 items tend to be historical—"When were you born?" "Are you married?" "Are your parents alive?" "Were either of them ever in a psychiatric hospital?"—questions neither difficult to ask nor time-consuming, but questions that help one make a clinical diagnosis.

The SPE averaged 2 hours in length. An inference was made that this exam may have been too lengthy or too ambitious to have been done reliably and uniformly in 810 community subjects. I want to point out that the ECA household interview schedule, which was administered across five sites to over 15,000 subjects, contained over 1000 items, *not* counting the DIS probe structure. The household interviews averaged 90 minutes in length. The SPE is not really an ambitious undertaking compared with the household interview.

The second issue I want to clarify concerns Dr. Burke's point regarding subject variance over time. We carefully looked for subject variance over time at the Hopkins site. We first looked at the DIS-to-clinical-reappraisal interval. In Baltimore, the median interval between the DIS and clinician reexamination was 12 days; the mode was 7 days, and the mean was 21 days. Seventy-five percent of our clinical reappraisal examinations were completed within 28 days. We analyzed our DIS-clinical reappraisal comparisons in four ways, looking for discrepancies in subjects for whom the interval was 1 week, 2 weeks, 3 weeks, or 3+ weeks. Overall, the DIS-clinical reappraisal comparisons did not vary at all with the duration of interval between the two exams.

We also considered subject variance in another way. For each diagnosis (with the exception of simple phobia), we studied the written and dictated case records of subjects who fell in the off-diagonal cells—that is, persons who fell in the "B" and "C" cells in a 2 × 2 table. The case records for each subject included a 1- to 6-page single-spaced typewritten narrative formulation made by each clinical reappraisal psychiatrist at the conclusion of each examination. We looked for subjects whose clinical status could have changed during the DIS-clinical reappraisal interval. We found only *one* case out of the entire study in which the subject's status changed during the DIS to clinical reappraisal interval: a woman who began abusing alcohol (shortly after the DIS interview) as a maladaptive response to abandonment by her live-in boyfriend.

If we stand back for a moment and get away from analyzing cells and off-diagonals, we should not be very surprised at these findings because most of these disorders tend to be chronic or have episodes of long duration: schizophrenia, major depression, alcohol dependence, dysthymic disorder. If you really think about it, we shouldn't have expected to see much change over a short time interval, or much fluctuation in disorder status.

A third issue I wish to clarify is that of criterion variance with regard to inclusion rules used to make diagnoses. While it probably is accurate to say that criteria sometimes varied between the DIS and our clinical reappraisal examinations, this statement requires further clarification.

An example of criterion variance frequently cited is the definition of insomnia. To us, the DIS does not clearly specify what is meant by insomnia; it asks something like "Have you ever had a period of two weeks or more when you had trouble falling asleep, staying asleep, or waking up too early?" The criterion for insomnia thus is whatever the subject thinks "trouble falling asleep" is. By contrast, in our clinical reappraisal, to rate insomnia related to a major depressive episode, we required persons to describe at least one or more hours of initial insomnia on more than 50% of days during a 2-week episode. We also inquired about sleep continuity disturbance and early-morning awakening using the same parameters. You might call this difference criterion variance, but at least there are clear criteria. You may argue that our criteria are wrong, but at least you know what they are, that they are reproducible, and that they can be tested. They don't vary with the subject's own interpretation.

My fourth point concerns exclusionary rules. We have gone to considerable lengths to look at the effect of DSM-III exclusionary rules on our DIS-clinical reappraisal discrepancies. For each discordant case in each DSM-III disorder category, we looked at all other DSM-III diagnoses. For example, for each person who received a DIS diagnosis of major depression but who did not get a psychiatrist's diagnosis of major depression, we looked for the presence of another psychiatrist's diagnosis which theoretically could have excluded major depression, such as dementia, delirium, and so on. We found none. We repeated this process for each discordant case for each DSM-III disorder. In no instance did we find that DSM-III exclusionary rules implemented by our psychiatrists accounted for a discrepancy between a DIS diagnosis and a psychiatrist's diagnosis. So although the hypothetical point can be made that comparing DIS diagnoses without exclusionary rules to clinical diagnoses with DSM-III exclusionary rules isn't tidy, the fact of the matter is that differential implementation of exclusionary rules did not account for any of the *observed* DIS-clinician disagreements in our study. Our data permit us to lay the issue of exclusionary rules to rest, at least with regard to our findings.

My last point concerns the temporal clustering of symptoms as a possible reason for DIS–SPE discrepancies. Dr. Burke cited the example of panic disorder, for which our study found particularly disappointing results: no concordance whatsoever. Dr. Burke pointed out that a subject could receive a diagnosis of DIS-panic disorder if he or she only had one panic attack during the prior month but had had three attacks during a 3-week period in the more recent past; he further speculated that psychiatrists using the SPE could only detect panic disorder if a study subject had three discrete panic attacks during the month preceding the clinical reappraisal examination. In fact, the SPE "stem question" for panic attacks, PSE-9 question no. 14, probes for *any* panic attacks during the month prior to the examination. We found no cases of DIS-panic disorder who had even *one* panic attack during the one month prior to the examination. Temporal clustering of symptoms had nothing to do with why the DIS panic disorder fared so poorly in our study.

We attempted to further investigate how well the DIS discriminates anxiety with autonomic symptoms. We cross-tabulated results from the DIS-anxiety stem question (which reads "Have you ever had a spell or attack when all of a sudden you felt frightened, anxious, or uneasy?") with SPE and PSE-9 items that deal with any type of autonomic anxiety. The sensitivity and specificity of the DIS panic disorder stem questions were still disappointing. I interpret this to mean that our poor results regarding DIS-panic disorder have less to do with problems of temporal clustering of symptoms or of rules for recency of disorder than with problems in the DIS stem questions.

Joseph Fleiss: I would like to rise to the defense of the kappa statistic. The data Dr. Burke reported which showed that, for a fixed sensitivity and specificity, kappa declines as prevalence declines, is absolutely on the mark. That is exactly the way it should be. As prevalence declines, I think one should and must demand better sensitivity and better specificity than when prevalence is close to 50–50. An analogy would be in the measurement of ambient temperature and human body temperature. A standard error of measurement of 2° Fahrenheit is tolerable for measuring ambient temperature throughout the year and would yield a very large value for the intraclass correlation coefficient, an analog of kappa. But, for measuring human body temperature, a standard error of 2° would not just be intolerable, it might be fatal. The reliability would be terrible, as it should be. If prevalence is low and kappa is low, that means that sensitivity and specificity, however good they appear, aren't good enough.

Helzer: It is obvious that this particular issue is going to create some debate. I and Dr. Spitznagle wrote a paper on this subject soon to be published in the *Archives of General Psychiatry*. We felt that it is important to stress that it is very difficult to compare kappa values across studies or within a study where there are large differences in base rate of disorder. That can occur, obviously, in epidemiologic studies, but it also can occur in clinical studies. With the kappa statistic, the confounding takes place in terms of the agreement between the raters and the base rate of the disorder, and because of this we suggested the need to consider and search for alternative statistics.

In the paper we discuss other alternatives. We recommended the Y statistic because we felt that it is the best one available, but we did not think any statistic was really perfect in both conditions of pure reliability and pure validity and in studies between reliability and validity, as many of these are.

Benjamin Pasamanick: I see now why panic disorders and dysthymia were omitted from the 6-month prevalence paper in the *Archives*, but you gave no data on the agreement on dysthymia. What was it?

You also stated that there was no evidence about the reliability of physicians, although you gave some examples of good reliability. I also am guilty of talking about lack of validity in psychiatric diagnoses. This is not wholly true. We do have some validity, particularly in disorders such as major depression which we can associate with response to therapy. In view of the distressingly low kappa values, I think this would be very important to do in the ECA study.

Helzer: We fully concur with your last remark. In fact, in the ECA, as Dr. Burke pointed out, we hope to actually apply the LEAD standard that Dr. Spitzer has recommended and Dr. Burke proposed. The reexamination samples in the ECA studies provide us an opportunity to do that. We have lay interviewer data on a sample of subjects selected from the general population and we have clinician data on the same subjects. Our hope is to follow them longitudinally to test predictive validity as well as response to any treatment they might receive by comparing the lay diagnoses and the physician diagnoses both in cases where they concur and cases where they disagree.

Bruce Dohrenwend: I have two questions. The first is about reliability. In view of the controversy about the appropriate statistics, and especially in view of your analogy with a tennis match between clinical examination instruments and the DIS, wouldn't it be useful to compare the reliabilities of the DIS with comparable test-retest or cointerviewer reliabilities for such instruments as SADS and PSE? The second question is, Why are the results so much better in Germany than they are here?

Burke: In answer to your first question, I agree we need more studies of that type. In fact, it was one of my suggestions that we now need studies of reliability rather than more of these inconclusive comparison studies.

Dohrenwend: But don't they exist in the literature? Aren't there kappas calculated for the reliability of SADS and PSE, and what are they?

Burke: There certainly are papers, for example, by Gershon, two papers by Keller, and a paper by Andreasen, that have used the SADS-L and have reported very good reliability. Those have been largely in clinical samples. One of Dr. Bromet's points was that she has looked at reliability over a long interval in a community population, and there it isn't so good. But the experts on these instruments are here—Dr. Wing is here, as are Dr. Endicott, Dr. Spitzer, and Dr. Wittchen.

Robert Spitzer: I too would like to come to the defense of the beleaguered kappa. Some people may have assumed that one of the problems with kappa is that, as the prevalence of the category decreases, kappa inherently has an upper limit. That, of course, is not the case. For example, in the DSM-III field trials we had some very sizable kappas for some extremely rare categories, such as certain paraphilias.

The problem occurs when one rater says that the category is common and the other says that it is rare. This situation does place an upper limit on kappa, but this is appropriate because in such a situation there is a real disagreement between the two raters. I do not understand the logic of looking for another statistic that will give you a nicer, higher number. Why not face the fact that, when dealing with a rare disorder, it is more difficult to obtain agreement, but agreement can be found and indexed appropriately with kappa.

Helzer: Obviously if both raters agree in 100% of cases, even if there is only one case and thus a base rate of one, the kappa will be perfect.

The point we are making is that, even if you hold sensitivity and specificity constant at a high level, the value of the kappa statistic is a function of the base rate. That makes it difficult to make direct comparisons between studies where the base rate varies.

Spitzer: If you are using the terms "sensitivity" and "specificity," then you have already assumed that you have a validity criterion. And if you have a validity criterion, you really should not talk about kappa; you should talk about sensitivity and specificity. But if you are really talking about agreement, which is the reliability issue, when neither assessment is a standard, then I don't see how you can argue issues of sensitivity and specificity. You have to do it one way or the other.

Helzer: In the *Archives* article we point out the differing conditions, that is a pure-validity situation versus a pure-reliability situation versus the situation that we see more frequently, one that is neither pure validity nor pure reliability. The terms sensitivity and specificity continue to be used even in situations which are not pure validity, because they are a useful way of denoting particular kinds of agreement or disagreement.

14

A Two-Stage Approach for Case Identification and Diagnosis: First-Stage Instruments

PATRICK E. SHROUT, ANDREW E. SKODOL,
AND BRUCE P. DOHRENWEND
Columbia University and New York State Psychiatric Institute

Within this volume we have the opportunity to review the exciting advances that have been made in psychiatric epidemiology during the past several decades. Many of these advances have been made possible by the development of improved diagnostic systems and of diagnostic assessment methods. While it is satisfying to note how much progress has been made, it is also important to remind ourselves that there are still many challenges that need to be faced before we are sure that we have the unbiased estimates of the prevalence and incidence of mental disorders in the United States that are needed in order to assess risk factors associated with various subpopulations, such as those defined by sex or region. This chapter explains why a single-stage epidemiologic survey is likely to give biased prevalence estimates and discusses an infrequently used survey design that yields minimally biased estimates. This design is the multistage survey design, in which an inexpensive first-stage screen is applied to a large sample of respondents, and an authoritative diagnostic method is applied to a selected subsample of the initial respondents. Statistical and empirical results are available to aid researchers in planning multistage research designs.

We begin with the proposition that no diagnostic interview administered by lay interviewers yields errorless classification. Given that this is true, it can be shown that prevalence rates based solely on such an interview, even if estimated from very large samples, will tend to be biased. This hard statistical truth is not new, but bears repeating even as diagnostic methods and conventions improve.

To illustrate this fact, suppose we wish to study the rate of a disorder in some population thought to be at increased risk for that disorder, and we chose a diagnostic instrument based on its published sensitivity and specificity. Sensitivity is the proportion of persons with the disorder who are identified correctly as cases, and specificity is the proportion of persons without the disorder who are identified correctly as noncases. If we had available a diagnostic measure with a known sensitivity of 95% and a specificity also of 95%, we would consider ourselves fortunate indeed. Most will agree that such low levels of misclassification are unusual. It would be a mistake however, to think that these low levels are negligible.

Suppose further that the true prevalence of the rare disorder is 2%. No sample estimate will yield exactly this number, but on the average an unbiased estimator will be less than the true prevalence about as often as it is greater than the true prevalence. The prevalence estimate based on the fallible diagnostic measure with 95% sensitivity and specificity, however, would not be unbiased; on the average, it would yield a prevalence estimate of nearly 7%. The bias that results from using a measure with apparently high sensitivities and specificities would lead us to believe that there is nearly a 3.5-fold increase in risk, when there is in fact no increase! We briefly review the mathematical basis for this worrisome conclusion.

Suppose that we knew the true diagnostic status of a population of persons; then the cross-classification of true status with observed status can be represented for a dichotomous distinction as in Table 14.1. Following Tenenbein (1970), let θ represent the proportion of *true cases* who are misclassified as noncases; we will call this proportion the false-negative rate. Let ϕ be the proportion of the *true noncases* who are misclassified as cases; this we will call the false-positive rate. Let p be the true prevalence, that is, the proportion of the total population who are cases, and let π be the observed prevalence. It is well known in the statistical literature (e.g., Bross, 1954; Sutcliffe, 1965; Tenenbein, 1971) that π will usually be a biased estimate of p if θ and ϕ are not zero. The amount of bias is given by the formula

$$\pi - p = \phi(1 - p) - \theta p. \tag{1}$$

It is clear that false-positives and false-negatives only "cancel out" if the false-positive rate is exactly $\phi = \theta p / (1 - p)$. For rare disorders, this equality will hold only if the false-positive rate is much smaller than the false-negative rate;

Table 14.1. Classification of True Disorder Status and Fallible Measure

	Fallible Measure of Disorder		
True Status	Case (+)	Noncase (−)	Total
Case (+)	$p(1 - \theta)$	$p\theta$	p
Noncase (−)	$(1 - p)\phi$	$(1 - \phi)(1 - p)$	$(1 - p)$

when the two error rates are of comparable sizes, the observed prevalence rate will tend to be an overestimate.

Although long available, this statistical result has been largely ignored because it is based on the assumption that true diagnostic status can be known. While statisticians can easily show the importance of some theoretical results—for example, that unreliability attenuates validity, or that small sample sizes make it difficult to achieve significance—they have a difficult time proving that prevalence estimates from fallible measures are biased, because there is no obvious criterion that can be used to demonstrate the result empirically. The result, however, is real and should not be ignored.

In practice, we need to use a corollary of the result. If a diagnostic procedure can be defined that can be said to be as good as possible, then any less reliable or less valid diagnostic method will yield prevalence estimates that are biased relative to the ideal procedure. In the following discussion, we assume that the ideal diagnostic method is an initial structured or semistructured assessment by a trained, experienced clinician and a follow-up interview to verify the diagnosis. Ignoring the cost of such a procedure, most will agree that this ideal is more likely to be accurate than a diagnosis obtained from an interview administered at one point in time by a lay interviewer. We will refer to this ideal diagnosis as the criterion method.

TWO-STAGE PROCEDURE FOR CASE DETECTION

The obvious problem with setting as a criterion a complicated procedure that requires an experienced diagnostician is the cost of such a procedure. The cost can be reduced if the criterion is used only on a subsample of persons, all of whom have been surveyed initially with a less costly but less accurate screening measure. Figure 14.1 and Table 14.2 show schematically a general design for a two-stage study. A sample of N persons is drawn from the population and classified into one of two categories by the fallible screen. Of the πN persons who are positive on the screen, a fraction f_1 are followed immediately with the criterion method. In addition to these, a fraction f_2 of the $(1 - \pi)N$ persons who were negative on the screen are also followed with the criterion. For simplicity, let us assume that we are interested only in a single disorder, and that the criterion can classify persons as either having or not having the disorder. Let us say that a proportion, λ_1, of those screened positive who are followed and another proportion, λ_2, of those screened negative who are followed have the disorder. Thus, λ_1 can be interpreted as the positive predictive value of the screen, and λ_2 can be interpreted as one minus the negative predictive value. Alternatively, λ_1 and λ_2 can be thought of as the true prevalence rates in the screened positive group and in the screened negative group.

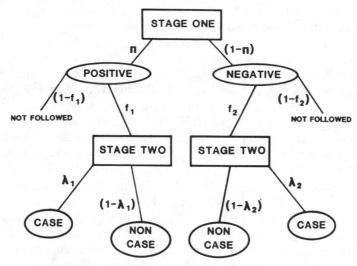

Figure 14.1. A diagram of a two-stage design.

Bross (1954) and others (e.g., Deming, 1977; Tenenbein, 1970) have shown that an unbiased estimate of the prevalence according to the criterion can be written,

$$\hat{p} = \hat{\lambda}_1 \, \hat{\pi} + \hat{\lambda}_2 \, (1 - \hat{\pi}). \tag{2}$$

The asymptotic variance of this estimate can be shown to be

$$V(p) = \frac{1}{N} \left[\pi(1 - \pi)(\lambda_1 - \lambda_2)^2 + \frac{\pi}{f_1} \lambda_1 (1 - \lambda_1) + \frac{(1 - \pi)}{f_2} \lambda_2 (1 - \lambda_2) \right]. \tag{3}$$

Table 14.2. Schematic Data Layout from Two-stage Survey

	First-Stage Screening Results	
Criterion	Case (+)	Noncase (−)
Case (+)	$f_1\pi\lambda_1$	$f_2(1 - \pi)\lambda_2$
Noncase (−)	$f_1\pi(1 - \lambda_1)$	$f_2(1 - \pi)(1 - \lambda_2)$
Not seen (?)	$(1 - f_1)\pi$	$(1 - f_2)(1 - \pi)$
Total	π	$(1 - \pi)$

This variance estimate will be useful not only in evaluating the precision of prevalence estimates from two-stage studies, but also in designing studies that yield the desired estimate precision. These uses will be discussed later.

Since the advantages of two-stage designs have been known for three decades, it is disappointing that they have not been employed more widely. Two-stage designs have been advocated by Diamond and Lilienfeld (1962) for general use in epidemiology, and in psychiatric epidemiology they have been promoted by Cooper and Morgan (1973) as well as by many others, including Dohrenwend and Shrout (1981). An outstanding example of the feasibility of the design has been provided by Henderson and his colleagues (Duncan-Jones & Henderson, 1978; Henderson, Duncan-Jones, Byrne, Scott, & Adcock, 1979) in their studies of psychiatric disorder in Canberra, Australia.

The two-stage design is not only useful for estimating prevalence; it is also a natural design for economically identifying treated and untreated cases in general populations for prospective studies. Some applications of two- or multistage designs may be less concerned with total expense than with the wealth of data that results from applying contrasting diagnostic methods to the same respondents. Dohrenwend and Shrout (1981) have recommended multistage designs for methodological research aimed at evaluating competing instruments. Their research design called for following up all persons with a second interview, and following up persons with diagnostic discrepancies with one or more additional assessments. The redundant information obtained in the various interviews is crucial for a critical evaluation of the strengths and weaknesses of each interview.

DESIGNING TWO-STAGE STUDIES

Perhaps the reason that two-stage designs are not employed more often is the apparent complexity of the procedure. First and second-stage assessment methods must be selected, and the overall proportion of respondents included in the second stage, as well as the relative proportions of those screened positive and those screened negative, must be determined. Fortunately, there are helpful statistical results that bear on the design questions, and there are some empirical findings that make the choice of the first-stage interview easier. We will first review the statistical results, and then report some empirical results.

Let us assume that for choices of the first-stage screen and the second-stage diagnostic evaluation, the relative cost of the assessments (c_1/c_2) is known, as is the expected proportion, π, of respondents who will be positive on the screen. We also assume that estimates of the positive and negative predictive values, λ_1, $1 - \lambda_2$, of the first-stage instruments are available. With this information, the investigator can choose the proportions of screened positive and negative to be followed (f_1 and f_2), as well as the overall sample size, N.

If estimating prevalence is the central aim of the study, the optimal proportions of screened positive and negative to be followed can be calculated. Deming (1977) derived expressions for f_1 and f_2 that will minimize the standard error of the estimate of p.

$$f_1 = \frac{c_1}{c_2}\left[\frac{\lambda_1(1 - \lambda_1)}{\pi(1 - \pi)(\lambda_1 - \lambda_2)^2}\right]^{\frac{1}{2}},$$

and

$$f_2 = \frac{c_1}{c_2}\left[\frac{\lambda_2(1 - \lambda_2)}{\pi(1 - \pi)(\lambda_1 - \lambda_2)^2}\right]^{\frac{1}{2}}. \tag{4}$$

If the relative costs c_1 and c_2 are similar, and the difference between λ_1 and λ_2 is small, the Eq. (4) may actually produce estimates of the proportions that are larger than one. If both estimates are one or larger, no economy is obtained by applying a two-stage procedure. In such a case the investigator must either apply the criterion diagnostic method to all respondents in the sample or find a first-stage screening instrument that makes fewer misclassifications.

The relative sizes of f_1 and f_2 in Eq. (4) vary as function of the caseness rate within the positive and negative screen groups. If the screening instrument is at all successful in identifying cases of the disorder under study, then λ_1 will be larger than λ_2, and consequently a larger proportion of the screened positives would be followed than of the screened negatives. What may not be apparent from Eqs. (4) is that the actual number of persons to be followed from the screened negative group may be larger than the number of persons followed from the screened positive group since the size of the group screened negative will be larger than the size of the group screened positive. Deming (1977) evaluated these equations for a number of hypothetical values, and he concluded that the two-stage procedure is most useful when the underlying prevalence rate is low and when there is a big difference in the cost of administering the screen and the cost of performing the criterion diagnosis.

The equations reviewed above can be used to design a two-stage study that yields an estimated prevalence with an acceptably narrow 95% confidence bound. As Deming noted, however, caution should be exercised in substituting sample estimates of λ_1, λ_2, and π for the parameters in the equations. Special attention should be given to the appropriateness of the samples used to obtain the estimates and to the sizes of the samples used. A cautious approach would dictate using a range of values to ensure that the design recommendations are robust.

The fact that the allocation rule given in Eq. (4) suggests that relatively few of the screened positives be followed for diagnostic evaluation in the second stage may disappoint those who hope to identify a group of confirmed cases for case-control research. Clearly the optimal design for estimating prevalence is not optimal for case identification. Indeed, if one were interested in following cases to study their relapse rates, and if economy is the principal criterion for designing the survey, one might choose to set f_1 to one and f_2 to zero. In actual practice, it would be unfortunate if no screened negatives were followed, since without an estimate of λ_2, it is impossible to estimate prevalence. Moreover, questions about the representativeness of the sample of cases can only be addressed by comparing cases detected as true positives with cases identified as false-negatives on the screen.

One can use the equation for the standard error of the estimate of p to evaluate the efficiency loss resulting from the use of nonoptimal choices of f_1 and f_2. Deming (1977) concluded that for prevalences in the range of 10% and larger, the loss of efficiency may be small for values of f_1 and f_2 far from optimal. For studies of rare disorders, however, departures of f_1 and f_2 from the optimal values may result in appreciable losses in efficiency.

EMPIRICAL EVALUATION OF POTENTIAL SCREENING MEASURES

In the discussion above, it was assumed that a screening instrument is available that is related to the disorder of interest. We also assumed that the parameters λ_1, λ_2, and π were either known or could be estimated. In fact, there are many psychological and psychiatric instruments that have been proposed as measures of psychiatric disorder. We might consider as a first-stage screening instrument any measure that is brief, easy to administer, and tested in community populations. Prime candidates for the screening measure might be instruments that a decade ago were themselves considered to be measures of psychiatric "caseness."

We report here the ability of three symptom scales to differentiate known psychiatric cases from apparent noncases sampled from the community in northern Manhattan. The three scales are the Demoralization scale of the Psychiatric Epidemiology Research Interview (Dohrenwend, Shrout, Egri, & Mendelsohn, 1980), the Center for Epidemiologic Studies Depression scale (Radloff, 1977), and the Global Severity Index of the SCL-90-R (Derogatis, 1977). The first measure typically employs a 1-year time frame, and the other two measures typically employ a 1-week time frame, but in our research we modified all three to use a 1-month time frame.

The Demoralization scale was selected for study because of its similarity to measures of caseness that were developed for the major postwar studies of mental disorder in North America. Link and Dohrenwend (1981) have shown that it is strongly related to such scales as Langner's 22 items, and the HOS and Dohrenwend *et al.* (1980) have argued that the findings of the postwar epidemiologic studies can be better understood if their measures are interpreted in terms of Frank's (1975) concept of demoralization. The measure we employed has 27 items, each of which is scored on a 5-point scale.

The CESD was developed at NIMH to provide a brief assessment of depression in nonclinical samples, and has been widely used as a measure of depression. Myers and Weissman (1980) and Roberts and Vernon (1983) have concluded from comparisons of CESD scores with RDC diagnoses made on the basis of SADS interviews that the CESD is only a rough indicator of clinical depression, but that it may be useful as a screening measure. Both studies employed samples of community respondents who were administered the CESD and then followed with the SADS structured clinical interview. They reported false-positive rates of 17% and 6%, and false-negative rates of 40% and 36%, respectively, for a conventional cutpoint of 16 on the scale.

The SCL90-R Global Severity Scale (GSI) is an index constructed from responses to 90 symptom items covering a variety of complaints in addition to depressive symptoms. Derogatis (1977) claims that the GSI is the "best single indicator of the current level of depth of the [psychological] disorder" (p. 12). The measure was selected in this comparison for its breadth of symptom coverage; unlike the CESD, the GSI is designed to measure other psychopathology in addition to depression.

Subjects and Methods

The three measures were administered, along with various PERI symptom measures, role measures, and life events, to samples of patients and of community respondents. The patients were recruited principally from the outpatient clinics and inpatient services at Columbia-Presbyterian Medical Center in New York, and were interviewed either in the treatment setting or in their homes by interviewers who read the questions and recorded the responses. Spanish versions of all the measures were available, as were bilingual interviewers. In the analyses to be reported, only patients with DSM-III diagnoses of major depression ($N = 65$) or with nonaffective psychoses ($N = 49$) were included. (Since the second group was composed primarily of schizophrenics, we will refer to it as the schizophrenic group.) The DSM-III diagnoses were made by residents who were supervised by members of the biometrics department at New York State Psychiatric Institute, and each diagnosis was reviewed by the supervising psychiatrist.

The community sample was drawn from the Washington Heights section of Manhattan using telephone directories to locate households; respondents within households were selected randomly from among residents between the ages of 17 and 60. As with the patients, interviewers administered the questionnaire and recorded the responses. While not strictly representative of the

Washington Heights community, this sample did provide heterogeneity in age, ethnic group, sex, and social class. Demographic characteristics of the samples are shown in Table 14.3.

Since the only information available on the psychological status of the community respondents was that collected during the research interview, it was not possible to be sure that the community sample contained no cases of schizophrenia or major depression, but that possibility was minimized by eliminating persons who 1) currently were seeking treatment for a mental disorder, 2) reported a previous history of psychiatric hospitalization, or 3) reported having a "nervous breakdown" in the past. Of the 275 persons in the community who were given the interview, 47 (17%) were eliminated on the basis of these criteria. Since the rates of major depression and schizophrenia are low, it is likely that the vast majority of the 228 remaining community respondents were not current cases of these disorders.

The reader should be aware that the sample used in our analyses overlaps with, but is not identical to, the sample used in Chapter 10 by Dohrenwend *et al.* Their sample includes respondents who were interviewed in the same field operation with another version of the interview which did not include the measures of interest here, and their community noncase group excludes persons who had elevated levels of demoralization.

Results

While the three screening scales were conceptualized to measure different aspects of psychological distress or disorder, they are very highly correlated, both in the community and patient samples, as is shown in Table 14.4. Given the generality of Frank's (1975) demoralization concept, we are inclined to

Table 14.3. Characteristics of Case and Comparison Samples

	Depressed	Schizophrenic	Community
Total *N*	66	49	228
Sex			
Male	17 (26%)	29 (59%)	100 (44%)
Female	49 (74%)	20 (41%)	128 (56%)
Ethnic			
Black	17 (26%)	20 (40%)	66 (29%)
Hispanic	19 (29%)	16 (33%)	75 (33%)
White	30 (45%)	13 (27%)	87 (38%)
Education			
Not HS grad	18 (27%)	22 (45%)	65 (28%)
HS grad	29 (44%)	25 (51%)	101 (44%)
College grad	19 (29%)	2 (4%)	62 (27%)

Table 14.4. Correlations between Screening Scales

	SCL90 GSI	CESD	Demoralization
SCL90 GSI	—	.69	.83
CESD	.77	—	.76
Demoralization	.78	.78	—

Note: Shown above the diagonal are the correlations computed using the 115 patients, and shown below the diagonal are the correlations computed using 227 community respondents.

conclude that all three measures are tapping this nonspecific psychological distress.

The high correlations between the scales prepare us for the results of the comparisons of the depressed cases and community controls shown in Figure 14.2. This figure shows the tradeoff between false-positive and false-negative rates for a series of different rules for defining a screened positive for each of the scales. Instead of presenting the false-negative and false-positive rates for the scales using conventional cutpoints, we computed the error rates for a whole series of cutpoints. This series even includes extreme cutpoints, such as 55 out of the 60 possible on the CESD. Such extremely high cutpoints result in many false-negatives (but few false-positives), while extremely low cutpoints result in many false-positives (but few false-negatives). If one wishes to improve the false-negative rate by adjusting the cutpoint on the screen, it can only be done by increasing the false-positive rate. While the plot of false-negative rates with false-positive rates is related to the ROC curves of signal detection theory, it is presented here descriptively without making use of the formal elements of that theory.

The striking result in Figure 14.2 is that the three measures give essentially the same results across the entire range of cutpoints surveyed. If a cutpoint is sought that equalizes the false-negative and false-positive rates, for all three scales the constant rate would be about 20%, or 80% expressed as sensitivity and specificity.

While not explicit in the figure, the misclassification rates corresponding to the CESD cutpoint of 16 or more are 14% and 24%, respectively, for false-negative and false-positive rates. These results for the CESD are not dissimilar to the results of Myers and Weissman (1980) and of Roberts and Vernon (1983) in that they show that the CESD is associated with, but far from identical to, a clinical definition of depression. Our false-negative rate is somewhat better than the rates reported in the other two studies, no doubt due to the fact that their cases of major depression were selected from the community, while ours were recruited from treatment facilities. While not as

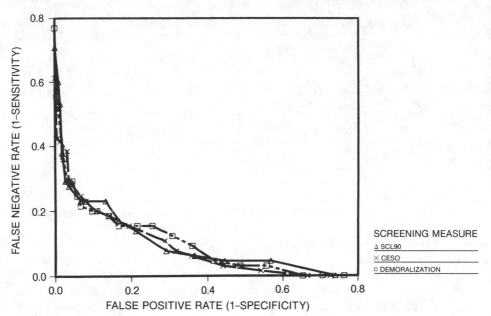

Figure 14.2. Plot of error rates of screening measures—depressive cases and community controls.

representative of all major depressed as the case groups in the other studies, our case-control design yielded substantially larger sample sizes and, consequently, more stable estimates of the error rates. Our conclusion that the CESD and the PERI Demoralization scale do not differ in their ability to discriminate persons with depression is consistent with results presented by Vernon and Roberts (1981).

Figure 14.3 shows the effectiveness of the three measures for screening cases of schizophrenia. Again the similarity of the three sets of curves is striking, especially since the CESD is not designed to screen this disorder, and since the SCL90-R contains items explicitly designed to measure psychoticism. Since the GSI of the SCL90 requires more than three times the number of questions as does each of the other two measures, we can conclude that it is the least economical of the three to be used as a first-stage screen for either depression or psychoticism.

When Figure 14.2 is compared to Figure 14.3, it is clear that all three measures are much more effective in screening cases of depression than cases of schizophrenia, and that the error rates for schizophrenia are high. If one is interested in screening a population for cases of nonaffective psychosis, one must consider other measures besides the SCL90 Global Severity index, a measure of demoralization, or the CESD. While often used in psychiatric research, these measures cannot be interpreted as indicators of generalized caseness.

When it is of interest to screen different kinds of cases of psychopathology in a population, it is likely that a multivariate screening rule will be needed. Such a rule might employ scales from a multidimensional instrument such as the Psychiatric Epidemiology Research Interview (Dohrenwend *et al.*, 1980). This instrument is especially promising for screening psychotics, since it contains a reliable scale that measures false beliefs and perceptions. Such a multidimensional rule is described in Shrout, Dohrenwend, & Levav (in press).

AN EXAMPLE OF A TWO-STAGE STUDY DESIGN

To illustrate the design of a two-stage study, let us use the results from Figure 14.2 to lay out a plan for measuring the prevalence of major depression in a population that is thought to have a 2% prevalence rate. (Note that if it is true that available prevalence estimates from single-stage studies are

Figure 14.3. Plot of error rates of screening measures—psychotic cases and community controls.

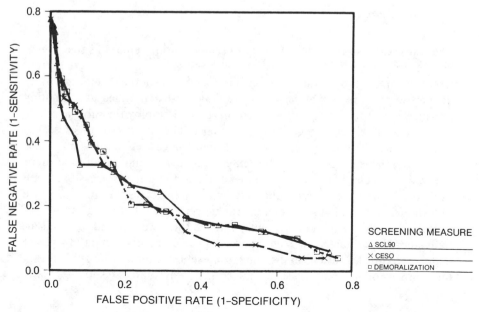

biased, then the true rate in the general population may in fact be this low.) From our consideration of the relative impact of false-negative and false-positive rates, we might adopt a screening rule for the first stage that has a very good specificity and a moderately high sensitivity. In Figure 14.2 we can find a point for the CESD that corresponds to an 8% false-positive rate and a 25%-false negative rate. The actual cutpoint associated with that point is 24: persons scoring 24 or more on the scale are operationally called screened positives.

Using Bayes' formula, as described in Fleiss (1981), we can calculate expected values of the prevalences in the screened positives and in the screened negatives using the assumed overall prevalence rate of 2% and the error rates from Figure 14.2. The expected rate of the disorder in the screened positive group is 16% and in the screened negative group it is .5%. The overall proportion of persons expected to be screened positive is 9%.

Let us assume that the ideal diagnostic procedure, involving two assessments by a clinician using a structured or semistructured interview, is about 40 times more expensive than administering the CESD. Using Eq. (4) we would find that the optimal sampling design requires that all the screened positives, and about a quarter of the screened negatives, be followed.

Suppose that we wished to obtain a 95% confidence bound on our prevalence estimate that ranges only two percentage points. If our estimates of error rates are accurate, we could obtain such precision by screening 1350 persons, and following 444 persons with the second-stage criterion method; 126 of those followed would have been screened positive and 318, negative.

CONCLUSIONS

The statistical results on the effects of misclassification remind us that prevalence estimates are likely be biased unless the classification procedure is error free. For rare disorders, the extent of this bias may be large. While error-free diagnostic procedures may never be available, research aimed at estimating prevalence of disorders in different groups should employ the most accurate assessment in existence, regardless of the cost. The expense of this research can be reduced by employing two-stage designs, since these designs may yield unbiased prevalence estimates while extensively evaluating only a fraction of the total subjects. Statistical guidelines for designing two-stage studies are available if the psychometric characteristics of the screening measures are known. Three potential screening measures were evaluated using samples of depressed and schizophrenic patients, and the three were found to be essentially indistinguishable; all were modestly useful in discriminating major depression, but less useful in discriminating schizophrenics. We suggest that multidimensional screening scales now under development should greatly improve the accuracy of first-stage screening instruments over those tested for purposes of this chapter.

ACKNOWLEDGMENTS

This work was supported from the following grants from the National Institute of Mental Health: MH37393, MH36208, and MH30906. Appreciation is expressed to J. L. Fleiss for comments on a draft of the paper.

REFERENCES

Bross, I. (1954). Misclassification in two by two tables. *Biometrics, 10*, 478–486.

Cooper, B., & Morgan, H. G. (1973). *Epidemiological psychiatry*. Springfield, IL: Charles C. Thomas.

Deming, W. E. (1977). An essay on screening, or on two phase sampling, applied to surveys of a community. *International Statistical Review, 45*, 29–37.

Derogatis, L. R. (1977). *SCL90 Revised Manual*. Baltimore: Clinical Psychometrics Research Unit, Johns Hopkins School of Medicine.

Diamond, E. L., & Lilienfeld, A. M. (1962). Effects of errors in classification and diagnosis in various types of epidemiological studies. *American Journal of Public Health, 52*, 1137–1144.

Dohrenwend, B. P., & Shrout, P. E. (1981). Toward the development of a two-stage procedure for case identification in psychiatric epidemiology. In R. Simmons (Ed.), *Research in community and mental health* (Vol. 2; pp. 295–323). Greenwich, Conn.: JAI Press.

Dohrenwend, B. P., Shrout, P. E., Egri, G., & Mendelsohn, F. S. (1980). Nonspecific psychological distress and other dimensions of psychopathology. *Archives of General Psychiatry, 37*, 1229–1236.

Duncan-Jones, P., & Henderson, S. (1978). The use of a two-stage design in a prevalence study. *Social Psychiatry, 13*, 231–237.

Fleiss, J. L. (1981). *Statistical methods for rates and proportions* (2nd ed.). New York: Wiley.

Frank, J. D. (1975). *Persuasion and healing*. Baltimore: Johns Hopkins University Press.

Henderson, S., Duncan-Jones, P., Byrne, D. G., Scott, R., Adcock, S. (1979). Psychiatric disorder in Canberra: A standardised study of prevalence. *Acta Psychiatrica Scandinavica, 60*, 355–374.

Link, B., & Dohrenwend, B. P. (1981). Formulation of hypotheses about the true prevalence of demoralization in the United States. In B. P. Dohrenwend & B. S. Dohrenwend (Eds.), *Mental illness in the United States: Epidemiological estimates* (pp. 114–132). New York: Praeger.

Myers, J. K., & Weissman, M. M. (1980). Use of a self-report symptom scale to detect depression in a community sample. *American Journal of Psychiatry, 137*, 1081–1083.

Radloff, L. S. (1977). The CESD scale: A self report depression scale for research in the general population. *Applied Psychological Measurement, 1*, 385–401.

Roberts, R. E., & Vernon, S. W. (1983). The center for epidemiologic studies depression scale: Its use in a community sample. *American Journal of Psychiatry, 140*, 41–46.

Shrout, P. E., Dohrenwend, B. P., & Levav, I. (in press). A discriminant rule for screening cases of diverse diagnostic types: Preliminary results. *Journal of Consulting and Clinical Psychology*.

Sutcliffe, J. P. (1965). A probability model for errors of classification: I. General considerations. *Psychometrika, 30,* 129–155.

Tenenbein, A. (1970). A double sampling scheme for estimating from binomial data with misclassifications. *Journal of the American Statistical Association, 65,* 1350–1361.

Tenenbein, A. (1971). A double sampling scheme for estimating from binomial data with misclassifications: Sample size determination. *Biometrics, 27,* 935–944.

Vernon, S. W., & Roberts, R. E. (1981). Measuring nonspecific psychological distress and other dimensions of psychopathology: Further observations on the problem. *Archives of General Psychiatry, 38,* 1239–1247.

DISCUSSION

Ernest Gruenberg: I was very positively impressed with the first part of your talk, but were you conscious of the fact that what you described as a multistage design is exactly the design that was used in the Baltimore ECA clinical reappraisal study? And of the fact that the clinical reappraisal sample we performed was the second stage exactly as you have defined the second-stage study, in which all of those who screened positive were interviewed by appraisers and a 17% random sample of all those who were negative were also reinterviewed by the best available method, a psychiatrist's standardized examination.

The reason I asked whether you were aware of these facts is that there is an excellent screen buried in the DIS to use for your two-stage design. It is a screen that Mike von Korff and Jim Anthony extracted from the DIS and is what they called the "stem DIS questions" for each of the DSM-III diagnoses. By just taking the first question asked to get into each detailed structure—only those questions, and ignore the whole structure—you select 100% of those who would ever get a DIS diagnosis, plus those who would not get a diagnosis but might have something else. That screen was very successful in picking up almost all the Axis I cases. Detailed analysis has not yet been done as to how weak it was, that is, how often an Axis I diagnosis was picked up in the screen negatives.

There is a strong connection between what you were talking about and the Hopkins Clinical Reappraisal design. I thought I would call it to your attention.

Shrout: Thank you for your question; it gives me a chance to congratulate you on the design used in Baltimore.

I intentionally avoided talking about Baltimore and the ECA because I did not want the controversies and results of that program to distract the audience from my central points. Many of these points have been made in the statistical literature more than a decade before your study and the ECA studies in general. One of the key points I wanted to make is that, relative to a given gold standard, a single-stage prevalence study employing a fallible diagnostic rule will usually give biased results. I realize that there is disagreement about what the gold standard should be and that some persons are unhappy with the standard employed in Baltimore. I tried to make my talk somewhat less controversial by letting people choose whatever gold standard they wished. I personally applaud the Baltimore reappraisal, and I hope to see the results soon.

Lee Robins: I thought your chapter was really interesting, and I agree with you that the two-stage design can be very useful, but let me raise some problems. It seems to me that you are making some assumptions that don't accord with our experience. We have found that both sensitivity and specificity fluctuate enormously with the prevalence rate in the population. When we did our psychiatric evaluation in a clinical sample, we found that we had the kind of pattern you described—approximately equal sensitivity and specificity for depression (the common disorder in that clinical sample) when we measured lay interviewers' results against those of physicians. However, when we used the same interview and same method of comparison in a general population sample where depression was rare, we got very much better specificity than sensitivity. This finding has been typical for other disorders as well. Depression is an extreme example because about half of our clinical population has had a depression, as compared with 5% of our general population sample. In the general population, sensitivities tend to be very much lower than specificities, while specificities are high. We get specificities at the 98 or 99% level for most disorders in the general population, not at the 95% level you called "good." As a result, we find little evidence for biased estimates of prevalence in our general population samples. The fact that such biases could happen, about which you are correct, does not mean that they *do* happen very often in epidemiologic studies. The rising specificity seems to compensate nicely for the falling sensitivity when one moves from the clinic to the community.

Shrout: I thank you for pointing out that the proper sensitivities and specificities that should be used in the statistical analysis are those obtained in the population being studied. It is encouraging to hear that your specificities are very high, but for a rare disorder, .98 might not be good enough. I wanted a dramatic example to illustrate my point, and I was able to obtain one using a specificity value that many people would claim to be good. A 95% specificity and sensitivity results in a threefold increase in prevalence over a true 2% rate. Many of the rates that are being reported in the ECA, especially for subgroups, are 1% or less. The rarer the disorder, the more serious the lack of perfect specificity will be. So I think the question of bias is worth constant reexamination. If it turns out that in validity studies done with community samples, you find that the adjustments for the bias are trivial, then so be it. But I think that these analyses should be reported, since the effects of apparently small amounts of error can be counterintuitively large.

Charles Holzer: Since you have already addressed the issue of bias, I want to address the issue of cost. Are you assuming that the cost of the first-stage screen is fixed, regardless of whether it comes out positive or negative, and similarly for the second-stage screen? I would think that under the second-stage circumstance, such as when administering the DIS or when the psychiatrist is doing the interview, the interview length is shortened when it is coming out negative.

Shrout: I am assuming a very costly second stage, regardless of whether respondents have symptoms or not. I am also assuming that prevalence estimates that are unbiased are going to cost more than biased estimates from one-stage surveys done with fallible measures. In some cases one might be lucky and save money by appending a screening measure such as the CES-D onto another survey. If the CES-D could be added on a survey that is already being done, its cost could be fixed and really very minimal.

Holzer: I was making my comment more as an assertion. Most instruments have built into them some degree of potential skip-out or shortening, and so there is a degree of the two-stage idea built into a single interview or questionnaire.

Shrout: I don't believe in skipping out. I like data. I believe in collecting redundant data; the more times you can ask the same question, the more likely it is that you are going to get the right answer.

John Rice: An alternative that we are using to study relatives in the NIMH-CRB Collaborative Depression study is to use two independent assessments (i.e., blind interviews) 6 years apart. Our rationale is that if there is a problem with low specificity, then false-positives can be eliminated by requiring stability of diagnosis. For example, if the specificity were .9, so that 1 of 10 true noncases was a false-positive, then we expect only 1 in 100 to be misclassified twice. This approach is similar to the repeated measures idea of utilizing independent measures at disparate points in time to deal with error. It would seem that, in the two-stage approach, there is still the problem of not having a gold standard, so that one has to worry about two sets of sensitivity and specificity parameters.

Shrout: Making a given stage as reliable and as valid as possible has been the focus of much of the work in the past decade, and the fruit of this labor is now being harvested in terms of recent survey results. For rare disorders, it seems unlikely to me that a single-stage survey will give unbiased results, unless (as Dr. Robins has said) there is good empirical evidence that specificity and sensitivity are not a problem in that population. To provide such empirical evidence one must assume a gold standard, or at least be able to specify the best diagnostic procedure available. The process of deciding what is the best diagnostic criterion is as much a philosophical question as an empirical one. In making the decision, one must try to anticipate and to address the criticisms of all critics whom one hopes will believe the results.

Rice: Maybe ours is a special case, in the sense that our first and second stages are both full diagnostic assessments.

Darrel Regier: One of the issues that I have not seen addressed by any statistics, and which was an important consideration with the ECA, was the effect of potential dropouts between the first- and second-stage intervention. I wonder if your statistical model takes into account the effect of dropouts between these two stages, particularly if the dropout rate were biased in some sense, such as by a differential dropout rate for those with more severe disorders.

Shrout: I did not consider the dropout rate. Without such additional complications, the formula for the standard error of the prevalence is already somewhat intimidating. Actual applications of the two-stage method will have to take the problem of dropouts into account. The best way to handle this problem, however, is to avoid dropouts and achieve high response rates. High compliance rates can be obtained; in Puerto Rico, Drs. Canino and Bird currently are getting response rates better than 91%. It is possible to get such rates, perhaps not in New York, perhaps not in Baltimore, but it is possible in many places.

Joseph Fleiss: The standards that we have are high, I know, but I will repeat what I said earlier. They are not high enough. The specificity of 98% for a procedure applied to estimating prevalence when the true prevalence is 2% may produce an estimate of approximately 4%. That is a 100% error. Thus, 98% specificity may not be good enough.

IMPLICATIONS OF EPIDEMIOLOGIC FINDINGS FOR POLICY AND PROGRAM PLANNING

15

Need and Demand for Mental Health Services in an Urban Community: An Exploration Based on Household Interviews

SAM SHAPIRO, ELIZABETH A. SKINNER, and PEARL S. GERMAN
Health Services Research and Development Center, Department of Health Policy and Management, School of Hygiene and Public Health, Johns Hopkins University
MORTON KRAMER
Department of Mental Hygiene, School of Hygiene and Public Health, Johns Hopkins University
ALAN ROMANOSKI
Department of Psychiatry and Behavioral Sciences, School of Medicine, Johns Hopkins University

A major driving force behind efforts to estimate need and unmet need for mental health services for the noninstitutionalized population is the importance of assessing the adequacy and appropriateness of available ambulatory health care resources. Of concern are services in the general medical or specialty sectors, health care behavior of the population and provider practices when mental and emotional problems occur, and inequities affecting access to care. Information related to these issues would presumably provide a more rational basis than we have to identify manpower, facilities, and health insurance requirements, and link effectively the ill with a suitable source of care (Regier, Shapiro, Kessler, & Taube, 1984).

It is important to recognize at the outset that the development of estimates of need faces frustrating issues common to both physical and mental disorders, that is, difficulty in defining the concept of need and operationalizing it into a set of widely accepted measures (Ware, Manning, Duan, Wells, & Newhouse, 1984). Need can be viewed from two vantage points—the consumer's and the provider's. In the former, the concern is with a complex set of perceptions, values, and other factors that facilitate or create barriers to health services. The endpoint is the observed utilization of services plus care identified by the consumer as needed but not obtained. This is independent of the provider's appraisal of the appropriateness of the care sought (Aday, Fleming, & Andersen, 1984).

307

From the medical community's standpoint, what is often meant by need is the health care expert's view of requirements for primary or secondary prevention of disease and diagnosis, treatment, or rehabilitation in the presence of specified signs, symptoms, or conditions. The degree of certainty of benefit varies with knowledge of the natural history of the condition and the availability of interventions that are effective at different stages of the condition. Further, agreement may be greater on whether care should be obtained than on the nature, source, duration, or volume of care required (or its outcome).

Methods to take into account both the consumer's and provider's views are being developed. The objective has been to see how far we can go in determining measures of need and unmet need using observations from the community studies in the NIMH Epidemiologic Catchment Area (ECA) program of research.

This chapter gives results of the second phase in this effort at the Eastern Baltimore site, one of five ECA areas. The first phase utilized information from a baseline household survey of adults in the area to make such estimates (Shapiro, Skinner, Kramer, Steinwachs, & Regier, 1985); with the recent availability of observations from follow-up surveys over a 1-year period, a new phase in the derivation of estimates of need becomes possible.

In both phases, the indicators of mental health problems are reports of a visit to a provider for emotional problems, a DIS/DSM-III diagnosis, GHQ score of four or more symptoms from a 20-item version of this instrument, and a report of at least one day of inability to carry out usual activities due to an emotional problem. Clearly, any definition of need based on this information has a restricted meaning, and there is no inference to be drawn about appropriateness of source of care, adequacy of treatment, and so on.

METHODS

Although, by now, many aspects of the ECA program are well known, it is worth noting that from the early planning days of the ECA, the program offered special opportunities for grappling with the difficult problem of deriving estimates of need and unmet need for mental health care and their correlates of need (Regier *et al.*, 1984). Central to such exploration was the provision for collecting information on the prevalence and incidence of mental disorders, personal and health characteristics including use of health and mental health services, and sources of care.

Baseline household interviews have been conducted with probability samples of 3000–3500 community noninstitutionalized residents, age 18 or older, in each of five defined geographic areas in various parts of the United States; smaller-scale surveys have been carried out among the institutionalized (Eaton *et al.*, 1984). Because of special interest in the aged, those age 65 or older were oversampled in some of the areas, including Eastern Baltimore. Respondents were reinterviewed in person with substantially the same instrument, one year later, and by telephone (or in person in one site) with an abbreviated questionnaire 6 months after the baseline, thereby making possible longitudinal analysis.

The survey instrument in both face-to-face interviews included the Diagnostic Interview Schedule (DIS), a fully structured questionnaire administered by trained lay interviewers (Robins, Helzer, Croughan, & Ratcliff, 1981). Responses to the DIS are used to generate selected psychiatric diagnoses according to operationalized DSM-III criteria and a Mini-Mental State Examination Score. Recency of meeting the diagnostic criteria is determined and for the inquiry into need, the period used is the 6 months prior to the interview.

In the Eastern Baltimore site, the interviews in the home as well as the intervening telephone interviews included 20 items drawn from the General Health Questionnaire (GHQ) developed by Goldberg (1972). More specifically, these 20 items consist of the 12 "best item" set identified in Goldberg's original work, 6 items drawn from among the 8 next best items, and 2 additional items selected because of their relevance to depressive symptoms. The 20-item GHQ is designed to cover current symptoms of distress and to identify individuals at high risk of having a diagnosable emotional disorder. The number of positive responses provides a gradient of risk but for analytic purposes, high risk is defined as being positive on 4 or more GHQ items. This cutpoint is based on an analysis by Goldberg of his 20-item version of the GHQ (Goldberg, 1978).

The questionnaire in the survey offers other possibilities for identifying individuals with some manifestation of emotional problems. Among these are report of psychotropic medication, positive response to an inquiry into whether the respondent had recently been unable to carry out usual activities for at least a day because of an emotional or nervous problem, and combinations of selected items in the DIS which do not meet criteria for a diagnosis but reflect emotional symptomatology. The item on inability to carry out usual activities was selected for this analysis since it adds a direct indicator of impairment that occurred in close proximity to the interview and provides a different dimension of emotional disturbance than a DIS diagnosis or high GHQ score.

The Eastern Baltimore site is located in a large, densely populated urban area of Baltimore City. It covers three contiguous mental health catchment areas with a combined population of 241,000; about 175,000 are age 18 and older. The population is somewhat older than in many other urban areas (18% of the adults were age 65 or older) and has relatively high proportions of nonwhites (35%) and persons on Medicaid or in a near-poor status (35%).

The field survey was designed to obtain interviews in the household with one person randomly selected from those age 18–64 and with everyone age 65 and older; proxy respondents were accepted for 2.7% who were ill or had language problems. The overall response rate in the baseline survey was 78%, yielding 3481 completed interviews. All measures derived are weighted to take into account differential sampling probabilities and response rates; adjustments are made to the 1980 decennial census counts by age, race, and sex. The follow-up 6-month telephone and 1-year household interviews were confined to the baseline survey interviewees. Response rates were 83% and 81%, respectively.

To determine the nature and extent to which biases may have resulted from nonresponse in these follow-up surveys, baseline characteristics relevant for the analysis in this chapter have been examined for respondents and nonrespondents. The results indicate only minor differences, none of which would affect the measures derived. Of greater consequence are what appear to be changes in response to questions related to mental and emotional conditions and mental health care. This is illustrated in Table 15.1 for three of the key variables (manifestations of emotional disorders) used in developing estimates of need.

The decrease in the proportion with DIS diagnoses is due in large measure to a sharp drop in the prevalence of phobias, from 13.4% to 6.4% between the two surveys, the evaluation of which is still under way. The reasons for decreases in positive responses to the GHQ and disability days are likely to remain unexplained.

Another difference that is significant for the use of longitudinal observations in this study concerns the proportion who made a visit during the prior

Table 15.1. Manifestations at Baseline and 1-Year Resurvey

Manifestation	Percent Baseline†	Percent 1-Year Reinterview
Number of Persons*	3481	2767
DIS/DSM III disorders, recent**	23.4	18.0
GHQ score, 4 or more	15.5	11.6
One or more disability days due to emotional problems††	5.1	2.2
No manifestation	67.9	74.4

*Unweighted; percentages based on weighted data.

**Past six months. Includes Mini-Mental State Examination, scores 0–17; cognitive impairment (severe).

†Percentages are for all persons interviewed at baseline; excluding nonrespondents at the 1-year resurvey changes the proportions slightly: DIS, 23.3%; GHQ 4+, 14.6%; disability, 5.1%

††Past 3 months in baseline interview; past 6 months in 1-year interview.

6 months to a general medical provider or mental health specialist for an emotional problem or disorder. In the baseline survey, 7.1% of those surveyed belonged in this category, almost evenly divided between these two sectors of care; in the 1-year resurvey the figure was 6.1%. The difference is not statistically significant ($p > .10$), but it is possible that some decrease did occur due to a change in the structure of the questionnaire designed to reduce a moderate degree of overstatement of utilization of mental health services in the baseline survey.

In the discussion that follows, we consider first the approach taken and results obtained in measuring need from the baseline information (Phase 1); then we turn to the longitudinal sources of information (Phase 2).

MEASURES OF NEED AND UNMET NEED: PHASE 1 (BASELINE SURVEY)

In determining need for mental health services, four variables were used from the baseline survey.

1. Mental health services use—defined as a visit made during the prior 6 months for an emotional problem to a general medical care provider or specialty mental health resources (e.g., psychiatrist, psychologist, psychiatric social worker).
2. Three manifestations of emotional problems identified previously:
   a. DIS diagnosis within 6 months of the interview;
   b. GHQ score of 4 or more positive symptoms;
   c. Disability day—inability to carry out usual activities in the past 3 months for at least an entire day because of emotional problem.

Need for mental health services was defined as either having received care (met need) or, in the absence of such care, having more than one manifestation (unmet need). In effect, the concept of need linked the consumer's perception of need as evidenced most clearly by behavior (i.e., mental health visits) with manifestations interpreted as reflecting unmet need whether or not the consumer recognized a need for service or would act on it. The requirement of at least two manifestations to be present when no visits were made was aimed at increasing confidence that we were including individuals who had symptoms indicative of "pain or suffering" of more than a transient nature. As indicated in Table 15.2, having multiple manifestations was more likely to lead to this type of visit than having just one manifestation.

The bold numbers in the table represent the components of need for mental health care defined above. Met and unmet need are quite similar

Table 15.2. Manifestation of Emotional Problems and Mental Health Visits, Baseline Survey

Manifestation of Emotional Problems	Number of Persons*	Percent		
		Total	With Mental Health Visits**	No Mental Health Visits
All Persons	3,481	100.0	7.1†	92.9
2 or more manifestations	344	9.5	3.1	6.4††
1 manifestation only	832	23.0	2.1	20.9
No manifestations	2,305	67.6	2.0	65.6

Note: Manifestations refer to DIS/DSM-III disorder present in prior 6 months, including
cognitive impairment (severe); GHQ score of 4 or more, one or more disability days due to
emotional problem in prior 3 months.
  *Unweighted; percentages based on weighted data.
  **Visit to mental health specialist or general medical provider for mental health reasons
in prior 6 months.
  †Met need for mental health services.
  ††Unmet need for mental health services.

(7.1% and 6.4%, respectively), and total need is measured at 13.5% of the
adults in the Eastern Baltimore area. Exploration of the utility of these
measures in identifying relative risks for mental health service needs in
different segments of a community's population was begun in Phase 1 (Shapiro *et al.*, 1985). For example, multivariate analysis showed that need for
such care was influenced by a variety of demographic and socioeconomic
factors: it was low among the aged and high among women, persons living
alone, and those on Medicaid. The proportion of need that was unmet varied
less, but for two groups, the aged and nonwhites, it was relatively large.
Those on Medicaid through public assistance, an especially high-need subgroup, were more likely to have their need met than the near-poor. When
each DIS disorder was examined, many individuals found to be in need had
not seen a provider in the prior six months; the proportions ranged from
close to 50% for schizophrenic disorder to 75% for cognitive impairment.

MEASURES OF NEED AND UNMET NEED:
PHASE 2 (LONGITUDINAL DATA)

A major limitation of the measures just discussed is the uncertainty that they
do distinguish between emotional problems that may be transient and those
that are more enduring. The availability of information from the 1-year
follow-up survey in the ECA provides a basis for partially dealing with this

situation. The present analysis of longitudinal data addresses several of the relevant questions:

1. Is need status at baseline predictive of the status 1 year later?
2. What changes take place in manifestation of mental or emotional conditions between baseline and 1-year resurvey?
3. What is the influence of persistence (or recurrence) of manifestations on mental health visits?
4. How does utilizing longitudinal information on mental health manifestations affect measures of met and unmet need?

Predictive Value of Baseline Criteria of Need

Table 15.3 gives the proportion of persons in need for mental health services at baseline who met the same criteria 1 year later; similarly for those who did not meet the need criteria at baseline. Two things stand out: first, almost two-fifths (36.6%) continued to be in need; and second, despite this drop, we are clearly not dealing with a random phenomenon. Need established at baseline identified a subgroup in the population with a risk of being in need a year later that was six to seven times the corresponding risk among those not previously in need (5.8%). Assumptions to take into account biases that might have resulted in reductions in prevalence of manifestations and use of

Table 15.3. Distribution of Individuals with Need at 1-Year Resurvey by Need at Baseline Survey

Status at Baseline Survey	Number of Persons**	Status at One Year Resurvey*			
			In Need		Not in Need
		Total	Mental Health Visits†	No Mental Health Visit, 2+ Manifestations	
Total	2,768	10.0	6.1	3.9	90.0
In need	285	36.6	24.4	12.2	63.4
With mental health visit** (need met)	173	44.7	34.1	10.6	55.3
No mental health visit, 2+ manifestations (unmet need)	112	27.8	13.7	14.1	72.3
Not in need	2,482	5.8	3.2	2.6	94.2

*Based on criteria used for baseline status.
**Unweighted; percentages based on weighted data.
†Visit to mental health specialist or general medical care provider for mental health reasons in prior 6 months.

mental health services between the baseline and reinterviews do not affect these relationships materially.

From Table 15.3, it is also apparent that those who had made a mental health visit during the 6-month period before the baseline survey were more likely to be classified as in need later on (44.7%) than was the case for the "unmet need" subgroup (27.8%). This simply reflects the fact that one of the criteria for establishing need is demand for mental health services and about one-third (34.1%) of the individuals who had made a visit for an emotional problem prior to the baseline again reported such a visit at the reinterview. In comparison, only 13.7% of those in need at baseline, but who had made no mental health visit, did visit a provider for an emotional problem a year later. One interpretation is that repetitive episodes of care are more frequent than initiating care, a not uncommon observation in health services generally.

Changes in Mental Health Manifestations between Baseline and 1-Year Resurvey

The upper section of Table 15.4 presents information on the extent to which individuals with DIS diagnoses at baseline had manifestations of emotional problems a year later; this is independent of whether they had made a mental health visit. In 40.1% of the cases, a DIS diagnosis was made again (sum of 24.9% and 15.2%) and an additional 8.6% had one or both of the other manifestations, leaving 51.3% with no manifestation at all.

The co-occurrence of a DIS diagnosis and another manifestation at baseline increased the risk of having a DIS diagnosis or other manifestation a year later (61.8%) as compared with the situation for those who had only a DIS diagnosis at baseline (41.1%).

The added risk for later manifestations associated with having both a GHQ score of 4+ and disability due to an emotional problem is also apparent in the lower section of Table 15.4, which is restricted to persons with no DIS disorder at baseline. Here, we see that 1 year later, 60.3% had some mental health manifestation as compared with 42.5% among those with only one manifestation at baseline. The bottom row indicates that a small but nontrivial proportion, 15.3%, change from no manifestation to some manifestation.

Influence of Persistence (or Recurrence) of Mental Health Manifestations on Mental Health Use

The probability of a mental health visit in the 6-month period prior to the 1-year resurvey is affected by the nature of the manifestations of emotional problems that persist or recur and changes in these manifestations.

The upper part of Table 15.5 provides the information for persons who had a DIS disorder at baseline. Of interest are the very low proportions

Table 15.4. Distribution of Manifestations at 1-Year Resurvey by Manifestations at Baseline Survey

| | | | Percent at 1-Year Resurvey with: | | | |
| | | | DIS/DSM-III Disorder, Recent** | | GHQ and/or Disability Days (No DIS) | No Manifestations |
Baseline Survey	Number of Persons*	Total	DIS Only	With Other Manifestations		
Total	2,768	100.0	12.8	5.3	7.6	74.3
DIS/DSM-III disorder, recent**	699	100.0	24.9	15.2	8.6	51.3
DIS only	422	100.0	27.2	8.1	5.8	58.9
With other manifestations	247	100.0	20.8	27.5	13.5	38.2
No DIS/DSM-III disorder, recent	2,099	100.0	9.1	2.4	7.3	81.3
GHQ and disability days	31	100.0	19.1	14.6	26.6	39.7
GHQ or disability days	230	100.0	13.8	8.3	20.4	57.6
No manifestation	1,838	100.0	8.4	1.5	5.4	84.6

*Unweighted; percentages based on weighted data. Sum of row percentages may not add to 100.0% due to rounding.

**During 6 months prior to survey. Includes cognitive impairment (severe).

Table 15.5. Percent with Mental Health Visits in 6 Months Prior to 1-Year Resurvey by Manifestations at Baseline and 1-Year Resurvey

Status at Baseline Survey		Status at 1-Year Resurvey			
		DIS/DSM-III Disorder, Recent*		GHQ and/or Disability Days (No DIS)	No Manifestations
	Total	DIS Only	With Other Manifestations		
		Percent with Mental Health Visit**			
Total	6.1	11.4	33.4	13.1	2.5
DIS/DSM-III disorder, recent*	12.7	14.5	37.7	21.8	2.9
DIS only	6.7	6.5	26.7	18.1	2.9
With other manifestations	23.2	32.7	43.4	24.6	2.9
No DIS/DSM-III disorder, recent	4.1	8.9	25.0	9.9	2.4
GHQ and disability days	26.6	36.4	69.4	14.3	14.3
GHQ or disability days	8.9	18.7	35.1	3.6	4.7
No manifestation	3.2	6.2	13.3	12.3	2.2

*During 6 months prior to survey. Includes cognitive impairment (severe).
**Percentages show proportion of persons in each cell with visit to mental health specialist or general medical care provider for mental health reasons in prior 6 months.

making a mental health visit among those who no longer had any of the manifestations at the resurvey (2.9%) or continued to have only a DIS disorder (6.5%). The likelihood of such a visit increased sharply (43.4%) when manifestations persisted (recurred) among those who, at baseline, had a DIS disorder plus distress and/or impairment.

The importance of multiple manifestations at baseline for subsequent mental health visits is demonstrated further in the lower part of Table 15.5. Here the information is limited to the smaller number of individuals with no DIS diagnosis at baseline. Particularly significant are the relatively high proportions with a mental health visit among those who at baseline have distress (GHQ) and impairment (disability days), and subsequently have a DIS disorder.

A New Estimate of Met and Unmet Need

Two approaches have been taken to the derivation of estimates of need, using information on manifestations of emotional problems included in this analysis and visits to providers in the general medical or mental health specialty sectors for a mental health problem. One is to confine the data to observations in the 1-year resurvey and apply as criteria a mental health visit in the prior 6 months (need met) or, when no visit was made, two or more manifestations (need unmet). The resulting figures are:

	In Need
Met	6.1%
Unmet	5.1%
Total	11.2%

The other approach brings to bear the longitudinal information in the ECA surveys. The change is to include in the category of unmet need individuals who have a DIS disorder only at both baseline and 1-year resurvey and did not make a mental health visit. The rationale is that persistence of a DIS diagnosis is evidence of need, albeit unrecognized. Table 15.6 shows that 3.8% belong in this category and that the total classified as in need increases to 15.0%, with 8.9% having unmet need. The bottom figure in the table indicates that four out of five persons met none of the criteria of being in need at either baseline or resurvey.

DISCUSSION

This chapter has examined the extent to which the classification of individuals as being in need for mental health services is predictive of their future need status and how longitudinal information might affect measures of met and

Table 15.6. Need at 1-Year Resurvey

Number of Persons (unweighted)	2,768
In need	15.0%
Mental health visits in 6 months prior to resurvey (need met)	6.1
No mental health visits (need unmet)	8.9
Persistent DIS, no other manifestation	3.8
Two or more manifestations at resurvey	5.1
Not in need	85.0
Two or more manifestations at baseline only	4.5
Need criteria not met at baseline or resurvey	80.5

unmet need. The data come from interviews with a probability sample of adults in the Eastern Baltimore ECA, at two points in time, one year apart.

The baseline survey showed that 7.1% of the individuals satisfied the criterion for "need met" by virtue of having made a mental health visit to a formal provider of care in the prior 6 months. Another 6.4% did not make such a visit but had more than one of three manifestations of emotional problems; DIS disorder, distress (GHQ score of 4 or more), and impairment (more than one day's disability due to an emotional problem); they were classified "need unmet."

Observations from the 1-year resurvey demonstrated that while there was substantial change from "in need" to "not in need," the presence of multiple manifestations of emotional problems in one period (i.e., baseline) is indicative of mental health problems that persist or recur. The affected individuals are likely to continue to show some manifestations a year later and about half seek care for emotional problems. The net effect is to have a similar proportion classified in need at the resurvey (11.2%) as at the baseline, when the same criteria are applied.

The longitudinal data focus our attention differently on the DIS information than on the baseline cross-sectional information. Results from applying the DIS are of special interest because they are the source in the ECA surveys for deriving psychiatric diagnoses. In this study, very few individuals with persistent or recurrent DIS conditions alone made a mental health visit. Lack of recognition of an emotional problem may be partially responsible for this situation. For example, information available in the survey on whether an individual believed that he or she now had an emotional or nervous condition shows that those with a DIS disorder only were far less likely to respond in the affirmative than those with other manifestations (10.6% vs. 30.8%). This may not be surprising since the questions on distress and impairment due to an emotional problem were direct and bore down on the current situation, whereas the DIS is a lengthy instrument with complex algorithms to derive specific disorders. Nevertheless, persistence of a DIS disorder cannot be ignored as an indicator of need, at a minimum for making a visit to a formal provider of care. When this is taken into account, unmet need increases substantially at the resurvey; that is, from 5.1% to 8.9%, and the total in need becomes 15.0%.

This exploration of met and unmet need for mental health services is based on a concept that consists of two components. One is a judgment that combinations of the DIS, distress, and impairment are indicators of a need for a mental health visit. The other is dependent on the individual's care-seeking behavior based on his or her perception of need, regardless of how the provider would assess the necessity for the visit or the nature of the condition presented. The fact of a visit is equated to met need. Although this has the restricted meaning that the individual acted on a felt need, the criterion turned out to be a strong predictor of future need; close to half of those who reported such a visit at baseline met the need criteria a year later.

The process of developing measures of need for mental health services is far from complete. Information from telephone interviews conducted at about the midpoint between baseline and 1-year resurvey will make it possible to reconstruct utilization of mental health services, including inpatient care, over a full year. Also, while the DIS does not include all disorders in DSM-III, we should learn more when we examine specific diagnoses, symptoms, and syndromes identified through the DIS. Further, new insights can be expected with the availability of information from the assessments of need that were made in the psychiatric examinations conducted on probability subsamples of the ECA respondents in Eastern Baltimore. However, whatever methodology is applied, our understanding of met and unmet need will remain unclear until we are able to link the information available from the ECA on the population to characteristics and practices of the usual sources of care selected by people, including provider recognition of mental and emotional problems, treatment, and referral practices.

ACKNOWLEDGMENTS

The Epidemiologic Catchment Area Program is a series of five epidemiologic research studies performed by independent research teams in collaboration with staff of the Division of Biometry and Epidemiology (DBE) of the National Institute of Mental Health (NIMH). The NIMH principal collaborators are Darrell A. Regier, Ben Z. Locke, and Jack D. Burke; the NIMH project officer is Carl A. Taube. The principal investigators and coinvestigators from the five sites are: Yale University, UO1 MH 34224—Jerome K. Myers, Myrna M. Weissman, and Gary L. Tischler; Johns Hopkins University, UO1 MH33870—Morton Kramer, Ernest Gruenberg, and Sam Shapiro; Washington University, St. Louis, UO1 MH 33883—Lee Robins and John Helzer; Duke University, UOI MH 35386—Dan Blazer and Linda George; University of California, Los Angeles, UOl MH 35865—Marvin Karno, Richard L. Hough, Javier I. Escober, M. Audrey Burnam, and Dianne M. Timbers.

REFERENCES

Aday, L. A., Fleming, G. V., & Andersen, R. (1984). *Access to medical care in the U.S.: Who has it, who doesn't.* Chicago: Pluribus Press and Center for Health Administration Studies, University of Chicago.

Eaton, W. W., Holzer, C. E., von Korff, M., Anthony, J. C., Helzer, J. E., George, L., Burnam, M. A., Boyd, J. H., Burke, J. D., & Regier, D. A. (1984). The design of the Epidemiologic Catchment Area surveys: The control and measurement of error. *Archives of General Psychiatry, 41,* 942–948.

Goldberg, D. P. (1972). *The detection of psychiatric illness by questionnaire.* London: Oxford University Press.

Goldberg, D. P. (1978). *The Manual for the General Health Questionnaire.* London: National Foundation for Educational Research.

Regier, D. A., Myers, J. D., Kramer, M., Robins, L. N., Blazer, D. G., Hough, R. L., Eaton, W. W., & Locke, B. Z. (1984). The NIMH Epidemiologic Catchment Area Program: Historical context, major objectives, and study population characteristics. *Archives of General Psychiatry, 41,* 934–941.

Regier, D. A., Shapiro, S., Kessler, L. G., & Taube, C. A. (1984). Epidemiology and health services resource allocation policy of alcohol, drug abuse, and mental disorders. *Public Health Reports, 99,* 483–492.

Robins, L. N., Helzer, J. E., Croughan, J., & Ratcliff, K. S. (1981). National Institute of Mental Health Diagnostic Interview Schedule: Its history, characteristics, and validity. *Archives of General Psychiatry, 38,* 381–389.

Shapiro, S., Skinner, E. A., Kramer, M., Steinwachs, D. M., & Regier, D. A. (1985). Measuring need for mental health services in a general population. *Medical Care, 23,* 1033–1043.

Ware, J. E., Manning, W. G., Duan, N., Wells, K. B., & Newhouse, J. P. (1984). Health status and use of outpatient mental health services. *American Psychologist, 39,* 1090–1100.

16

Mental Health Service Policy Implications of Epidemiologic Data

DARREL A. REGIER
National Institute of Mental Health

This chapter addresses an issue of long-standing importance to those concerned with mental health policy issues, namely, the interface between policy and the research base with which it may be associated. Although there are several other policies on professional staffing and reserach support that need attention, the specific mental health policy issue addressed here concerns the allocation of mental health service resources.

The scarcity of research findings to support or refute the many policy options in this arena continues to frustrate mental health professionals and elected officials alike. Suggested remedies include rapid, ad hoc policy-directed research studies that are often too late to have the desired effects.

What has become increasingly clear, though, is that some aspects of health policy may be severely hampered by the absence of a systematic and cumulative research base in several of the related fields of psychopathology, epidemiology, and services research   including health economics and financing research. This is not to say that ad hoc, rapid evaluations do not have their place in the policy field, but it is necessary to emphasize that there are some structural aspects of the mental health and health care delivery system in general that require a better understanding before many of the policy options available to government agencies or academic and professional groups can be evaluated properly.

MENTAL HEALTH POLICY DETERMINANTS

Before proceeding, it may be helpful to divide up the health policy field and to point out where the emphasis will be placed in this chapter. In the best research tradition, we may conceptualize health policy as a dependent variable contingent on multiple determinants otherwise known as independent variables. At least four of these independent variables that determine health services policy are:

1. Political idealism.
2. Political pragmatism.
3. Implementation expertise.
4. Research data base.

Political Idealism

In the area of political philosophy or idealism, policy decisions are based not so much upon the needs of policy recipients as they are upon a philosophy of the proper role of government in our society. If a determination is made that the federal government should not be in the business of direct service delivery or even of monitoring categorical programs of service delivery, such a policy decision will not be dependent upon a research data base that speaks to the narrow issue of who is or is not receiving adequate services under the existing system. The decision to institute a policy of block grants was not based on data showing that federal categorical programs were ineffective, but on a political belief that health and mental health service programs are the proper responsibility of state and local governments or the private sector.

David Stockman (1981) points out other aspects of this area of policy determination by presenting a view of the medical marketplace that recommends fundamental shifts both in the supply side and demand side of how the health care delivery system is structured. Policy shifts advocated by Stockman are based not so much on research data as they are on economic theory of how the medical care system can operate more efficiently. Other opposing political theories of the ideal role of government in health care have produced systems such as the National Health Service of Great Britain.

Political Pragmatism

The second determinant of care, in what I am presenting as a hierarchy of sorts, is what I call the political pragmatism determinant of health policy. Once the overall framework of political ideology is established, it will still be necessary to respond to "single issue" constituency groups or individuals who demand access to care. A need will also continue at some government level whether federal, state, or local to allocate available resources and in some cases to cut back on previous allocations in response to economic scarcity. The policy issues involved in resource allocation are often made on the basis of pragmatic political considerations which nonetheless may be influenced by available research data. As a result, research data may have a greater chance of affecting or interacting with this variable than that of political idealism.

Implementation Expertise

The third policy determinant is implementation expertise. Regardless of whether a mental health service policy is driven by an ideological theory or a pragmatic attempt to meet patient needs, the outcome will be largely effected by the skills of the service administrators and providers. The literature (Pressman & Wildavsky, 1973) is full of presumed examples of outstanding policies which are flawed in their implementation by inept or undedicated managers. Other works on implementation (Regier, 1979) point out that, because of prior political compromise, the seeds of their own destruction are often planted within policies which are ultimately doomed to failure despite the best efforts of dedicated and capable managers. However, it is also true that an adequate information base is absolutely essential if a manager is to take best advantage of available resources to meet recipient demands. The burgeoning interest in management information systems to monitor and evaluate the implementation of service programs is an area that draws heavily on descriptive epidemiologic and services research data bases. Hence this variable may also potentially be influenced by research data, even if such data are considered totally irrelevant by the idealist or insufficient by the pragmatist.

Research Data Base

Finally, it is important to recognize that even the most scientifically sound research data base is but one determinant of health policy, although it may be used as a touchstone to justify policy formulation. More frequently such a data base is needed to monitor and evaluate the implementation of policy objectives if available assessment technology exists. In all too many cases the basic research capability to specify diagnoses, disability, service need, treatment type, and treatment outcome are not adequate to support simple cost benefit equations. As a result the evaluation of much of our health policy is made on grounds other than whether it serves the intended recipients well. Instead, such policies are tested on the basis of whether they meet philosophical criteria or adequately address concerns of the most vocal constituency group.

With this realistic framework in mind, the remainder of the chapter is directed primarily to the development of a research data base that can both advance our understanding of the distribution and determinants of mental disorders as well as our understanding of the distribution and determinants of mental health service use. Such a data base can also serve as an independent variable in the determination of mental health policy. It is a variable that may be used with differential skill but one that should be used as a common denominator by policy advocates of any persuasion.

The three fields of mental health psychopathology, epidemiology, and health services research will be reviewed briefly to indicate their importance to this issue and to demonstrate areas where more knowledge is needed and where promising developments exist. The objective is to provide an information base on which to assess the functioning of our system of mental health care delivery and to assist in the inevitable midcourse corrections that are necessary for any policy to evolve and mature over time.

Gaps in the existing research base leave the mental health area more vulnerable to political ups and downs than such similar gaps do for the general health field. This is due to at least three separate issues (Goldman, Taube, Regier, & Witkin, 1983) including the historic separation of physical and mental health, the stigma of mental disorders, and the greater historical reliance of mental health treatment on the public, politically managed sector. As a result of these factors, it is necessary to have even better data in the mental health area to keep pace than it is in the physical health area. Evidence of this is clear not only in the public sector, but also within the private insurance industry, which has indicated a selective tendency to decrease mental health benefits in the face of overall economic austerity.

POLICY-RELATED RESEARCH DATA BASE

Basic research and technological advances continue to have a major impact on the development of the entire health service delivery system by contributing to our understanding of disease and increasing the range of our therapeutic options. However, what I will be focusing on today are three interrelated areas of research that have potential implications for a more direct influence on mental health service allocation policy. These research areas include psychopathology, epidemiology, and services research.

Psychopathology

Psychopathology is a relatively new arrival as a front-line participant in mental health policy determinations. The advent of Diagnosis Related Groups (DRGs) [Health Care Financing Administration (HCFA), 1983] has forced a reevaluation of the adequacy of our current diagnostic systems to predict longitudinal course and therapeutic requirements. DRGs have constituted in effect a new challenge for the whole of medicine to determine the practical utility of diagnoses for making resource allocation decisions about the extent of care required by such diagnoses. Although it is clear that DRGs involve a mix of diagnoses and procedures, they may prove to be a spur for greater application of the methods advanced by Robins and Guze (1970, 1972) for establishing diagnostic validity in psychiatry. These methods included careful clinical description, exclusion of other disorders, laboratory studies, follow-up studies, and family and genetic studies. Weissman and Klerman (1978) have added two additional criteria including response to treatment and correlation with psychological or social variables as indicators of validity. All of these approaches will be tested in the future with particular attention to follow-up studies, treatment response, and social or psychological correlates that affect the length of stay in inpatient settings.

The research challenge in psychopathology affecting service allocations will be to determine if current comprehensive diagnostic systems, such as *the Diagnostic Statistical Manual, Third Edition* (DSM-III; American Psychiatric Association, 1980), can develop improved measures of severity, clinical history, functional status, disability, and social circumstance that would be more useful in predicting longitudinal course and service needs. To have the maximum policy impact, recommendations for refining the existing 15 alcohol, drug abuse, and mental disorder DRG categories will need to be made that incorporate a different mix of diagnoses and other variables. However, the development of more homogeneous subgroups of current disorders or new disorders that can target therapeutic approaches more effectively will eventually have policy as well as clinical significance.

Recent developments in psychopathology have also been critical for epidemiology which is dependent on the availability of clearly defined criteria for identifying a "case" or individual with a diagnosis. The advances in psychopathology over recent years—which included the Feighner Criteria (Feighner, Robins, Guze, Woodruff, & Winokur, 1972) and Research Diagnostic Criteria (RDC) (Spitzer, Endicott, & Robins, 1978), along with the Renard Diagnostic Interview (RDI) (Helzer, Robins, Croughan, & Weiner, 1981) and the Schedule for Affective Disorders and Schizophrenia (SADS) (Endicott & Spitzer, 1978)—were essential for the development of DSM-III. The DSM-III criteria have in turn generated associated instruments which include the NIMH Diagnostic Interview Schedule (DIS) (Robins, Helzer, Croughan, Williams, & Spitzer, 1981) and the Structured Clinical Interview for DSM-III (SCID) (Spitzer, 1983). With these advances in psychopathology and case identification in hand, it has been feasible to launch an entire new generation of epidemiological studies beginning with the Epidemiologic Catchment Area (ECA) program (Regier *et al.*, 1984).

Epidemiology Research

At the outset it is important to note that epidemiology, like psychopathology, has scientific purposes other than informing health service policy. Epidemiology has been considered a basic integrant of clinical research in the rest of medicine (Shepherd, 1978, 1982, 1983) and as the basis for the organization of extramural psychiatry in Europe (Stromgren, Dupont, & Nielsen, 1980).

The methods developed in clinical epidemiology provide a population-based strategy for studying illness rates (prevalence, incidence) screening tests (sensitivity and specificity), multiple and interactive risk factors of illness (risk ratio, odds ratio), longitudinal course of illness, treatment effectiveness in clinical trials, and preventive intervention trials (population-attributable risk) (Regier & Burke, 1984). The development of an improved knowledge of risk factors and treatment effectiveness adds to the general advance of health services in the same manner as basic research and other technological advances.

Within epidemiology there have been three divisions, which include descriptive epidemiology, analytic epidemiology, and experimental epidemiology.

Descriptive Epidemiology. The most basic public health mandate for any health field is a determination of the prevalence rate of disorders in a population. The major gaps in our understanding of the distribution of mental disorders in the population as defined by current criteria became readily apparent at the time of the President's Commission on Mental Health in 1978. With a concerted effort of U.S. and international experts in psychopathology, case-identification instruments, epidemiology, and services research, the ECA program was launched in 1978. This program, which is ongoing, has already produced an enormous advance in our understanding of the scope and distribution of specific mental disorders in large community populations. Other chapters in this volume provide additional details on the rates of specific disorders and their relationship with service use.

Such descriptive epidemiology studies to determine both treated and untreated prevalence rates are useful for planning mental health services and for providing a large data base of use in psychopathology studies. For example, we now know that approximately 19% of the adult population can be diagnosed as having had at least one mental disorder in the past 6 months (Myers *et al.*, 1984). Of those with any such disorder, only 20% received any mental health service in this same 6–month time period (Shapiro *et al.*, 1984) and only 50% have received any such service in their lifetime memory. Hence, mental health service planners should clearly not attempt to develop specialty services for all persons with mental disorders, but try to determine the targeted population they wish to serve in the most efficient manner. However, the striking question raised by these data is why are the 80% with mental disorders not being served and what is the consequence of their lack of care?

Analytic Epidemiology. Although much remains to be done in analyzing the ECA data base, one of its greatest potential contributions is the provision of clearly defined cases for doing retrospective case control studies in community populations or prospective studies of patients to determine the longitudinal course of a representative sample of persons with a specific mental disorder. Prospective studies of representative community cohorts without disorders are now possible to assess "exposures" to risk factors that may be associated with mental disorder onset or incidence rates. Such a prospective cohort study has already been initiated at the St. Louis site in which a cohort exposed to several natural disasters is being followed up to assess the impact of this risk factor on incidence rates of new disorders.

This type of research has the greatest potential for identifying both risk factors and protective factors affecting development of specific disorders—a scientific basis for future prevention research and services.

Experimental Epidemiology. In other fields of medicine, it is interesting to note that large-scale clinical trials of medications or therapeutic techniques such as coronary bypass surgery are conducted by epidemiologists in conjunction with their clinical treatment colleagues. Likewise, large-scale, population-based, preventive intervention trials such as those using vaccines to prevent infectious diseases are also designed and monitored by epidemiologists and statisticians. Within the field of psychiatry, the need for these research designs led to importing prospective cohort, double-blind clinical intervention trial methods to an astute group of clinician pioneers like Jonathan Cole and Gerald Klerman. Although these psychopharmacology investigators, including others like Jerome Levine (1979), did not come from epidemiology backgrounds, they have made major contributions to the development of clinical trial methodology, which is used in epidemiological studies throughout medicine.

As the field of psychiatric epidemiology develops, we would anticipate a greater cross-fertilization between epidemiologically-trained psychiatrists, statisticians, and other disciplines, and clinical treatment specialists to develop clinical drug trials and preventive interventions. This will bring psychiatric epidemiology and clinical research into the mainstream of similar research fields now relatively well developed for infectious disease, cardiovascular disease, cancer, and other general medical areas.

Health Services Research

In the same way that a research data base is only one determinant of health policy, the presence of a disorder is only one determinant of health service use. Epidemiology tends to focus on improving our understanding of psychopathology, including its distribution, determinants, and treatment. Health services research uses the diagnosis as a starting point and must add other variables to diagnosis which ultimately contribute to the determination of who receives health services and the quantity and quality of those services. I have identified five factors: 1) nondiagnostic patient characteristics; 2) treatment effectiveness characteristics; 3) health service provider characteristics; 4) health facility characteristics, and 5) the organization and financing of care. Although a full development of each of these service-use determining variables is beyond the scope of this chapter, I will summarize a few of the concepts.

Nondiagnostic Patient Characteristics. The finding in the ECA that 80% of individuals with at least one mental disorder receive no mental health treatment illustrates the importance of nondiagnostic patient characteristics in predicting who will use mental health services.

In an early and influential study of mental health service use, Tischler, Heinsz, Myers, & Boswell (1975) demonstrated that mental disorder symptomatology was not nearly as good a predictor of health service use as the social supports available to individuals with such symptoms. Single-parent families were much more likely to seek mental health services than those with a more stable social support system. In a more recent study using the ECA data, Regier, Shapiro, Kessler, and Taube (1984) and Shapiro *et al.* (1985) have identified the relative contribution of mental disorder diagnosis, symptom level, and disability level to the prediction of mental health service use. Tischler and Leaf (1985) have also considered the contribution of subjective psychological impairment and nonspecific stress measures to predicting service use. This area remains one of importance for assessing future psychopathology and DRG financing issues.

For those interested in psychopathology, an obvious question is, Should these nondiagnostic patient characteristics be emphasized in Axis IV or V of DSM-III? Or are there other elements of psychopathology such as "defense mechanisms," as advocated by George Valliant (personal communication, 1984), that would assist in predicting service need and use.

Treatment Effectiveness. Although controlled clinical trials are essential for establishing the efficacy of therapeutic interventions, it is ultimately necessary to apply new medications or therapeutic approaches in routine clinical populations. The application of such therapies varies markedly by the service delivery setting in which they are used. One would expect primary-care physicians to require a much more standardized therapeutic approach than psychiatrists who are able to spend a greater amount of time and have a greater amount of expertise in dealing with clinical variation of mental disorders. Hence, clinical services research may use the prospective cohort intervention technique of experimental epidemiology to assess the effectiveness of a treatment of depression in primary care with careful attention to the homogeneity of conditions studied in such nonresearch settings. It has already been possible to assess the effectiveness of screening tests and diagnostic information as an intervention to improve the identification of patients with mental disorders in primary-care settings (Hoeper, Nycz, Kessler, Burke, & Pierce, 1984). In this type of study, the major attempt is to carry out a secondary prevention effort to reduce duration and disability associated with a pre-existing mental disorder by drawing attention to the need for treatment (Shapiro *et al.*, 1983).

If successful screening for patients with disorders can take place in primary-care settings, it would be feasible to identify routinely a large proportion of the 80% with such a diagnosis who never seek care. However, the benefits of such screening would clearly be dependent on demonstrations that effective treatment can be applied for each diagnosis, either in the primary-care setting or on referral.

Provider Characteristics. The decision to use mental health services is dependent on many characteristics of health care professionals as well as the charactcristics of patients. Shepherd, Cooper, Brown, and Kalton (1980) and Stromgren (1980) were early obscrvers who noted marked discrepancies in rates at which individual physicians could recognize the presence of a mental disorder. The likelihood of recognition resulting in treatment as well as the duration and intensity of treatment are dependent on the provider's assessment of probable benefit, both to the patient and to the provider. Richman and Brown (1979) have noted the marked increase in mental health services provided by Canadian general practitioners when they could be reimbursed for such services. Treatment orientation of providers in primary care, specialty mental health, general medical/nursing home, and other human service sectors of the De Facto Mental Health Service System will greatly influence service use (Regier, Goldberg, & Taube, 1978). Such orientations will be affected by treatment idcology, perceived treatment effectiveness, and the facility characteristics and financing mechanisms for providing care.

Facility Characteristics. One of the benefits of a study such as the ECA will be to assess the differences in mental health service utilization that occur when a different mix of services are available in a given community. It is clear that utilization is the final product of a combination of supply and demand such that an increased supply of facilities can be expected to increase the demand in use for them. Shapiro *et al.* (1984) have shown that 6-month use of specialty outpatient mental hcalth services varies in the first three ECA sites from a low of 2.2% of all persons in St. Louis, to a high of 4.0% of all persons in New Haven. This is an issue of growing concern to hospital rate-setting commissions and to those conccrned with the organization of services and facilities to provide more efficient systems of care for designated populations.

Financing. The financing of health carc introduces a basic economic factor into our understanding of the use of mental health services. Productive interactions with health economists require us to use theoretical models that equate the health care system with other types of service industries. The interrelationship of psychopathology, epidemiology, and health services research is nowhere more graphically illustrated than in the development of DRGs as a financing mechanism for the treatment of Medicare patients.

The absence of basic health services research data to support the DRGs in psychiatry has had a major impact on the dcvelopment of health policy for the alcohol, drug-abuse, and mental health fields. Taube, Lee, and Forthofer (1984) were able to demonstrate that whereas 30–50% of the length-of-stay variance could be explained by DRGs in general medicine, less than 5% could be explained by using the Health Care Financing Administration (HCFA) DRGs for alcohol, drug abuse, and mental disorders. This has resulted in an intensive effort on the part of the Alcohol, Drug Abuse, and Mental Health Administration to cooperate with HCFA in identifying better measures of mental health service need for use in future prospective financing policies.

CONCLUSIONS

What implications, then, are we able to draw from the current political context and the available data for future mental health service policy? Unlike the period following release of Hollingshead and Redlich's *Social Class and Mental Illness* (1958) and the other major epidemiologic studies of the 1950s and early 1960s, it is unlikely that a major new, federally sponsored mental health service program will be launched. The reasons for the current response may be summarized in relation to the previously described independent variables affecting health policy:

1. The political ideology at present strongly supports the allocation of mental health service government responsibilities to state and local levels and encourages much greater investment in private mental health services.

2. Political pragmatism now requires a greater targeting of existing resources to increase the effectiveness of treatment for specific types of disorders. Hence, greater attention is being accorded to categorical service programs such as substance-abuse treatment centers, Community Support Programs (CSPs) for the chronically mentally ill, Alzheimer's disease treatment programs, and even phobia clinics, rather than large service delivery system programs.

3. With regard to implementation of the current political ideology, the intent to place providers more at risk for services has resulted in the development of DRGs. A great deal of effort is now being directed toward improving the usefulness of DRGs to predict mental health service needs and inpatient length of stay. Such an undertaking requires a careful use of data from psychopathology, epidemiology, and health services research.

4. Finally, there is a great need to improve the specificity of our data bases in all three of these research areas as we attempt to conduct longitudinal studies of those with mental disorders—both treated and untreated—in the population. This research will be essential to deter-

mine the types of disorders and associated conditions that are most in need and most able to benefit from available treatment methods.

This chapter covers a wide range of conceptual issues dealing with the relationship of research to health policy. Within research, a particular focus has been drawn to the interrelationships between psychopathology, epidemiology, and health services research, which may contribute to a policy-relevant research data base. We anticipate that future developments in each of these three research fields will have a major impact on the other associated fields as well as on mental health service policy. Hence, conferences that provide a forum for linking the three research fields with the assessment of their health policy implications should provide a useful stimulus for addressing the major research issues identified.

Despite the optimism that major advances in these fields are now possible, it is important to remember that any impact on mental health service allocation policy will be mediated by the political idealists and pragmatists as well as the front-line administrators and clinicians. It is particularly these latter professionals who must ultimately implement the fruits of research and policy for the patients with mental disorders whom both are designed to serve.

REFERENCES

American Psychiatric Association (1980). *Diagnostic and Statistical Manual of Mental Disorders* (3rd ed.). Washington, DC: Author.

Endicott, J., & Spitzer, R. L. (1978). A diagnostic interview: The Schedule for Affective Disorders and Schizophrenia. Archives of General Psychiatry, *35*, 837-844.

Feighner, J. P., Robins, E., Guze, S. B., Woodruff, R. A., & Winokur, G. (1972). Diagnostic criteria for use in psychiatric research. *Archives of General Psychiatry, 26*, 57-63.

Goldman, H. H., Taube, C. A., Regier, D. A., & Witkin, M. (1983). The multiple functions of the state mental hospital. *American Journal of Psychiatry, 140*(3), 296-300.

Health Care Financing Administration (1983). *Interim final rule; Medicare program: Prospective payments for Medicare inpatient hospital services.* 42 CFR Pts. 405, 409, 489.

Helzer, J. E., Robins, L. N., Croughan, J. L., & Weiner, A. (1981). Renard Diagnostic Interview. *Archives of General Psychiatry, 38*, 393-398.

Hoeper, E. W., Nycz, G. R., Kessler, L. G., Burke, J. D., & Pierce, E. W. (1984). The usefulness of screening for mental illness. *Lancet, i*, 33-35.

Hollingshead, A. B., & Redlich, F. C. (1958). *Social class and mental illness: A community study.* New York: Wiley.

Levine, J. (Ed.). (1979). Coordinating clinical trials in psychopharmacology: Planning, documentation, and analysis. DHEW Pub. No (ADM) 79-803.

Myers, J. K., Weissman, M. M., Tischler, G. L., Holzer, C. E. III, Leaf, P. J., Orvaschel, H., Anthony, J. C., Boyd, J. H., Burke, J. D., Jr., Kramer, M., & Stoltzman, R. (1984). Six-month prevalence of psychiatric disorders in three communities: 1980-1982. *Archives of General Psychiatry, 41*, 971-978.

Pressman, J. L., & Wildavsky, A. (1973). *Implementation*. Berkeley: University of California Press.

Regier, D. A., Goldberg, I. D., & Taube, C. A. (1978). The de facto U.S. mental health services system: A public health perspective. *Archives of General Psychiatry, 35,* 685–693.

Regier, M. C. (1979). *Social policy inaction: Perspectives on the implementation of alcoholism reforms*. Lexington, MA: D.C. Heath.

Regier, D., & Burke, J. (1984). Epidemiology. In H. I. Kaplan & B. J. Sadock (Eds.), *Comprehensive textbook of psychiatry* (4th ed.; pp. 1035–1072). Baltimore: Williams & Wilkins.

Regier, D. A., Myers, J. K., Kramer, M., Robins, L. N., Blazer, D. G., Hough, R. L., Eaton, W. W., & Locke, B. Z. (1984). The NIMH Epidemiologic Catchment Area (ECA) program: Historical context, major objectives, and study population characteristics. *Archives of General Psychiatry, 41,* 949–958.

Regier, D. A., Shapiro, S., Kessler, L. G., & Taube, C. A. (1984). Epidemiology and health service resource allocation policy for alcohol, drug abuse, and mental disorders. *Public Health Reports, 99,* 483–492.

Richman, A., & Brown, M. G. (1979). Reimbursement by Medicare for mental health services by general practitioners—clinical, epidemiologic and cost containment implications of the Canadian experience. *Mental Health Services in General Health Care* (Vol. 1). IOM Publication 79-004, Washington, DC.

Robins, E., & Guze, S. B. (1970). Establishment of diagnostic validity in psychiatric illness: Its application to schizophrenia. *American Journal of Psychiatry, 126,* 107–111.

Robins, E., & Guze, S. B. (1972). Classification of affective disorders: The primary-secondary, the endogenous-reactive, and the neurotic-psychotic concepts. In T. A. Williams, M. M. Katz, & J. A. Schield (Eds.), *Recent advances in the psychobiology of the depressive illness* (pp. 283–293). Washington, DC: U.S. Government Printing Office.

Robins, L. N., Helzer, J. E., Croughan, J., Williams, J. B. W., & Spitzer, R. L. (1981). NIMH Diagnostic Interview Schedule: Version III. Rockville, Md., NIMH (mimeo.).

Shapiro, S., German, P. S., Turner, R. W., Klein, L. E., von Korff, M., Kramer, M., Teitelbaum, M., Folstein, M., & Skinner, E. A. (1983). Secondary prevention with adult patients in primary care settings. Final Report for Contract No. 278-81-0025 (DB), December.

Shapiro, S., Skinner, E. A., Kessler, L. G., von Korff, M., German, P. S., Tischler, G. L., Leaf, P. J., Benham, L., Cottler, L., & Regier, D. A. (1984). Utilization of health and mental health services: Three Epidemiologic Catchment Area sites. *Archives of General Psychiatry, 41,* 971–978.

Shapiro, S., Skinner, E. A., Kramer, M., Steinwachs, D. M., Regier, D. A., & Kessler, L. G. (1985). Measuring need for mental health services in a general population. *Medical Care, 23,* 1033–1043.

Shepherd, M. (1978). Epidemiology and clinical psychiatry. *British Journal of Psychiatry, 133,* 289–98.

Shepherd, M. (1982). Psychiatric research in medical perspective. *Archives of Psychiatr Nervenkr, 232,* 501–506.

Shepherd, M. (1983). The application of the epidemiological method in psychiatry. *Acta Psychiatrica Scandinavica* (Supplement 296), *65,* 9–23.

Shepherd, M., Cooper, B., Brown, A. C., & Kalton, G. W. (1980). *Psychiatric illness in general practice* (2nd ed.). London: Oxford University Press.

Spitzer, M. D., Endicott, J., & Robins, E. (1978). Research diagnostic criteria. *Archives of General Psychiatry, 35,* 773–782.

Spitzer, R. L. (1983). Psychiatric diagnosis: Are clinicians still necessary? *Comprehensive Psychiatry, 24*, 99–411.

Stockman, D. A. (1981). Premises for a medical marketplace: A neoconservative's vision of how to transform the health system. *Health Affairs, 1*, 6–18.

Stromgren, E. (1980). Who takes care? How and where? And why?: Epidemiological research as basis for the organization of extramural psychiatry. *Acta Psychiatrica Scandinavica, 62*, 9–14.

Stromgren, E., Dupont, A., & Nielsen, J. A. (Eds.). (1980). Epidemiological research as basis for the organization of extramural psychiatry. *Acta Psychiatrica Scandinavica* (Supplement 285), *62*.

Taube, C. A., Lee, E. S., & Forthofer, R. N. (1984). Diagnosis-related groups for mental disorders, alcoholism, and drug abuse: Evaluation and alternatives. *Hospital & Community Psychiatry, 35*, 452–455.

The President's Commission on Mental Health (1978). *Task Panel Reports Subcommittee to the President's Commission on Mental Health.* Washington, DC, Stock No. 040-00-00393-2, Volume 1.

Tischler, G. L., Heinsz, J. E., Myers, J. K., & Boswell, P. C. (1975). Utilization of mental health services: I. Patienthood and the prevalence of symptomatology in the community. *Archives of General Psychiatry, 32*, 411–418.

Tischler, G. L., & Leaf, P. J. (1985, February). *The direct measurement of need: A clinician's perspective.* Paper presented at the NIMH Needs Assessment Conference, Rockville, MD.

Weissman, M. M., & Klerman, G. L. (1978). Epidemiology of mental disorders: Emerging trends in the United States. *Archives of General Psychiatry, 35*, 705–712.

17

Implementation of Service Programs Suggested by Research Findings: The View from within NIMH

HERBERT PARDES
Columbia University

Sometimes it is appropriate to be proud. The advances subsumed in the NIMH Epidemiologic Catchment Area (ECA) project allow such an opportunity. Simultaneously, Northeasterners from a tradition of being afraid to admit their wealth lest somebody take it away from them, obsessionals who populate the academic field, and careful people who do not want to overstate have to examine reservations, potential problems, and potential challenges to our feeling of accomplishment.

Dan Freedman (1984) stated that the ECA project is "far more than a simple census. It is a landmark in the development of American contributions to the psychiatric knowledge base" (p. 931). I agree.

This chapter examines the context in which the ECA Program emerged. We examine implications of the ECA in today's setting. Finally, we raise a few questions designed to prevent us from becoming too self-satisfied.

HISTORICAL CONTEXT

One has to look at mental health over a period of time to appreciate broad changes (Pardes, 1984). In the 1940s, the mental health system consisted of large state mental hospitals and a small private-practice enterprise largely for people from the upper-socioeconomic strata of society. There was little in the way of treatment beyond shock therapies, some long-range psychotherapies, and a general inclination to rest, rehabilitation, and disengagement from obstensible pathogenic family and social contexts.

There was little in the way of outpatient mental health care or community outreach. There was also a focus on the continuum of psychological functioning and a notion that diagnostic categories were either artifacts or boxes into which one could fit patients by contortion.

334

The experience of reviewing patients' charts in a hospital and finding that if they had ten previous hospitalizations, they might have almost as many diagnoses was a widespread phenomenon.

Later, with the development of epidemiological surveys, we secured figures regarding the presence or absence of mental symptoms, using systems based on the notion of a continuum of mental health into psychiatric diseases. The information flowing from those surveys included the fact that a very large proportion (as high as 85%) of the American population suffered mental symptoms.

In the 1950s and the 1960s, we saw active development of the community mental health centers, the introduction of a variety of therapeutic agents, the deinstitutionalization of patients, the development of outpatient and outreach programs, and the resurgence of phenomenological psychiatry that emphasized an attention to diagnosis. But by the mid-1970s, a widespread perception was that the Community Mental Health Center Program, while helping to destigmatize mental health to an extent, and making services more widely available, was leaving many problems unattended. There was a sense that populations such as the elderly, children, the deinstitutionalized, and the minorities were not receiving full attention.

Against this backdrop the Presidential Commission on Mental Health was formed in the latter 1970s and suggested a new effort in the service areas in mental health. It is noteworthy that this new program called the Mental Health Systems Act, which included support for the interaction between mental health and general health and a focus on programs for underprivileged groups as well as a shift in the direction of greater state involvement was the major piece of health legislation passed during the Carter administration. This law was signed in October 1980. However, within seven months after the Reagan administration had taken office, this law had been scuttled. This is a sobering example of the impediments to our ability as a nation to launch programs to address perceived needs.

Fortunately, however, one of the other projects launched by the Presidential Commission on Mental Health was the ECA Program. The fact that we needed greater precision in our data regarding incidence and prevalence of mental disorders, and the fact that we could not in the words of Regier and his colleagues (Regier, Shapiro, Kessler, & Taube, 1984) "determine which disorders were found in the various service sectors" thereby making it "not possible to state specifically which type treatment resource should be increased" were important considerations in the launching of this program. The ECA was stimulated owing to perceptions of this sort by the President's Commission on Mental Health.

It is important to realize that this call for more specific data is akin to the increasing attention to diagnosis symbolized by the development of DSM-III and also the greater tendency to match specific treatments with specific disorders symbolized by the American Psychiatric Association's effort to produce a compendium of treatments recommended for specific illnesses. These trends have been indications of an era in psychiatry of refinement and differentiation of psychiatric concepts. This tendency to refinement is seen in research with efforts to disaggregate large categories of disorders into smaller groups. This disaggregation has been used with success in mental retardation resulting in a better understanding of disorders of galactosemia, phenylketonuria, and Down's syndrome. This understanding might have been developed far later had the tendency to think of all mental retardation as one disease prevailed.

The ECA findings demonstrate differentiated prevalence of various disorders, offering the possibility of examining correlations between those disorders and demographic factors, demonstrating service use patterns in relationship to those disorders, and demonstrating differences and consistencies in diverse parts of the country. The ECA represents a gold mine of data and one of the most important accomplishments stemming from the work of the Presidential Commission on Mental Health. It was encouraged by the many authorities in epidemiology and in psychiatric research.

CURRENT IMPACT

Given the use of this kind of data in a political situation which allows an objective response to new information, we likely would want to have further refinements of the treatments that fit these diagnoses. We might examine the existing service system and match it against what the needs appear to be, derived from our ECA data, and we might want to launch model programs, demonstration programs, or to institutionalize new services.

However, the forces that prevail today suggest decreases rather than increases of federally supported programs, a cutting of the federal budget expenditures, and a delegation to states and localities of service delivery responsibilities in mental health and mental illness. Some policymakers suggest a reduction even in research in health and mental health. Fortunately, this last statement is not a predominant view. On the other hand, when one puts forth information without some systematic attempt to guide its utilization, the information has no impact. The challenge is to disseminate this information and to make it matter at a time of conservatism regarding the launching of new efforts.

First, the research effort in mental health is so vigorous and so full of potential that forces calling for enhanced support likely will prevail over those who have recommended decreases. The use of brain imaging, the detection of transmitters and receptors and their many significant functions, the development of sophisticated techniques of molecular genetics, the matching of behavior and biology and other lines of investigation dovetail beautifully with the advances being made today in epidemiology. These ECA findings demonstrate that the ferment in the field is not confined to the neurosciences, but that a number of the sciences related to psychiatry are active, producing information that will possibly strengthen psychiatry's clinical potency. The more that we are able to diagnose accurately, the more that we can make precise statements about the epidemiology of psychiatric disorders, the more that we can match specific treatments to specific illnesses, the more effective we will be in offering relief from illness. Further, the increased epidemiological data should actually foster research inasmuch as the more information available about homogeneous categories of disorders, the more scientific progress is catalyzed.

This should also have a beneficial impact on stigma regarding mental illness. A more powerful momentum for changing the stigmatization of mental illness than the imploring of people to be kind, is the demonstration that clinicians have techniques for diagnosing and effectively treating disorders. Some of the increased readiness of well-known people such as Dick Cavett, Bert Yancy, Jennifer Jones, and others to advocate for mental health programs and of large-scale citizen groups such as the National Alliance for the Mentally Ill, the Mental Health Association, and the American Mental Health Fund to work to secure increased support for research is a result of the increasing knowledge base developing in the psychiatric field. The extraordinary wealth of information coming out of the Epidemiology Catchment Area Program is justification for greater support of good research in the same way as the discovery of the endorphins or the development of new treatment agents.

Current policy makers, however, are also reserved about the need for analysis of "person power" to address the problems on which the ECA Program focuses. A suggested analysis of the nature of work of mental health professionals was rejected by the Office of Management and Budget (OMB); it was one of the last acts in which I had any personal involvement before leaving the position of director of the National Institute of Mental Health in 1984 for the private sector. Our attempts to dissuade OMB were unsuccessful. The momentum from the ECA data to examine our service sectors and the providers in those sectors to know how to match more effectively our system to needs is diminished by policymakers who believe that the federal government should not concern themselves with those kinds of questions. Data regarding the kinds of diseases, the place in which those diseases arise, the demography to which they are related, all represent useful information not only for health planning, but also for health economics. If we know what the problems are and where they are, we can allocate our resources in a way to make them most effective. Such information can be used to reduce unnecessary costs.

To decide simply that we should not attend to manpower issues or to the services system is shortsighted and will result in long-term economic loss that will more than offset any temporary and small economic gain from not involving ourselves in these questions.

So put succinctly, my impression of the implications of the ECA findings are that:

1. They will strengthen our research by fitting with work in other areas of research designed to differentiate the various psychiatric disorders.

2. They will contribute to the development of *well*-conceived programs of prevention.

3. They will help the clinical care-providing community to achieve greater differentiation of the nature of disorders with which they are dealing and perhaps allow them to match more effectively treatments and illnesses.

4. They will contribute to the formidable process of destigmatizing the mental illness field by refining and sharpening the system and enhancing its clinical potency.

5. It is doubtful that the ECA will have any significant impact, however, on the service delivery system as such right now, although it will add information of value in work on Diagnosis Related Groups (DRGs) and prospective pay systems.

6. Attempts to force a recognition of these data in determining manpower policies will encounter resistance of many in authority today who are not interested.

QUESTIONS

We have to look comprehensively at the implications of the ECA. This is not to detract from the accomplishments, but to give a balanced appraisal of what has been produced and what the reservations might be.

First, we have to be careful about any premature closure on diagnostic categories. The more we can refine, the better. However, we must not imply that we have reached an ultimate system for diagnostic appraisal. The advance recommended by DSM-III and the ECA is of major consequence. It enables us to treat homogeneous groups, to research homogeneous groups, and to be able to communicate with each other. However, as Dennis Murphy (personal communication, 1983) has stated, there may be other ways by which the diagnostic system should be organized. Further, the diagnostic system is only our best attempt to translate what nature has wrought.

Second, the use of inference in clinical assessment is a very valuable tool. How to use and appraise that tool systematically is a problem. Were a psychiatrist appraising a potentially suicidal patient in an emergency room, information available to the effect that this person's family history included suicide attempts, that the person had had a number of depressive episodes, and that the person in fact had made a suicide attempt a year or two before, would all be valuable pieces of information. However, equally important would be the clinician's intuitive sense of the likelihood that at that particular moment that individual was likely to make a suicidal attempt. Whether one talks about decreased serotonin metabolites in the cerebrospinal fluid or genetic and family patterns of suicide attempts, one still has to assess the specific individual. How we can include the ability to evaluate motivation and a balance of psychological forces working within the individual is important in rounding out an appropriate clinical assessment. This is not to demean the value of diagnosis or phenomenological orientations, but simply to recognize that we court a danger of swinging too widely afield. We must not become convinced that by having whatever is the most appropriate category for a specific person's illness that we know the full story.

Third, there is a substantial unmet need or to be more precise an untreated prevalence. Having uncovered that, what are we going to do about it? Is there a way of determining how much of the untreated prevalence might better be left alone? Should we bother with any of it? I think that some of the further efforts of the people working on the ECA data should likely include a look at these difficult questions. It is interesting substantively, but it also has political and fiscal implications. Whatever the stance of the government, the facts should be gathered and clearly articulated.

Fourth, in line with earlier comments about the need to focus on clinical judgment and intuition, our research efforts should not become exclusively focused on approaches which embody a Kraepelinian perspective on psychiatry. In other words, the Hypothesis-Finding study, the use of clinical judgment, a look at clinical research questions without an exclusive focus on diagnosis should be supported. The research field should not restrict itself to any one regimented approach.

Specific questions regarding the ECA data are inappropriate in this chapter. This is a most carefully done study, and while there are differences of opinion as to how to assess its significance, one must admire the extraordinary care and the large-scale cooperation of many distinguished investigators in bringing this information to our attention.

One area that stands out, however, in terms of current policy, is the focus on prospective pay systems or DRGs. The recent work of Taube *et al.* (1984) showing that diagnosis explains less than 5% of the variation in the length of stay in the psychiatric setting is a sobering piece of information. DRGs depend on specific diagnostic projections, but diagnosis while helpful in many ways is of limited use in forecasting the amount of time necessary to treat a patient with a psychiatric disease. In a related way, Regier and his colleagues (Regier *et al.* 1984a; Regier *et al.* (1984b) have reported that 74% of persons with a recent DIS diagnosis did not seek treatment during a 6-month interval. They note that a combination of additional correlates such as the level of symptomatology and a measure of disability status would likely increase the ability to identify those who would seek some mental health service.

Worrisome is the antithetical positions of two forces regarding reimbursement and length of stay. One based on research shows that diagnosis is not enough, and that we need other considerations, and another based on a political philosophy is moving forward with the battle cry that DRGs save money and should be applied to all systems of health care without worrying about the nuances elaborated in the work of Regier and his colleagues. This is not the first time that policymakers have been oblivious of critical data; the prognosis for programmatic concerns is consequently, at best, guarded.

CONCLUSIONS

Dan Freedman (1984) states, "To the question of how much and what kind of psychiatric illness is 'out there' we need no longer blindly grope. It is surely not the picture of a 'bottomless pit' of an infinitude of psychopathology; nor is it a picture of trivial impairments, self-indulgences, or flaccidity of will. The regularities of definable and quite different disorders, each occurring with distinct frequencies should dissipate such myths" (p. 933). This comment is well taken.

The ECA study is an important step in this process of differentiation of clinical psychiatry. It has produced an enormous amount of useful data. The study should help catalyze additional research efforts and strengthen research efforts in other areas; it should strengthen our clinical treatment efforts; and it should help us in developing information on which to base intelligent prevention and intervention programs.

We will need to look carefully at how to use it to influence the development of our services systems as such. That effort will enjoy considerable opposition. It should, however, be an additional rationale for solid support for psychiatric research. Additionally, given the large number of young and sophisticated scientists needed to carry out these projects and to use the resulting data most effectively, this work should help demonstrate the need for support of the training of epidemiological scientists as well as neuroscientists and clinical scientists in psychiatry.

These questions are designed to sensitize us to retaining an open mind. Still, this is a time for the field to be proud and for the society to recognize that the ECA is an important contribution.

REFERENCES

Freedman, D. X. (1984). Psychiatric epidemiology counts. *Archives of General Psychiatry, 41*, 931–933.

Pardes, H. (1984). Viewpoint: Challenges facing psychiatry in the eighties. *Psychiatric Journal of the University of Ottawa, 9(4)*, 155–159.

Regier, D. A., Shapiro, S., Kessler, L. G., & Taube, C. A. (1984a). Epidemiology and health service resource allocation policy for alcohol, drug abuse and mental disorders. *Public Health Reports, 99*, 483–492.

Regier, D. A., Myers, J. K., Kramer, M., Robins, L. N., Blazer, D. G., Hough, R. L., Eaton, W. W., & Locke, B. Z., (1984b). The NIMH Epidemiologic Catchment Area (ECA) Program: Historical context, major objectives, and study population characteristics. *Archives of General Psychiatry, 41*, 949–958.

Taube, C. A., Lee, E. S., & Forthofer, R. N. (1984). Diagnosis-related groups for mental disorders, alcoholism and drug abuse: Evaluations and alternatives. *Hospital & Community Psychiatry, 35*, 452–455.

Panel Discussion

Charles Kahn: Dr. Rose has asked me to begin the panel discussion by commenting on the climate in Washington with respect to mental health needs. I would like to make a number of points about where we are now in Congress and where I think Medicare is going, and then share with you some thoughts about the future for payment for medical care and for programs for the elderly.

First, let me start by saying that the deficit is the primary theme right now in Congress. All current policymaking comes from a consideration of how a given program will affect the deficit. This has several implications. First, there is a mindset not to do anything new. Second, there is a mindset, at least on the domestic side, of how to live within constraint and how to cut back what we are currently doing. However we constructed this thing called the deficit—whether we did it because we refused in the past to sunset programs (letting ourselves get away with just funding everything and adding a few percentage points to every program we started since the 1930s) or whether we did it by cutting taxes, in 1981, to the extent that we did not have the fiscal capacity to fund continuation of programs—the fact remains that the deficit has put us into a situation where we have done away with all our flexibility. This is really a shame because there are unmet needs, and we are discovering those needs all the time.

Another aspect of letting the deficit issue control policymaking is that, instead of reassessing programs and trying to decide what our priority should be within existing programs, the tendency (especially from the Office of Management and Budget) has been just to terminate programs. I don't think that the question should be, "Should we have Amtrak?" but rather, assuming that we want passenger rail transit in this country, "What can we do to change Amtrak, to make it more what it should be?" But in this present deficit dilemma, it is very difficult to be reformist because there is really not much flexibility.

A related but separate issue is the issue of benefits. I will specifically address Medicare, but my remarks relate to the array of service programs that the federal government finances. In the current environment, it is difficult to think about how we would expand benefits when we will be lucky to retain the package of benefits we now offer Medicare beneficiaries. Beyond that, we have been burned consistently in the past when programs were brought on as benefits. The end-stage renal disease program is one example. The early projections, back in the early 1970s, when we began to pay for end-stage renal disease, for dialysis, and later for kidney transplants, were that the program would cost between $100–200 million a year. That program costs $2 billion a year today. This is an example of where there was a need, a critical need, but when the demand was financed, a situation evolved where the cost blossomed beyond all expectation. Give this example, and there are others, the fact is that congressional policymakers are reluctant to expand benefits, in a sense to pay for a new kind of provider, because of concern that the same thing will happen.

In terms of acute medical care, we also have good data now that give a very confusing message. Dr. John Wennberg at Dartmouth has come up with data on practice patterns that show a wide variation between practices. For example, he looked at hysterectomies in two comparable, adjacent towns in Maine. In one town there was a 70% probability that a woman would have a hysterectomy, and in another town down the road, in the same community, in the same state, there was a probability of 20%. These kinds of statistics were found throughout the country; Wennberg found them in Iowa, in Michigan, and in other states, for a whole host of procedures. What are the appropriate practice styles? I am not saying that 70% of the women in one town should not have had hysterectomies, or that 20% having hysterectomies was the "right" rate—perhaps a rate in between these extremes is the appropriate level—but the point is that, for what we pay for today, we get clear signals that we don't know what we are getting for our money. Regardless of your findings on mental health needs, the point from our perspective is that we have great difficulty thinking about paying for more things, debating with the psychiatrists whether we should pay for an increased number of visits than we do now under Medicare, when we don't know the benefit to the patient. We do know that when we have a system such as fees-for-service for medical services, we tend to get back mixed signals on what the practitioners do when they get the money and when the beneficiaries have the power to buy services.

So, in this environment of uncontrolled growth of expenditures for Medicare, a few years ago congressional leaders began to think about how to reform and put some cap on Medicare expenditures, and also how Medicare could be used as a vehicle to reform the health care system as a whole. It is important that Medicare reforms are thought of not just as affecting the elderly population but as relating to the whole health-care system.

I bring this up because, regardless of this deficit issue and regardless of specific Medicare items, fundamentally the issues that are raised by the ECA research are ones that are probably going to be dealt with more in the private sector than they will be in the public sector. In the end it may not be Medicare, or the government, that makes the decision whether or not more mental health services will be paid for, but the decision is going to be made in the private sector. Let me describe how that may come about.

At present, in terms of Medicare reform, we have a two-track strategy to come to grips with how we pay for Medicare services. One track is the one that you are all familiar with, and that is the prospective payment track. It is the track where we use DRGs as a methodology for paying for inpatient services under Part A. This track was instituted with the Tax Equity and Reform Act of 1982. The Secretary of Health and Human Services was required to do a study on the feasibility of a prospective payment system, and then one year later, with the Social Security Act, that program was put into line.

Actually the Social Security Act did two things. It put in line payment under DRGs for inpatient services, and it also called for about 27 different studies of various aspects of prospective payment. By doing so it set up an agenda for research and then for implementation of new programs, for paying physicians, for capital, for paying for graduate medical education— the whole array of areas that weren't dealt with specifically in that original Act. That is the movement that gets the most attention in terms of reforming Medicare. It is a regulatory movement. It is a movement that basically provides price control, a unit price for inpatient services that is set by the government, based on historical averages. Today I would argue that, over the next decade, what happens with DRGs and that whole movement will be relatively inconsequential compared with a more important reform, a reform that leads to my conclusion about how the private marketplace will affect the practice of psychiatry.

In the Tax Equity Reform Act there was another provision which allowed for Medicare beneficiaries to opt out of the Medicare program and to opt into HMOs, or something invented in the language of that act called "competitive medical plans." The point I want to make is that what Medicare is doing is to move in the direction of a voluntary voucher. It moves also in the direction of the government paying a specified amount to a plan, and the plan then deals with its set of providers, either in a group practice model or whatever model the HMO is in. Price then becomes the variant; other than meeting a relatively modest set of criteria the plan is pretty much on its own both to market to beneficiaries and to arrange the price between it and hospitals and other kinds of providers. That kind of model, where price in the marketplace is going to make the difference, is the one that you ought to be watching. It would seem to me that in the long run the strategy of psychiatry should be to figure out how you are going to fit into this prepaid mode. In a sense it should be: How do you get your colleagues, the administrators of these plans, and the public that are going to buy into these plans, to recognize that your services and the array of opportunities that those services provide ought to be in those packages?

I don't think the federal government can do that. In its current mindset, I don't think the federal government will mandate it. There has been great reluctance to do so in the past.

Let me make a final point. Medicare itself is an acute-care program. It was invented 20 years ago, and it was based on a model of health insurance not much different from Blue Cross and Blue Shield. Part A of Medicare is comparable to Blue Cross and Part B of Medicare is comparable to Blue Shield. Blue Cross and Blue Shield in the last couple of decades have been developed as a health insurance program for employed people ranging from young to middle-aged to families. It was not specifically designed for the elderly and their unique problems. I would argue that, as we get past this deficit debate, assuming that we solve it, congressional leaders are going to begin to look at Medicare and ask questions about whether the array of benefits and the focus of the program are really appropriate. Medicare does not provide payment for many health-promotion or disease-prevention-type activities. It doesn't cover health screening. It covers immunizations for pneumococcal pneumonia, but it doesn't cover flu immunizations. It doesn't cover hypertensive drugs. It doesn't cover any kind of preventive services for identifying potential high-risk people who could suffer from depression. It doesn't try to identify and reduce risk for an array of illnesses which could help reduce costs and improve quality of life.

As an acute-care program, Medicare has very minor long-term care provisions. I would argue that the benefits that are called "long-term care"— skilled nursing facility benefits and others—are really nothing more than the kinds of benefits one would expect in a program that deals with subacute issues, such as immediate posthospitalization. Because we have a large and growing aging population, and because we continue to expand the lifespan potential and expectations of our people, I think that long-term care is going to become a primary focus and that Medicare itself is going to have to do something about long-term care.

With all that in mind, if over the next three or four years we can come to grips with this thing called the deficit, and I include the other deficit we are looking at—the deficit in the Part A trust fund for Medicare which is projected to go belly up sometime in 1995—we can begin to ask some of these very important questions and to reexamine a host of issues, not just medical, but also social welfare issues in terms of income security as the aging population expands.

Hans Huessy: I am worried that we are always ready to change our programs in view of new research, and we forget to do the things that we already know and for which we don't need more research.

We know that our sickest patients are getting the least adequate psycho-pharmacologic treatment at the moment. We do not have well-trained psychiatrists in our state hospitals where these patients are located. Regardless of what the reimbursement system is, we must find some way of addressing that issue if we are going to do a responsible job of caring for our most ill and needy patients.

Sometimes a financial crunch situation can be used to change a pattern which otherwise cannot be changed. We are now financing a lot of treatment activities without evidence of benefit, because if you run a community mental health center the only way to finance it is to treat every person in sight. We waste a lot of money that way.

Our financing system makes us abuse hospital care because it pays for hospital care but does not pay for other models of care. We don't even know what the present financing costs are. The system is very secretive. If you try to find out what the costs are for Medicare, Medicaid, Social Security Disability, SSI, and so on, it is difficult to do so. NIMH has engaged a private company to study the Social Security tapes, and so at least that part of the information should be available, but it is not at the moment. We don't know how much money we are spending. You cannot get the most for your dollar or design anything better if you don't even know what you are spending.

Our system also encourages increased professionalization of all services. The more diplomas one has, the easier it is to get paid. We have many needs in the care of chronic patients where nonprofessionals do the best job, but we are making it harder and harder to use them. One area where the budget crunch might help is to clarify where we are wasting money and thus help get more mileage for our dollar.

Kahn: I agree. In terms of acute care in hospitals, we have begun to examine monetary allocations. Regardless of whether paying by averages under a DRG system is fair, it has forced institutions to reexamine what they do. On the acute hospital side they now know better what they can do with their resources, and I think that has led to better management.

For care out of hospital, though, it is much more difficult to come to grips with the problem. We have tended to be very blunt with our policies. A few years ago it became fashionable to send patients out onto the streets, to do away with state hospitals. Legislators at the state level found that very attractive because it saved a lot of bucks. They sent patients out of the state hospitals and closed down beds, but they did not provide any services outside the hospital. Now we have the tremendous problem of the homeless. In the current fiscal environment I do not know how that will be dealt with. I think that ultimately policymakers would prefer to find ways to capitate those people, whether the mentally retarded or the chronically mentally ill, that require some level of institutionalization, ranging from group homes to being in hospitals. Then the marketplace could respond to their needs.

This may be too idealistic, and the marketplace may not respond well. The financing has to be rich enough, and in the present budget climate I doubt that it will be. There are bills in Congress, but I am not confident that we are going to do much substantively for these people during the next year.

Herbert Pardes: The questions just raised are very sensitive ones. The point regarding the need to have better professional care in state hospitals is well taken. However, I would suggest that we be careful. It is good to be internally critical, but I think it best to put that in context. It is not just the mental health care system in which a better ordering of resource allocation would be helpful; I would suggest that the mental health care system involves only a small part of the questionable resource allocations in health.

The mental health care system does have data demonstrating effectiveness of treatment which are as good as the data for most of the other health care systems. The Congressional Office of Technology report in 1979 demonstrated that only about 15% of all medical treatments were ever shown to be safe and effective.

The climate today, as perceived by a cold-blooded objective political analyst, is such that people will be happy to take anything that you offer to cut. But don't be assured that that cut will be offset by any replacement elsewhere. Also, there is a tendency at a time of constricted resources for everybody to point fingers at someone else. In our field, the psychotherapists will point fingers at the excessive use of psychopharmacology; the psychopharmacologists will point fingers at the early-prevention advocates. This is politically dangerous because there is nothing that fiscal planners in a budget crunch would like more than to have us offer up parts of our system for reduction. They are not in a mood to put up additional monies. That doesn't mean that one shouldn't try to work with political policymakers as best as possible, but one should listen to what they are advocating. The overwhelming mandate is to find some way to cut this deficit wherever one can.

Robert Cloninger: We have heard from each of the panel that there is a clear realization in Congress of many unmet needs in the mental health arena, and we have also been told that we need to be more effective, integrated lobbyists and advocates. Exactly what form should that advocacy take? Should it be in clarifying what the need is and the cost effectiveness of reform? How can we be effective as an organization, as clinicians, or as individual researchers?

Pardes: That is a very apt question. First of all, I believe that when one makes a good case about a component of the mental health care system, there is an important halo effect on the perception of the entire mental health care system.

One of the exciting things in health today is a real ferment within research related to mental health. When being an advocate you certainly want to emphasize those developments having distinct benefits for the actual care system. You have to compare what happened, as I tried to do earlier, over the course of several decades. It is important to state that the clinical psychiatric delivery system is constantly trying to improve itself, and that there are advances. The ECA findings that a large number of people out there have real disorders and really hurt is important, but it is also important to talk of the economic implications of effective programs. The work of Richard Wyatt, which demonstrated that lithium use saved about $6 billion in the last 15 years, is important. Wyatt has also recently developed projections about what would happen economically, given a certain investment in research which had some impact on schizophrenia in, let us say, 10 or 20 years. Data such as that on offset can be useful.

In the short run, the strategy should be, "Hunker down and hope that we can get through the next few years as best we can." The long-run strategy is to keep building the knowledge base of this field and show that we can help people. I think that is happening increasingly and makes me feel some optimism for the long haul.

Kahn: In terms of Congress, you first need to recognize that most members and most staff know very little about mental illness. They are culture-bound and tend to believe most of the clichés. Even though the culture has become a lot more open to mental illness, for example, accepting that alcoholism is a disease not to be shunned but to be met head on, in terms of other types of mental illness Congress has to be better educated. You should assume that we don't know very much about it and don't understand it very well.

Second, in the current governmental environment, it is going to be very difficult to deal with the problem of cost offset. You almost have to wait until we get away from the current mindset of budget-cutting and no new programs.

Let me give one brief example. The Institute of Medicine recently came out with a study that showed that we have plateaued in our success at reducing infant mortality and morbidity. The primary reason for this is that we really have not come to grips with low birth weight. We have done a very good job in neonatal intensive care of helping children to survive, but we have peaked in terms of the utility of this. The Institute of Medicine report indicated that there have been a number of projects in different parts of the country which show that, if you do good prevention and put pregnant mothers through good prenatal services and high-risk programs, you can keep babies out of neonatal intensive care. Our response to this report, from the policy standpoint, was for Senator Durenberger to put in a little bill, a technical bill which would have given states the option to expand the benefits under Medicaid that they would provide to pregnant mothers. The cost of this would probably be somewhere around $70–150 million from the federal government, and then money from the states if they chose to expand the benefits they could offer. I promise you that if this program just kept a small percentage of babies out of neonatal intensive care, it would save a lot of money, but the Congressional Budget Office (the office that does our projections for budgetary policy) is just going to be looking at the part of the program they can quantify—that there would be more visits if they funded it and if all the states bought into it. They know more visits are more expensive, and that is the only side of the ledger they currently would look at. So, we have a dilemma. This little technical bill really wouldn't cost that much money, and it would save a lot of money both in terms of keeping babies out of neonatal units and in preventing retardation, which frequently accompanies low birth weight, with all the other costs to society of that problem. But we won't pass that bill because in the current environment we cannot show the offset in such a way that the policymaking process will accept it. I think it is going to be a couple of years until we can get it through. It is a crying shame, and I don't know what to do about it.

Jean Endicott: A question for Mr. Shapiro. I am curious about the characteristics of people who did not have a DIS diagnosis but who reported missing at least one day of work because of nervous, mental, or other kinds of problems. That seemed to be a very high predictor of service use and of the perceived need for services.

Sam Shapiro: I cannot give you a precise response. We know that a large proportion of those with two manifestations (distress, impairment, or a DIS diagnosis) were not under treatment. We know that some of the social and demographic characteristics, such as age, income, or minority-group status, were heavily related to distress and impairment and thus were vulnerability markers.

Darrel Regier: We have not yet analyzed differences between those with and without a DIS diagnosis who had a disability day for mental health reasons. However, from this study and others we know that it requires more than diagnosis to predict service use and that it is important to add level of disability (whether measured on the Global Assessment Scale or other measures) to diagnosis. In that regard, one issue that we will face in the future is whether we should develop a more useful multiaxial diagnostic system that will help us stage our diagnoses and assess level of impairment. Such changes would be useful clinically and for some service policy implications, such as those related to DRGs.

Robert Spitzer: The discussion up to now has focused on the general implications of the ECA findings for public policy, and it is certainly clear from the ECA study that there are many people out there with diagnosable mental disorders who are receiving no or minimal treatment. There are also people going for help who do not have a DIS/DSM-III disorder. Could Dr. Regier and Mr. Shapiro be a little more specific regarding particular findings and how they would bear on a rational public policy? Suppose we did have an administration which said, "We know there is a lot of unmet need, and we are prepared to help." What specific findings do you have which would help us in setting up specific programs?

For example, I understand the ECA results showed an unexpectedly large number of individuals with anxiety disorders, many of whom do not go to mental health professionals for care. Does this mean that we should set up anxiety clinics? Or is the existence of all these mild, simple phobias an interesting fact that we don't need to do anything about? Can we link specific findings to specific recommendations, or are we only dealing with some general statement that "there are a lot of sick people out there, and we want more help for everything"?

Regier: Research rarely provides a clear clarion call for an immediate service policy or program. However, there are some hints about things that we need to look at. For example, the fact that individuals with cognitive impairment have the lowest rate of service use in the population and that these individuals are present disproportionately among the elderly, indicates something about the adequacy of services for this population. We should try to look more carefully at the characteristics of the service system that result in only 4–7% of all individuals with severe cognitive impairment receiving any kind of mental health services. What prevents them from getting that care? Is it a Medicare financing system with an outpatient treatment cap of $250 a year for mental illness that prevents them from getting adequate treatment? We know that some changes have occurred (almost anticipating the ECA finding) in the services for Alzheimer's disease that came about as a result of greater concern over inadequate care for this population.

HCFA performed a sleight-of-hand trick—they changed Alzheimer's disease from a "mental" to a "neurological" disorder, and thereby avoided the cap. Proponents of this policy saw it as the art of doing what is politically feasible to improve services for a population that was not getting adequate care. There may well be other, similar efforts for improving services based on data from this study, but I doubt that we will see a massive new federally sponsored services program.

Before recommending any changes in services policy based on ECA data, we need to know what the difference is between those individuals with specific disorders who receive care and those who do not receive care. I think Dr. Pardes's statement about the need for improved data concerning the effectiveness of care and the longitudinal course of these illnesses is most important. Such data should enable us to be more specific about the consequences of not providing services for individuals with a specific diagnosis and level of disability.

Additionally, we should use the ECA data base to begin studies of risk factors and causes of mental disorders. We are now able to use epidemiologic methods, such as case control and prospective cohort studies, in a much more powerful way. We should be moving into areas that cancer epidemiology has entered, including what they call "molecular epidemiology." Such studies attempt to locate biological correlates of disorders identified in epidemiologic studies, as well as psychosocial factors that may suggest intervention from both therapeutic and preventive standpoints.

In summary, the ECA analyses thus far have not led to very direct service program implications. But the ECA program clearly contributes to a sense of hope, based on evidence, of a much more scientifically sound understanding of mental disorders and their treatment. Such advances can, in fact, be conveyed to our patient constituents, their families, and to Congress, in order to help us compete more effectively for federal dollars with the other health fields—including cancer and heart disease, fields which have been extraordinarily effective in using such advances to obtain additional research support.

Shapiro: In addition to what Dr. Regier has been saying, it is important to bear in mind that part of the process under way at all the ECA sites, not only the eastern Baltimore site, is directed at methods for identifying high-risk groups. Then we will be in a better position to start thinking in terms of intervention trials. In the present climate of cost constraints there may be questions about the feasibility of such trials, but some should certainly be possible even under current budget conditions. We can gain a great deal of knowledge through additional observational types of studies, including those providing long-term follow-up, but at some point we are going to be faced with the very difficult question of how we can really understand the significance of unmet need without some type of intervention trial—some kind of experiment that would select the high-risk group for unmet need, attempt to intervene, and see what difference that makes.

I also want to comment about related information that has come out of the ECA program, reported recently in the *Archives*. Both Dr. Regier and I indicated that only a very small proportion of the people who had DIS disorders received care for mental or emotional problems within a defined time frame. We have to place that finding in the context of another important observation made at all the ECA sites: that persons with DIS disorders are high utilizers of both general ambulatory care and of inpatient care for physical conditions. If we bring these two pieces of information together, the unmet-need issue becomes quite significant for global medical care costs. The issue of the possible effect of mental health services on reducing general medical care costs emerges forcefully when we direct attention at the unmet-need group.

Incidentally, the report on low birth weight to which Mr. Kahn referred struck home with me because I was on the Institute of Medicine Committee that produced it. One lesson to be learned is that it is important to keep marshalling facts, and that it is unpredictable when this marshalling will have a productive effect.

Robert Rose: Let me raise a rather radical question. It relates to Dr. Cloninger's question about what we can do.

It seems to me that a significant amount of this discussion so far could be interpreted as saying that, although the magnitude of loss of future productivity is an interesting argument, it does not have much impact. In other words, preventive dollars do not have a great deal of salience at this time.

Perhaps the greatest implication of the ECA data is the need for us to educate people about the importance of getting care. A significant number of people with ECA diagnoses do not seek help, and we are aware that this is related to the stigma of the mental illness issue. If the system goes toward a voucher plan, we are going to have to be more influential in educating people to recognize that they have a problem and to seek appropriate care. This may be an overinterpretation, but I wonder if that is not the really telling issue for the next five years.

Pardes: You are touching on one of the basic problems of mental illness. People don't recognize that they have an illness, and they certainly don't think that they are going to become mentally ill.

If you put any 10 people in a room and ask them what to do with $1 million that is left for the total research budget in the United States, even people who are mental health advocates would probably say, "Put it in heart disease and cancer research," because everybody is concerned that they will develop those, but nobody thinks they are going to contract a psychiatric disorder. We have a glaring problem: when the federal government decides it will not be involved and that the private sector will take care of it, you give up one of the most important ways to address psychiatric problems, that is, a national view saying that occasionally we have to take action or institute a program even though it might not necessarily be favored actively by the majority of citizens.

James Barrett: A question for Mr. Shapiro. I got a little uncomfortable as I heard certain aspects of your presentation. My discomfort concerned the way you were defining unmet need. It was the presence of a DIS diagnosis, or some combination of this and other measures, but it was a global measure. It had departed from a focus on specific disorders, which to me is the strength of the ECA methodology. It also evoked a *déja vu* of the 1960s when we also had global measures of mental illness and programs for "mental health" as a global concept. How easy it was to dismember those programs quickly when they were so general and without specific goals. Alex Leighton, in his book *Caring for the Mentally Ill*, has written eloquently about what happened to psychiatric services when this global approach was used.

One of the ECA's strengths is the ability to look at need from the point of view of individual diagnoses, but I am concerned about the implication that a DIS diagnosis specifically equals need. That need is going to vary depending on which individual diagnosis is examined. And a related issue is whether programs are needed at all for certain mild disorders. David Goldberg writes about the "worried well" to refer to people with diagnosed disorders, such as some anxiety disorders, that are fairly time limited. I don't want to sound antitherapeutic, but I want to bring the discussion back to a focus on individual disorders and their needs. Dr. Pardes and Mr. Kahn both indicated that it is much more effective for obtaining national funding to come in and say, "Here is a treatment for *this*, and it works," or "it saves money," or whatever.

Shapiro: I agree with you that the value of the ECA program rests to a considerable degree on the ability to look at specific diagnoses. We have a paper in press that begins to examine specific diagnoses in relation to need for mental health services, although, since that information is only from a single site, there are important constraints on how far we can go in our recommendations. On the other hand, one of the strengths of the ECA program is the ability to bring together reasonably similar types of information, not only diagnostic data from the DIS but also indicators of distress and impairment on many people, which moves us into another stage in developing data to understand better what "unmet needs" really are and what subgroups within the population are more seriously affected. I want to emphasize that in our future analyses a critically important element is specific diagnosis. We have not forgotten this aspect of the ECA.

Regier: You need both the specific and the global summary types of statements. By looking at the global summary information, we could make some comparisons with previous studies. Having roughly a 20% rate for all disorders is useful because you can compare it with the global measures for serious disorder that were used in the Stirling County or the Midtown Manhattan studies. Likewise, by looking at the overall rate, we first noted similarities between the gender group rates and examined the differences between groups. For example, women seem to have higher rates of depression and anxiety disorders; men have higher rates of substance-abuse and antisocial personality disorders. In other analyses, we have focused on specific disorders, which you referred to as a strength of the ECA. I commented earlier about cognitive impairment, where only 4–7% used mental health services in a 6-month period. In contrast, 50% of persons with schizophrenia used mental health services in that same 6-month period. The affective disorders have service-use rates in the 30% range, and the anxiety disorders, including phobias, experience 20% use rates. These disorders appear to be very different, with different treatment and clinical course implications. It will be important for us to understand each disorder and associated service use in detail as well as in the context of the overview that Mr. Shapiro was providing.

Joseph Zubin: It might be out of character to raise any doubts about the frequency of unmet needs, which is probably the most important question facing this panel, but I was glad that Dr. Regier pointed out that he was not just going to attempt to satisfy all unmet need, but that he was going to try to learn from what was done. For example, for half of those who have unmet needs, give them what planners think they need, but keep the other half as controls to see whether or not it is really important to meet some of those needs.

I want to address not so much the present as the future. There is some danger that if we were today to set up a bureaucracy that will fill all the needs for this current moment, without paying attention to the demographic dynamics, we might eventually come to the point where, because of the self-preserving nature of bureaucracy, we will be filling needs that are no longer necessary. How can we control the situation so as to prevent the perpetuation of what we are doing now from getting us into difficulties later? It is important to understand and plan for the effects of projected demographic changes.

I would remind you of an example. In 1950, there was a shortage of teachers, and the explanation was that "people don't like to be teachers." But there was also a shortage of physicists, chemists, psychologists, and so on. The reason was that the lower birth rate in the 1930s dropped the reservoir of available people; consequently there were not enough young people to go into teaching, and of course the subsequent rise in the birth rate produced many more children. So there was a big hiatus between the supply of potential teachers and the number of children to be taught. However, there was no drop in schizophrenia. About 30 years ago Dr. E. I. Burdock and I explained this finding as follows: We suggested that when there are fewer very ill schizophrenics to be hospitalized, then milder cases are admitted. They are released after a short stay, and that perhaps is how the mental hygiene movement got such a good name in the 1960s—we were discharging milder patients, "curing schizophrenia," so to speak. So if we ignore the dynamics of demography, and instead pay continued attention to the self-serving demands of the bureaucracy, we may get into trouble.

Bruce Dohrenwend: It is now 28 years since Hollingshead and Redlich published their monograph, *Social Class and Mental Illness*, and it is interesting that no ringing recommendation has come out of the present study as it did from that study. One policy recommendation was that there was a need for a $5 psychotherapist. This recommendation was related to their finding of a strong inverse relationship between social class and mental illness. I don't know that the particular substance of this recommendation needs to be debated, but what it did point to was the importance of economics.

Another factor that the Hollingshead and Redlich report highlighted was the crucial role of public attitudes. One of the great advances of the ECA program is that it has done epidemiologic research in tandem with health services research, and that is certainly needed as a basis for policy. What the ECA program has not done is anything on economics or on public attitudes which, along with work on efficacy, are also needed. In the ECA program, are there plans to address attitudes, what Hollingshead and Redlich called "lay appraisal processes," the public counterpart of psychiatric diagnoses?

Regier: At present we have some questions that address individual concepts of mental illness, as well as respondents' concepts about their own mental health. However, these data vary somewhat from site to site and have not yet been published.

Another perspective on this issue has resulted from the overall prevalence rates, the 19%, or 1 in 5 with mental disorders, that has been so emphasized by the press. We have had many questions about the meaning of such a high rate. A British newsman was particularly graphic in asking, "Is everybody in the United States mad?" However, these questions have opened up the opportunity to bring mental disorders into the same context as physical disorders, where the public expects to find the full range of disabilities. Everybody with a mental disorder is not disabled. There are the common colds as well as the cancers of mental disorders.

In discussing this issue, we have compared mental disorder service use and prevalence data with comparable data for chronic physical disorders. We find that not every person with chronic circulatory disease or respiratory disease goes to a physician in a particular year. It should not be that striking to find 20% of the population with disorders affecting the brain and behavior when comparable rates are found for other organ systems. For example, the NCHS Health Interview Survey found 25% with chronic circulatory disorders and 27% with chronic respiratory disorders in a 1-year period. The public attitude challenge we face is to bring mental disorder epidemiology and mental disorders into the mainstream of health care, so that such disorders and the people afflicted can be destigmatized to some degree.

Name Index

Subject Index